Philosophy of Economics

D1474011

Julian Reiss's *Philosophy of Economics: A Contemporary Introduction* is far and away the best text on the subject. It is comprehensive, well-organized, sensible, and clearly written. It is the first text that I've ever been eager to use in teaching the subject. I expect that everyone interested in philosophy of economics, whether with a background in philosophy or with a background in economics, will learn a great deal from Reiss's masterful treatment.

Daniel M. Hausman, University of Wisconsin-Madison

Economists can no longer avoid the agenda of problems in the philosophy of economics, if they ever could. Equally, political and moral philosophers ignore economics at their own intellectual peril. Julian Reiss takes us on an insider's tour of the most important issues in this domain, teaching economists and philosophers what they need to know about how each of their disciplines have an impact on the other. For completeness, currency and clarity, *Philosophy of Economics: A Contemporary Introduction* cannot be beat.

Alex Rosenberg, Duke University

Philosophy of Economics: A Contemporary Introduction is the first systematic textbook in the philosophy of economics. It introduces the epistemological, metaphysical and ethical problems that arise in economics, and presents detailed discussions of the solutions that have been offered.

Throughout, philosophical issues are illustrated by and analysed in the context of concrete cases drawn from contemporary economics, the history of economic ideas, and actual economic events. This demonstrates the relevance of philosophy of economics both for the science of economics and for the economy.

This text will provide an excellent introduction to the philosophy of economics for students and interested general readers alike.

Julian Reiss is Professor of Philosophy at Durham University. He has a degree in Economics and Finance from the University of St Gallen and a PhD in Philosophy from the London School of Economics. His main research interests are methodologies of the sciences, philosophy of economics, and science and values. He is the author of *Error in Economics: Towards a More Evidence-Based Methodology* (2008), *Philosophy of Economics: A Contemporary Introduction* (2013), and some 40 papers in leading philosophy and social science journals and edited collections.

Routledge Contemporary Introductions to Philosophy
Series editor: Paul K. Moser, Loyola University of Chicago

This innovative, well-structured series is for students who have already done an introductory course in philosophy. Each book introduces a core general subject in contemporary philosophy and offers students an accessible but substantial transition from introductory to higher-level college work in that subject. The series is accessible to non-specialists and each book clearly motivates and expounds the problems and positions introduced. An orientating chapter briefly introduces its topic and reminds readers of any crucial material they need to have retained from a typical introductory course. Considerable attention is given to explaining the central philosophical problems of a subject and the main competing solutions and arguments for those solutions. The primary aim is to educate students in the main problems, positions and arguments of contemporary philosophy rather than to convince students of a single position.

Ancient Philosophy
Christopher Shields

Classical Philosophy
Christopher Shields

Classical Modern Philosophy
Jeffrey Tlumak

Continental Philosophy
Andrew Cutrofello

Epistemology
Third Edition
Robert Audi

Ethics
Second Edition
Harry J. Gensler

Metaphysics
Third Edition
Michael J. Loux

Philosophy of Art
Noël Carroll

Philosophy of Biology
Alex Rosenberg and Daniel W. McShea

Philosophy of Economics
Julian Reiss

Philosophy of Language
Second Edition
Willam G. Lycan

Philosophy of Mathematics
Second Edition
James Robert Brown

Philosophy of Mind
Third Edition
John Heil

Philosophy of Perception
William Fish

Philosophy of Psychology
José Luis Bermudez

Philosophy of Religion
Keith E. Yandell

Philosophy of Science
Third Edition
Alex Rosenberg

Social and Political Philosophy
John Christman

Forthcoming:

Free Will
Michael McKenna

Metaethics
Mark van Roojen

Moral Psychology
Valerie Tiberius

Philosophy of Literature
John Gibson

Philosophy of Economics

A Contemporary Introduction

Julian Reiss

Routledge
Taylor & Francis Group

NEW YORK AND LONDON

First published 2013
by Routledge
711 Third Avenue, New York, NY 10017

Simultaneously published in the UK
by Routledge
2 Park Square, Milton Park, Abingdon, Oxon OX14 4RN

Routledge is an imprint of the Taylor & Francis Group, an informa business

Library of Congress Cataloguing in Publication Data
Reiss, Julian.
Philosophy of economics : a contemporary introduction / By Julian Reiss. -- 1st ed.
   p. cm. -- (Routledge Contemporary Introductions to Philosophy)
   Includes bibliographical references and index.
   1. Economics--Philosophy. I. Title.
   HB72.R4425 2013   330.01--dc23

ISBN: 978-0-415-88116-6 (hbk)
ISBN: 978-0-415-88117-3 (pbk)
ISBN: 978-0-203-55906-2 (ebk)

Typeset in Garamond Pro and Gill Sans
by Bookcraft Ltd, Stroud, Gloucestershire

SFI Certified Sourcing
www.sfiprogram.org
SFI-00453

Printed and bound in the United States of America
by Edwards Brothers, Inc.

To EIPE

Contents

Figures

Tables

Acknowledgments

Dan Hausman read a draft version of the entire manuscript and provided extensive feedback, for which I am very grateful. His comments have greatly helped to improve the book. But my intellectual debts to Dan go well beyond that. Dan supervised my PhD thesis for my first two years at LSE, and has continued to contribute to my intellectual development through comments on my articles and book chapters and discussions until this very day. Nancy Cartwright's influence on my views concerning laws, causation and evidence should be clear from Chapters 5, 6 and 10. She has also read and commented on previous versions of the manuscript, for which I am very grateful. I discussed previous versions of the manuscript with the EIPE reading group section "C" (Conrad Heilmann, François Claveau, Willem van der Deijl, Luis Mireles Flores, Darian Heim, Vaios Koliofotis, Attilia Ruzzene, Johanna Thoma, Melissa Vergara Fernandez and Philippe Verreault-Julien), to whom I owe a debt of gratitude. Individual chapters have much profited from comments by Anna Alexandrova, David Birke, Till Grüne-Yanoff, Francesco Guala, Conrad Heilmann, Caterina Marchionni, Robert Northcott, Ingrid Robeyns and Johanna Thoma. Philippe Verreault-Julien contributed a great deal to the production of the manuscript and provided his own comments. I owe him enormous thanks. I would also like to thank the students of the 2010/11 and 2011/12 courses in Philosophy of Economics at the Erasmus School of Economics for laboring through drafts of the manuscript, as well as the tutors—François Claveau, Joost Hengstmengel, Clemens Hirsch, Freddy van Houten, Luis Mireles Flores, Attilia Ruzzene, Melissa Vergara Fernandez—and Jack Vromen, who teaches Philosophy of Economics to Dutch-speaking students, for their feedback.

Chapter 7 was previously published as 'The Explanation Paradox', in *Journal of Economic Methodology* **19**(1): 43–62 (2012). Parts of Chapter 8 were previously published in Chapter 2 of my book *Error in Economics: Towards a More Evidence-Based Methodology*. London and New York: Routledge, 2008.

I dedicate this book to the Erasmus Institute of Philosophy and Economics (EIPE), where the bulk of it was written and whose students, colleagues and visitors have provided the kind of intellectual environment without which a book like this would never have existed.

Bloopers and oversights remain my responsibility, as always.

1   The Why, What and How of Philosophy of Economics

- Overview
- Two Opposing Paradigms
- The Philosophy of Economics: Interpreting Theory, Methodology and Ethics
- The Aims of Economics and the Problem of Purpose
- Study Questions
- Suggested Readings

Overview

The philosophy of economics is at the same time an ancient and a very recent discipline. It is ancient in that the world's greatest economists beginning with Aristotle were also or mainly philosophers, and many of their contributions should be classified as contributions to the *philosophy* of economics rather than the *science* of economics, narrowly understood. With the increasing specialization and professionalization of academic disciplines that occurred in the nineteenth century, economics was separated from philosophy and developed, especially after the Second World War, a mainstream paradigm that was hostile to philosophical reflection. At the same time, philosophers of science were mainly interested in natural science and thus tended to ignore economics and other social sciences. It is only in the last 30 or so years that we can once more experience a mutual interest and exchange, and witness the development of academic institutions that focus on the intersection of economics and philosophy. In that sense, then, the discipline is a novel one. This chapter will explore why philosophy of economics is a subject worth studying, explaining its various branches and the overall approach and narratives in evidence in this book.

Two Opposing Paradigms

When I am being introduced to someone I haven't met before and my new acquaintance asks me what I am doing, they often look at me in surprise, puzzlement or sheer disbelief when I tell them that I am a "philosopher of economics." Aren't philosophy and economics two completely different kettles of fish? Isn't economics a science that deals in facts which can be expressed in figures and equations, and isn't philosophy a discipline belonging to the humanities, more akin to the arts than the sciences, and dealing with ideas rather than data? Somewhat more provocatively, aren't economists cold-hearted proponents of free markets and individual responsibility and philosophers naive believers in idealistic principles and the human good?

No doubt there is something to these stereotypes. Observing economists and philosophers at their respective academic conferences gives some evidence beyond the platitudes that the two fields are indeed dominated by quite different cultures. But to some extent both disciplines have become more open to ideas from the outside, and values other than their own now play a role in each discipline. To give just a couple of examples of sub-disciplines of economics and philosophy where untypical attitudes have a great influence on the debate, take happiness economics and formal ethics. Happiness economics studies the causes and effects of subjective well-being. It is highly interdisciplinary and often combines economic analysis with work from other fields such as psychology, sociology and philosophy. It is different from traditional welfare economics in that it rests on a radically different concept of well-being (see Chapter 12 for details). Whether this or that concept of well-being is adequate is of course one of the major issues any philosopher working on ethical theory has to address. Formal ethics, in turn, is a branch of philosophy that addresses traditional philosophical issues using tools drawn from economics such as rational-choice theory and game theory. The values of rigor and mathematical elegance, formally more characteristic of economics than of philosophy departments, surely influence the debate in no small measure.

The separation of economics and philosophy into two disciplines has in fact occurred fairly recently and is to a large extent artificial. Indeed, many of the world's greatest economists were also, or even mainly, philosophers: Adam Smith, David Hume, John Stuart Mill, Karl Marx, William Stanley Jevons, to some extent John Maynard Keynes and more recently Amartya Sen. Aristotle is often said to be the first economist, but of course he is better known as one of the greatest philosophers of all time.

The separation into distinct disciplines has to do with the general trend towards greater specialization that all sciences have experienced and continue to experience but also with a more specific stance towards science, including social science. This stance, sometimes called "modernism" (McCloskey 1983), takes the view that (a) science investigates facts, and only facts; (b) factual knowledge is exhausted by what can be ascertained on the basis of observations and experiments.

Both clauses (a) and (b) serve to separate the science of economics from other kinds of inquiry. Science, we are told, examines facts, or what there is, and not values, or what ought to be. According to this view, the economist *qua* scientist abstains from value judgments. Objective, scientific knowledge is value-free. Value judgments are a problem for ethicists. Moreover, in order to be objective, our knowledge has to be based on observable features of the world. Science deals with verifiable states of affairs, not with speculations that go beyond what is accessible to the senses. A classic statement of this perspective stems from the greatest of the empiricists, David Hume:

> When we run over libraries, persuaded of these principles, what havoc must we make? If we take in our hand any volume; of divinity or school metaphysics, for instance; let us ask, *Does it contain any abstract reasoning concerning quantity or number?* No. *Does it contain any experimental reasoning concerning matter of fact and existence?* No. Commit it then to the flames: For it can contain nothing but sophistry and illusion.
> (Hume 1999 [1748]: 211; original emphasis)

Less radical thinkers of this orientation would perhaps stop short of Hume's call to arms but they'd nevertheless agree that there is a clear separation between science, which is based on numbers and observable facts, and metaphysics, which is based on hypothesis and speculation.

We are therefore facing a dichotomy: what is versus what ought to be; and what is ascertainable by observation versus what is speculative. According to this view, then, economists *qua* scientists stay on the safe side of these dichotomies. By contrast, philosophers *qua* ethicists deal with value judgments and what ought to be; philosophers *qua* metaphysicians deal with speculations about the ultimate constituents of reality.

Parallel developments in both economics and philosophy in the second half of the twentieth century have helped to overcome these dichotomies. On the one hand, at least some economists, while still emphasizing the distinction between so-called positive (or factual) and normative (or evaluative) economics have come to realize that they cannot shy away from value judgments altogether. Especially through the work of Amartya Sen it has transpired that an economist *qua* scientist needs to engage in ethical query (e.g., Sen 1987). On the other hand, economists have stopped insisting that economic knowledge is exhausted by what is observable. To give one example, economists now actively participate in discussions concerning the notion of cause, a concept once deemed too metaphysical for scientists (Hoover 2009). To give another, the notion of "revealed preference," once endorsed by the profession because it allows economists to avoid making assumptions concerning unobservable states of affairs, has come under severe attack (Hausman 2012).

Philosophy as a discipline has changed, too. While continuing to deal with traditional ethical questions such as those concerning the nature of the good and principles of justice, as well as traditional metaphysical questions such as those concerning the nature of causality and laws of nature, philosophers do so in ways increasingly informed by and continuous with science. Much of recent philosophy therefore resembles science to some extent, for example in the use of empirical information, mathematical modeling and sometimes even experimental methods.

In other words, economics and philosophy have drawn closer to each other by economists having started to ask questions that were once considered philosophical in the pejorative sense of "non-scientific," and by philosophers having started to address their questions in ways that resemble science more closely than traditional philosophy. A consequence of this convergence is that a lot of work that is now being done in economics and philosophy departments, discussed at academic conferences and published in economics journals or philosophy journals resists straightforward categorization as either "straight economics" or "straight philosophy." It is work at this intersection of economics and philosophy that this book is concerned with.

The recent (2008–) financial crisis provides an independent reason why philosophy of economics is an area of research of potentially very high significance, both academic and practical. Many commentators, among them Nobel prize-winning economists, have blamed the crisis on a failure of economics as a discipline. Here are some prominent voices:

> Of all the economic bubbles that have been pricked [since 2008], few have burst more spectacularly than the reputation of economics itself.
>
> (*The Economist* 2009)

> Last year, everything came apart.
> Few economists saw our current crisis coming, but this predictive failure was the least of the field's problems. More important was the profession's blindness to the very possibility of catastrophic failures in a market economy.
>
> (Krugman 2009a)

> The main cause of the crisis was the behavior of the banks—largely a result of misguided incentives unrestrained by good regulation. …
> There is one other set of accomplices—the economists who provided the arguments that those in the financial markets found so convenient and self-serving. These economists provided models—based on unrealistic assumptions of perfect information, perfect competition, and perfect markets—in which regulation was unnecessary.
>
> (Stiglitz 2009)

Paraphrasing Krugman and Stiglitz, we might say that among the causes of the financial crisis were economic models that were idealized to such an extent and in such a way that they couldn't be used for salient purposes such as predicting financial crises like the present one and underwriting policy interventions such as banking regulation. But are these critics justified in their allegations? Are they right in their rejection of current mainstream models and in blaming the crisis on these models? An unsympathetic observer might point out that both Krugman and Stiglitz have axes to grind. Specifically, both are supporters of alternative economic paradigms. Krugman's article pursues an unashamed Keynesian agenda; Stiglitz is well known for his advocacy of models of imperfect and incomplete information (which have, of course, different regulatory implications).

Krugman and Stiglitz thus criticize mainstream economics for using bad theories—theories that make assumptions about markets that are unrealistic, theories that do not allow for "catastrophic failure" despite its apparent empirical reality. Krugman's article points to another aspect. In his analysis of what went wrong Krugman writes, "As I see it, the economics profession went astray because economists, as a group, mistook beauty, clad in impressive-looking mathematics, for truth" (Krugman 2009a). Krugman, in other words, criticizes economists for using bad methodology: pursuing mathematical elegance rather than truth leads to models that both fail to predict significant economic events and fail to provide good policy advice.

Philosophers, or more specifically philosophers of science, think about questions concerning theory assessment and scientific methodology professionally. More generally speaking, philosophers of science are interested in metaphysical and epistemological issues raised by the sciences. Metaphysical issues are those pertaining to the most fundamental building blocks of nature and society such as objects, properties, individuals, laws of nature, social norms, causality and modality (possibility and necessity). Epistemological issues concern the ways in which scientists find out about these in experiments, measurements and observation. If philosophers of science are any good at their jobs, the tools, concepts and theories they come up with should help us judge whether Krugman's and Stiglitz's points concerning theory assessment and methodology are as compelling as they make them seem.

There is a third aspect. Some have argued, like Stiglitz, that the behavior of the banks was one of the main causes of the crisis. But unlike him, they do not see the failure in unrealistic idealizations but rather in inappropriate moral foundations of the economics future bankers are taught at business schools. An article in the British newspaper *The Guardian* argues:

> It is business schools, after all, which flooded the banking world with graduates of their prestigious MBA courses. They then helped the economy to nosedive.
>
> One US website recently dubbed business schools the "academies of the apocalypse" and named and shamed dozens of international high-flying MBAs—"toxic bankers and scammers"—from Harvard MBA graduate Henry Paulson, secretary of the treasury under President Bush, who spoke

> vehemently against government regulation of Wall Street, to deposed
> HBOS [Halifax Bank of Scotland] chief executive Andy Hornsby.
>
> (James 2009)

And it is not only the failure of business schools to integrate courses on
corporate social responsibility and business ethics that is to blame, as the
Guardian article continues to suggest. Rather, the economic paradigm
students are taught, in business schools and universities, can be used—or
abused—to justify Gordon Gekko's "greed is good" maxim. One of the
first things economics students learn is that there is a mechanism called the
"invisible hand" by which markets magically transform the pursuit of self-
interest into social benefit. Slightly more advanced students learn that Adam
Smith's invisible-hand hypothesis has been confirmed mathematically by the
so-called first fundamental theorem of welfare economics.

If the financial crisis is a social bad, as most of us would agree, and if it was
brought about by freely operating markets, there must be a mistake in the
invisible-hand idea. Perhaps greed isn't so good after all. At any rate, there is
some reason to doubt whether economics rests on a solid ethical foundation.

Once more, philosophers should be in a good position to advance debates
concerning ethical foundations. Ethics is one of the major branches of
philosophy, and philosophers have been debating problems of ethics since
the very beginning of Western philosophy. So surely they should have come
up with some concepts, tools and ideas to aid economists?

The Philosophy of Economics: Interpreting Theory, Methodology and Ethics

Philosophers of economics are philosophers whose work focuses on the
theoretical, methodological and ethical foundations of economics. It is no
accident therefore that I selected criticisms of economics which point to
theoretical, methodological and ethical challenges the financial crisis raises.
In this section I will explain in slightly more detail what these three branches
of philosophy of economics comprise.

The main theoretical framework in economics is given by theories of
rational choice. These come in various guises, applicable to situations of
certainty, risk, uncertainty, strategic situations and group decisions. To
examine the foundations of rational-choice theory means to examine the
axioms and principles that underlie such theories, to assess whether they
are justifiable as axioms and principles of *rational* choice and adequate as
descriptive accounts of *actual* choice.

Not every economic theory is one of rational choice, however. There are
also macro theories such as the Solow–Swan growth model, the quantity
theory of money, the IS/LM model and numerous microeconomic laws such
as Say's law, Hotelling's law, the laws of supply and demand. To examine
the foundations of economic theory also means to examine how to interpret

economic models and laws and ask about the metaphysical underpinnings of economics: Are there laws of nature in economics? What role do causal relations play? Are there only individuals or also social wholes?

Part I of this book will look in detail at a selection of these issues. Chapter 3 will examine rational-choice theory under certainty and risk and Chapter 4 game theory. Choice theory under uncertainty will be discussed briefly in Chapter 14. The notions of law, causation and causal mechanism will be examined in Chapters 5 and 6. Chapter 7 studies models and idealization in economics.

The second branch of philosophy of economics is methodology, which, as the name suggests, looks at the methods economists employ in testing their theories and establishing facts, laws and causal relations. Economists usually refer to something very specific when they use the term method: "A Three-Stage Optimization Method to Construct Time Series International Input–Output Database"; "A Quadratic Approximation Method for Agency Models with Frequent Actions"; "An Instrumental Variable Estimation Method of Nonparametric Models." Philosophers talk more abstractly and are more concerned about foundational issues. For them, there are observational and experimental methods. Observational methods generate data passively. Relevant for economics are mainly the measurement of economic indicators such as GDP, unemployment and inflation and the statistical analysis of data using regression. Experimental methods give economists a more active role: they design the set-up, manipulate a variable, observe and record the result and only then analyze it statistically. Experimental economics is now a thriving field within economics, and the use of randomized experiments has become popular in development economics in recent years.

To examine the methodological foundations of economics means to learn how these methods work, under which conditions they work, and what kinds of questions they can answer. Part II of this book is devoted to these issues. Chapter 8 will do so for the measurement of economic indicators, Chapter 9 for econometric methods, Chapter 10 for economic experiments and Chapter 11 for randomized field studies.

The third branch of philosophy of economics comprises the *ethical aspects of economics*. Economics involves ethical issues to no small degree. Consider a famous passage from Milton Friedman's essay "The Methodology of Positive Economics":

> An obvious and not unimportant example is minimum-wage legislation. Underneath the welter of arguments offered for and against such legislation there is an underlying consensus on the objective of achieving a "living wage" for all, to use the ambiguous phrase so common in such discussions. The difference of opinion is largely grounded on an implicit or explicit difference in predictions about the efficacy of this particular means in furthering the agreed-on end.
>
> (M. Friedman 1953: 5)

Friedman here claims that a "living wage for all" is an agreed-upon end while the means to achieve this end are disputed among economists. I doubt that at Friedman's time there was indeed widespread consensus regarding this policy objective but let us assume he was right. Does consensus regarding a policy objective mean that to take means to achieve it is morally justified? Is the end itself justified? Is rational discussion possible or are differences in value judgments "differences about which men can ultimately only fight" (M. Friedman 1953: 5)? These are the kinds of questions a philosopher of economics asks when he is concerned with the ethical aspects of economics.

Welfare economics is the branch of economics that addresses normative questions such as these. To examine the ethical foundations of economics mainly means to examine the ethical foundations of welfare economics, and that means to examine welfare, principles of distributive justice and ethical issues the market raises. Part III of this book will look at these matters, in this order, in Chapters 12–14.

I said earlier that to examine the ethical foundations of economics *mainly* means to examine the ethical foundations of welfare economics, because in fact ethical judgments abound even in what is called "positive" economics (that is, descriptive or explanatory economics). This is because many of the methods economists employ require ethical judgments in order to function well. This is especially noteworthy in the case of consumer price inflation measurement: to measure consumer price inflation appropriately judgments about the value of changes in the quality of goods have to be made; but such judgments require a notion of consumer welfare and are therefore ethical in nature (see Chapter 8).

Chapter 15 is a concluding chapter that aims to bring together various strands of thought encountered in the book. It discusses libertarian paternalism, a recent highly acclaimed and controversial policy proposal. As we will see, to understand this proposal, knowledge about rational-choice theory, experimental methodology, theories of well-being, justice and market failure is crucial. My hope is that readers will feel more confident about assessing such a proposal after reading the book than before.

The Aims of Economics and the Problem of Purpose

Economists pursue a variety of aims using a variety of scientific tools and methods. A classical statement due to Carl Menger ascribes the tripartite goal of explanation–prediction–control to economics (Menger 1963). According to this view, economists aim to explain past events and regularities; they further aim to anticipate future events and thereby help with policy and planning; and lastly they aim to provide recipes for successful interventions in the economy.

Menger's account is a nice starting point for a discussion of the aims of economics but it is incomplete. The description of economic phenomena using indicators and statistics is an auxiliary aim for the more ultimate goal of explanation–prediction–control but it is also a highly important aim in itself (cf. Sen 1983a). That the inflation and growth rates in a country X are such-and-such, and that Y percent of its inhabitants live in poverty is important information, quite independently of whether that information is used for further scientific or practical purposes.

Economists also contribute to a number of normative discussions. To provide adequate normative accounts of rationality, well-being and, perhaps, justice must therefore be regarded as among the aims of economics. Not every working economist actually participates in these foundational debates but the times where these debates were left exclusively to philosophers are long gone.

The reason to engage in this rudimentary discussion of the aims of economics here is that many of the discussions that follow are meaningless unless conducted in the context of a relatively well-specified scientific purpose, and the aims introduced here can provide such a purpose. For example, there is no sense in which it is advisable or not advisable *simpliciter* for economists to investigate causal mechanisms. But it may be advisable for economists to investigate mechanisms given they aim to explain economic phenomena, because according to a widely held view descriptions of mechanisms provide explanations of outcomes of interest. Similarly, it is at least ambiguous to ask whether rational-choice theory is adequate as such. But it may well be adequate as a descriptive account of how people actually make choices or as a normative account of how people ought to make choices, or both, or neither.

Scientific practices, then, should be evaluated against a purpose, preferably one that is pursued by the scientists themselves and not imposed from outside by a philosopher. If that is so, a complication arises: most scientific practices are used for a variety of purposes and their adequacy or appropriateness is relative to that purpose. Causal mechanisms, for instance, are investigated for at least three purposes. First, as already mentioned, they are used to explain economic phenomena. The second and third uses relate to causal inference. It is often difficult to ascertain whether one economic variable (say, money) causes another (say, nominal income) by means of statistical analyses alone, essentially because all statistical models are underdetermined by data (see Chapter 9). When underdetermination is a serious problem, it is sometimes recommended to investigate possible mechanisms through which X might cause Y:

> However consistent may be the relation between monetary change and economic change, and however strong the evidence for the autonomy of the monetary changes, we shall not be persuaded that the monetary changes are the source of the economic changes unless we can specify in some detail the *mechanism* that connects the one with the other.
>
> (Friedman and Schwarz 1963: 59; emphasis added)

The third use is to ascertain the generalizability of already established causal claims. What is true of the economic system of the United States in the period 1867 to 1960 might not hold true thereafter or for other countries. Knowledge of mechanisms has been recommended as useful for deciding whether causal claims can be exported from one setting to another.

A methodological recommendation to investigate the causal mechanism(s) responsible for some economic phenomenon of interest may therefore be a good recommendation in one context but a bad one in another. This, however, creates a problem: each of the three branches of philosophy of economics is in fact itself multidimensional because each theory, method and ethical principle should be evaluated relative to a purpose, and the purposes of economics are multifarious.

I have simplified my life to some extent by focusing on one salient purpose in Part I: the explanation of economic phenomena. I do not think that explanation is the only aim of economics, or that it is particularly important. But focusing on explanation provides a nice narrative and organizing principle for Part I. I therefore begin with an introductory discussion of the topic of scientific explanation in Chapter 2. Other purposes will be salient in Part II (especially description in Chapter 8 and policy in Chapter 11) and Part III (for instance, moral reflection and policy in Chapter 12).

Part III on ethics is similarly simplified. Welfare, markets and justice could be discussed from all sorts of perspectives. I have decided to take the "greed is good" maxim—or rather, its academic counterpart, namely, the invisible-hand hypothesis—as organizing principle. As I will explain in Chapter 12, markets transform the individual pursuit of self-interest into social benefit only under a number of controversial assumptions. These assumptions include assumptions about human welfare, the nature of markets and what matters to society. The ethical topics discussed in Part III are selected with a view to assessing the plausibility and moral justifiability of these assumptions behind the invisible-hand hypothesis.

Study Questions

1   Try to think of one case each for the theoretical, methodological and ethical challenge discussed in the first section of this chapter. How can philosophy of economics help to answer it?
2   If you are an economics student, think about your curriculum. Which of your courses raise philosophical issues? Do you think they will be addressed in this book?
3   The last section of this chapter, dealing with "The Aims of Economics and the Problem of Purpose," mentions description, prediction, explanation, control and normative reflection as aims of economics. Are there other aims? Is there a hierarchy among the different aims?
4   To what extent are the problems in philosophy of science similar to those in philosophy of other sciences? To what extent are they different?
5   "A good economist has to be a good philosopher." Discuss.

Suggested Readings

This is the introductory chapter to an introductory text on philosophy of economics, so further readings should be other textbooks on philosophy of economics. Alas, there are none, at least not on the field as it is understood here. The closest one can get in aims and scope is probably Dan Hausman's *The Inexact and Separate Science of Economics* (Hausman 1992a), though this book excludes the ethical aspects of economics (but see Hausman and McPherson 2006). Its appendix contains an excellent introduction to the philosophy of science, and many of its discussions of, for instance, *ceteris paribus* laws, Mill's philosophy of economics, Milton Friedman's instrumentalism, Paul Samuelson's operationalism and the preference reversal phenomenon are still among the best one can find on these topics. There are a number of fairly introductory books on the narrower topic of economic methodology, most of which are older and have a historical focus. An exception is the recent Boumans and Davis 2010; other, earlier texts include Blaug 1992 and Caldwell 1982. Hands 2001 is accessible and comprehensive. There are also a number of handbooks in philosophy of economics such as Davis and Hands 2011 or Kincaid and Ross 2009. Most articles in the latter are closer to research papers than introductions or overviews, however. Roger Backhouse's entry in the *New Palgrave* is also a useful starting point (Backhouse 2008). For an anthology with classic and contemporary readings, see Hausman 2008.

Part I

Interpreting Economic Theory

2 Explaining Economic Phenomena

Overview

This chapter asks what it means for a theory, an account or a model to "explain" a phenomenon of scientific interest. As we will see, the notion of (scientific) explanation has traditionally been closely related to that of a *scientific law*: according to this view, which has been endorsed by both philosophers and economists, to explain an economic phenomenon means to subsume it under a law. The chapter examines this so-called "deductive-nomological model of explanation." The account is widely regarded as mistaken nowadays, but a discussion of its deficiencies nevertheless serves as a good starting point because it is just these deficiencies that have made philosophers and social scientists look for more satisfactory alternatives, and much of the remainder of Part I discusses issues related to these alternatives.

Explanation as an Aim of Economics

To explain economic phenomena is an important aim of economics. This much can be seen from quotations such as the following (emphases added):

> The example of used cars captures the essence of the problem. From time to time one hears either mention of or surprise at the large price difference between new cars and those which have just left the showroom. The usual lunch table justification for this phenomenon is the pure joy of owning a "new" car. We offer a different *explanation*.
>
> (Akerlof 1970: 489)

> High taxation and negative public savings must have adverse effects on aggregate saving: they reduce the disposable income of the formal private sector, and the resources thus mobilized are not used to increase public savings. This may be an important part of the *explanation* behind the low saving equilibrium.
>
> (Rodrik 2007: 80)

> Our argument in a nutshell is that both the financial explosion in recent decades and the financial implosion now taking place are to be *explained* mainly in reference to stagnation tendencies within the underlying economy. A number of other *explanations* for the current crisis (most of them focusing on the proximate causes) have been given by economists and media pundits.
>
> (Foster and Magdoff 2009: 120)

> Many other *explanations* have, needless to say, been offered for the great East–West divergence: differences in topography, resource endowments, culture, attitudes towards science and technology, even differences in human evolution. Yet there remains a credible hypothesis that China's problems were as much financial as they were resource-based.
>
> (Ferguson 2008: 286)

In each of these cases, a hypothesis, an account, a model, a "story"—each a form of an economic *theory*—is offered as an explanation of some economic phenomenon of interest. The explanation of economic phenomena is clearly an important aim of economics. Some philosophers of the social sciences and methodologists would go as far as to claim that explanation is the only aim of the social sciences. Critical realist economists/methodologists such as Tony Lawson are a good example:

> In addition, the impossibility of engineering, and the absence of spontaneously occurring, closed social systems, necessitates a reliance on

non-predictive, purely explanatory, criteria of theory development and assessment in the social sciences.

(Lawson 1997: 35)

Others believe that explanation is not the only aim but that it has a special status. Thus, economist/social theorist/philosopher Jon Elster argues that the non-explanatory aims of social science are auxiliary (Elster 2007: 9): "The main task of the social sciences is to explain social phenomena. It is not the only task, but it is the most important one, to which others are subordinated or on which they depend."

The problem with the more radical view such as Lawson's is that it makes much economic practice seem futile. Economists invest a great deal in forecasting models and in testing policy claims. We will see many examples for these endeavors in Part II of this book. If engineering is impossible, why build models and experiments of mechanism design? And why have many government auctions of electromagnetic spectrum licenses been heralded as successes for economics if they might as well have been based on guesswork? While I am a critical commentator on economic practice myself, I think that across-the-board condemnations of pursuing certain aims, aims which in addition are of great practical importance, are exaggerated (for some arguments along these lines, see Reiss 2007a). Economists do, and should, pursue a variety of aims. Which of these is most important does not, luckily, have to be settled here. We will simply accept that the explanation of economic phenomena is one important aim of economics.

"Explaining economic phenomena" involves two philosophical terms, (scientific) "explanation" and "phenomenon." Let us begin by examining what a phenomenon is.

Phenomena

The Greek verb *phainomai* means "to appear", so in the most general terms a phenomenon is an appearance of sorts. There is a long philosophical tradition according to which in order to be a phenomenon something must be perceived by the senses, experienced by an individual. Phenomena in this sense are contrasted with the reality behind the appearances, in Kant's terminology, for example, with the "noumena" or "things in themselves" (Kant 1998 [1787]: A249).

In the contemporary philosophy of science literature, the term has lost its connection with the immediacy of experience. To the contrary, in contemporary usage a phenomenon is usually unobservable: "Phenomena are detected through the use of [observable] data, but in most cases are not observable in any interesting sense of the term" (Bogen and Woodward 1988: 306). A phenomenon is something that is inferred on the basis of observable data. If, for instance, I claim that the inflation rate in the Netherlands in the year to March 2011 has been 1.95 percent (as measured by the consumer price index), I make a claim about a (strictly speaking) unobservable phenomenon: individual price tags can be observed but the inflation rate is inferred on the basis of quite an intricate measurement procedure (see Chapter 8).

Obviously, not everything that transcends the immediacy of sense experience would be called a phenomenon. Rather, a phenomenon is something that is significant, something of scientific interest: "A phenomenon is *noteworthy*. A phenomenon is *discernible*. A phenomenon is commonly an event or process of certain type that occurs regularly under definite circumstances" (Hacking 1983: 221; original emphasis). A phenomenon is therefore something that calls for theoretical explanation. It is an event or process whose existence we have ascertained so that we can take it as a starting point for our scientific investigations.

A further characteristic is that phenomena are to some extent idealized. James Bogen and James Woodward contrast phenomena with *data* (Bogen and Woodward 1988; Woodward 1989, 2000). Woodward writes:

> When data play this role they reflect the causal influence of the phenomena for which they are evidence but they also reflect the operation of local and idiosyncratic features of the measurement devices and experimental designs that produce them.
>
> (Woodward 2000: S163–4)

It is these idiosyncratic features of the data that we aim to idealize away in order to be able to discern the phenomenon of interest. Economists have long understood that theories do not explain facts but idealized versions thereof. This idea is reflected in their notion of a *stylized fact*, which was introduced by Nicholas Kaldor as follows:

> Since facts, as recorded by statisticians, are always subject to numerous snags and qualifications, and for that reason are incapable of being accurately summarized, the theorist, in my view, should be free to start off with a "stylized" view of the facts—i.e. concentrate on broad tendencies, ignoring individual detail.
>
> (Kaldor 1961: 178)

In the passage quoted above, Ian Hacking says that phenomena are events or processes of a certain *type*. What he means by that is that these events or processes can be instantiated many times and in different locations, and that they have regular features. Phenomena of this kind exist in economics: business cycles, the "liquidity effect," or Kaldor's stylized facts (Kaldor 1957):

•   the shares of national income received by labor and capital are roughly constant over long periods of time;

- the rate of growth of the capital stock is roughly constant over long periods of time;
- the rate of growth of output per worker is roughly constant over long periods of time;
- the capital/output ratio is roughly constant over long periods of time;
- the rate of return on investment is roughly constant over long periods of time;
- the real wage grows over time.

Many of the events or processes economists seek to analyze are, however, unique. They are not *types* but *tokens*. They are particulars located in space and time and instantiated only once or, if they are the instantiations of a general type, the economist regards them as particulars. Examples include:

- the rise of the dotcom industry;
- the financial crisis of the late 2000s;
- (more contentiously) the victory of capitalism over socialism.

The financial crisis of the late 2000s can illustrate the difference between types and tokens. On the one hand, this particular crisis shared many aspects of other crises—the bursting of an asset bubble, the ensuing credit crunch, the effect of the credit crunch on the "real" economy—and as such it is an instance of the general type "financial crisis." On the other hand, it had a number of peculiarities. Perhaps the fact that the asset bubble occurred in the subprime housing market made a difference to how the crisis evolved; according to some analysts, its root cause was a shift in global economic power from the West to India and China (Ross 2010b). These features are not shared by other crises, and they are what make this crisis unique. Economists interested in these features examine the crisis as a "token phenomenon."

In sum, a phenomenon in the technical sense used in this book is an effect or process that:

- is (usually unobservable but) measurable;
- is of scientific interest or "noteworthy";
- must be inferred from the data using more or less sophisticated techniques;
- is to some extent idealized;
- comes in two kinds: types (repeatable) and tokens (unique).

Why-Questions, Explanandum and Explanans

In the most general sense, explanations are answers to why-questions: "Why did you arrive late?" "Because I missed the train." "Why do many people live much longer today than they used to?" "Because of better hygiene and nutrition." In a scientific explanation, the why-question concerns the phenomenon of interest. We might ask, for instance, "Why did the recent financial crisis happen?" or "Why did it happen when it did?" or "Why was this crisis much more severe than any other crisis since the Great Depression?"

Of course, not every answer to a why-question is also an explanation, much less a *scientific* explanation. If I were asked to explain the financial crisis, and I answered that it happened when it did because of a full moon on the day the US Treasury decided not to save Lehman Brothers, I'd be more likely to be committed to an institution than win the Nobel Memorial Prize. In other words, we want the explanation to be connected to the phenomenon in some way, and in the right way. A full moon does not seem to have the right kind of connection with the outbreak of a financial crisis in order to be acceptable as an explanation.

It is useful to introduce some further terminology at this point. According to the so-called "deductive-nomological model" (or "D-N model") of scientific explanation, which I am focusing on in this chapter and which has come to be accepted as the "received view" of scientific explanation since the 1960s, a scientific explanation falls into two parts: an *explanandum* (from Latin: "the thing to be explained"), a description of the phenomenon of interest, and an *explanans* (from Latin: "the explaining thing"), the sentences that are thought to give an account of the phenomenon (Hempel and Oppenheim 1948). The logical positivists thought that the right kind of connection between the explanans and the explanandum was that of logical consequence: the explanandum must follow from the explanans as a matter of logic.

In other words, an explanation is a *logically valid argument*: the explanans comprises the premises of the argument and the explanandum its conclusion, and the conclusion cannot be false if all of the premises are true. Here is a (stylized) example of such an explanation:

> All men are mortal.
> Michael Jackson was a man.
> (Therefore,) Michael Jackson was mortal.

The first two sentences are the explanans, the third is the explanandum. The explanans deductively entails the explanandum.

Not every logically valid argument is, however, a scientific explanation. If our phenomenon of interest is the existence of light, and thus our why-question "Why is there light?" the following argument would not be acceptable as a *scientific* explanation:

> And God said, "Let there be light!"
> Whatever God says will happen.
> There was light.

Even more trivially, any statement implies itself: "There was light" implies "There was light." But an explanandum doesn't double up as explanans. So there must be conditions on what is acceptable among the premisses that jointly make up the explanans for the argument to be a scientific explanation.

Scientific Laws

The logical positivists imposed two main conditions. First, the sentences in the explanans must be true or at least verifiable and verified. The argument that is to serve as a scientific explanation should not only be *valid* but also *sound*. My "full-moon explanation" of the financial crisis would not convince the staunchest believer in the causal power of the moon if it was not true that on the day Lehman Brothers failed there was a full moon. (As it happens, Lehman Brothers filed for bankruptcy on September 15, 2008, and there was a full moon on that day. So far, so good for this explanation.)

Second, the premisses must contain at least one scientific law non-redundantly. This condition in fact comprises three requirements: at least one of the premisses must be a law; the law must be "scientific"; and removing the law(s) from the set of premisses renders the argument invalid. This condition shows that the "Let there be light!" explanation is not a scientific explanation. Even if we believed that the argument was valid and sound (i.e., we believed that God said this, and that whatever God says will happen), and that the "law" that whatever God says will happen is not redundant, the argument doesn't qualify as a *scientific* explanation: a law it may be that whatever God says will happen, but it is not a scientific law.

But what *is* a scientific law? Unfortunately, the logical positivists could not come up with a satisfactory answer to that question, even after many years of trying. Some features were thought to be uncontroversial. A scientific law is a regularity or universal generalization of the form "All *C*s are *E*s" or "Whenever *C*, then *E*"; in terms of first-order predicate logic, "For all *x*, $Cx \rightarrow Ex$." Here are some examples: "All swans are white"; "All samples of bismuth melt at 271°C"; "Free-falling bodies fall with uniform acceleration."

For such a law to be a *scientific* law, it also has to be contingent (that is, not logically true), verifiable and supported by evidence. "All bachelors are men" is not a scientific law because it is a truth of logic. "Whatever God says will happen" is contingent; it may well be true but it is not verifiable—what observations could be made that show this statement to be false? "Higgs bosons have a mean lifetime of 1 zeptosecond" is contingent, verifiable but currently unsupported by evidence. The three generalizations mentioned in the previous paragraph, by contrast, have the characteristic of a scientific law: we can observe instances, make measurements or conduct experiments in order to test the claim. The generalization "All swans are white" could be, and indeed was, falsified by the observation of a black swan; "All samples of bismuth melt at 271°C" by measuring the temperature of a melting sample of pure bismuth (and finding it to be different from 271°); and "Free-falling bodies fall with uniform acceleration" by releasing bodies of different masses from a height and finding them to accelerate with different speeds.

But there are many generalizations that are verifiable and verified but not genuine scientific laws. It may be a true generalization that all coins in Marnix's pocket are euro coins but this isn't a law. Or compare the two statements: "There is no sphere of gold that is larger than 20 kilometers in diameter" and "There is no sphere of uranium-235 that is larger than 20 kilometers in diameter." The latter is a genuine law: the critical mass of uranium-235 is 52 kilos, which is a sphere of about 17 centimeters. Beyond the critical mass, a nuclear chain reaction will start. By contrast, that there is no sphere of gold of that dimension is merely accidentally true (see Hausman 1992a: appendix).

Various criteria have been proposed to distinguish between "accidental" generalizations such as that about gold and genuinely nomological (law-like) generalization such as that about uranium. Suffice it to say that all have failed. One proposal has been to simply list all genuine scientific laws. While this wouldn't give us a criterion to determine what is a scientific law, it would help the D-N model because the model requires only that there be scientific laws, not a general criterion that enables us to decide what they are. Thus, "All samples of bismuth melt at 271°C" is a genuine law but "All coins in my pocket are euro coins" isn't.

Defining lawhood by listing paradigms is a viable option in economics— there are many statements that have been called laws. Here is a sample:

- *Engel's law*: "As incomes rise, the proportion of income spent on food falls, even if actual expenditure on food rises."
- *Law of diminishing returns*: "In all productive processes, adding more of one factor of production, while holding all others constant, will at some point yield lower per-unit returns."
- *Gresham's law*: "Bad money drives out good money."
- *Say's law*: "[All] products are paid for with products."
- *Laws of supply and demand*: "If the supply of a commodity increases (decreases) while the demand for it stays the same, the price decreases (increases); if the demand for a commodity increases (decreases) while the supply remains the same, the price increases (decreases)."
- *Iron law of wages*: "Real wages always tend, in the long run, toward the minimum wage necessary to sustain the life of the worker."
- *Okun's law*: "For every 1 percent increase in the unemployment rate, a country's GDP will be at an additional 2 percent lower than its potential GDP."

Despite this wealth of laws in economics (Wikipedia lists some 22 economic laws!), we will see in a moment that the deductive-nomological model of explanation is not a good model for explanation in economics. In fact, it is now generally believed to be deficient (e.g., Salmon 1989). It will turn out that discussing the model is very useful, however, because its various drawbacks have triggered the search for alternatives, and it is these alternatives that will be discussed in the remainder of Part I of this book.

The D-N Model and Its Discontents

In sum, the D-N model says the following. A scientific explanation is a logically valid and sound argument ("deductive") that contains at least one scientific law non-redundantly ("nomological"). Schematically:

Laws $L1, L2, \dots Ln$
Initial conditions $C1, C2, \dots Cn$
Therefore, E (the explanandum or phenomenon of interest).

Example: Why does this piece of chalk fall when I release it?

All massive objects released near the surface of the Earth fall. (Law)
The piece of chalk I am holding is a massive object. (Initial condition)
Therefore, the chalk falls when released. (Explanandum)

Practically every aspect of the model has been criticized since its first publication. Here I will discuss only three criticisms that are relevant to applications in the social sciences and, in particular, economics.

First, some philosophers have argued that human behavior does not fall under laws. Most notably, Donald Davidson has argued that D-N explanation of human behavior would require laws that connect mental events such as beliefs and desires with physical events such as actions, but there cannot be any psycho-physical laws. Davidson's argument that there are no psycho-physical laws is long and intricate (see Davidson 1970), and largely irrelevant for the purposes of this book. Setting these metaphysical considerations aside, it is still the case that human behavior seems to eschew lawlikeness, if by a law we mean a "universal generalization." All principles that describe human motivations—take Mill's "All humans seek wealth and avoid labour" or the contemporary economists' "People (always) prefer more to less"—are subject to qualification and counterexample. Thus, even if Davidson's metaphysical arguments were unsound, there simply wouldn't be, strictly speaking, any laws to get the D-N model off the ground.

And yet, it seems as though many explanations of human behavior are successful. Suppose that Sally is thirsty, and she believes that drinking water will quench her thirst. Sally's thirst is a reason for her drinking, and it explains her action *qua* being a reason. The rational-choice model economics uses is a more sophisticated example of this mode of explanation by reason. That model postulates that people have preferences among the various alternatives they can choose, and they have beliefs about what alternatives are available to them. These beliefs about available alternatives together with the preferences among the alternatives provide the reasons for the agent's choices, and they explain the agent's choices. I will look at this model of explanation in Chapters 3 and 4.

Second, even generalizations that do not cite human motivations or beliefs are seldom strictly universal. This is in fact true of generalizations in both natural and social sciences. No body will fall with uniform acceleration when there are disturbing forces. The melting point of bismuth will not be 271°C if the air pressure is altered significantly. All generalizations are therefore rough, subject to qualifications and exceptions.

As an example from economics, take the iron law of wages. Even in the formulation given above, a qualification is expressed: "Real wages always tend, in the long run, towards the minimum wage necessary to sustain the life of the worker." Real wages *tend* towards sustenance levels, they do not always approach these levels. David Ricardo remarked about the iron law:

> Notwithstanding the tendency of wages to conform to their natural rate, their market rate may, in an improving society, for an indefinite period, be constantly above it; for no sooner may the impulse, which an increased capital gives to a new demand for labor, be obeyed, than another increase of capital may produce the same effect; and thus, if the increase of capital be gradual and constant, the demand for labor may give a continued stimulus to an increase of people.

(Ricardo 1817)

Law statements therefore do not (usually) express universal generalizations but rather *causal tendencies* or *ceteris paribus laws*. A causal tendency obtains when some factor pushes another in a certain direction, even when its operation is interfered with by a disturbing factor. We might say that there is a tendency for an oil-price shock to drive up domestic prices. However, if there are other downward pressures on prices (for example, increasing competition), the oil shock might never *result* in increased inflation. Prices will still be higher than in the hypothetical situation in which there is no oil shock.

Ceteris paribus laws are similar. They hold only under certain conditions—"other things being equal," or, better, "other things being right." The quotation from Ricardo mentions some of the conditions that must be right in order for the iron law to result in wages approaching sustenance levels. All generalizations in economics are subject to such a *ceteris paribus* qualification.

Causal tendencies and *ceteris paribus* laws are explanatory, however. The oil-price shock can be cited to explain why prices are higher than they would have been without the shock—even though prices did not, in fact, increase. And *ceteris paribus* laws explain when the conditions under which the law holds can be specified precisely enough, and these conditions hold in a given case. These two forms of causal explanation will be looked at in Chapter 5.

Third, it is not clear whether laws *qua* regularities (whether accidental or genuine) are explanatory at all. Consider again Okun's law, which says that "for every 1 percent increase in the unemployment rate, a country's GDP will be at an additional 2 percent lower than its potential GDP" and suppose that, contrary to fact, this a strict and non-accidental law.

Is it explanatory? It seems rather that it is an empirical regularity that is itself seeking to be explained. Being confronted with the "law," we are inclined to ask, "Why does this regularity hold?" The reason is that few regularities in the social sciences (insofar as there are any regularities) are brute, not subject to further scrutiny. Rather, empirical generalizations such as Okun's law hold *on account of a deeper socio-economic structure*, and only if the underlying structure operates in a certain way, an empirical regularity will ensure.

A good explanation in economics will therefore ask for the detailed causal process or *mechanism* that is responsible for the phenomenon of interest. In the case of Okun's law, the phenomenon is an empirical regularity. In other cases it might be a singular event. Either way, a mere regularity that connects an input and an output—no matter how stable and lawlike that regularity is—does not explain why there is a connection between input and output. To investigate a mechanism means to open the black box between input and output and to illuminate why regularities hold and outcomes happen. We will return to social mechanisms in Chapter 6.

Conclusions

Scientific explanation is a major aim of all science, and economics is no exception. Economists explain to gain understanding of the economy and in order to make more accurate prescriptions and devise better policies. As the introduction to Part I of this book, this chapter has focused on the logical positivist so-called deductive-nomological model of explanation. According to this model, explanations are deductive arguments that contain at least one scientific law among their premises. The D-N model is now generally regarded as inadequate. Nevertheless, its discussion is useful as a starting point because of the terminology that was first introduced in the context of the model and that is still being used by philosophers, and because many of its deficiencies have triggered searches for alternatives that are more defensible. We looked at three deficiencies in particular:

- there are no psychological laws;
- genuine laws (universal or strict regularities) are rare, be it in social science or in science generally speaking;
- laws by themselves do not seem (highly) explanatory.

These deficiencies, finally, motivate the following alternatives to D-N explanation: rational-choice explanation; explanation in terms of causal tendencies and *ceteris paribus* laws; and mechanistic explanation.

Study Questions

1 "Economics must seek to be an explanatory science." Discuss.
2 Are there laws in economics? Come up with a number of arguments in favor and against.
3 What distinguishes genuine laws from merely accidental generalizations?
4 This chapter discussed three main problems of the D-N model of explanation. Do you see further problems? (Hint: one additional problem will be discussed in Chapter 5.)
5 Take a (token) phenomenon of your choice (e.g., the recent financial crisis, the collapse of the tiger economies or the rise of the USA as dominant economic power) and construct a D-N explanation of it. What obstacles do you encounter?

Suggested Readings

Any good introduction to philosophy of science or philosophy of social science will contain a chapter on explanation which could serve as a starting point for further examination of the topic. I first learned about the topic from Salmon 1992 and would still recommend it as general introduction. A splendid short book focusing on explanation in social science is D. Little 1991. I also learned much from Kincaid 1996. The state-of-the-art statement of the "received view" of scientific explanation of the logical positivists is Hempel 1965. For an in-depth historical overview of the development of philosophical thinking about explanation between 1960 and 1980, see Salmon 1989. See also the critical essays in Kitcher and Salmon 1989.

Part IA

Rationality

3 Rational-Choice Theory

Overview

According to one widely held view, human behavior is caused by intentions and motivations and therefore resists subsumption under natural laws. Rather, explanations of human behavior should describe the *reasons for actions*. The two chapters of this part deal with rationality at the individual level (Chapter 3) and at the level of interactions between individuals (Chapter 4). Both levels share the folk-psychological model according to which behavior is caused by the interaction of beliefs, opportunities and desires. They also share the idea that to explain an outcome means to rationalize it. According to this view, an account that portrays humans as erratic and unpredictable would not be explanatory as it would fail to elucidate the rational grounds for action.

Folk Psychology

There is a common-sense view that human behavior can and ought to be explained by the acting person's beliefs and desires. Why did Willy go on a diet? He believed he was overweight and hoped to lose some pounds. Why did Sally drink the water? Because she was thirsty and believed that drinking water would quench her thirst. To give economic examples, why did the US Treasury allow the investment bank Lehman Brothers to fail? Because the then Treasurer, Hank Paulson, thought it would be bad to saddle taxpayers with paying to save a private company that screwed up, and he believed that bailing Lehman out would do just that. At a more theoretical level, why do businessmen invest in the production of a good up to a point where marginal costs equal marginal revenue? Because they aim to maximize profits.

The view that human behavior can and ought to be explained by citing beliefs and desires is called folk psychology. Sometimes folk psychology is understood as "the body of information people have about the mind," which in turn is regarded as the "basis for our capacity to attribute mental states and to predict and explain actions" (Nichols 2002: 134).

Although often treated as synonyms, it is useful to distinguish between mere behavior on the one hand and "action" or "choice" on the other. Behavior is the more general notion that describes physical movements of the body that originate within the individual. Not every movement of the body is also behavior. Traveling from Amsterdam to London by airplane moves the traveler's body but one wouldn't describe it as the traveler's behavior. Behavior is caused by the agent, as when I type these sentences or scratch my ear. Behavior can be intentional or unintentional. Twisting and turning during sleep or reflexes such as the sudden pulling away of one's hand from a hot stove constitute unintentional or "mere" behavior. Actions are intentional behavior, caused by the beliefs and desires of humans and thus the topic of folk psychology.

Decisions are somewhat in between beliefs and desires on the one hand and actions on the other. Sally's desire to drink some wine together with her belief that there is some chilled Chardonnay in the fridge explains her decision to get herself a glass. But decisions do not automatically lead to choices. She might make up her mind but then fail to convert the decision into action, because of weakness of will, forgetfulness or change of mind.

We have to impose some constraints on the beliefs and desires for them to serve as an explanation of the human action of interest. Sally's desire to be a superstar together with her belief that the Chinese have the best cuisine in the world doesn't explain her choice to go to Harvard rather than Columbia to study medicine. Beliefs and desires have to be connected with the chosen action in the right way in order to explain the action.

The typical form for a belief such that together with the agent's desire to X explains the action A is "A helps to promote X" or sometimes "A constitutes (the fulfillment of) X." Sally's wanting to be a superstar and her belief that performing with her band on TV will help her realize that goal jointly explain her decision to accept the offer from the TV station. In the case of choosing Harvard over Columbia the desire might be to go to the best medical school in the USA together with the belief that Harvard is the best school. In this case the action simply constitutes the fulfillment of her desire.

Beliefs and desires are thus *reasons for action*. But not every reason someone might have to act in certain ways also explains her actions. Sally might have perfectly good reasons to go to Harvard—her desire to go to the best medical school in the States, to become a highly acclaimed brain surgeon or what have you. But in fact she might decide to go to Harvard because she values the beauty of the Indian summers in Boston extremely highly. Thus, not every reason an individual might have to perform an action also constitutes the reason that explains his or her action. Rather, it is the reason the individual *acted on* that explains the action. When one acts on a reason such that the action is an effective means to one's end, one is said to act in accordance with instrumental rationality (Way forthcoming).

There are two ideas built into the concept of "acting on a reason" according to Donald Davidson: besides the idea of rationality there is also the idea of cause (Davidson 1974). He thinks that an explanatory reason is a rational cause. It is a cause in that it helps to *bring about* the action. It is neither necessary nor sufficient for the action. Had Sally not acted on her desire to admire Boston's Indian summers, she might have decided to go to Harvard anyway because it's the best school. And it's not sufficient because it will only jointly with many other factors determine the action (as mentioned, these factors will include the absence of weakness of will, for instance).

Rationality is required for a different reason. The motivations and beliefs that lead people to act are not typically transparent to outsiders such as social scientists. If Sally is our friend, we can ask her about her original motivation, and even if one cannot always take what people say at face value (and this is true even if we disregard intentional lying: people are often bad judges of their own motivations), we will have far more information that allows us to determine what was the actual reason she did act on than a social scientist analyzing an individual or a group or groups of individuals. A social scientist relies on evidence mostly in the form of observable behavior. But in order to infer motivations or beliefs from behavior (or other accessible forms of evidence), one must make fairly strong assumptions concerning the system of beliefs and desires people have. If individuals acted very erratically (though always on reasons!) it would be impossible to infer beliefs or desires or both from their actions (see Hausman 2000).

Models of rationality are essentially one way to constrain the beliefs and desires people are allowed to have in order for their actions to be explainable by a social scientist. In the next two sections I will describe in some detail two models of rationality that have received a great deal of attention in economics: a model of decision-making under certainty, *ordinal-choice theory*; and a model of decision-making under risk, *cardinal-choice theory*. In the following chapter I will go on to discuss decision-making in strategic situations, also known as *game theory*. First, though, let us look at decisions under certainty.

Ordinal-Choice Theory

Preferences

Economists explain action by preferences which represent beliefs and desires. Preferences differ in various respects from desires. Most fundamentally, preferences are comparative, desires are absolute. When one says that Sally desires to enjoy Indian summers, nothing is entailed about other desires she might hold. In particular, desires can conflict without contradiction: Sally might desire both the beauty of Boston Indian summers as well as the unique buzz of living in New York City, fully knowing that she can't have both, and by stating her desires she would not contradict herself. But she would contradict herself if she said she (strictly) prefers Boston to New York and New York to Boston.

What Sally might say without contradicting herself is that she prefers Boston to New York *qua* weather and New York to Boston *qua* buzz. We can call this concept of preferences "partial evaluative ranking." It ranks alternatives with respect to certain qualities or attributes people value. In this conception, people can have as many rankings as the alternatives have attributes people value.

People can also rank alternatives overall or "all things considered" (Hausman 2012). Apart from asking her which city she prefers *qua* weather and which *qua* buzz, we can ask her what she prefers all things considered. Ordinary language permits both uses of the term "prefers." Economists (and decision theorists) tend to employ the latter conception. For example, Richard Jeffrey, a well-known logician and decision theorist, wrote:

> But throughout, I am concerned with preference *all things considered*, so that one can prefer buying a Datsun to buying a Porsche even though one prefers the Porsche qua fast (e.g., since one prefers the Datsun qua cheap, and takes that desideratum to outweigh speed under the circumstances). *Pref* = preference *tout court* = preference on the balance.
>
> (Jeffrey 1990: 225; original emphasis)

The advantages of explaining action in terms of preferences rather than desires, and taking preferences to be "preferences on the balance" from the point of view of the economist or other social scientist are easy to see. Sally's desire to enjoy many Indian summers will not automatically explain her decision to move to Boston rather than New York because she might also have a desire to enjoy the New York City buzz. A preference for Boston over New York does not explain her decision, either, if it is a partial preference and therefore compatible with a partial preference the other way. But citing Sally's preference for Boston over New York *all things considered* goes a long way towards explaining her decision.

Thus far I have compared preferences with desires. A desire is a particular state of mind, a mental entity. Economists do not always feel comfortable when mental states are invoked in explaining phenomena of interest. Mental states are unobservable to everyone but the individual who has them, and therefore of dubious scientific value if one thinks that a proper science deals only with verifiable states of affairs, as, among others, the logical positivists did. Indeed, statements from papers written by the pioneers in what later has come to be known as the "revealed-preference theory" of consumer behavior give testimony that worries about introspection and the scientific status were among their motivations (all of the following quotations are taken from Sen 1973: 242). Paul Samuelson, for one, argued that he aimed to "develop the theory of consumer's behavior freed from any vestigial traces of the utility concept" (Samuelson 1938: 71). What he meant by "the utility concept" was the idea used by the classical utilitarians Jeremy Bentham, James and John Stuart Mill and Henry Sidgwick, and that was pleasure or happiness—a mental state (for more detailed discussions of utilitarianism, see Chapters 12 and 14). A decade later in a paper developing the revealed-preference theory Ian Little claimed "that a theory of consumer's demand can be based solely on consistent behavior," which for him meant that "the new formulation is scientifically more respectable [since] if an individual's behavior is consistent, then it must be possible to explain that behavior without reference to anything other than behavior" (I. Little 1949: 90, 97). Note the focus on explanation in this quotation. A final example is due to John Hicks, who said that: "the econometric theory of demand does study human beings, but only as entities having certain patterns of market behavior; it makes no claim, no pretence, to be able to see inside their heads" (Hicks 1956: 6).

In this early work on consumer demand, preferences were *identified* with choices. A clear statement of the identification comes from the paper by Ian Little already cited:

> The verb "to prefer" can either mean "to choose" or "to like better," and these two senses are frequently confused in the economic literature. The fact that an individual chooses A rather than B is far from conclusive evidence that he likes A better. But whether he likes A better or not should be completely irrelevant to the theory of price.
>
> (I. Little 1949: 91–2)

The idea that preference and choice are synonymous and that consumption theory can make do without non-choice data has become the "standard approach" to economic analysis. According to a recent paper:

> In the standard approach, the terms "utility maximization" and "choice" are synonymous. A utility function is always an ordinal index that describes how the individual ranks various outcomes and how he behaves (chooses) given his constraints (available options). The relevant

data are revealed preference data; that is, consumption choices given the individual's constraints. These data are used to calibrate the model (i.e., to identify the particular parameters) and the resulting calibrated models are used to predict future choices and perhaps equilibrium variables such as prices. Hence, standard (positive) theory identifies choice parameters from past behavior and relates these parameters to future behavior and equilibrium variables.

Standard economics focuses on revealed preference because economic data come in this form. Economic data can—at best—reveal what the agent wants (or has chosen) in a particular situation. Such data do not enable the economist to distinguish between what the agent intended to choose and what he ended up choosing; what he chose and what he ought to have chosen.

(Gul and Pesendorfer 2008: 7–8)

Clearly, if economists want to explain economic phenomena using preferences they *must* be able to estimate preferences from data accessible to them, and individuals' mental states are not normally accessible. But the identification of preference with choice on which revealed-preference theory is based is too crude a means for achieving accessibility. Preferences are closely related to choices: preferences may *cause* and help to *explain* choices; preferences may be invoked to *justify* choices; in fortuitous circumstances, we can use preference data to make *predictions* about choices. But to identify the two would be a mistake (Hausman 2012: ch. 3).

To begin with, it is clear that we have preferences over vastly more states of affairs than we can ever hope (or dread) to be in the position to choose from. Here's a famous passage from Hume meant to illustrate a completely different point but which may serve as an example: "'Tis not contrary to reason to prefer the destruction of the whole world to the scratching of my finger" (Hume 1960 [1739], "Of the Passions," part III, section 3). Most of us will have the opposite preference but never be in the position to choose between the two. In fact, most of the things we have preferences over we do not choose. I prefer to live in good health (rather than die a violent premature death), to have more money than Bill Gates (rather than have what I have), the next president of Russia to be sane (rather than insane). I can choose none of these things. I can choose the apple over the chocolate éclair for pudding; I can choose a career in the pharmaceutical industry over one in philosophy; I can choose to campaign for more democracy in Russia over staying put. But I never choose among those more ultimate things that concern me a great deal.

Economists may object that they are not in the business of providing an analysis of the ordinary concept of preference but rather in the business of science, where they can choose to define a technical concept as they please (as long as it is scientifically valuable). In other words, economists may *stipulate* a concept of preference which may only be loosely connected to our ordinary concept.

Unfortunately, the scientific value of the technical concept of preference as choice is dubious as well. One problem is that defining preference as choice makes it conceptually impossible for people to make counter-preferential choices (Sen 1977). And yet, counter-preferential choice is surely a genuine phenomenon. People make all sorts of mistakes when they choose due to inattentiveness, weakness of will or false beliefs. The other day I chose to watch the movie *J. Edgar* (directed by Clint Eastwood), believing that it would be a drama. I prefer drama to comedy (the only available alternative at the time). The movie turned out to be a romance, which I hate even more than comedies. I was also told that Leonardo DiCaprio had learned to act since *Titanic*. On top of being misled about the nature of the movie I was lied to. I counter-preferentially chose romance over comedy because I was ill-informed.

Economists could in principle stick to their guns and deny the existence (or economic importance) of counter-preferential choice. I hear there are still economists around who deny the existence (or economic importance) of involuntary unemployment or asset bubbles. That move would not help, however, because of an assumption economists make concerning preferences, and in fact need to make if they want to predict and explain choice behavior from observations of past choice behavior. The assumption is that preferences are *stable* during a reasonable passage of time. This is how Hal Varian puts it:

> When we talk of determining people's preferences from observing their behavior, we have to assume that the preferences will remain unchanged while we observe the behavior. Over very long time spans, this is not very reasonable. But for the monthly or quarterly time spans that economists usually deal with, it seems unlikely that a particular consumer's tastes would change radically. Thus we will adopt a maintained hypothesis that the consumer's preferences are stable over the time period for which we observe his or her choice behavior.
>
> (Varian 2010: 118)

If people are not allowed to make mistakes, it is very unlikely that preferences are stable, even over short periods of time. Three days ago I "preferred" comedy over romance, yesterday romance over comedy, and today comedy over romance again. Such "preferences" no one can work with. What happened in fact is that I have had a stable *mental ranking* of alternatives but made a mistake in my *choice* yesterday. A conception of preference as mental ranking is more useful (Hausman 2012).

Another reason why preferences shouldn't be understood as choices is that in the more interesting parts of economic theory, beliefs and expectations over future states of affairs are needed in addition to preferences in order to explain choices. This is certainly the case for decision-making under risk (see below) and for game theory (see Chapter 4). Beliefs and expectations are mental states. To banish preferences understood as mental rankings because they are unobservable or subjective would mean one would have to banish beliefs and expectations too. One would throw out the baby with the bath water. Decisions under uncertainty and risk and game theory do not make sense without beliefs. And therefore preferences cannot be choices (cf. Hausman 2000, 2012). Henceforth, we will understand preferences as mental rankings of alternatives, "all things considered."

Choice Problems

The economic world does not come neatly parsed into clear-cut choice problems. Rather, an economist must formalize a given, naturally occurring situation into a choice problem. The way this is done determines the branch of choice theory relevant to the problem, and how the problem is to be solved. To give a simple and stupid example, suppose I am about to make breakfast and have to decide whether to have my coffee black (without milk) or white (with milk). One could formalize this as a simple choice between two goods (black coffee, white coffee) and apply decision theory under certainty. I might have a preference for white coffee over black, and since white coffee is available one could use decision theory to predict my choosing white coffee. But there are many more ways to conceive of the situation. We can build some uncertainty into it. I might prefer white coffee to black, but not when the milk is sour. I don't know for sure whether the milk is sour, but I can make reasonable guesses about it. If I know the probability that the milk is sour, then the problem is one of decision-making under risk, which will be examined in the next section.

There are yet other ways to think about the situation. Suppose I live with a flatmate, and he is responsible for buying milk. Now my best decision depends on his action, and his action might in turn depend on mine (he might or might not know for instance that I *really* like my coffee with milk and get very upset if there isn't any; his decision to buy milk might depend on his fear of my reproach). We're now in a game-theoretic situation.

Finally, my decision might depend on all sorts of contextual features. My decision to put milk in my coffee was immanent when I was making breakfast. That was an important piece of information, because I have white coffee for breakfast but black coffee after lunch. So my preferences are not over goods as such but rather over, say, "consumption bundles" which include relevant contextual features. An example due to Amartya Sen illustrates this point:

> Suppose the person faces a choice at a dinner table between having the last remaining apple in the fruit basket (*y*) and having nothing instead (*x*), forgoing the nice-looking apple. She decides to behave decently and picks nothing (*x*), rather than the one apple (*y*). If, instead, the basket had contained two apples, and she had encountered the choice between

having nothing (*x*), having one nice apple (*y*) and having another nice one (*z*), she could reasonably enough choose one (*y*), without violating any rule of good behavior.

(Sen 1993: 501)

The seemingly same act ("taking an apple from a fruit basket") can be a variety of different things, depending on whether there is more fruit in the basket but also of course on the social norms that are in place when the decision is being made—as Ken Binmore comments on Sen's example (Binmore 2009: 9): "The people in Sen's story inhabit some last bastion of civilization where Miss Manners still reigns supreme"—and other contextual features such as earlier decisions. Someone's preference for having an apple or not surely depends on whether he's already had a dozen or rather none, and if he is starving to death, he can safely decide to take the last apple even in the presence of Miss Manners. Care must be exercised when designing a choice problem.

For now I will ignore this issue and assume that the alternatives between which an agent chooses are sufficiently well described to apply decision theory coherently but come back to the issue further below.

Axioms and Preference Representation

Economists conceive of preferences as weak orders (in the mathematical or set-theoretic sense) over a set of available alternatives $x_1, x_2, ..., x_n$ in **X**. I will use the symbol "≥" to mean "weakly prefers," that is, either "strictly prefers" or "is indifferent to." In order to constitute a weak order, preferences must satisfy a number of formal properties. One is transitivity:

Transitivity: For all x_i, x_j, x_k in **X** if $x_i \geq x_j$, and $x_j \geq x_k$, then $x_i \geq x_k$.

If Sally prefers Harvard to Columbia, and Columbia to Johns Hopkins, she must also prefer Harvard to Johns Hopkins. The second main axiom is completeness:

Completeness: For all x_i, x_j in **X**, either $x_i \geq x_j$ or $x_j \geq x_i$ or both.

Completeness says that an agent is able to rank *all* available alternatives. For instance, Sally knows for any pair among the 134 institutions in the USA which award the degree of Doctor of Medicine whether she prefers one or the other or is indifferent between the two.

If one wants to represent preferences by means of a continuous utility function, as is often convenient, one has to assume that individuals' preferences satisfy an additional property:

Continuity: For all x_j in **X**, $\{x_i : x_i \geq x_j\}$ and $\{x_i : x_i \leq x_j\}$ are closed sets.

The axiom says that if an individual prefers each alternative in a series x_1, x_2, ... to another alternative y, and the series converges to some alternative x_n, then the individual also prefers x_n to y.

When people's preferences satisfy these properties, they can be represented by a utility function that is unique up to a positive order-preserving transformation. What this means is that one can associate all available alternatives with numbers in such a way she strictly prefers an alternative with a higher number to an alternative with a lower number (and is indifferent between two alternatives with the same number). The association of numbers with alternatives is arbitrary as long as it preserves the order among the alternatives. Table 3.1 gives an example of an individual's preferences among brands of beer, where a brand that is higher up in the table (and is associated with a higher number) is preferred to any brand that appears lower in the table (and is associated with a lower number).

Table 3.1 Ordinal Utility

Brand	Utility		
Budvar	2	1,002	–11.8
Jupiler	1	1,001	–11.9
Carlsberg, Heineken	0	1,000	–12

This individual prefers Budvar to Jupiler and either beer to both Carlsberg and Heineken, and is indifferent between Carlsberg and Heineken. The different sets of numbers express nothing beyond this. In particular the absolute values of and differences or ratios between the levels of utility are meaningless. A number is only meaningful relative to the other numbers and only with respect to where it appears in the ranking. One can only address the question: "Is 1,002 more or less than or equal to 1,001?" not "How much more than 1,001 is 1,002?"

Transitivity and completeness are the main axioms of this model of choice. Are these axioms defensible? There are two main ways to defend them. We could either try to argue that the axioms are *normatively* accurate, in that a convincing case that people's preferences *ought to* satisfy them can be made. Or we could try to argue that the axioms are *descriptively* accurate, in that they are useful in predicting and explaining people's actual choices. Let us consider both kinds of defense.

Rationality and Ordinal-Choice Theory

The most common normative justification of the transitivity requirement is to point out that agents whose preferences are intransitive may be subject to exploitation. If Sally prefers Columbia to Johns Hopkins, she would probably pay some money if she had a place at Johns Hopkins and was offered to swap. Now that she has a place at Columbia she'd pay some money for a place at Harvard. With intransitive preferences, she will now prefer Johns Hopkins to Harvard, once more pay money to get the place and end up where she started. This so-called "money-pump argument" in favor of transitivity was suggested by Frank Ramsey (1931 [1926]) and then developed by Davidson *et al.* (1955).

The money-pump argument is subject to a number of limitations, two of which I will consider here. First, people can be pumped only when they act on their preferences. Above I argued that preferences are not the same as choices. One might have intransitive preferences but never act on them and thus not be subject to exploitation. When one is offered trades, one might soon realize the risk of exploitation, amend one's preferences for the purpose of the trade and revert (or not) to intransitive preferences afterwards.

Second, the money-pump argument might be too strong to make its intended point. Let us suppose for the moment that an individual's preferences are indeed revealed by his choices. In order to prevent people from being money pumps, they do not necessarily have to have transitive preferences *at each point in time* but rather *over time*. Contrapositively, one can have transitive preferences at each point in time and still be victim to money pumpers because one's preferences change in such a way as to make them intransitive over time. Denote as "$>_t$" someone's preference at time t. Thus, an individual might have the following preferences: $x >_t y$, $y >_t z$ and $x >_t z$. That individual is in possession of z and is offered to trade it for y at an amount of money. He agrees. At time $t + 1$, the preferences have changed to: $x >_{t+1} z$, $z >_{t+1} y$ and $x >_{t+1} y$. He is offered a trade of the y that is now in his possession for x, and he agrees. At time $t + 2$, his preferences are now: $x >_{t+2} z$, $z >_{t+2} y$ and $x >_{t+2} z$. At this point, he is offered to trade the x that he now has for a z, which, once more, he agrees to. This individual's preferences are transitive throughout and yet he is being money-pumped because they are *dynamically* inconsistent. I will say a few more things about dynamic consistency below. For now, let me just state that there is nothing irrational as such with changing preferences.

Another argument that has been made is that the transitivity of preference is part of the meaning of the term "preference":

> The theory ... is so powerful and simple, and so constitutive of concepts assumed by further satisfactory theory ... that we must strain to fit our findings, or interpretations, to fit the theory. If length is not transitive, what does it mean to use a number of measure length at all? We could find or invent an answer, but unless or until we do, we must strive to interpret "longer than" so that it comes out transitive. Similarly for "preferred to."
>
> (Davidson 1980: 273; see also Broome 1991)

Davidson's defense is question-begging. If "preferred to" is analogous to "longer than," then "preferred to" must obey transitivity. But whether or not preference is relevantly like length is the question that is at stake here. We should not presuppose an answer.

Finally, there seem to be cases where decision-makers have good reason to entertain intransitive preferences. Paul Anand describes such a case:

> [I]magine that you are at a friend's dinner party and your host is about to offer you some fruit. If you are proffered an orange or small apple, you would rather have the orange, and if the choice is between a large apple and an orange you decide you would rather have the large apple. As it happens your friend is out of oranges and emerges from the kitchen with two apples, one large and one small. How should you choose? Etiquette seems to suggest that one might take the small apple and I find it difficult to see why such a choice must be judged irrational.
>
> (Anand 1993: 344)

The completeness property is even less well justifiable on rationality considerations (see for instance Elster 2007: 194; Gilboa *et al.* 2011). Robert Aumann once wrote:

> [O]f all the axioms of the utility theory, the completeness axiom is perhaps the most questionable. Like others, it is inaccurate as a description of real life; but unlike them we find it hard to accept even from the normative viewpoint.
>
> (Aumann 1962: 446)

If I'm offered "death by hanging" or "death by lethal injection" I might reasonably not have a preference for one over the other. And that wouldn't mean that I am *indifferent* between the two modes of dying. I am simply not able to rank the two options. Perhaps to the extent that preferences are used for explanations, this lack of justification does not matter too much. In a decision situation one is often forced to choose among alternatives, even in the absence of good reasons to go one way or the other. Perhaps economists are mainly interested in giving accounts for such situations. But, still, that is not a justification for the completeness axiom as an axiom of rationality.

There is an important difference between the absence of a preference between two options and indifference. Suppose one takes human life and money as incommensurable. One might then be given a choice between losing a human life and losing $10,000,000. One's absence of a preference then should not be interpreted as indifference, as the so-called "small-improvement argument" shows (Peterson 2009: 170). If one was really indifferent, then a small amount of money should tip the balance. So if one is really indifferent between saving a life and not expending $10,000,000, then one should prefer not to expend $10,000,000 minus one cent. However, if one thinks of the two options as incommensurable, one will resist this conclusion.

In sum, the two major axioms of ordinal decision theory are not incontrovertible from the point of view of rationality. Meeting a money pumper and accepting his offers, one had better have dynamically consistent preferences. But this tells us little about other situations. Likewise, when one is forced to make a choice, one will, but the choice does not necessarily reveal a pre-existing preference.

Ordinal-Choice Theory as Explanatory Theory

Actual decision-makers frequently violate the transitivity axiom. Economists have been concerned with the phenomenon since the late 1970s, when experimental work done by psychologists on the so-called "preference reversals" phenomenon was brought to their attention (Grether and Plott 1979). In the psychological experiments (Lichtenstein and Slovic 1971, 1973), subjects were asked to state their preference between lotteries. Pairs of lotteries were designed such that one offered a very high probability of winning a relatively small amount of money (the "P-bet"), and the other a smaller chance of winning a larger amount of money (the "$-bet"). The expected values of the two lotteries were roughly equal. Lichtenstein and Slovic predicted that people who chose P-bets would often pay more for a $-bet because in choice situations individuals' decisions are influenced primarily by the probability of winning or losing, whereas buying and selling prices are determined by dollar values. Their predictions were borne out in the data produced by their experiments.

Economists David Grether and Charles Plott began their paper with an acknowledgment of the significance of these findings:

> A body of data and theory has been developing within psychology which should be of interest to economists. Taken at face value the data are simply inconsistent with preference theory and have broad implications about research priorities within economics. The inconsistency is deeper than the mere lack of transitivity or even stochastic transitivity. It suggests that no optimization principles of any sort lie behind even the simplest of human choices and that the uniformities in human choice behavior which lie behind market behavior may result from principles which are of a completely different sort from those generally accepted.
>
> (Grether and Plott 1979: 623)

In their paper, Grether and Plott report the results of their own experiments in which they attempted to control for various alternative explanations of data such as insufficient incentives and indifference between lotteries (in Lichtenstein and Slovic's experiments, subjects did not have the option of stating that they were indifferent between lotteries; Grether and Plott included that option but it was seldom taken). They concluded:

> Needless to say, the results we obtained were not those expected when we initiated this study. Our design controlled for all the economic-theoretic explanations of the phenomenon which we could find. The preference reversal phenomenon which is inconsistent with the traditional statement of preference theory remains.
>
> (Grether and Plott 1979: 634)

Economists take intransitive preferences seriously enough to develop choice theories without the transitivity axiom. One alternative to standard rational-choice theory that allows for intransitive preferences is regret theory (Loomes and Sugden 1982).

It is much harder to test the completeness axiom empirically because most economists take a very close relationship between choice and preference for granted. If, for instance, a subject refuses to choose between alternatives, this will often be interpreted as evidence for indifference. Nevertheless, Duncan Luce (2005 [1959]) observed that people sometimes seem to choose alternatives probabilistically rather than deterministically (e.g., x is chosen over y in p% of cases and y over x in $(1 - p)$% of cases). This could be interpreted as deterministic preferences switching back and forth all the time or, more plausibly, as stable *stochastic* preferences. Stochastic preferences conflict with the completeness axiom, which says that people always prefer either x over y or y over x or are indifferent between the two.

Cardinal-Choice Theory

The value of many of the consequences of our choices depends on factors we cannot influence and that we do not know with complete certainty. Suppose Marnix is planning a birthday party for his twins, and he has to choose whether to plan a trip to the municipal outdoor swimming pool or the bowling center. The twins, and thus Marnix, would strongly prefer going to the swimming pool, but only if the weather is sunny. If the weather is bad, this is the least preferred option. They rank bowling in between, and the "bad weather" alternative higher than the "good weather" alternative because of the regret they'd feel if they went bowling knowing how much they would have enjoyed swimming in the sun. How should they decide?

Risk and Uncertainty

Alas, no one knows for sure what the weather will be like. But we may reasonably assume that the uncertainty surrounding weather events can be described by a probability distribution over these events. In Frank Knight's terminology (Knight 1921), the decision-maker is thus facing *risk*, not (radical) *uncertainty*. In decision-making under certainty, which outcome obtains is known. Sally, for example, was assumed to have full knowledge of the consequences of her choice between going to Harvard and going to Columbia. In decision-making under risk, it is not known what outcome will obtain, but it is known what outcome might obtain and with what probability. Outcomes are thus assumed to be generated by a stable process analogous to the rolling of a die or the spinning of a roulette wheel and the ball landing on a certain number. In decision-making under uncertainty it is neither known which outcome will obtain nor the probability with which it will occur. In fact, such a probability might not even exist. Arguably, most decisions actual economic agents face are characterized by this latter kind of uncertainty. In this book I will focus on decisions under risk because the associated decision theory is much better developed and easier to understand (but see Peterson 2009: ch. 3; Resnik 1987: ch. 2; Mitchell 2009).

Axioms and Preference Representation

There are three main differences between decision-making under certainty and under risk. First, the alternatives (over which the agent has preferences) are interpreted as *prospects*, which are defined as the pairing of the consequences of an action with the probabilities of these consequences occurring when the action is taken (Hargreaves Heap *et al*. 1992: 9). Essentially, prospects are lotteries. Suppose the probability of the weather's being good is p. The choice Marnix is facing is between one lottery that gives him p^*u(swimming | good weather) + $(1 - p)^*u$(swimming | bad weather), where $u(A \mid S)$ is the utility of action A given state of the world S, and another that gives him p^*u(bowling | good weather) + $(1 - p)^*u$(bowling | bad weather).

Second, in order to construct a representation of the agent's preferences by a(n expected) utility function, a variety of additional assumptions are required. The most important of these is an independence axiom, sometimes called Strong Independence (Hargreaves Heap *et al*. 1992: 9):

> *Strong Independence*: If $y = (x_i, x_j; p, 1 - p)$ and $x_i \sim y_i$,
> then $y \sim (y_i, x_j; p, 1 - p)$.

Strong Independence says that any component of a prospect can be replaced by another prospect to which the agent is indifferent, and the agent will be indifferent between the original and the new prospect. Hargreaves Heap *et al*. explain an implication of the axiom:

> Suppose that you are indifferent between $100 for certain and a 50–50 chance of receiving $250. Furthermore suppose that there are two prospects (I and II) which are identical except for one component: in I there is $100 with probability 1/5 and in II there is a 50–50 chance of $250

with probability 1/5. Strong Independence implies that you will be indifferent between I and II, since they differ only with respect to this component and you are indifferent between the two options for this component. It is sometimes felt that this is an unreasonable inference, since the $100 is no longer certain in the comparison between I and II. Yet, is it really reasonable to have this indifference upset by the mere presence of other prizes? Strong Independence answers "no."

(Hargreaves Heap *et al.* 1992: 10)

One of the reasons for mentioning Strong Independence here is that one of the most famous paradoxes in decision theory concerns a violation of the axiom (see below).

Third, if an agent's preferences satisfy all axioms, these can be represented by an expected-utility function that is *unique up to a positive affine transformation*. Thus, if an agent's preferences can be represented by an expected-utility function u, any function $u' = a + bu$ (where a, $b > 0$) can represent the agent's preferences equally well.

What an affine transformation means is best illustrated by an example of a quantity that is, like expected utility, measured on a cardinal scale: temperature. In order to determine a specific scale for measuring temperature, two points are fixed arbitrarily. In case of the Celsius scale, these are the melting point and the boiling point of water, and they are arbitrarily associated with $0°$ and $100°$. Once these are fixed, however, any other temperature is determined. That the melting point of bismuth, for instance, is $271°C$ is not arbitrary, given the two fixed points of the Celsius temperature scale.

A couple of things are noteworthy about the cardinal scale temperature. First, as mentioned above, it is unique up to an affine transformation. For example, to convert Celsius (C) into Fahrenheit (F), the formula $F = 32 + 9/5\ C$ is used. Second, ratios of differences are meaningful. While it does not make sense to say either that it is twice as hot in New York (where temperature is measured in Fahrenheit) as in London (where it is measured in Celsius) nor that the difference between the temperature in New York and London is such-and-such, it is perfectly meaningful to say that the difference between London's temperature today and yesterday is twice as large as the difference between New York's temperature today and yesterday.

Using these properties of cardinal scales, one can construct a utility function from people's judgments and expressions of indifference as follows. Arbitrarily (but sensibly) fix the lowest- and highest-ranking alternatives as 0 and 1, respectively. In our example, u(swimming | good weather) = 1 and u(swimming | bad weather) = 0. Then ask Marnix, "At what probability of good weather p are you indifferent between going bowling for sure and playing a lottery of going swimming in good weather with probability p and going swimming in bad weather with probability $1 - p$?" Finally, define the expected utility of outcomes to be equal to that probability.

Risk Attitudes

Expected-utility functions have the so-called expected-utility property. That is, the utilities they assign to prospects are the sum of the utilities of the payoffs, weighted by their probabilities. Thus, if $w = [(x, p), (y, 1 - p)]$, then $EU(w) = p*u(x) + (1 - p)*u(y)$.

Using this property, we can define various attitudes towards risk, depending on how the expected utility of a prospect relates to the utility of its expected value. Three attitudes are usually distinguished:

- *Risk-neutrality* means that an agent is *indifferent* between playing a lottery and receiving the expected value of the prospect for certain; that is, his expected utility of the prospect is identical to the utility of its expected value: $EU(w) = p*u(x) + (1 - p)*u(y) = u(p*x + (1 - p)y) = u(E(w))$. Firms in the theory of the firm (e.g., insurers) are often assumed to be risk-neutral.
- *Risk-aversion* means that an agent prefers receiving the expected value of the prospect for sure to playing the lottery: $EU(w)<u(E(w))$. Risk-aversion is often assumed for consumers. "Probabilistic insurances," for instance, in which the insured person receives the insurance sum with a probability less than 1 are rarely observed in the market. In the context of insuring their belongings, consumers are risk-averse.
- Being *risk-loving* means that an agent prefers playing the lottery to receiving its expected value for sure: $EU(w)>u(E(w))$. That some consumers are risk-loving must be assumed to explain gambling behavior because most gambles are "unfair" (gamblers receive less than the cost of playing the lottery on average). Interestingly, casino gambles are much fairer than the much more popular state lottery. In roulette, for example, the "house edge" (the average amount the player loses relative to any bet made) is a little above 5 percent in American roulette and 2.7 percent in European roulette, while the average player of a state lottery loses more than half of his ticket costs.

Expected-utility explanations are arguably somewhat deeper than explanations in terms of decision-making under certainty. To explain the choice of an apple if one could have had a banana by saying that the agent preferred an apple is not very illuminating. One way to interpret expected-utility theory (EUT) is to say that it constructs preferences over prospects from preferences over outcomes, given a risk attitude (cf. Hausman 2012). Assuming that people satisfy the axioms of EUT, they can be said to choose the prospect that maximizes their expected utility. But since the latter can be expressed as a weighted sum of utilities over outcomes, we can regard these utilities as basic and understand EUT as deriving preferences over prospects.

Consider a farmer who faces the choice between two crops, with the associated payoffs as described in Table 3.2.

Table 3.2 The Prudent Farmer

Weather	Crop A (€; utility)	Crop B (€; utility)
Bad (p = ½)	€10,000; 10	€15,000; 36
Good (1 − p = ½)	€30,000; 60	€20,000; 50
Average income	€20,000	€17,500
Average utility	35	43

We can easily see that the farmer is risk-averse because he derives higher utility from crop B, even though crop A gives him a higher average income.

To explain his choice, we can cite the preferences he has over the different outcomes and the beliefs he has about the probabilities of the weather. Most economists would say that the farmer's preferences over the prospects are given and basic. But this is implausible, and it prevents EUT being a genuinely explanatory theory. It is implausible because people will have more stable and basic preferences over things they ultimately care about. The farmer in this case cares about his income and the consumption associated with it, not about playing a lottery. (This may be different in other contexts. People might gamble solely for the enjoyment of the game and not for the money they might or might not win. In most cases, however, the enjoyment derives from the consequences of the choices, not from the choices themselves.)

The other reason for privileging this interpretation is explanation. If preferences over prospects were given, all an economist could say is that the farmer chose crop B because he preferred to do so—as in the case of decision-making under certainty. If one takes only preferences over outcomes as given and those over prospects or lotteries as derived, one can tell a more nuanced story about why farmer chose as he did.

Rationality and Expected-Utility Theory

The normative and descriptive aspects of expected-utility theory are interwoven, so I'll begin with a famous experimental observation of violation of Strong Independence: the Allais paradox (see Allais 1953). The Allais paradox is a choice problem designed by Nobel prize-winning economist Maurice Allais. Table 3.3 lists some of the choices subjects are given in experiments.

It turns out that most people choose A1 over A2, and most people choose A4 over A3. Importantly, the same individuals often choose A1 as well as A4, which violates Strong Independence. That axiom says that equal outcomes added to each of the two choices should have no effect on the relative desirability of one prospect over the other; equal outcomes should "cancel out." Experimental evidence suggests that they don't. People seem to prefer an amount for sure (€1,000 following act A1) to a gamble in which they have some chance of winning a higher amount but also some (albeit minimal)

Table 3.3 The Allais Paradox

States	S1 (p = 0.89)	S2 (p = 0.1)	S3 (p = 0.01)
Acts			
A1	€1,000	€1,000	€1,000
A2	€1,000	€5,000	€0
A3	€0	€1,000	€1,000
A4	€0	€5,000	€0

chance of winning nothing (A2). By contrast, if they are in a betting situation anyway (such as in the choice between A3 and A4), they prefer the lottery with the higher expected payoff.

It is important to see that it is not risk-aversion as such that explains these choices. Risk-aversion is consistent with expected-utility theory—the degree of risk-aversion can be measured by the curvature of the utility function (formally, it is measured by the ratio of its second derivative to its first derivative). Typical choices in the Allais paradox are *not* consistent with expected-utility theory. There is *no* utility function that is consistent with a preference of A1 over A2 and A4 over A3. To see this, compute the utility differences between the two pairs of acts (for any utility function):

$$u(A1) - u(A2) = u(\text{€1k}) - [0.89u(\text{€1k}) + 0.1u(\text{€5k}) + 0.01u(0)]$$
$$= 0.11u(\text{€1k}) - [0.1u(\text{€5k}) + 0.01u(0)]$$
$$u(A3) - u(A4) = 0.89u(0) + 0.11u(\text{€1k}) - [0.9u(0) + 0.1u(\text{€5k})]$$
$$= 0.11u(\text{€1k}) - [0.1u(\text{€5k}) + 0.01u(0)].$$

Many people confronted with these choices will, however, stick to them and insist that their choices are not irrational. Leonard Savage, one of the founders of modern decision theory, argued in response that in state S1 it does not matter, in either choice, which lottery is picked; this state should consequently be ignored. Decision-makers should base their decisions on features that differ between lotteries. In states S2 and S3 the payoffs differ between the lotteries, but the differences are exactly identical. Therefore, people should choose A1 over A2 if and only if they choose A3 over A4. This idea is called the "sure-thing principle" (Savage 1972: 21ff.).

Not everyone agrees with the sure-thing principle (McClennen 1988). In particular, it has been argued that Savage's principle begs the question as to why we ought to ignore the sure-thing outcomes. Perhaps Savage has given us an explanation of why violations sometimes occur, but he has not positively shown that we ought not to violate the principle. And there is certainly a relevant different between the pairs A1/A2 and A3/A4. If I were to end up in state S3 after choosing A2, I will regret my choice a great deal. I could have had a good amount of money for sure. I chose to gamble and lost. That was silly. In the choice between A3 and A4, the odds that I end up with nothing are overwhelming anyway. I'd consider myself lucky if I did win but not winning wasn't silly. Quite to the contrary, it would have been unreasonable to forfeit a good chance of a considerable higher gain for a minimally smaller chance of losing. I would not regret my choice.

Expected-Utility Theory as Explanatory Theory

There are various other paradoxes like Allais', one of which I will discuss here. I will only point out that people often violate the axioms of expected-utility theory, but not ask whether it is reasonable to do so.

Ellsberg's Paradox. Ellsberg's paradox (see Ellsberg 1961), first noticed by Daniel Ellsberg when he was a PhD student in Harvard in the 1950s, also demonstrates a violation of Strong Independence. It involves choosing from an urn with different-colored balls whose composition is not precisely known. It therefore involves uncertainty, and not mere risk.

In the example, you are supposed to have an urn containing 30 red balls and 60 other balls that are either black or yellow. You know that there are 60 black and yellow balls in total, but not how many of each there are. The urn is well mixed, so each individual ball is as likely to be drawn as any other. You are now given two choices between two prospects each:

> Choice 1
> Option A: You receive €100 if you draw a red ball.
> Option B: You receive €100 if you draw a black ball.
>
> Choice 2
> Option C: You receive €100 if you draw a red or yellow ball.
> Option D: You receive €100 if you draw a black or yellow ball.

Since the prizes are exactly the same, it follows from EUT that you will prefer prospect A to prospect B if and only if you believe that drawing a red ball is more likely than drawing a black ball. Further, there would be no clear preference between the choices if you thought that a red ball was as likely as a black ball. Similarly it follows that you will prefer prospect C to prospect D if and only if you believe that drawing a red or yellow ball is more likely than drawing a black or yellow ball. It might seem intuitive that, if drawing a red ball is more likely than drawing a black ball, then drawing a red or yellow ball is also more likely than drawing a black or yellow ball. So, supposing you prefer prospect A to prospect B, it follows that you will also prefer prospect C to prospect D. In experiments, however, most people strictly prefer prospect A to prospect B and prospect D to prospect C.

To see that this violates EUT, again compute the differences of expected utilities between the lotteries:

$$u(A) - u(B) = \tfrac{1}{3}u(\text{€}100) - p_{\text{Black}}u(\text{€}100)$$
$$u(C) - u(D) = \tfrac{1}{3}u(\text{€}100) + (\tfrac{2}{3} - p_{\text{Black}})u(\text{€}100) - \tfrac{2}{3}u(\text{€}100) = \tfrac{1}{3}u(\text{€}100)$$
$$- p_{\text{Black}}u(\text{€}100).$$

People choose in such a way as to avoid gambles with unknown probabilities. Since the proportion of black balls is not known, they choose A over B. Since the proportion of yellow balls is not known, they choose D over C. This too violates the sure-thing principle.

Stability, Invariance and Justifiers

Whether or not to accept experimental data as violations of expected-utility theory depends on the experimenter's beliefs about the stability of subjects' preferences and about how subjects construe a choice problem (see the section on "Choice Problems" above). The two assumptions interact. Any *apparent* violation of an axiom of the theory can always be interpreted as any of three things:

- the subjects' preferences *genuinely* violate the axioms of the theory;
- the subjects' preferences have changed during the course of the experiment;
- the experimenter has overlooked a relevant feature of the context that affects the subjects' preferences.

As we saw above, economists assume that subjects' preferences are stable for the goals and purposes of an economic investigation. Let us formulate this idea as a principle (cf. Binmore 2009: 9):

> *Stability.* Individuals' preferences are stable over the period of the investigation.

Stability is not enough, however. This is because even assuming stability any apparent violation could be explained by the fact that a subject interprets the choice situation differently than the experimenter; she sees a difference between two choices where the experimenter sees none. Thus let us formulate a second principle (cf. Hausman 2012: 16):

> *Invariance.* Individuals' preferences are invariant to irrelevant changes in the context of making the decision.

I have given some examples of contextual features that do not appear to be irrelevant to subjects' preference orderings above. But not just any contextual feature is allowed to change the preference ordering. Economists, for instance, insist that the presenting of *irrelevant alternatives* should not matter to one's preferences, as illustrated by an anecdote involving the late Sidney

Morgenbesser, a philosopher at Columbia University, who, apparently, is better remembered for his wit than his publications, and about whom the following tale is told:

> According to the story, Morgenbesser was in a New York diner ordering dessert. The waitress told him he had two choices, apple pie and blueberry pie. "Apple," Morgenbesser said.
>   A few minutes later the waitress came back and told him, oh yes, they also have cherry pie.
>   "In that case," said Morgenbesser, "I'll have the blueberry."
>
> (Poundstone 2008: 50)

In the story, the availability of a further alternative, cherry pie, should not matter to the preference between apple and blueberry pie. Such a preference change, induced by an irrelevant alternative becoming available, is regarded as irrational by economists.

What features shall we allow to induce preference changes? It is clearly *not* irrational to prefer to drive on the right side of the road when on the Continent and on the left when in Britain. Nor is it irrational to prefer coffee to tea for breakfast and tea to coffee at teatime. It is also not irrational to prefer having a piece of chocolate cake to having nothing when that piece is the first and to prefer having nothing to having another piece when one has already had four. The mere passage of time does *not* seem to be a choice-relevant factor, however (as is illustrated by the fact that most economists regard hyperbolic discounting as an anomaly; see Chapter 15).

These considerations also show that there is a problem, which one could formulate as a dilemma for the economist. Standard rational-choice theory is usually regarded as a formal, as opposed to substantive, theory of rationality (e.g., Hausman and McPherson 2006; Hausman 2012). Here is one way of putting the issue:

> [T]hat an agent is rational from [rational-choice theory]'s point of view does not mean that the course of action she will choose is objectively optimal. Desires do not have to align with any objective measure of "goodness": I may want to risk swimming in a crocodile-infested lake; I may desire to smoke or drink even though I know it harms me. Optimality is determined by the agent's desires, not the converse.
>
> (Paternotte 2011: 307–8)

The idea goes a long way back, to both David Hume and Max Weber. Hume thought that "Reason is, and ought only to be the slave of the passions, and can never pretend to any other office than to serve and obey them" (Hume 1960 [1739]). People value this and that; reason has no say in what they ought to value. I should mention in passing that an assumption along the lines that people always prefer more money to less would be inconsistent with this

Humean principle. If economists have nothing to say about what individuals ought to value, they surely cannot assume that individuals always value more money higher than less.

Max Weber's influence stems from his view of objectivity in the social sciences. Weber thought, like David Hume, that there was a clear distinction between facts and values (Weber 1949). The social sciences, being sciences of human behavior, cannot avoid dealing with values altogether. Weber then thought that the social sciences can preserve objectivity by restricting the values that are allowed to play a role in scientific investigations to the values held by agents under investigation. The social scientist should not influence the study by adding his or her own values. Rather, he or she should take the analyzed agents' ends as given and proceed from there.

Against the backdrop of Hume's ideas about "reason versus passions" and Weber's views on objectivity, we can easily see the significance of the distinction between formal and substantive theories of rationality. Rationality is clearly an evaluative notion. A rational action is one that is commendable, and an irrational action is one that is not. One cannot consistently say that a certain choice would be irrational and at the same time that the agent ought to do it. But, according to the economist's view, it is the agent's values that matter in the evaluation, not the economist's. The economist provides only some formal constraints of consistency.

The problem is that invariance is not a merely formal principle. If we left it to the agent to determine what counts as a "relevant" feature of the context, no choice would ever be irrational. Preferring beer to wine at one instant and wine to beer at the next will not reveal intransitive preferences, because the agent will be a few heartbeats older, and he might consider that fact relevant (age is surely relevant in the limit: there is no inconsistency in preferring sweet to savory as a child and savory to sweet as an adult).

To see how difficult it can be to determine whether a contextual feature is relevant or not, consider an example that is very similar to Morgenbesser's choice between apple and blueberry pie. Recall that Morgenbesser was making fun of someone violating invariance by reversing his preference when a new option became available. The example considered now shows that it doesn't always seem irrational to reverse one's preferences when new options become available or unavailable. The next day, the waitress asks Morgenbesser if he'd like chicken or steak. He chooses steak. After a minute, the waitress comes back and says they have a daily special, USDA prime rib. Morgenbesser says he would like that instead. Another minute passes and the waitress comes back again, announcing that the last prime rib has just gone to the customer who is sitting at the table next to his. "In which case," Morgenbesser says, "I'd like to have the chicken."

Now that he could have had prime rib, every bite of the ordinary steak would remind him of the forgone opportunity and make him feel regretful. He therefore chooses chicken in order to avoid such feelings of regret. It is at least not clear that this should be regarded as a piece of flawed reasoning.

Hence, sometimes the becoming available or unavailable of an alternative can induce a rational preference change, at other times a change in preference is irrational.

This is not merely a philosopher's worry. In Chapter 10 below I will describe in more detail a series of experiments on intransitive preferences conducted by economists Graham Loomes, Chris Starmer and Robert Sugden (Loomes *et al.* 1991). Loomes *et al.* point out that the results of earlier experiments on intransitive preferences such as the preference-reversal experiments by Slovic and Lichtenstein or Grether and Plott can be explained away by accounts other than ones involving intransitive preferences. One of the alternative accounts is that people regard choice-tasks and valuation-tasks as different kinds of problems, and consequently have different preferences. Another is that subjects do not regard the series of tasks as independent but instead treat it as a single lottery. In both cases (and others) the transitivity axiom can be saved. (Albeit at the expense of violating Strong Independence; that axiom is, however, more controversial anyway.) In their own experiments, Loomes *et al.* control for these and other alternative explanations of the results. But they too must make assumptions such as stability and invariance for the preferred interpretation of their results because there are always some differences between any two choice situations.

John Broome has a principle, similar to invariance, that helps to the construction of choice problems (Broome 1991: 103):

> *Principle of Individuation by Justifiers.* Outcomes should be distinguished as different if and only if they differ in a way that makes it rational to have a preference between them.

Broome's principle makes plain that one needs to make assumption about the nature of rationality when one designs a choice problem. Economists will not like this principle because they do not like to make substantive assumptions about rationality, which is why I concealed that matter by using a seemingly more innocuous term such as "relevant." But relevance, too, is something the economist has to decide on the basis of considerations about the nature of rationality.

The dilemma the economist faces, then, is this. He can either stick with the "formal axioms" of completeness, transitivity, Strong Independence and so on and refuse to assume the principles of stability and invariance. But then rational-choice theory will be useless for all explanatory and predictive purposes because people could have fully rational preferences that constantly change or are immensely context-dependent. Alternatively he can assume stability and invariance but only at the expense of making rational-choice theory a substantive theory, a theory laden not just with values but with *the economist's* values. The economist then has to decide whether, say, presenting an analogous problem as a choice-task and as a valuation-task is the same thing; more generally, whether framing a problem one way or another may reasonably affect someone's preferences; what relevant alternatives are;

whether, to what extent and what social norms may matter; whether to conceive of a series of choices as a single-choice problem or indeed a series of independent choices; and so on.

Conclusions

The empirical violations of rational-choice theory give the whole idea of explanation by reasons a somewhat ironic twist. The reason to look for rational-choice explanations of actions is that, at least according to Donald Davidson, there are no strict laws that relate mental events such as beliefs and desires with physical events such as bodily behavior. But the project of trying to explain human behavior is not yet doomed because we can explain behavior by citing reasons for action.

Social scientists must learn the reasons for action from observable behavior or otherwise accessible evidence. This means that they have to impose fairly stringent consistency and stability constraints on behavior in order for it to be interpretable in terms of rational-choice theory. But of course, human behavior isn't particularly consistent and stable—this is why there are no psycho-physical laws to begin with. If human behavior is not consistent and stable, the project of trying to explain it in terms of reasons for action is somewhat less promising.

Study Questions

1 Ought your preferences to be complete? Ought they to be transitive? Discuss.
2 Do we normally know the probability of outcomes which obtain in the future? How good is expected-utility theory as a model of choice?
3 Explain the difference between the Allais and Ellsberg paradoxes.
4 What are, in your view, contextual features that should make a difference to an individual's preference ordering?
5 Are unstable preferences irrational?

Suggested Readings

The best introduction to rational-choice theory is, to my mind, Resnik 1987. Somewhat more advanced and critical is Hargreaves Heap *et al.* 1992. Other very useful texts include Gilboa 2010 and Peterson 2009. Hausman 2012 provides a comprehensive treatment of the nature of preferences and the use of the concept in economics. Ratcliffe 2007 is a good and critical discussion of folk psychology.

4   Game Theory

- Overview
- Whither the Euro?
- Some Games and Some Formalism
- Game Theory's Payoffs
- Game Theory and Rationality
- Game Theory as Explanatory Theory
- Study Questions
- Suggested Readings

Overview

In this chapter I will look at some pressing philosophical issues concerning game theory in both its descriptive as well as its prescriptive modes. After some motivation and preliminaries, I will introduce the game-theoretic formalism along with famous games that have proved to be of philosophical interest. I will then look at some arguments in the debate whether game theory is an empirically more or less empty formalism or a substantive theory and finally whether it is a normative theory of rational choice.

Whither the Euro?

When this chapter was written (December 2011), the euro still existed as the official currency of the eurozone of 17 of the 27 member states of the EU. Here is a prediction: when the chapter is being read, the euro will no longer exist in that form. It might continue to exist as a common currency for a core EU, but if so, the financial architecture behind it will be quite different.

One of the most important issues dividing the EU today is whether to introduce so-called European bonds or "Stability bonds," sovereign debt backed collectively by all eurozone member states, in order to save the common currency. So far sovereign debt within the eurozone has been *denominated* in euros but *guaranteed* only by the issuing country. Is it a good idea to change that and to introduce a system of joint liability?

Any economic argument makes idealizing assumptions (see Chapter 7), so let us begin by caricaturing the actual situation. There are two blocs of euro-zone states, the "North" and the "South." Within each bloc, national poli-cies are completely homogeneous so that we can treat each bloc as a single economic agent. Both North and South have a menu of fiscal policy options. Simplifying—caricaturing—again, let us assume that there are only two available fiscal policies: being "frugal" or being "profligate." A "frugal" policy is one that encourages saving, that reduces the fiscal deficit or even pays back government debt. A "profligate" policy is one that encourages consumption, that does not mind running budget deficits and that will pile up government debt. If both blocs are profligate, total eurozone government debts will soon run out of control, interest rates will surge and, on occasion, interventions by the European Central Bank (ECB) in the form of direct purchases of government bonds will enable continued spending. These interventions will fuel inflation, which will rise to 10 or more percent per year. The currency will be devaluated relative to the US dollar and the yuan. Let us call this scenario "currency erosion." Neither bloc particularly likes it.

What about other scenarios? Let us suppose that both blocs are strong enough to shoulder the other's debt as long as at least one of them is frugal. That is, if either North or South but not both are frugal, sovereign debt will rise at best modestly, inflation will be contained and the euro remain strong relative to other currencies. Whichever bloc is profligate will of course consume much more than the frugal one; and employees in the frugal bloc will work, to some extent, in order to subsidize the other bloc's consumption.

What policies do North and South prefer? Let us begin with the stereo-type. The North with its Protestant and principled ethics prefers to be frugal no matter what—for frugal is what one ought to be. The preferences of the Catholic and utilitarian South are more complicated. It likes best the North to finance its lavish consumption: i.e., itself to be profligate when the North is frugal. With joint liability it is free to act in this way—the North guar-antees its government debt, after all. We can assign this situation an arbi-trary number, let's say 5. The South likes least the counterfactual situation in which the South works in order to finance lavish consumption in the North—this is unheard of. Assign this situation the number 0. Being frugal when the North is frugal is intermediate, perhaps 3. Currency erosion is liked much less but still preferred to being a sucker to the North, so let's give it a 1.

In the beginning, the North will be frugal and the South profligate. But the North, though principled, is certainly not pea-brained and will soon learn that it could profit from the Eurobond system if it started consuming and had others pay for it. They of course will not like the currency to erode, but will like even less continuing to be a sucker to the South. Being frugal alongside the other is still an option they like, though not quite as much as having others paying for an opulent lifestyle. In other words, the North's preferences are now a mirror image of those of the South.

If we now call the numbers (which are arbitrary as long as they preserve the ordering of policy options) "payoffs," North and South "players," the policy options "strategies" and arrange the whole shenanigans in a matrix such that player 1's strategies appear in the rows and player 2's strategies in the columns, we have what economists call a "game" (see Figure 4.1).

How do we make a prediction about what players will do in a game? Focus on the North's actions first. Suppose—counterfactually—that the South plays "frugal." If the North is frugal itself, it will end up with a payoff of 3. If, by contrast, it plays "profligate," it will end up with 5. So it will play "profligate." This is precisely what the numbers mean: a higher payoff just means that that strategy will be played given the chance, no mistakes are being made etc. If the South plays "profligate" the North will end up with 0 when it plays "frugal" but 1 when it plays "profligate." In that situation, too, it will play "profligate." That is, no matter what the South does, the North will play "profligate"—despite its initial Kantian ethics. Since the South's preferences are a mirror image of those of the North, the exact same reasoning applies to the South, so they will end up both playing "profligate," the currency will erode and the union dissolve. The bottom line is: perhaps it's not such a good idea to have countries with different interests guarantee one another's debt.

Game theory is the branch of economics which concerns itself with strategic situations such as this. The game I mockingly called the "Eurobonds game" is in fact a version of the Prisoner's Dilemma, one of the most important and most widely discussed games analyzed by the theory. To some, Game theory has been the main driver of theoretical progress in economics in the last 30 or so years (Kincaid and Ross 2009). To others, it is a mere "branch of applied mathematics" (Rosenberg 1992: 248). It is thus controversial whether game theory is a substantive empirical theory that allows making predictions and explains phenomena of interest. What appears to be less controversial is the understanding of game theory as the theory of rational choice in situations of strategic interaction (this is certainly how the founders of game theory saw it; see von Neumann and Morgenstern 1944).

		South	
		Frugal	Profligate
North	Frugal	(3, 3)	(0, 5)
North	Profligate	(5, 0)	(1, 1)

Figure 4.1 The Eurobonds Game

But appearances deceive. While most philosophers and economists agree that there *is* a prescriptive reading of the theory, it is by no means clear what this reading amounts to. We can illustrate this in a simple and intuitive way using our Eurobonds Game. If the two players play the strategies they most prefer, they end up in a situation they both dislike—currency erosion. Given the players know this, to many observers playing "profligate" does not seem so rational after all, especially when there seems to be a Pareto-superior set of strategies available ("frugal," "frugal"). Economists tend to respond that the Pareto-superior set of strategies is only seemingly available. This is because if one of the players did play that strategy, the other would have a massive incentive *not* to do so himself, which is predicted by the first player, who will therefore also stick with playing "profligate." But who is to say that *this* reasoning is compelling?

The set of strategies ("profligate," "profligate") is called a "Nash equilibrium." As we will see below, the justification for why rational agents ought to play Nash-equilibrium strategies is very thin. Moreover, the Prisoner's Dilemma is a very unusual game in that it has a unique Nash equilibrium. Most games have many such equilibria, and there are no good principles to guide players in selecting a specific Nash equilibrium. It is therefore often not quite clear what "the" rational course of action in a given strategic situation amounts to.

Some Games and Some Formalism

The folk of economics are *economic agents*. Economic agents have *preferences*, which means that they can order the options available to them. When the value of the different options an agent faces depends on what other agents do (that is, when they are in strategic situations), the agents are said to play a *game*, and they are referred to as *players*. Players in games select among *strategies*. A strategy is a sequence of actions that tells a player what to do in response to other players' possible strategies. There are two main forms to represent a game: strategic (or normal) and extensive. The *strategic form* is a matrix, as in Figure 4.1. The *extensive form* resembles a tree, as in Figure 4.2, where the same game is represented in this alternative mode. When I was first taught game theory, our teacher referred to extensive forms as Baselitz-style trees, for obvious reasons.

In strategic form, the players' strategies are arranged in the *rows* and *columns* of the matrix, and there is a convention to list player 1's strategies in the rows, and player 2's strategies in the columns. (Games with more than two players exist of course, but we will not consider them in this chapter.) In extensive form, players' decision points are represented by *nodes*, and their strategies by *branches* (or arrows) emanating from the nodes. In either form, the *outcome* of the game is a set of *payoffs* to the players, and payoffs are ordinal utilities assigned to players (or cardinal utilities when mixed strategies are allowed; mixed strategies will be introduced below).

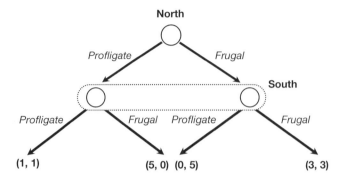

Figure 4.2 The Eurobonds Game in Extensive Form

To solve a game, one has to find its equilibrium or set of equilibria. The most important equilibrium concept is that of the *Nash equilibrium*. A Nash equilibrium is a set of strategies such that no player can improve her payoff by changing her strategy, given the strategies of the other players. One way to find a Nash equilibrium in a strategic-form game is by eliminating *strictly dominated strategies*. A strategy is said to be strictly dominated whenever it is inferior to all other strategies regardless of what the other player does. Thus, in the matrix of Figure 4.1 playing "frugal" is a strictly dominated strategy for player 1, North, because playing "profligate" is superior independently of whether player 2, South, plays "frugal" or "profligate." We can therefore eliminate the top row. The same reasoning applies to player 2, so here we can eliminate the left column. There remains a single set of strategies ("profligate," "profligate"), which constitutes the unique Nash equilibrium of the game.

But as mentioned above, the Prisoner's Dilemma is an unusual game. Consider a second game philosophers enjoy discussing, the Stag-Hunt Game (Figure 4.3).

The story associated with it stems from Jean-Jacques Rousseau's *Discourse on Inequality* in which he describes the advantages of social cooperation:

		Hunter 2	
		Stag	Hare
Hunter 1	Stag	(3, 3)	(0, 2)
	Hare	(2, 0)	(1, 1)

Figure 4.3 The Stag-Hunt Game

Was a deer to be taken? Everyone saw that to succeed he must faithfully stand to his post; but suppose a hare to have slipped by within reach of any one of them, it is not to be doubted that he pursued it without scruple, and when he had seized his prey never reproached himself with having made his companions miss theirs.

(Rousseau 2002 [1755]: 116)

This passage is often interpreted as describing the following situation (cf. Skyrms 2004). Two individuals go out on a hunt. Each can individually choose to hunt a stag or hunt a hare. Each player must choose an action without knowing the choice of the other. If an individual hunts a stag, he must have the cooperation of his partner in order to succeed. An individual can get a hare by himself, but a hare is worth less than a stag.

The first thing to notice about the Stag-Hunt Game is that there are no dominated strategies. "Hare" is the inferior strategy only when the other hunter plays "stag," and "stag" is inferior when the other plays "hare." We can nevertheless find Nash equilibria, namely ("stag," "stag") and ("hare," "hare"): when one hunter plays "stag," the other hunter cannot improve his payoff by playing "hare"; the same is true for "hare."

There is an obvious sense in which ("stag," "stag") is a "better" solution than ("hare," "hare"): both players receive a higher payoff, which means that both players prefer that outcome. But the Nash equilibrium concept by itself does not allow us to choose among different equilibria. To do so, various "refinements" of the concept have been proposed which we will consider below.

The main difference between strategic- and extensive-form games is that the latter allows the representation of sequential moves. Suppose, counter to fact, that in the Eurobonds Game the North moves first and plays "frugal." If the South knows this, it will play "profligate" and the outcome will be (0, 5). If the North plays "profligate" and the South knows this, it will also play "profligate," resulting in (1, 1). The North will anticipate the South's move and therefore play "profligate." Figure 4.2 shows this sequence of moves. However, in the original set-up, the players were assumed to move simultaneously or, more accurately, ignorant of the other player's move. In extensive games such assumptions about knowledge can be represented by the device of an *information set*. The dotted lines around the South's nodes indicate that the South does not know whether it is at the left or at the right node.

In other sequential games the first mover's actions are known. Consider Figure 4.4, called the Ultimatum Game. In an Ultimatum Game (another philosophers' favorite), player 1 (the "proposer") divides a cake and player 2 (the "responder") responds by either accepting the division, in which case both players receive the amount allocated by player 1, or rejecting it, in which case both players receive zero.

(Figure 4.4 is simplified; more accurate would be a representation in which there are as many branches from the proposer node as there are ways

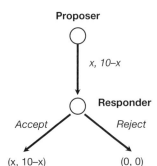

Figure 4.4 The Ultimatum Game

to divide the cake; for instance, one for 10–0, one for 9–1, and so on.) In this game, the responder will accept any offer greater than zero, which will be predicted by the proposer, who therefore offers the minimum amount possible. Sequential games are solved by what is called *backward induction*. Backward induction reasons from outcomes backwards to earlier decision problems. I will say more about the method below. In this simple game, there are only two stages. The responder makes the final (second) move, accepting or rejecting the offer. He will prefer to accept any non-zero offer. Knowing this, the proposer decides about the size of the offer. Maximizing, he will offer the smallest amount the responder will still accept, i.e., the smallest possible non-zero offer.

There are two final distinctions I want to introduce. The first is the distinction between *one-shot* and *repeated* games. *Finitely* repeated games are analyzed in exactly the same manner as one-shot (sequential) games, by backward induction. Suppose the Eurobonds Game of Figure 4.2 was repeated 20 times. At the very last stage, South would still do better by playing "profligate," which would be predicted by the North. The North would at the second-but-last stage also play "profligate," which in turn would be predicted by the South. This reasoning continues all the way to stage one.

Infinitely repeated games (or games in which agents do not know the number of rounds that are being played) are really a different matter. Here "always play 'profligate'" is no longer a dominant strategy (Aumann 1959). Rather, other strategies have higher payoffs. One such strategy is known as "tit-for-tat." "Tit-for-tat" means that the player starts by playing a "nice" strategy (in this case, "frugal") and then observes what the other player does. If the other player's move is also "nice," he continues doing the same. If the other player plays selfishly (in this case, "profligate"), the first player retaliates by doing so himself now and in future games (Rapoport and Chammah 1965).

Finally, there is a distinction between *pure* and *mixed* strategies. So far we have considered only pure strategies, by which deterministic strategies are meant: an agent makes up his mind and plays the chosen strategy. In the mixed case, a strategy is assigned a probability by the player, who then lets a random device determine which way he chooses. When there are only two options, one can think of the agent's decision as one about how to load a coin (and let the coin toss determine which strategy is in fact chosen).

A simple mixed strategy can be illustrated by the children's game Rock–Paper–Scissors. As can easily be seen in Figure 4.5, there is no Nash equilibrium in pure strategies. If player 1 plays "rock," player 2's best response is "paper"; player 1's best response to that is "scissors," to which player 2 best responds by playing "rock" and so on. If the players had a random device (such as a three-sided coin), how would they "load" it? Suppose player 1 assigns probabilities 90%/5%/5% to the three options. After a while, player 2 would learn these probabilities from player 1's actions, respond by playing "paper" most of the time and therefore win most of the time. The only way to avoid this is by assigning equal probabilities to the three strategies.

More generally speaking, a mixed-strategy Nash equilibrium is found by assigning probabilities to the different strategies such as to make the other players indifferent to what strategy one plays. In a symmetric game such as Rock–Paper–Scissors this is easy to see, but asymmetric games can be solved analogously (Varian 2010: 540).

This ends our brief survey of game-theoretic techniques. No doubt, this was a most rudimentary introduction. As we will see below (and in other chapters), it is enough to appreciate some of the most pressing philosophical problems of game theory. Before delving into these problems, we have to examine the nature of the utilities involved in game theory in slightly more detail.

Game Theory's Payoffs

Economists sometimes use "preference" and "choice" interchangeably. That is, they identify preferences with choices. Given that (ordinal) utility is nothing but an index of preference, one can say: "In the standard approach,

		Player 2		
		Rock	Paper	Scissors
Player 1	Rock	(0, 0)	(–1, 1)	(1, –1)
	Paper	(1, –1)	(0, 0)	(–1, 1)
	Scissors	(–1, 1)	(1, –1)	(0, 0)

Figure 4.5 Rock–Paper–Scissors

the terms 'utility maximization' and 'choice' are synonymous" (Gul and Pesendorfer 2008: 7). This standard approach is the theory of revealed preferences.

We saw in Chapter 3 that revealed-preference theory is untenable as a general theory of preferences for decision theory. Here we will make some additional observations concerning the use of "preference" in game theory. A theory which identified preference with actual choices is a non-starter for game theory applications, because it would be impossible to write down the structure of most games. When both agents are rational in the Eurobonds Game (Figure 4.2), the top left of the diagram will never be reached. And yet, we assign utilities to these outcomes. Or think of Rock–Paper–Scissors. If we identified preferences with choices all we could infer from people playing the game is that they prefer whatever move they make to the other two. Observing them using each strategy a third of the time would lead us to believe that they are indifferent between the three moves. But of course, they are not. Utility cannot mean "preferences as revealed in actual choices."

Some economists therefore say that preferences are identical to *hypothetical* choices:

> In game theory, we are usually interested in deducing how rational people will play games by observing their behavior when making deci-sions in one-person decision problems. In the Prisoner's Dilemma, we therefore begin by asking what decision Adam *would make* if he *knew* in advance that Eve had chosen dove.
>
> If Adam *would* choose hawk, we would write a larger payoff in the bottom-left cell of his payoff matrix than in the top-left cell. These payoffs may be identified with Adam's utilities for the outcomes (dove, hawk) and (dove, dove), but notice that our story makes it nonsense to say that Adam chooses the former because its utility is greater. The reverse is true. We made the utility of (dove, hawk) greater than the utility of (dove, dove) because we were told that Adam would choose the former. In opting for (dove, hawk) when (dove, dove) is available, we say that Adam reveals a preference for (dove, hawk), which we indicate by assigning it a larger utility than (dove, dove).
>
> (Binmore 2007: 13–14; emphasis added)

Rational-choice theory, accordingly, is a theory of consistent behavior. What we learn about a person's preferences licenses inferences about what that person will do in a similar situation. Unfortunately, this won't do for game theory, either. One problem is that players have preferences over outcomes they are never in the position to choose (cf. Hausman 2012: 34). In an ulti-matum game, the proposer clearly prefers the respondent to accept as long as he offers a positive amount (as indicated by his payoff $x > 0$). But he is never in the position to choose between these outcomes, that choice is up to player 2. Of course, one could ask player 1 what he would do if he had to choose between the outcome (*x*, accept) and (*x*, reject). But to do so would be the same as to ask him about his preference between the two situations. The *choice* is up to player 2.

Another problem with identifying preferences and hypothetical choices is that people could not make mistakes. If preferences just were choices (actual or hypothetical) people could not fail to maximize their utility. On the one hand, it is implausible that people never make mistakes in their choices, and therefore a theory that makes it conceptually impossible to make mistakes should be rejected. On the other hand, some of the difficulties economists debate regarding equilibrium selection presuppose that people can make mistakes (see below). Hence, to the extent that we want to be able to make sense of these debates, the revealed-preference theory cannot be used in the context of game theory.

The upshot is that the utilities assigned to outcomes in the games described in this chapter are an index of preference satisfaction, and "preference" here refers to some mental state. All we need is that people can mentally rank the available outcomes. Higher utilities indicate a higher mental rank.

As young teenagers at school we enjoyed writing up what we then called "love lists": if you were a boy you'd rank every girl in class from "like the most" to "like the least," and vice versa for girls. Of course, we boys were never in the position to choose. And yet, we were all more than eager to construct love lists. For the intents and purposes of this chapter, this is what is meant by having preferences.

Game Theory and Rationality

Among other things, game theory purports to answer the question: How does one act rationally in strategic situations? In this section we will see that game theory is not always completely clear about how to answer that question. We will first ask whether game theory's main solution concept, the Nash equilibrium, is philosophically well founded. After that we will look at a number of its refinements.

Is It Always Rational to Play a Nash Equilibrium in One-Shot Games?

Do agents have compelling reason to always play Nash equilibria and to only play Nash equilibria in one-shot games? Are there perhaps considerations that might lead a rational agent to make an out-of-equilibrium move? In this section I will examine a number of arguments that have been made in defense of the Nash equilibrium as a solution concept for one-shot games. More complex games will be considered below.

The most frequently heard defense of the Nash equilibrium is that it constitutes a self-enforcing agreement (e.g., Hargreaves Heap *et al.* 1992: 101). Suppose North and South could meet before playing the Eurobonds

Game. They look at the structure of the game and observe that both could profit by playing "frugal." They therefore agree to do so. In our actual case this was called the "Euro-Plus Pact," which was adopted in 2011 in order to pave the way for Eurobonds. What are the chances of the players sticking to their agreement? In the structure of Figure 4.1, nil. Unless there is external enforcement—which there is neither in the Eurobonds Game nor in reality—the incentives are strong not to honor the agreement. To promise to stick to a certain course of action in such a situation amounts to no more than "cheap talk."

By contrast, if the players agreed beforehand to play "profligate" instead, neither would have an incentive to deviate. "Thus, the Nash equilibrium can be seen as the only sustainable outcome of rational negotiations in the absence of externally enforceable agreements" (Hargreaves Heap *et al.* 1992: 102). Are all and only Nash equilibria self-enforcing? It appears not. Consider the game in Figure 4.6 (Risse 2000: 366).

Here ("bottom," "right") is the only Nash equilibrium. But both players have incentives to deviate from it, provided they believe that the other does so too. Why wouldn't rational players believe that other rational players do something that is better for them?

Another example is the Stag-Hunt Game of Figure 4.3. Here ("stag," "stag") is a Nash equilibrium but a fragile one. Suppose the hunters meet beforehand and agree on the Pareto-superior outcome. To stick to the agreement requires a lot of trust. What if hunter 1 suspects hunter 2 of not honoring the agreement (because hunter 1 knows that hunter 2 is very suspicious, say, and therefore might not trust hunter 1 either, or simply because he may make a mistake)? He might then decide to play "hare," which secures him a payoff of at least 1. The same reasoning applies to hunter 2, of course. Thus, while ("stag," "stag") is the Pareto-superior outcome ("hare," "hare") is the less risky outcome. Less risky outcomes can be preferable in situation where one cannot be so sure that others are trusting (even if one is trusting oneself) or when people are prone to make mistakes.

		Player 2		
		Left	Centre	Right
Player 1	Top	(4, 6)	(5, 4)	(0, 0)
	Middle	(5, 7)	(4, 8)	(0, 0)
	Bottom	(0, 0)	(0, 0)	(1, 1)

Figure 4.6 A Non-Self-Enforcing Nash Equilibrium

Risk considerations also motivate the next game (Figure 4.7) which shows that a self-enforcing agreement does not have to be a Nash equilibrium (Risse 2000: 368).

If the players have a chance to negotiate before playing, ("bottom," "right") suggests itself as point of agreement. Of course it is true that both players have incentives to deviate from this outcome. But if they did as they preferred, they would risk ending up with nothing, as long as they believe that the other might also not honor the agreement.

Lesson: the self-enforcing agreement argument cannot be used as a justification of the Nash equilibrium because it is neither the case that all Nash equilibria are self-enforcing agreements nor that all self-agreements have to be Nash equilibria.

Another influential defense of the concept is that playing a Nash equilibrium is required by the players' rationality and common knowledge thereof. Consider the Figure 4.8 (Hargreaves Heap and Varoufakis 2004: game 2.9).

Here every strategy is a best reply to some strategy played by the opponent. If player 1 believed that player 2 would play "right," he will play "bottom." Why would player 1 believe that player 2 will play "right"? Perhaps because he believes that player 2 expects him to play "top," and "right" is an optimal

		Player 2	
		Left	Right
Player 1	Top	(0, 0)	(4, 2)
	Bottom	(2, 4)	(3, 3)

Figure 4.7 A Self-Enforcing Non-Nash Equilibrium

		Player 2		
		Left	Centre	Right
Player 1	Top	(3, 2)	(0, 0)	(2, 3)
	Middle	(0, 0)	(1, 1)	(0, 0)
	Bottom	(2, 3)	(0, 0)	(3, 2)

Figure 4.8 A Rationalizable Strategy

response to that. The problem with this kind of reasoning is that it cannot apply to everyone sharing the same beliefs: if the agents actually played a set of strategies such as ("bottom," "right"), at least one player's expectations would be frustrated. The only strategy set that avoids regretting one's beliefs or actions is the Nash-equilibrium strategy ("middle," "center").

The problem with this defense is that it is only plausible when there is a unique rational way for each player to play the game. But this is not always the case. Figure 4.9 shows that considerations of riskiness could sometimes trump the Nash equilibrium (Hargreaves Heap and Varoufakis 2004: game 2.11).

In this game ("top," "left") is the unique Nash equilibrium in pure strategies. Will rational players play it? If player 1 plays "top" he risks ending up in the ("top," "right") cell, which he prefers least because player 2 is indifferent between "left" and "right." The same reasoning applies to player 2's playing "left." By contrast, playing ("bottom," "right") means that both players end up with payoff 1, no matter what the other player does. Why would a rational agent not play a non-equilibrium strategy *guaranteeing* him a payoff which he can reach playing the Nash equilibrium only by assuming a great risk?

Another problem with this defense is that the idea that there is a specific kind of recommendation of what to do in strategic situations is somewhat incoherent. As Isaac Levi points out, an agent who wants to use the principles of rational choice critically cannot predict that he will act rationally (Levi 1997). But arguably, game theory portrays agents as deliberating about what they are going to do given the preference structure of the game and relevant beliefs. Game theory, so the objection goes, cannot assume that players know that they are rational, and therefore *a fortiori* it cannot assume that they know that the other players are rational.

		Player 2		
		Left	Centre	Right
Player 1	Top	(1, 1)	(2, 0)	(–2, 1)
	Middle	(0, 2)	(1, 1)	(2, 1)
	Bottom	(1, –2)	(1, 2)	(1, 1)

Figure 4.9 Risk-Dominant Non-Nash Equilibria

Refinements of the Nash Equilibrium

We could end our discussion of "game theory and rationality" right here because the Nash equilibrium is *the* central solution concept of the theory. But the above criticisms pertained only to one-shot games, and there are at least potential defenses of the Nash equilibrium as a result of rational learning (Kalai and Lehrer 1993) or evolution (Binmore 1987). I will not consider these defenses here and instead take a look at another fundamental problem of game theory as theory of rationality: there are almost always multiple Nash equilibria in a game, and game theory does not provide good advice about equilibrium selection. Thus, even if the Nash equilibrium were defensible from the point of view of rationality, no defense would gain much ground because "solve the game by finding the Nash equilibria" underdetermines what rational players should do in most games.

A class of games with multiple equilibria in which players mutually gain by performing the same action is called "coordination games." The structure of the simplest one is shown in Figure 4.10.

Suppose two drivers (or horse riders) have to coordinate whether to veer left or right in order to avoid a collision. Doing either would be fine as long as both do the same. How, in the absence of a government that can enforce rules, do rational agents decide which way to go?

Thomas Schelling proposed that most situations of this kind have "some focal point for each person's expectation of what the other expects him to expect to be expected to do" (Schelling 1960: 57). Back in the day when people traveled on horseback, keeping left may have been a focal point because most people are right-handed. By keeping left, horsemen could hold the reins in their left hand and keep their right hand free to greet the oncoming rider or pull out their sword (Parkinson 1957).

In this particular story, right-handed riders would probably have a *preference* for keeping on the left so that the payoffs in the ("left," "left") equilibrium should be higher than the payoffs in the alternative equilibrium. But in other situations the choice of equilibrium is driven by expectations alone. An example Schelling uses is this: "Name 'heads' or 'tails.' If you and

		Player 2	
		Left	Right
Player 1	Top	(1, 1)	(0, 0)
	Bottom	(0, 0)	(1, 1)

Figure 4.10 A Simple Coordination Game

your partner name the same, you both win a prize" (Schelling 1960: 56). Arguably, there is nothing intrinsically more valuable about "heads" than about tails; there is a reason to *expect* people to choose heads, though, and heads is therefore a focal point, because it is customarily mentioned first.

Focal points are a reasonable way to choose among equilibria, based on expectations of what people might do because of the existence of certain customs, habits or conventions. But it is not clear how to model focal points formally, which is why the theory remains rather undeveloped to this day. If considerations regarding focal points affect the payoffs (as they should at least sometimes), the focal-point strategy is also the Pareto-dominant strategy. This is another refinement of the Nash equilibrium: if there are multiple Nash equilibria, choose the Pareto-dominant outcome.

Pareto dominance sometimes conflicts, however, with another idea we have already encountered: risk dominance. The Stag-Hunt Game (Figure 4.3) shows as much. ("stag," "stag") is the Pareto-dominant outcome. If, however, for whatever reason, the other player chooses "hare," the hunter choosing "stag" ends up in the least preferred state. Playing "stag" is thus risky. By playing "hare," by contrast, the hunter can only gain: if the other hunter makes a mistake and plays "stag," the first ends up with a payoff that is *higher* than the equilibrium payoff.

Playing the risk-dominant rather than Pareto-dominant strategy has sometimes been defended on the basis of evolutionary considerations (Kandori *et al.* 1993; Young 1993). But is it always or even most of the time rational to play the risk-dominant strategy? To give up risk also means to give up the extra profit, and surely it is not always in one's best interest to do so. At any rate, civilization is to a large degree built on trust, and without mutual trust little economic interaction and development would be possible. To trust (the other not to make a mistake in this case) means to play "stag," despite being the risk-dominated strategy. Rationality considerations by themselves cannot decide between these two refinements, at least not generally.

To introduce another series of refinements, consider the Battle of the Sexes Game (Figure 4.11).

		Player 2	
		Bananarama	Schoenberg
Player 1	Bananarama	(4, 2)	(0, 0)
	Schoenberg	(0, 0)	(2, 4)

Figure 4.11 The Battle of the Sexes Game

A story that goes along with the game could be as follows. Unbeknownst to each other, one morning a couple bought tickets to different musical events on that same night. When they go for lunch that day, they agree to go to the same event come what may, but she had to run off to another meeting before they could decide which one. In an extraordinary stroke of bad luck, both of their iPhones die on them just after lunch, and both have out-of-office appointments all afternoon. Given they cannot communicate, how do they coordinate their evening? Player 1, Claire, prefers Bananarama to Schoenberg, and going to either concert with her partner to going alone. Player 2, Jeff, prefers Schoenberg to Bananarama, and also going to either concert with Claire to going alone.

There are two obvious Nash equilibria (in pure strategies), and that would be the end of the story if it wasn't for refinements of the concept. If that was the end of the story, game theory would really not be very helpful in determining what rational agents ought to do in strategic situations. Who would have thought that it's rational for Jeff to go to the Bananarama concert if Claire does and to the Schoenberg if she goes there (and vice versa for Claire)?

Luckily, there are further refinements, one of which we've in fact already encountered: the subgame-perfect Nash equilibrium. A strategy profile is a subgame-perfect equilibrium if it represents a Nash equilibrium of every subgame of the original game. The concept applies only to sequential games, so let us amend the story a little. Let us suppose that Claire works until 6 p.m. that day and Jeff until 7.30 p.m., and both know that. So Claire will make her decision first (which is known by Jeff). The resulting *sequential* game is depicted in Figure 4.12.

Informally speaking, a subgame is game that begins at any node of the original game and contains that node and all its successors (unless the subgame's initial node is in an information set which is not a singleton; in that case all nodes in that information set belong to the subgame). This

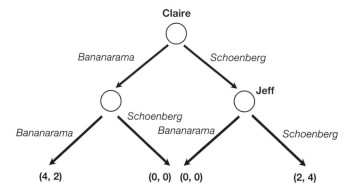

Figure 4.12 The Battle of the Sexes in Extensive Form

game has three subgames: the original three-node game (every game is a subgame of itself) and two games that begin at Jeff's decision points. The Eurobonds Game of Figure 4.2 has only two subgames: the original game and the subgame that begins with South's moves (because both nodes of that stage of the game are in the same information set).

As we have seen, one solves a game in extensive form by backward induction. Backward induction is a method to find the subgame-perfect equilibrium of a game. In the left node, Jeff would choose "Bananarama," and "Schoenberg" in the right node. Predicting that, Claire chooses "Bananarama," and thus the only subgame-perfect equilibrium in this game is ("Bananarama," "Bananarama"). The purpose of backward induction is to eliminate incredible threats. Jeff can threaten all he wants to go to Schoenberg, because once Claire has made up her mind, he could only lose by exercising his threat. By invoking an asymmetry—allowing Claire to move first—we can reduce the number of pure-strategy Nash equilibria from two to one.

The elimination of incredible threats creates a paradoxical situation, however, which can be illustrated by the four-stage Centipede Game of Figure 4.13. Its subgame-perfect solution is for player 1 to move "down" at the first stage (we are moving left to right instead of top to bottom). This is because at the last stage, player 2 would move "down," which is predicted by player 1, who would therefore move "down" at the third stage, and so on. At any intermediate stage, either player may ask: "How did we get here?" Consider stage 2. Given player 1's rational move at stage 1 was "down," the only explanation that we reached this stage is that player 1 is irrational or made a mistake. But if so, player 2 may expect that player 1 continues to play that way, and intend to stop at a later stage when the payoffs are higher. Rationality for player 2 in fact may *require* that he does not play "down" at stage 2 if he believes that player 1 is not fully rational. Suppose player 2 believes that player 1 moves "right" no matter what. If so, player 2's best move is to wait until the last stage of the game to move "down." Thus, if the players do not assume other players to be rational, their own rationality allows or asks of them to continue in the game. Indeed, in empirical tests of the game, subjects play a few rounds before ending the game (see for instance McKelvey and Palfrey 1992).

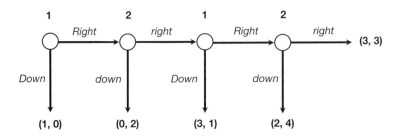

Figure 4.13 The Centipede Game

To *end up* in the subgame-perfect equilibrium outcome (1, 0), we therefore have to assume both players be perfectly rational and have common knowledge of rationality. But if we make these assumptions, we can never *reason* our way towards that outcome.

One standard way around this paradox in the literature is to invoke so-called "trembling hands" (Selten 1975). A player's hand trembles when she makes mistakes despite being fully rational. Player 1 might for instance be resolved to play "down" at the first node but then accidentally push the wrong button and go "right." As long as this happens with some positive probability, the game can be solved by backward induction.

The idea of a trembling-hand (perfect) equilibrium further refines the subgame-perfect equilibrium, as can be seen in the Tremble Game of Figure 4.14 (Rasmusen 2006: 111). In this game there are three Nash equilibria: ("top," "left"), ("top," "right") and ("bottom," "left"), two of which are subgame perfect: ("top," "left") and ("bottom," "left"). However, the possibility of trembling rules out ("bottom," "left") as an equilibrium. If player 2 has a chance of trembling, player 1 will prefer to play "top" in order to secure his payoff of 1. Player 2 chooses "left" because if player 1 trembles and plays "bottom" by mistake, she prefers "left" to "right." ("top," "left") is therefore the unique trembling-hand equilibrium.

The "standard way around" the paradox is not convincing. Depending on how large one player estimates the probability with which the other player's hand trembles and his own payoffs, it might well be rational to continue in the Centipede Game. It does not matter whether the opponent is assumed to be irrational or make mistakes, the consequences for each player's deliberations of what best to do next are the same. To respond that trembles occur randomly and with small probability does not help. In order to reach the final stage of the game quite a few trembles have to have occurred. Trembles influence results systematically.

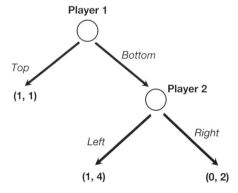

Figure 4.14 The Tremble Game

Let us examine a second paradox. In the Chain Store Game, a Dutch monopolist called Alban Heym has branches in 20 towns. The chain faces 20 potential competitors, one in each town, who can choose "enter" or "stay out." They do so sequentially and one at a time. If a potential competitor chooses "stay out," he receives a payoff of 1, while the monopolist receives a payoff of 5. If he chooses "enter," he receives a payoff of either 2 or 0, depending on the monopolist's response to his action. The monopolist must choose between two strategies, "cooperative" or "aggressive." If the monopolist chooses the former, he and the competitor receive a payoff of 2, and if he chooses the latter, each player receives a payoff of 0. The last round of the game is depicted in Figure 4.15.

The subgame-perfect equilibrium is easy to see. Entering into a price war, Alban Heym can only lose. The competitor knows this, and since he has a higher payoff when the market is shared than when he stays out of it, he will enter. ("enter," "cooperative") is the equilibrium reached by backward induction in this game.

But the managers of Alban Heym think they can outwit the competitor. They reason that if Alban Heym demonstrates being tough by playing "aggressive" in early rounds, potential entrants will be deterred and the chain store can reap higher profits (cf. Selten 1978). A game theorist might respond: "Look, your threat is not credible. You will most certainly not enter a price war in the final round—there is nothing to gain from it. Thus, the competitor will enter for sure. In the penultimate round, there is again no reason to fight. It will be costly, and it has no effect on the final round. Continue to reason thusly, and you will see that deterrence is not a valid strategy."

Indeed, the managers of Alban Heym made a mistake. If "aggressive" is a preferable strategy in early rounds of the game, then this should be reflected in the payoffs. The managers analyzed a different game, not the Chain Store Game. However, one can show that if there is a small amount

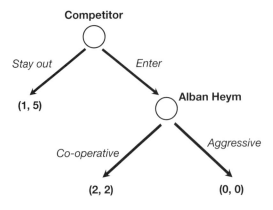

Figure 4.15 The Chain Store Game

of uncertainty about the payoffs, it may be rational for a monopolist to build up a reputation by fighting entry initially. This leads to another refinement of the subgame-perfect equilibrium called *sequential equilibrium* (Kreps and Wilson 1982).

The idea is that at least one player's profile is determined exogenously and unobservable to the other player. In the Chain Store Game, for instance, the monopolist may be "weak" or "strong" depending on whether his preferences are as in Figure 4.15 or the converse, as on the right-hand side of Figure 4.16.

The game is solved by finding for a player *i*, at each information set after which *i* is to play, the best reply to the strategies of the other players. In this game, Alban Heym can build a reputation of being tough and thereby deter potential entrants from trying to enter the market.

In each case considered above, the "refinement" of the Nash equilibrium consisted in adding a structural feature to the game which changed its nature. In no case was the refinement justified on the basis of considerations of what would be reasonable in a situation to do. One consequence is that the refinements often do not reduce indeterminacy but rather add to it. Both the Centipede and the Chain Store Game show that in order to settle on specific equilibria one has to weaken common knowledge assumptions, which means that one is moving away from attempting to defeat indeterminacy.

Game theory, understood as a theory of rational decision-making, is thus highly problematic. The Nash equilibrium is ill-justified. Even if it were justified, it would solve few problems because most games have multiple Nash equilibria. Thus far, the refinement program has produced few results that can be defended from the point of view of rationality and that have helped to reduce indeterminacy.

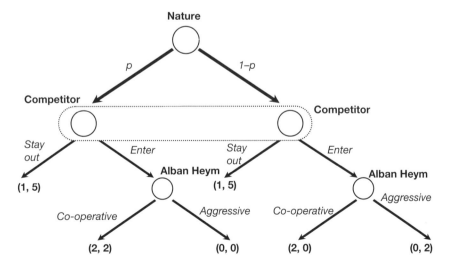

Figure 4.16 The Chain Store Game with Uncertainty

Game Theory as Explanatory Theory

It has sometimes been argued that game theory, as theory of rational choice, would be a very good candidate for an empirical theory of social phenomena (see for instance Grüne-Yanoff and Lehtinen 2012). A theory which predicts that people act rationally is self-fulfilling. People who accept the theory and therefore predict that other people behave rationally have an incentive to act rationally themselves. A theory which predicts that other people behave *ir*rationally does not have this benefit. Agents acting on such a theory have all the more reason to deviate from the theory because doing so will improve their performance. Rational-choice theories therefore have a stabilizing influence on social phenomena.

But of course this argument has any bite only to the extent that game theory is successful as a theory of rationality. As we saw in the last section, it is not. Not all is lost yet, though. Perhaps game theory isn't so good a theory of rationality but it might nevertheless be a useful predictive and explanatory theory. Perhaps the justification of playing a Nash equilibrium strategy in this or that refinement is wanting, but if people play the strategies the theory predicts anyway, who cares? As long as the theory has empirical content, or, more carefully, as long as it is useful for modeling empirical phenomena, it may have its virtues. In this section we will see that even as explanatory or predictive theory, game theory is very problematic.

In order to make predictions (only a theory that predicts empirical phenomena can also explain them), any theory must in one way or another be brought to bear on empirical phenomena. Most genuine theories transcend the realm of the observable, i.e., they contain terms that refer to unobservable states of affairs. If the arguments that were given here concerning the nature of preferences are correct, one of the core elements of game theory refers to something unobservable. Carl Hempel called the principles that connect a theory's theoretical (or unobservable) vocabulary with an observational vocabulary "bridge principles" (Hempel 1966). We need bridge principles for a theory to have empirical content.

The architecture of games is given by their payoff structure. As we saw in the previous section, the payoffs are utility indices indicating preference ranking. This is unfortunate. If they indicated material outcomes, the game theorist could straightforwardly determine which game is being played in a given situation because material outcomes are observable (perhaps not literally, but for all intents and purposes of the game theorist). The usual story that goes along with what I have called the Eurobonds Game is one about a proposal made to two prisoners, which is why the game is normally known as Prisoner's Dilemma:

> In the Prisoner's Dilemma, two prisoners … are being interrogated separately. If both confess, each is sentenced to eight years in prison; if

both deny their involvement, each is sentenced to one year. If just one confesses, he is released but the other prisoner is sentenced to ten years.

(Rasmusen 2006: 20; footnote suppressed)

The corresponding matrix could be written as shown in Figure 4.17.

		Prisoner 2	
		Confess	Deny
Prisoner 1	Confess	(8 years, 8 years)	(0, 10 years)
	Deny	(10 years, 0)	(1 year, 1 year)

Figure 4.17 The Prisoner's Dilemma in Game Form

The advantage of presenting games in this way—that application to empirical situations is easier—is frustrated by the fact that game theory could not make any predictions without knowledge of players' preferences. In some cases, what people prefer may be relatively straightforward, such as here. It is very reasonable to assume that almost everybody has the following preference ranking: acquittal > 1 year > 8 years > 10 years. In other words, it is reasonable to assume that utility is strictly decreasing by number of years in prison and therefore that the Eurobonds Game of Figure 4.2 is an adequate transformation of the game form of Figure 4.17 (for the notion of a game form, see Weibull 2004).

What is reasonable to assume in one case should not be blindly accepted as a rule more generally. In other words, one should allow the utility function:

$$U = U(M),$$

where M designates the material outcomes of a game, to vary between people and across situations. Although in early experimental applications of game theory, subjects were assumed to care only about their own material gains and losses, this is clearly *not* a substantive hypothesis of game theory as such. As game theorist and experimenter Ken Binmore remarks:

Actually, it isn't axiomatic in economics that people are relentlessly selfish. ... Everybody agrees that money isn't everything. Even Milton Friedman used to be kind to animals and give money to charity.

(Binmore 2007: 48)

Thus, institutions, social and cultural norms and other immaterial facts may affect people's valuations of the material outcomes of a game. It is by no means obvious for instance how people rank the different outcomes of the Ultimatum Game (Figure 4.4, above). If a strong fairness norm is at work, players might rank (material) outcomes as follows (5, 5) > (0, 0) > (6, 4) > (4, 6) > (7, 3), etc., which is not at all strictly increasing in material outcomes.

There is now a growing literature on what functional form U might take. For instance, in Fehr and Schmidt's theory of fairness, the utility function for two-person games has the following form (Fehr and Schmidt 1999: 822):

$$U_i(x) = x_i - \alpha_i \max\{x_j - x_i, 0\} - \beta_i \max\{x_i - x_j, 0\}, \ i \neq j,$$

where the x's are player i's and j's monetary payoffs and α and β are parameters measuring how disadvantageous and advantageous inequality affects a player's utility. In Cristina Bicchieri's formulation, social norms are explicit arguments in the function (Bicchieri 2006: 52):

$$U_i(s) = \pi_i(s) - k_i \max_{s_{-j} \neq L_{-j}} \max_{m \neq j} \{\pi_m(s_{-j}, N_j(s_{-j})) - \pi_m(s), 0\},$$

where $s = (s_1, s_2, ..., s_n)$ is a strategy profile, $\pi_i(s)$ is the material payoff function for player i and $k_i \geq 0$ is a constant representing a player's sensitivity to the relevant norm. A norm for player i is represented by the function $N_i: L_{-i} \rightarrow S_i$, where $L_{-i} \subseteq S_{-i}$, S_i is player i's strategy set and S_{-i} the set of strategy profiles for the other players.

Generally speaking, though, economists are loath to make any substantial assumptions about people's utility functions. They instead believe that one can learn people's preferences in one situation and use that knowledge to make predictions about what the same people will prefer in another situation. Learning about what people prefer in choice situations is called "preference elicitation." Often this is done by having experimental subjects play a subgame of a game of interest. Suppose we are interested in eliciting the players' preferences in the Eurobonds Game. First we have to write down the game in game form with material outcomes. For simplicity, let us assume that the main material outcome is growth rates. In extensive form, the game could then look as shown in Figure 4.18.

To elicit the South's preferences, we have it choose over strategies in the subgames (Figure 4.19).

To elicit the North's preferences we simply switch roles (we can do so because the material payoffs are symmetrical). If both North and South prefer "profligate" to "frugal" in both subgames we know that Figure 4.2 is a correct rendering of the game, and we can use game-theoretic tools to solve it and make a prediction.

The problem with this elicitation procedure is that it assumes that preferences are quite strongly context-independent. What that means, and why this is not always a reasonable and safe assumption to make, can be illustrated with the following game, called the "Trust Game" (Figure 4.20). Here an investor can choose between keeping his investment or transferring it to a trustee. If he does the latter the money is quintupled. The trustee then decides whether to keep the money or return half of it to the investor.

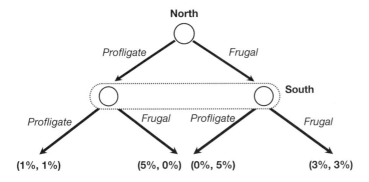

Figure 4.18 The Eurobonds Game in Game Form

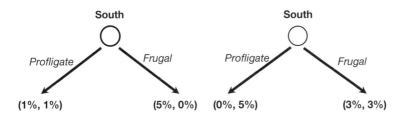

Figure 4.19 Two Subgames of the Eurobonds Game in Game Form

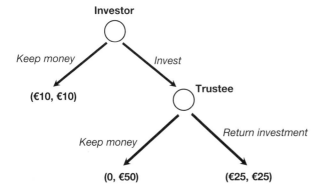

Figure 4.20 The Trust Game in Game Form

Consider the subgame beginning at the second decision node. On its own this subgame is in fact a version of the so-called Dictator Game in which a player decides whether or not to split a pie between herself and a second player. Unlike in the Ultimatum Game (recall Figure 4.4), in the Dictator Game the second player does not have the option to "reject," and the first player therefore does not have to fear punishment. It is thus in the subgame of the Trust Game. We can then expect people to choose similarly in both games, and indeed, the assumption that people choose similarly is implicitly made in using this elicitation procedure.

Suppose an individual chooses "Keep money" in the subgame when played on its own. Is it reasonable to expect her to do the same in the full game? When the full game is played, other norms may affect players' decisions than when only the subgame is played. If I am trusted I may wish to reward the trusting partner by returning his investment, even at a material cost to me, and even when the investor has no way to punish me for a selfish decision. Or I may act on equity considerations. Unlike in the Dictator Game, in the Trust Game the investor helps to produce the pie, and I might therefore think that she deserves a return or that I am obliged to pay her back because it is her money.

Be the normative considerations as they may, subjects do in fact choose differently in the Dictator Game and in the Investment Game (see for instance Cox 2004). This means that their preferences over outcomes are not context-independent. An aspect of the relevant context in this case is whether another player has moved first and thereby helped to create the opportunity to "reward" or "pay back." Without context independence, this particular elicitation procedure is invalid.

There are other problems with this procedure. Francesco Guala points out that it cannot be used to test games in which reciprocity matters (Guala 2006). That this is correct is not hard to see: if my being "nice" (in the sense of moving in such a way as to give a co-player a higher payoff than I could have done had I chosen differently) depends on my co-player's being "nice"; i.e., if my preferences depend on my co-player's preferences, one cannot learn about these preferences in situations where other players do not exist.

It is important to note, however, that game theory is not wedded to this particular elicitation procedure, or any other procedure for that matter. Weibull 2004, for instance, proposes for a slightly more complicated version of a Dictator Game in which four outcomes have to be ranked that "the experimentalist asks subject *A* to state her ordinal ranking of the four plays for each of the 24 possible (strict) ordinal rankings that *B* may have, and likewise for subject *B*." The experimenter could then find a matching pair, inform each player about the other's preference and make a prediction on that basis.

There are numerous problems with this proposal. First, it might be too far away from the revealed-preference approach for it to be appealing to econo-mists. Even if one refuses to *identify* preferences with choices, one could still hold that choices are *the best guide* to people's preferences and thus insist on people's preferences being elicited in choice tasks. Second and relatedly, as we saw in the previous chapter, people sometimes reverse their preferences between a valuation-task and a choice-task (Lichtenstein and Slovic 1971, 1973). It is therefore not clear that asking people to rank outcomes is a reliable guide to what they will do later in the choice-task. Third, there may be no matching pair of rankings. Fourth, even if the procedure worked for laboratory experiments, it is quite obviously completely unusable for predicting and explaining field phenomena.

There is a deeper issue which has nothing to do with any of the specific problems of specific elicitation procedures. Any theory needs bridge principles in order to be applicable to empirical phenomena for theory testing, prediction and explanation. In game theory, bridge principles come in two types. Type one are assumptions about the form of people's utility functions. As mentioned above, if people's utilities could be assumed to be strictly increasing (or decreasing) in their own material gains and losses (and independent of everything else), one could use observations of material outcomes together with the tools of the theory to derive predictions. That simple assumption is implausible, but nothing prevents economists from providing more complex functions in which other people's material gains and losses and social and cultural norms (to give a few examples) play a role. The other type of bridge principle are elicitation procedures. Here preferences are estimated without necessarily assuming that utility functions must have some specific form. The two types are sometimes used jointly. The utility functions in the literature on fairness and social norms all come with free parameters which have to be estimated from people's choice behavior. Here, then, a type-one assumption about the general form of a utility function is combined with a type-two elicitation procedure that fills in the details.

So far, so good. The problem is that none of these bridge principles is part of the core set of claims of the theory. Rather, there is quite a large menu of potential principles to choose from, and economists make free use of the menu in specific applications. But the choice is not systematic and well reasoned. *If* the assumption that people always prefer more money for themselves to less were part of game theory, then the theory could be used for predictions and explanations. But it's not (see the Binmore quotation above), and for a good reason: the theory would have been refuted in countless instances. *If* preference elicitation through choices in subgames were part of the core of game theory, preference interdependence could not be represented within the theory. But it's not, and for an equally good reason: preference interdependence is an empirically important phenomenon.

Economists do not like to make substantial assumptions of this kind. Their theory of rationality is a "formal," not a "substantial" theory, we are told. But a formal theory does not by itself allow the prediction and explanation of empirical phenomena. Thus bridge principles, which provide the theory with substance, are added on an ad hoc basis. The ad hocness of the conjoining of core theory with principles is problematic for both predictions and explanations. Genuine predictions cannot be made because it is known only after the fact which of a variety of bridge principles should be used in conjunction with the theory. After the fact we can always find some game-theoretical model that in conjunction with some bridge principle captures the phenomenon of interest. But have we thereby explained it? There are three main accounts, models or senses of explanation: rational-choice, causal and unification (see Chapters 2 and 7). Game theory is not a theory of rationality (or if it is, it's a very problematic one), and thus game-theoretic "explanations" are no rational-choice explanations. Game theorists are adamant that they do not intend to model the underlying decision processes of agents that are responsible for people's choices, and therefore they are no causal explanations, either. Nor are they unifying, as I will argue in Chapter 7. For now let us conclude that as long as there are no more systematic insights into what bridge principles should be regarded as part of the core of the theory (in other words, as long as there is no more systematic work on what utility functions people have—work of the kind we find in Fehr and his colleagues and in Bicchieri—and on elicitation procedures of the kind we find in Weibull), game theory remains deeply problematic, both as a theory of rational choice and as explanatory theory.

Study Questions

1   The Eurobonds Game caricatures the actual situation in which Europe found itself in 2012 quite badly. What are the most important differences? Do you think there is a core of truth within it?

2   Rewrite the games in the section on "Is It Always Rational to Play a Nash Equilibrium in One-Shot Games?" as sequential games. Is the Nash equilibrium now a more convincing solution concept?

3   Compare the criticism of game theory as explanatory theory in the section on "Game Theory as Explanatory Theory" with the criticism of rational-choice theory in the previous chapter. Are there commonalities between the two?

4   Model an empirical strategic situation (such as the Cuba crisis or firms competing for business) as a two-person one-shot game and solve it. What obstacles do you encounter?

5   In your view, what parameters should a utility function that is useful as a bridge principle to apply games to empirical situations have? Defend your answer.

Suggested Readings

Game theory began with von Neumann and Morgenstern 1944. A good critical introduction to the issues discussed here is the chapter on game theory in Hargreaves Heap *et al.* 1992. Grüne-Yanoff 2008, Grüne-Yanoff and Lehtinen 2012 and Ross 2010a are useful philosophical discussions. I learned about the importance of bridge principles for the application of game theory from Guala 2008.

Part IB

Causality

5 Causation and Causal Tendencies

Overview

Reasons are kinds of causes. But not everyone insists that causal explanations always have to cite reasons. The present chapter responds to the second deficiency of the deductive-nomological model of explanation, namely, that social phenomena, even in areas where human motivations are not directly concerned, seldom fall under a scientific law, conceived of as a strict regularity. Strict regularities are few and far between in the economic world. This is due to the circumstance that it is always possible, and often actually the case, that the operation of the law is disturbed by countervailing factors. A strict regularity therefore only holds when certain, often unrealistic conditions are in place. There are two major variants of such a "law with qualifications" view. The first asserts that laws express regularities subject to a *ceteris paribus* condition. The *ceteris paribus* condition makes the circumstances under which the regularity ensues manifest. The second understands laws as expressions of tendencies. According to this view, for example, the iron law of wages, say, doesn't state that wages always approach subsistence levels but rather that wages *tend* towards subsistence levels, which might mean that they in fact always exceed them.

The Rise of Causal Talk in Economics

For many a year, economists have tried to avoid talking explicitly about causes. As mentioned earlier in Chapter 1, "cause" and its cognates have a metaphysical tang. I can see the hammer swiftly approaching the tiny porcelain figurine, I can hear a shattering, I have a tingly feeling as some shards impact on my skin—but I do not, or so it is said, experience the causality of the cause. We see the hammer moving and the bits of porcelain flying, but we do not see how the hammer *breaks* the figurine, how it *turns it into* shards flying off in all directions, how it helped to *produce* scratches on my skin. According to Hume, what we can't see we can't know, and thus we can't know causal relations. The logical positivists borrowed skepticism about causation from Hume, and, until very recently, economists borrowed it from logical positivism.

Philosophers of science began to realize that science could ignore causal analysis only at the expense of hampering the achievement of important goals of sciences—such as scientific explanation and the development of effective strategies for policy—in the late 1970s and early 1980s (see for instance N. Cartwright 1979; Salmon 1984). In economics too the tide soon changed, and the use of causal notions experienced an upsurge in the 1990s, as a study by Kevin Hoover demonstrates (Hoover 2004). Figure 5.1 reproduces his findings.

One thing we should notice is that it is practically impossible to avoid causal talk altogether. To be sure, we can avoid using "cause" and its cognates.

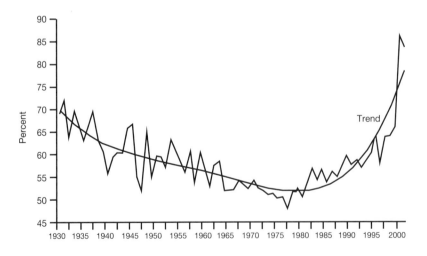

Figure 5.1 Causal Language in Econometrics

Source: Hoover 2004: 153.

Note: The figure shows the proportion of econometrics articles that use "cause" or a cognate in the full text.

But natural languages have zillions of so-called "causatives"—verbs expressing causation without using "cause" explicitly: "scrape, push, wet, carry, eat, burn, knock over, keep off, squash, make (e.g. noises, paper boats), hurt" (this list is due to Anscombe 1992 [1971]: 93). Above I highlighted the causatives describing our destructive hammer example: break, turn into, produce. And even in the first description there were two words expressing causation implicitly: shatter and impact. Perhaps it is possible to design a technical language that is free of causal implications, but to the extent that economists use natural language, and they use a great deal of it, they cannot avoid talking about causation.

Moreover, unlike, say, cosmology and archeology, economics is an inherently policy-oriented science. Economists play an important role in the formulation of social policies, be they economic or non-economic, and in institutional design. To give examples of non-(purely) economic policies to which economists contribute copiously, take policies relating to terrorism (e.g., Stiglitz and Bilmes 2008; Krueger 2007; Becker and Rubinstein 2011; Frey and Luechinger 2003) or to climate change (e.g., Stern 2009; Nordhaus 2008). For a recent example of economists being involved in institutional design, take the auctions of the telecom licenses (e.g., Binmore and Klemperer 2002).

To do policy analysis successfully, we have to know about causes. A recent, politically highly controversial, example concerns minimum wages. Standard economic wisdom has it that increasing minimum wages above the competitive level causes increases in unemployment. Since the mid-1990s, empirical studies of the phenomenon have multiplied, many of which appear to show that this is not the case, and that small increases in minimum wages can even lead to *decreasing* unemployment (e.g., Card and Krueger 1995). Some economists have used this new evidence to advocate more generous minimum-wage legislation in the United States and elsewhere (e.g., Krugman 2009b). Others are more skeptical about the quality of the studies and hence urge caution (Neumark and Wascher 2008). Whoever is right in this dispute, what is clear is that it is a dispute (a) among economists; (b) about a causal claim (whether increases in the minimum wage cause unemployment to go up or down).

Causation is, then, at the heart of disputes concerning social policies. But causation also plays an important role in the *explanation* of economic phenomena. Following the general narrative of Part I of this book, I will here focus on the connection between causation and explanation, reserving the methodological discussion concerning economic policies for later (Chapter 12 in particular). For now, therefore, let us return to the topic of scientific explanation.

Chapter 2 discussed three types of criticism of the deductive-nomological model of explanation. Here is another, famous, counterexample, apparently due to the philosopher Sylvain Bromberger (Salmon 1989: 47). A vertical flagpole of a certain height stands on flat ground. The sun is shining, so the flagpole casts a shadow of a certain length. Given the initial conditions of the position of the sun, the height of the flagpole as well as the law of rectilinear propagation of light, we can deductively derive the length of the shadow. If the length of the shadow is our explanandum, citing the facts about the position of the sun and the flagpole along with the appropriate law seems perfectly acceptable as scientific explanation. However, using facts about the length of the shadow and the height of the flagpole along with the law allows us to deduce the position of the sun, and facts about the length of the shadow and the position of the sun along with the law allow us to deduce the height of the flagpole. The latter two deductions do not seem to be bona fide scientific explanations, though. The length of the shadow does not seem to be a factor that helps to answer questions "Why is the sun at such-and-such a position?" and "Why does the flagpole have the height it does?'

The core of the problem seems to be that explanation is an asymmetric relation whereas deduction is symmetric. Given the law of rectilinear propagation of light, we can use facts about the position of the sun and the height of the flagpole to deduce the length of the shadow, and, vice versa, facts about the height of the flagpole and the length of the shadow to deduce the position of the sun. But the former, and not the latter relation is explanatory. If a set of initial conditions C together with a law L explains an outcome E, this does not entail that E (in conjunction perhaps with other initial conditions) together with the law L also explains C. The D-N model of explanation treats these two cases as equivalent, however.

Starting with Wesley Salmon's book *Scientific Explanation and the Causal Structure of the World* (Salmon 1984), many philosophers have come to regard the asymmetry of *causal* relations as capturing explanatory asymmetry, and have for this and other reasons adopted causal models of scientific explanation. Causal relations are clearly asymmetrical. HIV causes AIDS and not the other way around. The decision to let Lehman Brothers fail may have triggered the ensuing credit crunch, but very clearly the later credit crunch did not cause the earlier decision by the US Treasury. It is also intuitive that causes should explain their effects and not vice versa. The flagpole's intercepting the sunlight causes the shadow, and therefore adducing facts about its height explains the length of the shadow. But the shadow does not cause the position of the sun—and thus no facts about the length of the shadow should play a role in an explanation of the position of the sun.

In this book I will look at two models of causal explanation: explanation by causal tendencies in this chapter and mechanistic explanation in the next. These are not all the models of causal explanation there are but they are prominent in economics and deserve special attention. Before delving deeper into causal tendencies and mechanisms, however, I will say a few more general words about causation.

Correlation Is Not Causation: So What Is Causation?

The slogan "correlation is not causation" is well known among social scientists. Though it is well known, I will begin by briefly rehearsing what correlation is and why correlation cannot be causation—in order to motivate the following discussion of the ideas of what else causation might be.

Correlation is the degree of linear association among variables. There are various measures of correlation, but the most commonly used one is Pearson's correlation coefficient, which, for two variables X and Y, is defined as:

$$\rho_{x,y} = \text{corr}(X, Y) = \frac{\text{cov}(X, Y)}{\sigma_x \sigma_y} = \frac{E[(X - \mu_x) Y - \mu_y)]}{\sigma_x \sigma_y} ,$$

where ρ (or corr) is the correlation coefficient, cov(X, Y) denotes the covariance between X and Y (which is defined in the numerator of the fraction before the comma), σ is the variance, μ the population mean, and E( ) denotes the expected value. Intuitively, two variables are correlated whenever observing the value of one gives you information about the likely value of the other. For example, when X and Y are positively correlated and the value of X is high, then the value for Y is also likely to be high, and vice versa.

Most ostensibly, correlation, like deduction, is symmetrical whereas causation is asymmetrical—as we have seen. If a variable X is correlated with another variable Y, then Y is also correlated with X. But it is not true in general that if X causes Y, then Y causes X. So correlation cannot be causation. The asymmetry problem can be fixed relatively easily, however: define the (temporally) earlier variable as the cause and the later as the effect. Correlation plus time-ordering might well be causation.

But it isn't. There are more potential reasons for which an earlier variable X is correlated with a later variable Y than X being the cause of Y. One such reason is the existence a third variable (or set of variables) Z such that Z causes both X and Y. You observe an increase in petrol prices at filling stations (X). You later observe an increase in your electricity bills (Y). Do higher petrol prices cause higher electricity bills? Most certainly not. Rather, an increase in the price for crude oil (Z) is responsible for both.

Variables Z that are common causes for two correlated variables X and Y are often called confounders, and correspondingly the problem that the correlation between X and Y may be explained not only by a direct causal relation between X and Y but also a structure in which a third factor Z causes both X and Y is called the "problem of confounders" (Steel 2004) or the "third-factor problem" (Elster 2007). We will later (in Chapter 10) see how econometricians try to deal with this problem. For now, suffice it to say that confounding is a serious methodological issue in economics because it is very often possible to come up with a factor Z that could explain the correlation between X and Y but that is not measurable so one cannot test whether it is indeed Z that is responsible for the correlation. To give a famous example, Ronald Fisher, one of the founding fathers of modern statistics, doubted that the observed correlation between smoking and lung cancer can only be explained by smoking being the cause of lung cancer. Rather, he argued, there might be a third factor, some genetic disposition that is responsible for both: having that gene disposes an individual to smoke *and* to develop lung cancer later in life. At the height of this debate in the 1950s it was of course not possible yet to test whether people would have such a genetic disposition, and indeed it took several decades for a consensus to emerge in the medical community that smoking is the cause of lung cancer.

Confounding is one problem, and there are more. Sometimes correlations arise from characteristics of variables that have nothing to do with their causal relations. That is, there may be non-causal reasons for the existence of a correlation. Most countries' GDP will be highly correlated with their GNP, which will be the case not because GDP causes GNP but rather because the latter is measured partly in terms of the former: GNP can be measured by subtracting the net income from assets abroad from GDP. The two are conceptually, not causally related.

Another non-causal explanation for correlations has been brought to the attention of philosophers in a widely discussed paper by Elliott Sober (1987). Sober considers two (imaginary) time series, one describing the evolution of bread prices in Britain, and the other the evolution of sea levels in Venice, which are assumed to be both (a) monotonically increasing and (b) causally unrelated. These two series will be highly correlated but they are, *ex hypothesi*, not causally related. They are correlated because of a characteristic of the variables: their increase over time (a high value of one variable makes it likely that the other variable has a high value as well and vice versa). This too is a genuine issue in economics. Most time series in economics are non-stationary: their moments (means, variance, etc.) change with time. Non-stationary time series will often be correlated whether or not they are causally related (for a detailed discussion, see Reiss 2007b; Hoover 2003 challenges Sober's claim that the two series are correlated).

Correlation is not causation, then. So what *is* causation? The best place to begin looking for an answer is in David Hume's writings. Hume is far and away the most important contributor to the philosophy of causation among the modern philosophers, and even though he gave an ultimately unsatisfactory account, it is worth recalling it for both historical and systematic reasons. Historically, it is Hume's skepticism concerning causal relations that sparked a great deal of debate among philosophers, a debate that is still alive today. Immanuel Kant, famously, said that Hume ('s skepticism concerning causation) awoke him from his "dogmatic slumber" (Kant 2004 [1783]: 10). Ever since, philosophers have had to decide whether they are "Humeans" or "anti-Humeans" on causation. Even many of those who agree that Hume's own account of causation is untenable have tried to provide accounts that are as "Humean" as possible.

Systematically, Hume's is a regularity account, and from its failures we learn much about the nature of causation.

In brief, Hume thought that "X causes Y" is true whenever (Hume 1960 [1739]: abstract):

a X is universally associated with Y;
b Y follows X in time;
c X and Y are spatio-temporally contiguous (there are no time-wise or space-wise gaps between X and Y).

Hume was what has come to be called a "reductionist" about causation. What this means is that Hume held that causation is not among the fundamental building blocks of our (conception of the) world. We can translate all causal talk—talk about causings and preventings, triggerings and inhibitings, makings and unmakings—into talk about constant conjunction. Thus, if we say that "The banks' irresponsible behavior *caused* the financial crisis of the late 2000s" (paraphrased from Stiglitz 2009) what we really mean is that (a) irresponsible banking is universally associated with financial crises; (b) the banks' behavior predated the crisis; and (c) there are no gaps between the banks' behavior and the crisis.

As this example suggests, there are serious flaws in Hume's constant conjunction account. In fact, none of conditions (a)–(c) is necessary, nor are the three together jointly sufficient for causation. In addition, there is a deeper reason for why one should not regard constant conjunctions as essential to causation.

First, most factors we regard as causes are not universally associated with their effects. Irresponsible bank behavior may have led to a financial crisis *in this case*, but it hasn't in many other cases. To use a less controversial example, even though smoking causes lung cancer, it is neither the case that all smokers will develop cancer nor that all lung cancer patients have smoked. Universal association is not necessary for causation.

Second, not all effects follow their causes. A "classical" counterexample is due to Kant (1998 [1787]: A203), who argued that when putting a ball on a cushion creates a hollow, the cause ("placing the ball") occurs at the same time as the effect ("the creation of a hollow"). In econometrics, contemporaneous causation is a frequent phenomenon. Some quantum mechanical models involve backwards causation. None of these examples is incontrovertible. But they shed some doubt on the assumption that temporal priority of the cause is an essential element in causation.

Third, causes may act at a temporal or spatial distance. In Newtonian physics, forces act instantaneously, which entails that any motion here and now has effects on all other bodies in the universe here and now. And causes are often thought to lie dormant for a considerable time before they produce their effects. Just consider Freudians, who think that much of your current behavior was caused when you were a small child.

Fourth, constant conjunction, temporal priority of the cause and contiguity together are insufficient for causation. Many common causal structures can serve as examples. Suppose that one member of a theatre cast after another develops symptoms of stomach sickness until everyone has become sick. Does this mean that the bug is contagious, that is, that one member's being sick causes another member's being sick? Not necessarily. Even though you have constant conjunction ("*every* member of the cast …"), temporal priority ("one member after another …") and contiguity (supposing that they all live and work together and could have contracted a bug from each other), but the outbreak may well have been caused by some gone-off food that they all had eaten.

Few people—philosophers or scientists—therefore believe that Hume got it completely right. They have nevertheless tried to develop views on causation that are *as close as possible* to Hume's regularity account. I will consider one such view in this chapter, namely John Stuart Mill's, which builds on the idea that causes issue in some kind of constant conjunction. In the next chapter, I will discuss a view that can be regarded as developing Hume's idea that cause and effect are spatio-temporally "close by," that the cause "touches" the effect or is "connected" with it. Views that are loosely related to Hume's priority condition are relegated to Chapters 9 and 10 in Part II of this book, on methodology.

Causal Tendencies

John Stuart Mill was mentioned in Chapter 1 as a highly original contributor to both philosophy and economics. As a philosopher, he is best known for his liberalism (see Chapter 13), his contributions to utilitarianism (see Chapters 12 and 13), his defense of women's rights (in fact, he is considered to be one of the first feminists) and his contributions to philosophy of science. As an economist, he helped develop the ideas of comparative advantage, of economies of scale and of opportunity costs, and he wrote a text that would serve as the main economics textbook in the UK and elsewhere until well into the twentieth century (Mill 1963a [1848]). A major contribution to the *philosophy of economics* was the idea that causal claims in economics seldom express universal regularities—*pace* Hume (who, as we have seen, held that a causal claim entails a claim about a regularity)—but rather what he called *tendencies.*

Let us, with Mill and many others after him, call a statement expressing a regularity a "law." That is, let us say that a law is a statement of the form, "Whenever *X*, *Y*." Mill distinguished between laws of coexistence and laws of succession. Examples for laws of coexistence are "All swans are white" and "All prime numbers are indivisible." Causal laws are kinds of laws of succession.

A law, then, is a statement about a generalization that holds universally, such as "The distance d of a body falling for time t is equal to $0.5gt^2$

(where g is the Earth's gravitational constant)"; "All gases can be described by the ideal gas law: $PV = NkT$ (where P is the absolute pressure of the gas; V is the volume; N is the number of particles in the gas; k is Boltzmann's constant; and T is absolute temperature)"; or Say's law, "All supply creates its own demand." Mill noticed that if we understand these laws literally as descriptions of what actually (and regularly) happens in the world, they are false.

Take the law of falling bodies as an example. Everyone can check for him- or herself that it is false, without even having to use measurement instruments. Take a feather and a more compact body such as a marble, lift both of them up to the same height and drop them at the same time. The compact body will hit the ground first. This means that the distance d_c it traveled in a given time t is different from the distance d_f the feather traveled in the same time: $d_c \neq d_f$. So the law can be true of at most one of the two bodies, not of both. But since it is meant to apply to all bodies (it is not called the law of falling marbles, for instance), it is false.

The culprit is, of course, air resistance. Compact bodies and feathers fall at the same rate (which is well described by the law) in a vacuum, and when no other forces are present. Many (if not all) laws hold only in such ideal conditions. The gas law mentioned above is quite adamant about this: it is even called the "ideal" gas law (since it ignores molecular size and intermolecular attractions; it holds approximately for monoatomic gases at high temperatures and pressures). The laws of economics are no exception.

Strictly speaking, then, laws hold only under special conditions. Economists (and others) often refer to these conditions as "*ceteris paribus*" or "other things being equal." Though widely used, this terminology is in fact somewhat misleading. The law of falling bodies, for instance, does not hold "other things being *equal*" but rather "other things being *absent*": it predicts the distance a falling body travels in a given time provided no force except the Earth's gravity influences it; that is, it predicts what a falling body does "all other forces (except g) being absent."

With respect to the ideal gas law and Say's law it is not so much (or not only) the case that other things (forces, etc.) have to be absent for the law to hold (though that is true as well) but rather that the conditions have to be *just right*. For instance, the ideal gas law assumes that intermolecular forces are negligible; Say's law that commodities are produced in proportion to and in accordance with individuals' preferences. In other words, the *ceteris paribus* condition here should read "other things being *right*."

I will say more about the latter reading of *ceteris paribus* below. For now, let us note that a tendency claim is a claim that describes a regularity, which holds in isolation, when disturbing factors (such as air resistance) are absent. Another way of putting it is to say that a tendency claim is a claim about a regularity that *would hold* if disturbing factors *were absent*. This is the reading of *ceteris paribus* that Alfred Marshall used when he introduced the term to economics:

> The element of time is a chief cause of those difficulties in economic investigations which make it necessary for man with his limited powers to go step by step; breaking up a complex question, studying one bit at a time, and at last combining his partial solutions into a more or less complete solution of the whole riddle. In breaking it up, he segregates those disturbing causes, whose wanderings happen to be inconvenient, for the time in a pound called Ceteris Paribus. The study of some group of tendencies is isolated by the assumption other things being equal: the existence of other tendencies is not denied, but their disturbing effect is neglected for a time.
>
> (Marshall 1961 [1920]: 366)

This, then, is the first characteristic feature of a tendency: describing a tendency means to describe what happens in isolation from disturbing factors: "All laws of causation, in consequence of their being counteracted, require to be stated in words affirmative of tendencies only, and not of actual results" (Mill 1874 [1843]: 319). The law of falling body is a tendency law, which states: "that all heavy bodies *tend* to fall; and to this there is no exception, not even the sun and moon; for even they as every astronomer knows, tend towards the earth, with a force exactly equal to that with which the earth tends towards them" (Mill 1874 [1843]: 320; original emphasis).

An implication of this point is that it would be wrong to say that the laws are false or subject to exceptions. Rather, laws are true, even universally true, properly interpreted: not as descriptions of actual outcomes but rather as descriptions of tendencies. Mill writes:

> Doubtless, a man often asserts of an entire class what is only true of a part of it; but his error generally consists not in making too wide an assertion, but in making the wrong *kind* of assertion: he predicated an actual result, when he should only have predicated a *tendency* to that result—a power acting with a certain intensity in that direction.
>
> (Mill 1844: 161; original emphasis)

This last clause reveals a second characteristic of Mill's notion of tendencies, namely that they are causal: a "power" that is "acting" with a certain "intensity." Tendencies are factors that make things happen.

According to Mill, it may well be impossible to physically isolate the factor of interest from disturbing causes. As it is impossible to create a perfect vacuum, individuals motivated by nothing but the desire to accumulate wealth have not been observed (at the time Mill was writing, at any rate). The million-dollar question then is: what happens when "other things are *not* equal," *that is*, when disturbing factors such as air resistance do operate?

To this, Mill thought, the sciences provide two kinds of answer, two "models," so to speak. In physics (which at his time meant mostly mechanics) the different factors all have their respective laws, which combine using a principle he called the Composition of Causes. If, for instance, a falling body is pulled towards the Earth with a force g and a sudden gust of wind pushes it sideways with a force f, the resulting force can be computed using vector addition, as in Figure 5.2. Air resistance in this case can be modeled as a force in the opposite direction of g, slowing down the body's rate of fall.

The chemist's model is different. When a chemist combines different factors—different chemical elements, say—the result is not usually predictable from the laws that describe the behavior of the elements. Thus, the properties of water (H_2O), for instance being liquid, do not result from a combination of the properties of its constituents, hydrogen (H) and oxygen (O), which are both gases (Mill 1874 [1843]: 267).

Mill now thinks that economic factors combine like the factors of mechanics, not like those of chemistry (for an opposing view, see Marshall 1961 [1920]: 771):

> The laws of the phenomena of society are, and can be, nothing but the laws of the actions and passions of human beings united together in the social state. Men, however, in a state of society, are still men; their actions and passions are obedient to the laws of individual human nature. Men are not, when brought together, converted into another kind of substance, with different properties: as hydrogen and oxygen are different from water, or as hydrogen, oxygen, carbon and azote [i.e., nitrogen] are different from nerves, muscles, and tendons. Human beings in society have no properties but those which are derived from, and may be resolved into, the laws of nature of individual man. In social phenomena the Composition of Causes is the universal law.
>
> (Mill 1874 [1843]: 608)

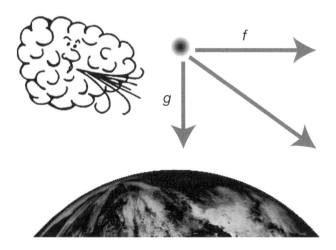

Figure 5.2 Two Tendencies Acting in Different Directions

This, then, is the third characteristic of Mill's tendencies: they produce stable contributions to outcomes that persist even in the presence of disturbing causes. In sum, tendencies have the following three features:

a   they are kinds of causes,
b   which produce a "characteristic effect" when operating in the absence of disturbing factors, but
c   which continue to contribute to outcomes when disturbing factors are present.

To give an economic example for how to interpret these three characteristics, consider the quantity theory of money. That theory says that (*ceteris paribus*!) changes in the money supply are proportional to changes in the price level. Sometimes it is stated in the form of Irving Fisher's "equation of exchange" $MV = PT$ (where M is the money stock, V the velocity of money, P the price level and T the "trade volume" or real value of commercial transactions; see I. Fisher 1911), but the simpler form $M \sim P$ (money is proportional to prices) is sufficient here. To interpret this law as a Millian tendency would require three things. One would first have to regard it as a causal statement: the changes in the money supply "cause" (influence, produce, affect ...) changes in the price level, and "with a certain intensity" (namely: proportionally).

Second, the precise statement is only true in the abstract, when disturbing causes are absent. For instance, even though an increasing money supply might exert an upward pressure on the price level, there might be other factors/causes that push in the opposite direction. Thus, we can imagine that a high rate of innovation and resulting decreases in transportation costs and higher productivity puts a downward pressure on prices. The result might be such that *the general level of prices decreases despite an increased money supply*!

Third, the money supply contributes to the overall result even though disturbing causes prevent it from having its full effect. To make matters really easy, suppose that the proportionality constant is unity so the law says that in the absence of disturbing factors, changes in money supply cause equal changes in the price level, and that money supply grew by 5 percent. Because of lower transportation costs and the rise in productivity, the price level decreased by 1 percent. The third characteristic of Mill's tendencies says that *the price level would have decreased even further (by 6 percent) if money supply hadn't grown*. That is, even though the actual result was a deflation—despite the increase in money supply—the increase in money still contributed to the outcome by proportionally decreasing the rate of deflation. The effect of an increased money supply is thus noticeable, even though the actual figures seem to provide an exception to the quantity theory.

Laws in economics are at best tendency laws. Some laws have that notion explicitly built into their statements. The iron law of wages, for example, has been stated as "real wages always tend, in the long run, toward the minimum wage necessary to sustain the life of the worker" (this is from Wikipedia).

Other laws are qualified by an explicit or implicit *ceteris paribus* clause, and one way to understand the meaning of a *ceteris paribus* clause is that it assumes the absence of disturbing factors. The "law of supply and demand," for instance, can be stated as:

> If the supply of a commodity increases (decreases) while the demand for it stays the same, the price decreases (increases); if the demand for a commodity increases (decreases) while the supply remains the same, the price increases (decreases).
>
> (Roberts 2004: 159)

This statement is to be read as qualified by an implicit *ceteris paribus* clause: "If nothing (such as a financial crisis) intervenes ..." Sometimes the clauses are made explicit such as here (notice also that the laws as stated here say something quite different from the "law of supply and demand" due to Roberts):

> The law of demand states that as the price of a good rises, the quantity demanded of the good falls, and as the price of a good falls, the quantity demanded of the good rises, *ceteris paribus*.
>
> (Arnold 2008: 54)

> The law of supply states that as the price of a good rises, the quantity supplied of the good rises, and as the price of a good falls, the quantity supplied of the good falls, *ceteris paribus*.
>
> (Arnold 2008: 66)

Do tendency laws explain? Yes and no. In very lucky circumstances the outcome has been produced by the causal factor in question, and no disturbing factors influenced the result. This is the case of the falling bodies when air resistance and other forces are absent. In such cases the law of falling bodies of course explains the outcome. When disturbing factors are present, outcomes can still be explained when two conditions are met: (a) the tendency laws of the disturbing factors are known; (b) the law of composition is known. In case of free fall, it is easy to include air resistance. The force due to air resistance can be assumed to be proportional to the speed: $f_{air} = kv(t)$, where k is the constant of proportionality (which depends on the shape of the object) and v is the speed (velocity) of the object. Since air resistance operates in the direction opposite gravity, to calculate total force, we just subtract it from gravity: $f_{total} = f_{gravity} - f_{air} = mg - kv(t)$.

In economics, the laws of the disturbing factors are not normally known. As Mill observed:

> It often reveals to us that the basis itself of our whole argument is insufficient; that the data, from which we had reasoned, comprise only a part,

and not always the most important part, of the circumstances by which the result is really determined. Such oversights are committed by very good reasoners, and even by a still rarer class, that of good observers. It is a kind of error to which those are peculiarly liable whose views are the largest and the most philosophical: for exactly in that are their minds more accustomed to dwell upon those laws, qualities, and tendencies, which are common to large classes of cases, and which belong to all place and all time; while it is often happens that circumstances almost peculiar to the particular case or era have a far greater share in governing that one case.

(Mill 1844: 154–5)

In a situation typical of economics, where a known factor (such as increases in the money supply) contributes to an outcome, but many other factors do too, most of whose contributions are not known, does a law such as that of the quantity theory explain? In my view, the known tendency law does not explain the outcome as such but rather the outcome relative to a counterfactual situation in which all the disturbing factors operated but the "main factor" (which is described by the known tendency law) did not. If, to go back to our example, the price level in fact decreased, the quantity theory does not explain the actual change in the level of prices. The explanandum concerns instead a *contrastive* question such as "Why did the price level decrease by 1 percent rather than a full 6 percent?" But of course, the counterfactual is very hard or even impossible to establish when neither the law of the disturbing factor nor the principle of combination is known. Here I have assumed that we know that in the absence of the change in the money supply, the price level would have dropped by 6 percent due to increased productivity. But we do not know how precisely productivity affects the general price level nor how that combines with changes in the money supply. If we don't know, our inferences can at best be qualitative. We might know that rising productivity exerts a downward pressure on prices, and money, an upward pressure. If the price level in fact drops, and given that productivity acted in the way it did and that nothing else affecting the price level occurred, we can explain that the price level dropped by only 1 percent rather than more by citing the tendency law.

Conclusions

Though it is not usually interpreted in this way, one can regard Mill's account of tendency laws as one way to "fix" Hume's regularity theory of causation. Tendency laws are statements about regularities. However, they are not statements about regularities as they occur actually or empirically but rather about regularities that would occur if there were no interferences.

This reading of Mill is not usually seen as an attempt to build on Hume because it involves reference to a counterfactual state of affairs—the world as it would be if there weren't any interferences (which, of course, there are). Hume, as we have seen, did not like things we cannot see, feel or taste, and a "what-would-have-been-if" is by definition not experienceable. Contemporary accounts of causation in terms of causal powers or capacities, which build on Mill's notion of a tendency, are therefore often viewed with suspicion for their alleged metaphysical content.

But as philosophers of economics we don't have to worry about that too much. Causes and counterfactuals are part and parcel of everyday life and economic science. If I hadn't drunk three beers, I wouldn't feel tipsy right now. I feel tipsy because I drank three beers. There is nothing suspicious about such claims. It is certainly the case that we couldn't do economic science without them. When we ask, "Who is to blame for the financial crisis?" (as economists have), we ask whether someone's actions are such that without them the crisis would not have happened. The 2011 Nobel prize in economics went to Chris Sims and Tom Sargent "for their empirical research on cause and effect in the macroeconomy" (see Nobelprize.org 2012). The list could go on and on. Arguably, thus, the burden of proof is on him who denies that causal and counterfactual statements are meaningless or unknowable.

Causes are difference-makers of a certain kind according to the tendency view. When a cause operates, it makes a difference relative to a counterfactual situation in which everything is held constant except for the operation of that cause. (It turns out that one has to be more careful with the characterization of the counterfactual situation; see for instance Hitchcock 2007. I ignore such niceties here.) Difference-making is one important intuition behind the concept of cause: to make an outcome happen means that the outcome would not have occurred, or would not have occurred in that precise way, had it not been for the cause.

There is another intuition behind the concept of cause: to cause something means to be connected with it in the right way. Effects do not pop into existence but rather evolve from the cause by means of a continuous process. That intuition is captured by the view of causes as mechanisms, to which I will turn next.

Study Questions

1   The slogan "correlation is not causation" seems to undermine much empirical work in the social sciences that tries to draw causal conclusions from regression (which is a kind of correlation). How do social scientists address this problem? Is their response satisfactory?
2   "The *ceteris paribus* clause makes any law-claim empirically vacuous." Discuss.
3   We have seen that Hume's regularity account suffers from numerous counterexamples. Do you see ways to improve the account so that the counterexamples do not arise?
4   Are all causes difference-makers?
5   Do we need causation for economic analysis? What would economics without the notion of cause look like?

Suggested Readings

Causation is now a hot topic in the philosophy of science, and the literature is vast and growing. "Classic" sources include Gasking 1955, Suppes 1970, Lewis 1973, Mackie 1974, Salmon 1984 and N. Cartwright 1979. The first five represent the five "standard approaches" to causation: manipulationist, probabilistic, counterfactual, regularity and transference. They are all Humean in nature. More recent proponents of the standard approaches are Woodward 2003 (manipulationist), Spirtes *et al.* 2000 (probabilistic), Hall *et al.* 2004 (counterfactual), Baumgartner 2008 (regularity) and Dowe 2004 (transference). The last defends a non-reductivist, anti-Humean view of causation. Cartwright subsequently developed it into a view of causes as capacities modeled on Mill's notion of a causal tendency (N. Cartwright 1989, 1999a). On counterfactuals in the social sciences, see Reiss 2012.

Because of the wealth of approaches and the problems with all of them, some philosophers have defended pluralist accounts of causation. Hitchcock 2007 provides a nice overview and discussion of the many ways in which one can be a causal pluralist. Reiss 2011 defends a pluralist view of causation that is motivated by inferentialist semantics.

6 Mechanisms

Overview

Another problem with the view of laws as strict regularities is that regularities, even where they exist, are hardly explanatory by themselves. Suppose we observe a case of wages approaching subsistence levels. If an economist, when asked why this happened, replied, "Because wages *always* approach subsistence levels," she would hardly win a prize for most insightful economic commentary. Establishing a regularity is at best part of the job. The regularity is itself explanation-seeking: we want to know why it holds, what is responsible for it to hold.

One response to this issue has been to demand that explanations must describe *mechanisms* that are *causally responsible* for a phenomenon of interest. Mechanism is a concept that is familiar to economists, compare "transmission mechanism," "price mechanism" or "mechanism design." Unfortunately, there is little agreement among either philosophers or social scientists about what mechanisms are and how precisely the description of a mechanism relates to explanation. These questions are taken up in the present chapter.

Hume on Money

As we saw in Chapter 5, according to Hume "spatio-temporal contiguity" was an essential characteristic of causation: causes do not operate across spatial or temporal gaps. Economics is full of apparent counterexamples. Economic causes often take some time before producing an effect—there are lags between variables. As any economist can testify, this is a frequent phenomenon. For an example let us turn to Hume's own economic work, which is somewhat less known than his philosophy. Hume contributed to our understanding of property rights, foreign trade, the theory of the interest rate and taxation. Hume is sometimes said to have exerted a significant influence on Adam Smith's economic thinking. First and foremost, however, Hume was one of the architects of the quantity theory of money, along with Nicolaus Copernicus, Jean Bodin, William Petty, John Stuart Mill, Irving Fisher and, more recently, Milton Friedman.

The quantity theory asserts that the prices in an economy are proportional to its money supply (see Chapter 5, section on "Causal Tendencies"). Apart from this effect on prices, does money affect other economic variables? Hume argues that it does not, by way of a thought experiment:

> For suppose, that, by miracle, every man in GREAT BRITAIN should have five pounds slipt into his pocket in one night; this would much more than double the whole money that is at present in the kingdom; yet there would not next day, nor for some time, be any more lenders, nor any variation in the interest [rate].
>
> (Hume 1752)

Hume, in other words, believed that money was neutral with respect to these variables. At the same time Hume observed that the influx of specie (gold and silver coins) from the Americas that had been occurring in the centuries before his writings was followed by a great increase in national wealth. Money, therefore, can stimulate genuine growth. How do these two propositions go together? Simply because money takes some time before it affects prices:

> To account, then, for this phenomenon, we must consider, that though the high price of commodities be a necessary consequence of the encrease of gold and silver, yet it follows not immediately upon that encrease; but some time is required before the money circulates through the whole state, and makes its effect be felt on all ranks of people. At first, no alteration is perceived; by degrees the price rises, first of one commodity, then of another; till the whole at last reaches a just proportion with the new quantity of specie which is in the kingdom.
>
> (Hume 1752: 47)

At the same time, in between the arrival of the new money and its full effect on prices making itself felt, money can stimulate real growth:

> In my opinion, it is only in this interval or intermediate situation, between the acquisition of money and rise of prices, that the encreasing quantity of gold and silver is favourable to industry. When any quantity of money is imported into a nation, it is not at first dispersed into many hands; but is confined to the coffers of a few persons, who immediately seek to employ it to advantage. Here are a set of manufacturers or merchants, we shall suppose, who have received returns of gold and silver for goods which they sent to CADIZ. They are thereby enabled to employ more workmen than formerly, who never dream of demanding higher wages, but are glad of employment from such good paymasters. If workmen become scarce, the manufacturer gives higher wages, but at first requires an encrease of labour; and this is willingly submitted to by the artisan, who can now eat and drink better, to compensate his additional toil and fatigue. He carries his money to market, where he, finds every thing at the same price as formerly, but returns with greater quantity and of better kinds, for the use of his family.
>
> (Hume 1752: 47–8)

Let me make three observations about these reflections of Hume's. First, money takes time to affect prices. Second, there is no "causal gap" between the arrival of money and the increase in prices. Rather, the two are connected through a continuous, gradual process. Three, money affects the economy in general and the price level in particular via a number of different channels. There are effects on commodities, wages and employment, and Hume at least considers effects on credit and interest rates. All of these can, in turn, affect the price level.

Methodologists call considerations such as these "mechanistic." If X and Y are social variables and X causes Y, we can expect X to influence Y *through* a mechanism or a set of mechanisms. The mechanism is that which connects cause and effect, that for which there is a causal relation between the variables to begin with. Mechanistic thinking has become very popular in recent philosophy of science and philosophy of the social sciences.

One of the reasons for their popularity is that mechanistic accounts are very plausibly regarded as explanatory. To describe the mechanism by which some variable (such as money) causes another (such as prices) means to tell a story about what structures and processes are underlying the relation between the variables. When an inflation occurs after an increase in the money supply and we explain this by citing the aggregate-level claim "money causes prices," we haven't added much to the original observation. When, however, we describe the mechanism by which money causes prices, we given an account of why the causal relation holds, which is a deeper and therefore arguably better explanation.

Four Notions of Causal Mechanism

So much for the good news. And now the bad news: there is no understanding whatsoever of what a mechanism is or how to best characterize the notion. Reviewing the philosophical literature one finds that there is at best agreement about the importance of mechanisms for scientific explanation and other goals of science but about as many definitions of mechanism as there are contributors to the debate. I haven't done any systematic study on the issue and thus the following has no basis more reliable than my own meandering experience, but in my view there are four notions of mechanism that can be found in the debate on causation and explanation in the social sciences:

- *Mechanism as individual causal relation.* Econometricians and others who model causal systems as systems of equations sometimes refer to whatever is represented by an individual equation as a "mechanism" (e.g., Simon and Rescher 1966; Pearl 2000). Mechanism in this sense contrasts with mere association and does not mean anything beyond causality. For instance, the aggregate relation "money causes prices" could well be described as the "monetary mechanism" in this sense.
- *Mechanism as mediating variable.* This notion builds on the idea that, in the social sciences and elsewhere, causes affect outcomes via intermediaries. Military service affects wages via its effect on schooling (among other things). Smoking affects the development of lung cancer via tar deposits in the lungs. When some researchers speak of "mechanistic strategies" for causal inference, they mean mechanisms in this sense (see for instance Morgan and Winship 2007: ch. 8). One way to identify, say, the effect of smoking on lung cancer when direct estimation is unreliable due to the likely presence of confounders would be to estimate the effect of smoking on tar deposits and the effect of tar deposits on lung cancer, and then multiplying the two (Pearl 2000: 83ff.). Importantly, it is not necessary that the "mediating" variable obtains at a lower level than the original cause and effect variables. Mechanisms in this sense can for instance obtain entirely at the social or aggregate level.
- *Mechanism as underlying structure or process.* Social or aggregate variables are constituted by entities and processes that lie at a deeper level. A change in money supply, for instance, might be implemented through a variety of instruments, and in a particular case an open-market operation, say, is simply what constitutes the change in money supply on that occasion. Similarly, a change in the general price level just is a weighted average of individual price changes. To provide a mechanism for an aggregate relation, then, is to describe how the entities and processes that underlie the aggregate variables are organized and interact with one another in such a way that the aggregate relation results. This notion plays an important role in the debate concerning "social mechanism" found

in recent philosophy of the social sciences (see for instance Reiss 2007a) and is the preferred notion by those who advocate methodological individualism (e.g., Hedström and Ylikoski 2010). It is also closely related to the debate on mechanisms in the biomedical sciences (e.g., Machamer *et al.* 2000).

- *Mechanism as a piece of theory.* Economists often mean by a mechanism not a thing in the world but rather a theory or part thereof. Thomas Schelling, for instance, writes: "a social mechanism is a plausible hypothesis, or set of plausible hypotheses, that could be the explanation of some social phenomenon, the explanation being in terms of interactions between individuals and other individuals, or between individuals and some social aggregate" (Schelling 1999: 32–3.). The main difference between this notion and the previous ones, apart from referring to a piece of theory rather than a thing in the world, is that these theoretical mechanisms are often highly idealized descriptions of the interactions among individuals. In the "Hired Gun Mechanism" (Andreoni and Gee 2011), for instance, individuals are assumed to be behave perfectly rationally, understand other players' optimal strategies, have stable preferences and so on. While the interactions described certainly obtain, if at all, at the level of individuals and not aggregates, they are unlikely to be realistic descriptions of who these individuals are and what they do.

Figure 6.1 illustrates the different concepts graphically.

Mechanisms as individual causal relations (as represented by structural equations in econometrics) and as mediating variables are mainly relevant in the context of causal inference, and will therefore be discussed in the methodology part of this book. Mechanisms as pieces of theory are closely related to models, which will be discussed in Chapter 7. Here I will therefore focus on mechanisms as underlying structures or processes.

Mechanisms as Underlying Structures or Processes

To get an intuitive grasp of the idea, let us consider an example: the monetary transmission mechanism (cf. Ireland 2008). Recall from the previous chapter that one way to read Fisher's equation of exchange is that changes in money supply *cause* proportional changes in prices. As is the case with most causal relations, money affects prices via a continuous process, which is called the monetary transmission mechanism. In Friedman and Schwartz's original sketch of it (Friedman and Schwartz 1963), roughly the following happens. The initial change in the growth rate of the money supply (implemented by, for example, an increase in the rate of open market purchases) causes an imbalance in the portfolios of the market participants: they hold too much liquidity relative to their preferences. They thus seek to adjust their portfolios and demand assets. Initially they buy assets that are similar to those sold to the Fed (that is, relatively risk-free titles), later they seek further

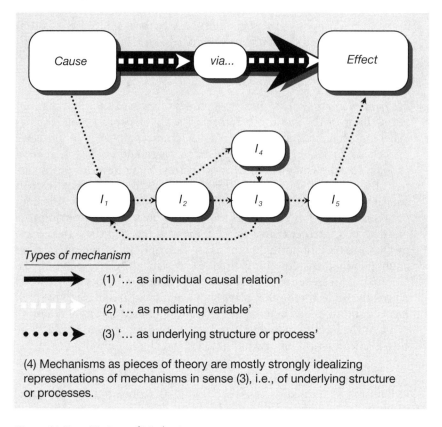

Figure 6.1 Four Notions of Mechanism

and also buy riskier securities. Increased demand will drive up the prices for these assets and, correspondingly, lower interest rates. Higher asset prices will make people feel wealthier and hence increase demand for non-financial goods and services. Increased aggregate demand will, in turn, increase income, employment and output. After a while, however, the prices of goods and services, too, will react to the higher demand and increase.

The quantity theory (in the form of the equation of exchange) thus describes an aggregate or macro-regularity (one that, of course, obtains at best as a tendency, not as a strict regularity): changes in the money supply cause proportional changes in the price level. To describe the transmission mechanism means, on the one hand, to describe what *constitutes* the changes mentioned in the quantity theory. Its quantity "change in the money supply" is highly abstract and concerns an aggregate or macro-variable. Describing the mechanism means to move a level down and to tell how a change in the abstract variable could be implemented. Here is some more detail:

Central bank liabilities include both components of the monetary base: currency and bank reserves. Hence, the central bank controls the monetary base. Indeed, monetary policy actions typically begin when the central bank changes the monetary base through an open market operation, purchasing other securities—most frequently, government bonds—to increase the monetary base or selling securities to decrease the monetary base.

(Ireland 2008)

To describe the transmission mechanism means, on the other hand, to describe the *process(es) through which* changes in the money supply as implemented will affect prices. Many macro-tendency claims can be regarded as "black box" causal claims. To investigate the mechanism is to open the black box and examine the detailed process that connects cause and effect.

Causal mechanisms have a number of noteworthy characteristics. First, like tendencies, they do not necessitate their effects. That is, it is not the case that when the mechanism has been triggered, it will come to completion, because intervening factors may disrupt their operation. A mechanism is a causal chain. As such it can break at every stage. One consequence of this is that while mechanisms can be used to explain an outcome once it has occurred, it is not normally possible to predict an outcome upon observing that this or that mechanism has been triggered.

Second, a given cause can be connected to its effect via any number of mechanisms, not just one. In our example, the different processes have been referred to as the "channels of monetary transmission" (Mishkin 1996):

- the traditional Keynesian *interest rate channel*;
- the *exchange rate channel* in open economies;
- *the asset price channel*;
- two *credit channels*:
  - the *bank lending channel*
  - the *balance sheet channel*.

Depending on how the different channels influence the outcome, it may be that the overall result is positive, negative or nil. In this particular case, all channels operate in the same direction: when money goes up, real variables such as prices and nominal income go up, and vice versa. Here is an example where two mechanisms operate in opposite directions:

A high marginal tax rate lowers the opportunity cost or "price" of leisure, and, as with any commodity whose price is reduced, thereby encourages people to consume more of it (and thus do less work). But, on the other hand, it also lowers people's incomes, and thereby may induce them to work harder so as to maintain their standard of living.

These two effects—the substitution and income effects, in economists'
parlance—operate in opposite directions, and their net effect is impossible to predict from theory alone.

(LeGrand 1982: 148; quoted from Elster 1998: 50)

An example loved by philosophers has the same structure (Hesslow 1976).
Birth-control pills (B) affect the incidence of deep-vein thrombosis (T) via
two channels. On the one hand, they produce a chemical (C) in the woman's
blood stream that increases the likelihood of thrombosis. On the other hand,
they prevent pregnancies (P), which themselves are a positive cause of thrombosis. Depending on the relative strength of the two channels, birth control
could increase, decrease or leave unchanged the likelihood of thrombosis, as
shown in Figure 6.2.

Thus, even when two variables X and Y are known to be connected by
a mechanism, and the mechanism is known to operate uninterrupted on
a given occasion, it is not guaranteed that the outcome can be predicted,
because of the possible existence of competing mechanisms, which affect the
outcome variable in the opposite direction.

Third, especially when there are several mechanisms it is not always clear
under what conditions which mechanism is or which mechanisms are triggered. Here is an example due to Jon Elster:

When people try to make up their mind whether to participate in a
cooperative venture, such as cleaning up litter from the lawn or voting in
a national election, they often look to see what others are doing. Some of
them will think as follows: "If most others cooperate, I too should do my
share, but if they don't I have no obligation to do so." Others will reason
in exactly the opposite way: "If most others cooperate, there is no need
for me to do so. If few others cooperate, my obligation to do so will be
stronger." In fact, most individuals are subject to both of these psychic
mechanisms, and it is hard to tell before the fact which will dominate.

(Elster 1989: 9)

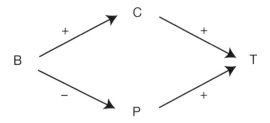

Figure 6.2 A Cause Influencing an Effect through Different Routes

All three characteristics serve to drive a wedge between the gaining of causal understanding of a situation through learning about a mechanism and the ability to use this knowledge for the practical purpose of prediction. Mechanistic knowledge might still help with predictions, but only in combination with other knowledge, such as that a mechanism can operate uninterruptedly, that either all mechanisms between a cause and an effect operate in the same direction or that mechanisms that adversely affect an outcome have been controlled in a given case or are not operational for other reasons and that the right mechanism has been triggered appropriately.

Mechanisms, Methodological Individualism and Micro-Foundations

The demand to explain aggregate or social regularities in terms of underlying mechanisms is reminiscent of a debate in the philosophy of the social sciences concerning so-called methodological individualism. Social mechanisms are often defined in terms of individuals and their actions: "Social mechanisms in particular are usually thought of as complexes of interactions among agents that underlie and account for macrosocial regularities" (Steel 2011: 298).

Moreover, those promoting theorizing in terms of social mechanisms, such as the advocates of analytical sociology, often also subscribe to methodological individualism and see in the mechanistic explanation of social phenomena a realization of the doctrine (e.g., Hedström and Ylikoski 2010; Hedström 2005; Hedström and Swedberg 1998).

The doctrine of methodological individualism goes back to Max Weber's insistence that social science be an interpretive science, and the debate concerns, among other things, the nature of a good social science explanation. Weber favored accounts of social phenomena in terms of the actions of individual agents because we can subjectively understand their motives for action (Weber 1968). This capacity of interpretively accessing the motives underlying actions allows us to understand why social phenomena occur in a way that is unique to the social sciences. An atom, billiard ball or chrysanthemum does not have any particular reason for behaving in the way it does, at least for all we know. Their behavior is entirely due to natural causal processes. Some of human behavior is, however, intentional, and it is this kind of behavior that is amenable to explanation by motivations or reasons.

Providing accounts of social phenomena in terms of individuals' actions is therefore a good thing because it gives us access to a form of explanation that is desirable and sets the social sciences apart from the natural sciences. The kind of explanation one thus achieves is "understanding though reducing the unfamiliar to the familiar" (Hempel 1966: 83; Hempel thought that scientific explanations can but do not have to have and typically don't have this characteristic). I understand other people's actions through their motives because their motives are familiar to me from reflection about my own intentions. The strange and mysterious—social outcomes—can thus be reduced to something ordinary.

Economists prefer rational-choice models of social phenomena and demand micro-foundations for macroeconomic theories. But we have to be careful not to hastily adopt Weber's defense of individualism for contemporary economics. Rational-choice models of the kind we find in economics today are far more tenuously related to Weberian methodological individualism than economists might realize.

It is true that Weber too implemented his explanatory strategy by a model of rational action. But this had more to do with two additional methodological convictions. One was that economics and sociology strive for explanatory generalizations rather than the historical explanation of particular outcomes in terms of the specific motives of the partaking individuals and therefore have to offer a general *model* of human action. The other was his methodological strategy to construct certain kinds of fictions—"ideal types"—that emphasize and exaggerate salient and analytically significant characteristics of social phenomenon of interest with the aim of classifying them into a scheme useful for the researcher's interpretive purposes.

Weber thus did not think of agents as behaving in accordance to his model. Rather:

> The construction of a purely rational course of action … serves the sociologist as a type (ideal type) which has the merit of clear understandability and lack of ambiguity. By comparison with this it is possible to understand the ways in which actual action is influenced by irrational factors of all sorts, such as affects and errors, in that they account for the deviation from the line of conduct which would be expected on the hypothesis that the action were purely rational.
>
> (Weber 1968: 6)

Like individualism, Weber's model of rational action is therefore a methodological device introduced for explanatory purposes. It is not clear at all whether a rational choice model we typically find in contemporary microeconomics can serve the same purposes. To begin with, not all decision-makers in microeconomic models are individual human agents. In general equilibrium theory, households and firms face one another. Among other things, households supply labor, and firms hire labor and produce goods. In public choice models, governments are often thought of as agents. Neither households nor firms nor governments are individuals: they are collectives.

The problem with microeconomics' basic units being collectives is that the relation between individual and collective agency is far from straightforward (e.g., Hardin 1982). Because of the existence of Prisoner's Dilemma-type incentive structures (see Chapter 4), common interests among individuals might not always realize at the collective level. Therefore, whatever a household, firm, government or "representative agent" preference represents, it cannot simply be assumed that it stands for the motivations of individual human agents. By itself this does not mean that there is anything wrong with micro-foundations. But it does mean that the Weberian defense of rational agency models, which is based on specific explanatory considerations, cannot be drawn on.

Another problem in applying Weber's defense is the high level of idealization employed in the models, with respect to both the setting in which agents find themselves and the cognitive abilities of the agents. We might well get some sort of understanding from, say, rational-expectations models, in which hyper-rational agents form expectations about the future values of variables on the basis of the true structural models for these variables, but it is not the kind of understanding we get through empathizing with an agent's motivations for action.

Perhaps this is for the better. The kind of understanding Weber sought has not always received the best press, especially in positivist circles (Hempel 1965; Salmon 1991). One of the problems is that many explanations that are accepted as quite truly scientific do the opposite: they "reduce" the familiar (such as middle-sized objects) to something very unfamiliar (a world of unobservable entities such as atoms, forces, quarks and strings). And perhaps this is just what contemporary micro-models aim to achieve. We will come back to this topic in the following chapter on models and idealizations.

For now, let us ask more generally whether there are good reasons to subscribe to methodological individualism. In brief, giving an account of a social phenomenon in terms of the motivations for individuals' actions is neither necessary nor sufficient for explaining the phenomenon. That individualist accounts are not necessary can be gleaned from the fact that there are alternative views about explanation. It is not easy to reject the idea that accounts citing the causal tendencies of macro-social or other non-individualist factors are genuinely explanatory without begging the question (by, for instance, defining explanation in terms of individualist mechanisms). Why and in what way accounts in terms of causal tendencies should be regarded as genuinely explanatory has been discussed above in Chapter 5.

Moreover, there are some reasons to believe that macro-behavior is more stable than micro-motives. As will be discussed in detail in Chapter 10 on economic experiments, individuals' actions appear to be extremely sensitive to the details of the situation the individuals find themselves in and the expectations they have about the right course of action in such a situation. To the extent that social science aims to provide general accounts of social phenomena, it seems therefore advantageous from an explanatory point of view to move to a level of description at which individual differences cancel out and behavior appears more stable. An increase in the money supply might always tend to exert an upward pressure on prices. But the mechanisms through which an increase, should it occur, realizes may be highly variable and not particularly interesting from a theoretical point of view.

In such a case the macro-tendency and not its micro-realization would be primary from an explanatory point of view.

That accounts in terms of individuals' actions and motives might not be sufficient for explanation I pointed to earlier when I mentioned the positivists' rejection of Weber's understanding of understanding. Explanation in terms of what seems familiar is both arbitrary as well as pre-scientific. It is arbitrary because what seems familiar to one person might not seem familiar to another. So-called "common sense" might be less common than is commonly presumed. Moreover, and this is the more important point, it is hard to see why we should accept an account just because the story it tells seems familiar to us. As mentioned above, science often progresses by postulating entities and kinds of behavior that seem strange to us. Social science too might advance by ignoring the appeal to "commonsensicals."

None of this is to say that accounts that derive descriptions of social phenomena from models of individual agency are not valuable. Not being necessary or sufficient for some purpose does not mean being useless. If we take for granted that individualistic accounts are not explanatory *qua* Weberian interpretive understanding (and we could challenge even that!), we might still argue that they may provide causal-mechanistic explanations, as I will describe shortly. One condition for that is that they give causally true accounts: a description of the mechanism for a relation between macro-social variables X and Y causally explains that relation only to the extent that there are cases in which the mechanism is indeed responsible for the macro relation. And if the account provides a (causally) false description of the underlying mechanism, it might still be explanatory, as we will see in Chapter 7.

Mechanistic Explanation

Whether at the individual level or at a meso (intermediate) level between macro and individual, a mechanistic description renders a phenomenon intelligible by showing how it came about, what constitutes it, or both. Mechanistic explanations have two kinds of explananda: outcomes (or facts) and aggregate relationships. A specific episode of inflation in some country can be explained mechanistically by a process such as a version of the transmission mechanism. Describing that mechanism shows how the inflation was produced, what brought it about. On the other hand, mechanistic descriptions can be used to explain an aggregate relationship such as that between monetary growth and inflation. The transmission mechanism explains why this relationship holds, why for instance monetary growth rates are positively correlated with inflation rates and not negatively correlated.

Simply put, a description of a mechanism helps to explain because what we seek from a scientific explanation to a large extent just is an explication of "how it works." We seek understanding and our understanding of a phenomenon is improved when the black box is opened and the nuts and bolts responsible for the phenomenon in question are revealed (these metaphors are Jon Elster's; see his 1989 and 2007). Of course, if we seek to gain understanding of a macro-social phenomenon through examining the underlying mechanism this means that we already have some understanding of the behavior of the parts. Let me make two remarks about this.

First, one might argue that the idea I just described, namely that of "deriving an understanding about the higher-level phenomenon from the understanding of the behavior of the mechanism(s) that produces and/or constitutes it" is circular, that the idea of understanding as such has been left unexplained. This might well be true, but arguably the circularity is not vicious. Any scientific advance has to build on previous work. Mechanistic explanation does not presuppose that there are any "rock-bottom" relations that are simple enough so as to be self-evident. Rather, any original scientific inquiry takes previous findings as given and derives new knowledge from them. But that doesn't mean that the bits of knowledge that have been presupposed in one inquiry cannot be challenged or sought to be refined in another one. And it is certainly the case that a relation that constitutes part of an explanatory mechanism can itself often be given a mechanistic explanation. Here is an example of a statement of the Keynesian "interest rate channel," a mechanism that explains the relation between money and inflation:

> A monetary tightening in the form of a shock to the Taylor rule that increases the short-term nominal interest rate translates into an increase in the real interest rate as well when nominal prices move sluggishly due to costly or staggered price setting. This rise in the real interest rate then causes households to cut back on their spending, as summarized by the IS curve. Finally, through the Phillips curve, the decline in output puts downward pressure on inflation, which adjusts only gradually after the shock.
>
> (Ireland 2008)

Each of these links can, in turn, be explained, and economists have explained them. The first link, for instance, is called the "liquidity effect," which has received much attention in the literature. In a survey paper, Chris Edmond and Pierre-Olivier Weill ask "how a collection of small segmentation frictions cumulates in the aggregate, and whether they add up to a quantitatively significant macro friction." This is significant, because "If they do, then the models of liquidity effects that we have discussed here would indeed be natural laboratories for the analysis of the monetary transmission mechanism" (Edmond and Weill 2009). Thus, a single link in one of the channels that together make up the transmission mechanism is itself explained by an "array" of micro-mechanisms.

Second, despite an appearance of similarity between this account of understanding and Weber's (discussed above), the two are not at all the same. The mechanistic account derives understanding of the phenomenon of interest from an understanding of the behavior of the parts of the mechanism that underlie it but that doesn't mean that the latter has to be one of Weberian interpretive understanding. There is nothing about the liquidity effect with which the researcher is more familiar than with the transmission mechanism as a whole or the aggregate relation between money and prices. To the contrary: the aggregate relation has been known since at least the sixteenth century, whereas the transmission mechanism and its parts are still a matter of dispute. To the extent that we are able understand the latter, that understanding derives from features of mechanisms that are unquestionably linked with the kinds of understanding we expect to get from science: causality and unification.

We understand causally to the extent that we have evidence that an observed relation is genuinely causal and not merely correlational. The potential advantages of mechanisms relative to aggregate relationships are twofold. First, the mechanism adds detail. If a mechanism for an aggregate relationship can be described, we don't merely see that it is a genuinely causal relationship, we also see how it is being produced. But this advantage comes at a certain cost: to the extent that we want explanations that cover many instances of a phenomenon, to add mechanistic detail might mean to restrict the number of applications. The relationship between money and prices may be extremely inclusive, perhaps even universal among economies with a certain monetary constitution and relatively free price-setting. The mechanisms through which the relationship operates may be far more local. On the other hand, it may be the case that it is easier to establish causality at the level of a link of the mechanism than at the level of the aggregate relationship. For instance, it may be very difficult to find or construct instruments to estimate aggregate relationship and far easier to find or construct instruments for a link in the mechanism (cf. Hamilton 1997, who argues as much about the liquidity effect; for an introduction to the instrumental variables technique to estimate causal relationships, see Chapter 10). Similarly, it may be possible to run experiments at micro-level, whereas macro-experiments are almost always unfeasible. But this is a matter that can only be decided on a case-by-case basis: often aggregate relationships might well be epistemically more easily accessible than a meso- or micro-relationship.

Another model of understanding is unification. We gain understanding by unifying complex and manifold phenomena and reducing them to a common core of principles. Wesley Salmon seems to have thought that in the natural sciences mechanisms can play such a unificatory role:

> We explain events by showing how they fit into the causal nexus. Since there seem to be a small number of fundamental causal mechanisms, and some extremely comprehensive laws that govern them, the ontic conception has as much right as the epistemic conception to take the unification of natural phenomena as a basic aspect of our comprehension of the

world. The unity lies in the pervasiveness of the underlying mechanisms upon which we depend for explanation.

(Salmon 1984: 276)

Again, much depends on the details of a case. The money–prices link is certainly much more unifying than the multifarious mechanisms proposed to explain it. In other cases there may be underlying structures that play a role in the generation of many aggregate phenomena. At any rate, the unification model of understanding/explanation will be considered in more detail in the next chapter.

Conclusions

Mechanisms are all the rage now in the philosophy of the social sciences, in the philosophy of the life sciences and in parts of general philosophy of science (especially in debates about causation). The reasons are not hard to appreciate. After the demise of positivism, causal explanation came to be regarded—again—as one of the more important aims of the enterprise of science, and the mechanistic model of causal explanation is one that fits well with much scientific practice, in the social sciences and elsewhere. I have been rather critical of the enthusiasm for mechanistic thinking myself (see Reiss 2007a), but it is hard to deny that mechanistic accounts can help with explaining social phenomena.

At the same time it is important to realize that the methodological literature on causal or social mechanisms that has appeared is to some extent irrelevant to contemporary economics. The models we find there look as though they could represent mechanisms—they certainly describe structures and processes that might underlie macro, social or aggregate relationships—but by and large they are too heavily idealized, including in their causal details, to be thought of as representations of actual mechanisms. At best, therefore, they should be thought of as representations of possible mechanisms. Possible mechanisms, however, do not explain social phenomena of interest. Whatever the models do, they do not explain in the causal-mechanistic sense. Nor do they explain in Weber's sense of providing interpretive understanding, as I argued above; even if they did, the victory would be transient as there are reasons to doubt that Weberian understanding is what economists seek or otherwise of great significance.

Paradise is lost, but not all. The next chapter will consider whether false models can explain. Later on, in Chapter 15, I will discuss a relatively recent movement in economics that can be understood as investigating the mechanisms that lead to decision-making more realistically—behavioral economics. About the latter, a prominent commentator said:

One area in which this is already happening is in behavioral economics, and the merging of economics and psychology, whose own experimental tradition is clearly focused on behavioral regularities. The experiments reviewed in Steven D. Levitt and John A. List (2008), often involving both economists and psychologists, cover such issues as loss aversion, procrastination, hyperbolic discounting, or the availability heuristic—all of which are examples of behavioral mechanisms that promise applicability beyond the specific experiments.

(Deaton 2010a: 450)

Study Questions

1   Do we need mechanisms in economics?
2   Do economists who demand that macro-theories be given micro-foundations pursue an agenda of mechanistic explanation?
3   What economic mechanisms have you come across in your studies? Do your examples fit the characterization given in this chapter?
4   Do all and only mechanisms explain phenomena of interest?
5   What other roles apart from explanation might economic mechanisms play?

Suggested Readings

Talk about mechanisms and their investigation is now very popular in various branches of social science and the philosophy of social science. Early proponents in social science include contributors to Hedström and Swedberg 1998, and in philosophy Mario Bunge (1997) and Jon Elster (1983 and 1989). A critical review of some of the work done in what I call the "New Mechanistic Philosophy" is Reiss 2007a. A recent review article is Hedström and Ylikoski 2010. See also Steel 2004.

General accounts of mechanisms, not directly related to social science, are Woodward 2002, Glennan 1996 and 2002, Machamer *et al.* 2000 and N. Cartwright 1999a (though she uses the term "nomological machine"). Glennan 2010 provides a mechanistic account of historical explanation.

On methodological individualism I would highly recommend Kincaid 1997 and chapter 5 of his 1996, as well as D. Little 1998.

Part IC

Models

7   Models, Idealization, Explanation

Overview

The theories of explanation discussed in Parts IA and IB are all different versions of *causal* explanation. Causal explanations have a peculiarity: they are not successful unless the account given is true of the phenomenon in question. The bursting of the asset price bubble in the American subprime market in 2007 does not explain the recession that followed it unless there was a bubble, the bubble burst and the bursting of the bubble caused the recession. Neither inexistent causal factor nor mere potential causal links explain.

   This fact about causal explanations doesn't sit easily with another couple of facts about economics, namely, that economics is heavily model-based (more specifically, that economic *explanations* are often based on models), and that all models are false in a variety of ways. Models always give simplified and often idealized accounts of the phenomena they are models of. But if models are false, explanations use models essentially and causal explanations have to be true, can economic explanations be causal? Part IC takes up this issue in a single chapter: Can false models explain? If so, how? Can the ideal of causal explanation be reconciled with the fact that all models are false?

Causal Explanation

The causal account of explanation is widely regarded as successful and, importantly, more successful than its alternatives—both as an account of scientific explanation in general and one of explanation in economics in particular. To explain a specific economic event is to cite its causes; to explain a general economic phenomenon is to describe the causal mechanism responsible for it.

The starting point for this chapter is the observation of a particular feature of causal explanations: causal explanations cannot be successful unless they are true. I took this idea from Nancy Cartwright, who, albeit to make a different point, wrote the following:

> My newly planted lemon tree is sick, the leaves yellow and dropping off. I finally explain this by saying that water has accumulated in the base of the planter: the water is the cause of the disease. I drill a hole in the base of the oak barrel where the lemon tree lives, and foul water flows out. That was the cause. Before I had drilled the hole, I could still give the explanation and to give that explanation was to present the supposed cause, the water. There must *be* such water for the explanation to be correct. An explanation of an effect by a cause has an existential component, not just an optional extra ingredient.
>
> (N. Cartwright 1983: 91; original emphasis)

Cheap money in the early 2000s does not explain the financial crisis of the late 2000s unless money was indeed cheap (in the sense that interest rates were lower than the rate that would have been "adequate" given the economic conditions) and unless cheap money was indeed the factor without which the financial crisis would not have occurred. The monetary transmission mechanism (or a description thereof) does not explain the aggregate relationship between money, the interest rate and real variables unless changes in real variables are, at least sometimes, brought about by the transmission mechanism.

The requirement that causal accounts be true in order to be explanatory is in fact the great downside of causal explanation. When phenomena are complex, and economic phenomena are, truth is hard to come by. Accounts given of economic phenomena are usually dramatically simplified and features that we know affect a result are represented in a systematically distorted way. Among economists, the slogan "all models are wrong, but some are useful" (due to statisticians Box and Draper 1987: 424) is well known. And yet, such models are regarded by economists and others as having more than heuristic value: Not always, to be sure, but often enough economic models succeed in explaining.

The issue I aim to tackle in this chapter is the question whether we can square the fact that all models contain significant falsehoods with the economists' aim to give genuinely explanatory accounts of economic phenomena: Do false models explain?

Economic Models

Economists see the world through models. Rather than discussing the matter generally and abstractly, let us examine a classic in the use of models in economics in some detail: Harold Hotelling's derivation of the principle of minimal differentiation, which has become to be known as "Hotelling's law" (Hotelling 1929). Hotelling's starting point is the observation that if one of a number of sellers of a good increases his price ever so slightly, he will not immediately lose all his business to competitors—against the predictions of earlier models by Cournot, Amoroso and Edgeworth:

> Many customers will still prefer to trade with him because they live nearer to his store than to the others, or because they have less freight to pay from his warehouse to their own, or because his mode of doing business is more to their liking, or because he sells other articles which they desire, or because he is a relative or fellow Elk or Baptist, or on account of some difference in service or quality, or for a combination of reasons.
> (Hotelling 1929: 44)

The reason for this is that another economics law, the law of one price, is itself at best a *ceteris paribus* law (see Chapter 5). The law says that in one market the same goods must sell at the same price—if they did not, customers would flock to the cheapest seller, forcing more expensive sellers to lower their prices or driving them out of the market. But that of course holds only if the goods are identical in every respect, including their spatial distance to the buyer, which is never strictly true of actual goods. Hotelling's model describes what happens when one of the conditions in the *ceteris paribus* clause is relaxed: specifically, when goods differ in their spatial distance to the buyer along a single dimension.

Suppose, then, that the buyers of a commodity are uniformly distributed along a line segment of length *l*. Two vendors *A* and *B* are at distances *a* and *b*, respectively, from each end of the line segment:

The cost of production for the good to *A* and *B* is assumed to be zero. Demand is perfectly inelastic; that is, each customer purchases one unit of

Figure 7.1 Hotelling's Model of Spatial Aggregation

the item, no matter what. Each buyer transports his purchase to the place where he consumes it at cost c per unit distance. Denote A's price by p_1, B's price by p_2 and let q_1 and q_2 denote the respective quantities.

Under these assumptions, B's price can exceed that of A without B losing *all* his customers to A. However, he must not let his price exceed A's by more than the transportation cost from A to B, which can be expressed as $c(l - a - b)$.

In this way, he will attract all the business of the line segment to his right, b, plus some of the business in between A and B, which is denoted by y. The same is true for A of course, *mutatis mutandis*, so that A attracts all the business to his left plus some of the business in between A and B, denoted by x. The lower A's price as compared to B's, the more business he can attract, *that is*, the greater is x.

The customer in between x and y (marked by the dotted line in Figure 7.1) is indifferent between A and B:

$$p_1 + cx = p_2 + cy.$$

Moreover, we know that:

$$l = a + x + y + b.$$

Solving for x and y, calculating profits = revenue = pq and substituting $a + x$ for q_1 and $b + y$ for q_2 yields:

$$\pi_1 = p_1 q_1 = p_1(a + x) = \tfrac{1}{2}(l + a - -b)\, p_1 - p_1^2/2c + (p_1 p_2/2c)$$
$$\pi_2 = p_2 q_2 = p_2(b + y) = \tfrac{1}{2}(l - a + b)\, p_2 - p_2^2/2c + (p_1 p_2/2c).$$

Setting the derivative with respect to price to zero and solving give the equations:

$$p_1 = c(l + (a - b)/3),$$
$$p_2 = c(l - (a - b)/3);$$

and

$$q_1 = \tfrac{1}{2}(l + (a - b)/3),$$
$$q_2 = \tfrac{1}{2}(l - (a - b)/3).$$

Profits then are given by:

$$\pi_1 = p_1 q_1 = c/2(l + (a - b)/3)^2,$$
$$\pi_2 = p_2 q_2 = c/2(l + (b - a)/3)^2.$$

So far we have assumed that A and B have fixed locations. Let us now relax that assumption. It can readily be seen from the profit equations that A will want to make *a* as large as possible and *B* will want to make *b* as large as possible. That is, they will move towards each other. If, in the above figure, *B* moves first, he will locate immediately to the right of *A*. In this case, *A* will move to *B*'s immediate right because that part of the line segment (in the figure: $x + y + b$) is larger than his segment on the left (*a*). Then *B* will move again to *A*'s right and so on until they are both at the center of the line, sharing the business half-and-half.

It is important to assume that *A* and *B* cannot occupy the same point on the line, because in this case they would enter into a price war, reducing profits for both. Hotelling remarks about this:

> From *B*'s standpoint the sharper competition with *A* due to proximity is offset by the greater body of buyers with whom he has an advantage. But the danger that the system will be overturned by the elimination of one competitor is increased. The intermediate segment of the market ($x + y$ > 0) acts as a cushion as well as a bone of contention; when it disappears we have Cournot's case, and Bertrand's objection applies.
>
> (Hotelling 1929: 52)

The two will therefore move as close as possible to each other without becoming identical. This, argues Hotelling, is precisely what we observe in a large number of economic and non-economic phenomena:

> In politics it is strikingly exemplified. The competition for votes between the Republican and Democratic parties does not lead to a clear drawing of issues, and adoption of two strongly contrasted positions between which the voter may choose. Instead, each party strives to make its platform as much like the other's as possible. …
>
> It leads some factories to make cheap shoes for the poor and others to make expensive shoes for the rich, but all the shoes are too much alike. Our cities become uneconomically large and the business districts within them are too concentrated. Methodist and Presbyterian churches are too much alike; cider is too homogeneous.
>
> (Hotelling 1929: 54 and 57)

The "too much alike" refers to the fact that the profit-maximizing equilibrium differs from the "social optimum" in the model. Indeed, if *A* located at one quarter of the line segment from the left and *B* at one quarter from the right, they would also divide the cake in half but customers would have to travel much less. But if *A* really did locate there, *B* would move to his immediate right, taking half of *A*'s profits. And so on. As an aside, note how Hotelling switches from a descriptive reading to a normative reading of the model. Shoes, churches and cider all are *too* homogeneous, cities *too* large and business districts *too* concentrated. I will say more about the fact–value issue in Chapter 8.

Idealizations

It is obvious that Hotelling's model is highly idealized relative to the phenomena it seeks to explain. The most literal application of the model would probably be to the location decisions of two businesses along a straight line such as shops on a Main Street or ice-cream vendors along a beach. Even for such applications—and the model, as we have seen, is meant to apply much more broadly—the model makes numerous assumptions we know to be false: we move in three- not in one-dimensional space; goods differ with respect to many aspects other than "distance from point of consumption"; customers are not uniformly distributed along a line and demand is seldom completely inelastic; sellers act on numerous motives, of which profit maximization is at best one.

There are many classifications of the different kinds of idealizations one might find in science. I find William Wimsatt's to be particularly useful:

1   A model may be of only very *local applicability*. This is a way of being false only if it is more broadly applied.
2   A model may be an *idealization* whose conditions of applicability are never found in nature (e.g., point masses, the uses of continuous variables for population sizes, etc.), but which has a range of cases to which it may be more or less accurately applied as an approximation.
3   A model may be *incomplete*—leaving out one or more causally relevant variables. (Here it is assumed that the included variables are causally relevant, and are so in at least roughly the manner described.)
4   The incompleteness of the model may lead to a *misdescription of the interactions* of the variables which are included, producing apparent interactions where there are none ("spurious" correlations), or apparent independence where there are interactions—as in the spurious "context independence" produced by biases in reductionist research strategies. Taylor (1985) analyzes the first kind of case for mathematical models in ecology, but most of his conclusions are generalizable to other contexts. (In these cases, it is assumed that the variables identified in the models are at least approximately correctly described.)
5   A model may give a *totally wrong-headed* picture of nature. Not only are the interactions wrong, but also a significant number of the entities and/or their properties do not exist.

(Wimsatt 2007: 101–2; original emphases)

On pain of trivializing (1), we should probably qualify "in its intended domain." No model explains everything; a model is always a partial representation of the world. But it is a substantial point to say that models often have local applicability, even in their intended domain. Unfortunately, it is not quite clear what a model's "intended domain" is or what "applicability" means.

Hotelling's paper gives some indication about where he intends his model to apply. He wants to draw our attention to the fact that consumers often deal with one seller rather than another despite a difference in price. He explains this by product differentiation. This suggests that the intended domain is economic settings in which producers can erect quasi-monopolies by differentiating their product from competitors and they can set prices in the light of maximizing profits. This cannot be the end of the story, because party politics are clearly within Hotelling's intended domain and parties at best maximize votes rather than profits, but let us ignore that here. What then might it mean for a model to be applied? Supposedly, it means to use the model to explain phenomena of interest and make predictions. The model might be falsified in this particular way if, for instance, two businesses do not compete via prices even though they could, or if they ended up in a price war because they produced identical goods.

That the model idealizes in sense (2) is clear, among other things, from the fact that its two producers move along a line that has no breadth or thickness. How significant such an idealization is depends on purpose and context. Hotelling himself sees a zero-dimensional market in economics in analogy to point masses in astronomy:

> To take another physical analogy, the earth is often in astronomical calculations considered as a point, and with substantially accurate results. But the precession of the equinoxes becomes explicable only when account is taken of the ellipsoidal bulge of the earth. So in the theory of value a market is usually considered as a point in which only one price can obtain; but for some purposes it is better to consider a market as an extended region.
>
> (Hotelling 1929: 45)

Moving from a zero-dimensional geography in which the law of one price holds to a one-dimensional geography where Hotelling's principle holds is the minimum adjustment he could make. Whether considering a market as a line is a harmless idealization depends on what aspects of the geometry are relevant for consumer decisions. It is often useful to consider cities as being two-dimensional. The shortest distance from A to B in two-dimensional space is of course a straight line or, when one cannot move in a straight line because of buildings and traffic, the closest approximation to a straight line. But when one travels by bike and the city is very hilly such as La Paz or San Francisco one usually fares better by taking the contours into account. Similarly, ice-cream vendors might have to take account of the breadth and gradient of the beach if these geographical features matter to consumers.

Hotelling's model is also false in sense (3). Customers care about much more than how far they have to travel to get a product, no matter what the geography. Hotelling mentions various examples himself: the sweetness of cider, whether the seller is a fellow Elk or Baptist, party ideologies. When producers can differentiate their goods with respect to more than one characteristic, whether or not all the different characteristics can usefully be captured in a single transportation cost parameter depends on whether the different characteristics interact in their bringing about the outcome. Do ice-cream vendors still move as closely together as possible when they can change both their location and the taste of the ice cream they sell?

Under (4) I would include assumptions to the effect that causal relations have specific functional forms in the absence of evidence that the modeled phenomena satisfy these functional forms. Transportation costs are assumed to be linear, consumer demand is assumed to be perfectly inelastic. These are at best approximations but more probably significantly wrong. Hotelling considers the case of elastic demand (Hotelling 1929: 56): "With elastic demand the observations we have made on the solution will still for the most part be qualitatively true; but the tendency for B to establish his business excessively close to A will be less marked." He asserts this without providing much evidence, however, and a result in which "B will definitely apart from extraneous circumstances choose a location at some distance from A" (Hotelling 1929: 56) is arguably a qualitatively different result than the principle of minimum differentiation.

A model is false in sense (5) when it gives a totally wrong-headed picture of nature, when the posited entities or properties do not exist. In economics this is a tricky type of idealization as the entities and properties it posits always have counterparts in our everyday ontology of the world. Economics doesn't explain phenomena by introducing strange things such as electrons, quarks and strings, the id and the unconscious, *l'élan vital* and *la volonté générale*. Rather, ordinary things such as households and firms, businesspeople, their plants and the goods they produce are transformed into something no less strange but with a clear analogue in everyday life. Typical economics models, let us say, assume businesspeople to have perfect calculation abilities and to care only about profits. But they are still businesspeople. Thus, in some sense, even if all actual businesspeople were particularly bad at math and cared mostly about world peace, these models would not give a totally wrong-headed picture of nature.

I would nevertheless say that an idealization falls into this category whenever the outcome of interest—say, minimal product differentiation—is produced by a causal mechanism that differs from the mechanism represented in the model. In the case at hand the mechanism includes a conscious product differentiation on the part of businesses aiming to create a spatial monopoly in order to maximize profits. Minimal product differentiation could be a result of other mechanisms—imitation, say, or chance—which may or may not be aimed at profit maximization. To the extent that such other mechanisms are at work, Hotelling's model gives a "totally wrong-headed picture of nature." To the extent, for instance, that politicians actually believe in the rightness of their politics, minimal differences between parties (where they exist) are misrepresented by Hotelling's model as being the result of a process of maximization.

Explanation

Hotelling's model, then, is false in all relevant senses (1)–(5) from Wimsatt's list. And yet, it is considered explanatory. The principle the model underwrites is often referred to as Hotelling's *law*. Moreover, and perhaps more importantly, it feels explanatory. If we haven't thought much about Hotelling's kinds of cases, it seems that we have genuinely learned something. We begin to see Hotelling situations all over the place. Why do electronics shops in London concentrate in Tottenham Court Road and music shops in Denmark Street? Why do art galleries in Paris cluster around rue de Seine? Why have so many hi-fi-related retailers set up business in calle Barquillo in Madrid that it has come to be known as "calle del Sonido" (street of sound)? And why the heck are most political parties practically indistinguishable? But we do not only come to see that, we also intuitively feel that Hotelling's model must capture something that is right.

We've now reached an impasse of the kind philosophers call a paradox: a set of statements, all of which seem individually acceptable or even unquestionable but which, when taken together, are jointly contradictory. These are the statements:

a   Economic models are false.
b   Economic models are nevertheless explanatory.
c   Only true accounts can explain.

When facing a paradox, one may respond by either giving up one or more of the jointly contradictory statements or else challenge our logic. I haven't come across anyone writing on economic models who has explicitly challenged logic (though their writings sometimes suggest otherwise). There are authors, however, who resolve the paradox by giving up a premiss. I will discuss one or more examples for each.

Economic Models Are True After All—in the Abstract

Let me begin with a disclaimer. Models do not have truth values. Whatever models are, and there is some debate about the "ontology of models" (see for instance Frigg and Hartmann 2012), it is most certainly not the case that models are sentences. But it is sentences that are true or false. For a very intuitive example, take the Phillips machine (or MOnetary National Income Analogue Computer, MONIAC). The Phillips machine is a model of the UK economy. It consists of a number of interconnected transparent plastic tanks and pipes, each of which represents an aspect of the UK economy. The flow of money through the economy is represented by colored water. The Phillips machine is not true or false, in the same manner as a tree is not true or false—*pace* Ernest Hemingway's "A thing is true at first light and a lie by noon" (Hemingway 1999). Statements are true or false *of* the Phillips machine—for example that its tanks and pipes are mounted on a wooden board—just as statements are true or false of a particular tree. And this remains the case whether the model is an analogue or physical model, or whether it is a mathematical or otherwise abstract model.

Consequently, when we say that a model is true or false, we speak elliptically. Suppose that when Bill Phillips built his machine, it was a representation of the UK economy that was adequate for his purposes. For instance, in the Phillips machine one can reduce expenditure by draining water from the pipe that is labeled "expenditure" and diverting it into a pipe that says "savings." This is an accurate representation insofar as savings reduce the funds available for expenditures in the UK economy. When I quoted the slogan "all models are false" approvingly above I meant to draw attention to the undisputed fact that all models also *mis*represent their targets in a myriad of respects. Whatever money in the UK economy is, it is not wet as the water in the Phillips machine is. Whatever banks are, they aren't plastic tanks filled with water. And so on. Thus, when we say colloquially "All models are false" what we mean is "All models misrepresent their targets in one way or another." In the case of an abstract model, we may alternatively say that some of the assumptions that define the model, and therefore are necessarily true of the model, are false of the target system of interest. As another alternative, we may say that a theoretical hypothesis, which states that some target system is like some model, is true or false.

One further remark. I mentioned a model's *target* above for a reason. Models do not represent or misrepresent, period. Rather, they represent well or accurately or not well at all specific target systems of interest. So the Phillips machine may have been a good representation (for certain purposes) of the UK economy, maybe also of other economies that share important characteristics with the UK's but not a good representation *simpliciter*. In what follows I will assume that such intended applications are either part of the model or else understood by the modeler. Similarly, when I speak of the "explanatoriness" of a model (or lack thereof) I will also mean that a model explains or does not explain specific systems or phenomena of interest. No model is explanatory *per se*.

Our first strategy to resolve our paradox is to claim that a model can be true despite or even in virtue of containing many falsehoods. More accurately, a model can misrepresent its target in some (presumably inessential) respects in order to correctly ("truthfully") represent other (presumably essential) respects. Another way of putting the issue is that models are true "in the abstract": they represent not what is true but rather what would be true in the absence of interferences (cf. the discussion of causal tendencies in Chapter 5). Nancy Cartwright (1989) developed such a view as a general perspective on science in great detail. The main advocate of a related view of models in economics is Uskali Mäki (e.g., 1992, 1994, 2005, 2009, 2011).

The core idea is that models can be thought of as Galilean thought experiments (N. Cartwright 1999b). In a Galilean thought experiment, an experimental situation is contemplated after mentally removing "disturbing factors"—factors different from the main cause under investigation, which nevertheless affect the outcome. To discover an instance of the law of falling bodies, say, the thought experimenter imagines a situation that is free from all factors that affect a body's rate of fall except the gravity of the Earth.

Mäki calls this mental process "isolation by idealization": the operation of one specific causal factor is isolated—in Galileo's case, the Earth's gravitational pull—by idealizing away every other factor—air resistance, other gravitational fields, other forces. The resulting model is "false" in many ways because these factors do affect all actual systems that we may choose as target systems of interest. But it is also "true" in one important way: it correctly captures the operation of the causal factor of interest, the gravity of the Earth. Mäki makes this point with respect to von Thünen's model of the isolated state:

> If there is a natural truth bearer here, it is neither this model as a whole nor just any arbitrary parts of it. It is rather a special component of the model, namely the causal power or mechanism that drives this simple model world: the Thünen mechanism. This truth bearer has a fair chance of being made true by its truth maker, the respective prominent causal "force" or mechanism in the real system. It is the mechanism that contributes to the transformation of distance into land use patterns through transportation costs and land values.
>
> (Mäki 2011: 60)

In Mäki's parlance, then, models are not true *per se* but they rather may contain truths such as truths about the causal powers or mechanisms of the target systems of interest. It would probably be more accurate to say (for instance) that a theoretical hypothesis stating that the model correctly represents a target system's causal power or mechanism can be true, but let us not get drawn away by a trifle.

This line of defense is perfectly legitimate for a variety of false modeling assumptions in science. In many domains of science, especially in mechanics, the method of analysis and synthesis has been employed with great success. Natural systems often do not obey neat scientific laws (in the sense of strict regularities; see Chapter 2) because they are too complex and too changing. So we experimentally create—in the lab or in the head—situations that are simpler, more manageable and free from outside influences. We learn what happens in these situations and use that knowledge to predict what happens in more complex, more natural situations. This is often possible because what we learn in the simplified system remains true, with qualifications of course, in the more complex system. It is not an accident that Galileo is often regarded as, on the one hand, the originator of the idea that natural systems can be analyzed as being composed of "phenomena"—universal and stable features, which are of scientific interest—and "accidents"—disturbing factors, which aren't—and, on the other hand, the inventor of the world's most famous and most successful thought experiments (McAllister 2004).

At first sight, economists are well aware of the method of analysis and synthesis, and regard their work as applications of this method. Our own Hotelling is a case in point. As he says about the principle of minimum differentiation:

> But there is an incentive to make the new product very much like the old, applying some slight change which will seem an improvement to as many buyers as possible without ever going far in this direction. The tremendous standardisation of our furniture, our houses, our clothing, our automobiles and our education are due in part to the economies of large-scale production, in part to fashion and imitation. But *over and above these forces* is the *effect* we have been discussing, the *tendency* to make only slight deviations in order to have for the new commodity as many buyers of the old as possible, to get, so to speak, between one's competitors and a mass of customers.
>
> (Hotelling 1929: 54; emphasis added)

Hotelling believes that his model does not represent a local causal principle with limited applicability—applicability only where the model's assumptions are met. Rather, it represents a more general tendency that persists (continues to affect outcomes) even in the presence of disturbing factors, which, in this case, are economies of scale, fashion and imitation.

The problem is only that the models of economics, Hotelling's included, are by and large very much unlike a Galilean thought experiment. Let us say with Mäki that a Galilean thought experiment isolates (the primary causal factor) by idealizing (away other causal factors). Is this really what typical economics models do?

Few of the assumptions in Hotelling's model aim to eliminate disturbing causal factors. Assuming businesses move along a line with no breadth or thickness is not assuming away the influence of geography; it is determining a specific geography in which Hotelling's results are true. Assuming that transportation costs are linear in distances is not assuming away the influence of transportation costs; it is determining a specific functional form of the effect of transportation costs on utility. Assuming that demand is perfectly inelastic is not assuming away the influence of demand; it is determining a specific functional form of the demand schedule. And so on.

One might object that the distinction I am making here is spurious, because to "assume away" a causal factor is in fact a special case of "assuming that"—the more general kind of idealization just described. To "assume away" air resistance is, so the objection goes, to assign a specific value to air resistance in the model—zero. Likewise, to "assume that," say, transportation costs are linear is to assign a specific value to the transportation cost parameter in the model.

However, there are at least three differences between Galilean and non-Galilean assumptions. First, in a Galilean thought experiment, the factor that has been "assumed away" does not normally appear. The assumption of no air resistance cannot be read off the model. It only surfaces when we ask "under what conditions would the result (given by the Galilean thought experiment) be true?" By contrast, the non-Galilean assumptions Hotelling employs are all an explicit part of the model, and they are assumptions without which no result at all could be calculated. That is, the assumption already appears when one calculates the model result, and not only when one uses the result to make a prediction about a phenomenon outside the model. Second, Galilean assumptions usually concern quantitative causal factors. Different media produce different degrees of resistance. Hotelling's assumptions are categorical. Different geographies are different kinds of thing and not the same kind of thing to a different degree. Third, Galilean assumptions usually concern a causal factor that has a natural zero. No air resistance is such a natural zero. Assuming that celestial bodies are point masses is another example: a point is the natural zero for the quantity "extension." Geographies and the functional form of transportation costs have no natural zero. The elasticity of demand may be considered to have a natural zero ("perfectly inelastic demand") but that particular value still appears in the model, and therefore elasticity is not "assumed away" but rather is part of the model.

The importance of making assumptions of the Galilean kind is made plain by the goal of a Galilean thought experiment, which is to learn what a causal factor does in isolation from disturbing factors (McMullin 1985; N. Cartwright 1989). To "assume away" air resistance in a thought experiment teaches us what a causal factor (in this case, gravity) does its own, when no disturbances (such as air resistance) are present. To "assume that" businesses are located on a straight line of length l, by contrast, does not teach us what the other causal factors (transportation costs, profit maximization, inelastic demand, etc.) do when geography is absent.

The problem with non-Galilean assumptions is that they make the model result specific to the situation that is being modeled. There is no way to tell from just inspecting the model that it is one subset of assumptions that is driving the result rather than another (cf. N. Cartwright 1999b). And therefore we do not know where to look for "truth in the model": all we know is that the model result depends on all of a model's assumptions and that many of the model's assumptions are false of any empirical situation we might wish to explain.

It is of course the case that in principle one can test a model result for robustness. Thus, in principle, we can determine which model assumptions drive a result, and from which assumptions results are to some extent independent. Some have even claimed that conducting robustness tests constitutes a significant part of economic practice (Kuorikoski *et al.* 2010). Indeed, many economic papers contain a section in which robustness is given *some* consideration, and sometimes economists check whether other economists' model results are robust. But by and large, robustness tests are not possible, and if possible and performed, their result is negative.

Hotelling's model is once more a case in point. The last two pages of his article concern modifications of the original model. Not a single calculation is made, all "extensions" appear to be based on guesswork. And there is a reason: robustness tests are very hard to perform, and not infrequently impossible, because the mathematics doesn't allow it altogether or is too difficult for the researcher in question. About relaxing the inelastic demand assumption, for instance, Hotelling says:

> The problem of the two merchants on a linear market might be varied by supposing that each consumer buys an amount of the commodity in question which depends on the delivered price. If one tries a particular demand function the mathematical complications will now be considerable, but for the most general problems elasticity must be assumed.
>
> (Hotelling 1929: 56)

A paragraph below that he asserts without proof: "With elastic demand the observations we have made on the solution will still for the most part be qualitatively true."

This turned out not to be the case—unless what we take as Hotelling's "observations" are broad enough to include minimum differentiation, maximum differentiation and everything in between. A recent survey article summarizes the following findings regarding changes in the elasticity assumption:

> The study of Hinloopen and Marrewijk (1999) examines a similar setup where transport costs are linear and the reservation price is constant across consumers. Given the reservation price is sufficiently high, the original Hotelling result holds in which no price equilibrium exists. If the reservation price is low, firms become local monopolists which leads to a continuum of equilibrium locations including maximum and intermediate differentiation. However, reservation prices in-between imply symmetric equilibrium locations where the distance between the firms is between one fourth and one half of the market. For a range of reservation prices there exists a negative relationship between this value and the amount of differentiation. Thus, summarizing we conclude that given a price equilibrium exists for the duopoly Hotelling model with uniformly distributed consumer preferences on the unit interval then the higher the elasticity of demand the less firms will differentiate.
>
> (Brenner 2001: 14–15)

The second sentence requires some comment. It is somewhat ironic that 50 years after Hotelling published his paper, his main result—that there is "stability in (price!) competition"—was shown to be incorrect (D'Aspremont *et al.* 1979). However, that was not too damaging for the minimum differentiation principle because there are a variety of settings in which that result holds, including a game-theoretic set-up without price competition (e.g., Osborne 2004: section 3.3) and one in which products and consumers are sufficiently heterogeneous (De Palma *et al.* 1985).

Let me mention just two further modifications of the original Hotelling set-up. When the number of competitors is three rather than two, there is no stability, because the one in the middle will always move to either side in order to regain its market (Lerner and Singer 1937). Finally, the exact functional form for transportation costs matters. D'Aspremont *et al.* 1979 showed Hotelling's original result to be incorrect but then went on to find an equilibrium in a setting that is as close as possible to Hotelling's. They found one in a setting that is *identical* to Hotelling's with the exception that transportation costs are now quadratic rather than linear—only that in this setting a principle of *maximum* differentiation holds!

With robustness out of the window, the distinction Mäki needs between "strategic falsehoods" introduced in order to isolate a causal power or mechanism of interest and the true descriptions of that causal power or mechanism cannot be sustained. The model result depends on the entire array of assumptions. Consequently, if these assumptions are false of an envisaged target system, we cannot expect the causal power or mechanism to operate in the target system. This is detrimental to our explanatory endeavor. Suppose we observe an instance of minimum differentiation as in Hotelling's cider or US politics. Does Hotelling's model explain that phenomenon under this reading of models? Not if we know some of the model assumptions to be false of the phenomenon and the result—the explanandum—to be dependent on these assumptions.

Economic Models Are Not Explanatory

A number of economic methodologists have denied that economic models are, by themselves, explanatory. Best known in the field is probably Dan Hausman's account of models as conceptual explorations. On this view, models as such do not make claims about the world. Rather, they define predicates, and modeling can be seen as an exercise in exploring conceptual possibilities. Only in conjunction with a theoretical hypothesis of the form "target system T is a system of the kind model M defines" does a model say something about the world and as a consequence may be explanatory (Hausman 1992a: section 5.2).

If models are physical or, more frequently, abstract entities, as has been defended here, Hausman's view that a model can only be informative in conjunction with a theoretical hypothesis or some such is of course correct. A physical thing or mathematical structure is not about anything. It is humans who make a thing into a model of some target system T by saying they will use the thing as a model of *T*. This can be done explicitly by speci-fying a theoretical hypothesis or implicitly simply by using the model. Thus, without agents, no representation and, *a fortiori*, no explanation.

The problem with Hausman's account from our point of view is that he just shifts the issue from one about false models to one about false theories. To him, a model plus a theoretical hypothesis is a theory, and thinking of models as conceptual explorations obviously doesn't help with the question of how false *theories* can be explanatory. We could simply reformulate every-thing that has been said so far as a problem not for models but for models plus their associated theoretical hypothesis. Hausman certainly does not hold that models plus hypotheses, to wit, theories are not explanatory.

Anna Alexandrova (Alexandrova 2008; Alexandrova and Northcott 2009) has given an account of models as open formulae, which also denies that models as such are explanatory. But she holds the stronger view that models, even including a specification of what they are models of, are not explanatory. Rather, models play a heuristic role in that they suggest causal hypotheses, which are then to be tested in experiments.

More specifically, Alexandrova holds that (2008: 396; original emphasis): "models function as frameworks for formulating hypotheses, or as *open formulae.*" An open formula is a schematic sentence of the form: "In a situ-ation of type *x* with some characteristics that may include $\{C_1 \ldots C_n\}$, a certain feature *F* causes a certain behavior *B*" (Alexandrova 2008: 392; foot-note suppressed). The free variable in the open formula is the *x*, the model specifies the *C*'s, *F*'s and *B*'s. Thus, for instance, an open formula suggested by an economic model may read: "In a situation of type *x*, which includes that values are private and some other conditions (the *C*'s) obtain, first-price auction rules (*F*) cause bids below true valuation (*B*)." To move from model to explanation we have to (a) identify an open formula on the basis of the model; (b) fill in the *x* so as to arrive at a causal hypothesis; and (c) confirm the causal hypothesis experimentally (Alexandrova 2008: 400).

It is clear, then, that in Alexandrova's account models do not play an explanatory role. Models are heuristic devices that suggest causal hypoth-eses, which, if experimentally confirmed, may be used in causal explanations of phenomena. But this throws the baby out with the bath water. Thousands of economic models have been adduced to explain real-world phenomena without ever having been tested in the lab or elsewhere. In the context of preparing experiments for policy, models may well serve the heuristic func-tion Alexandrova describes. To be fair, she does not claim more than that. More broadly, however, models are regarded as explanatory in themselves. One may of course deny that they are but then arguments have to be given, and it must be explained why a large part of the economics profession thinks otherwise. The open-formulae account therefore ignores rather than solves the problem.

Till Grüne-Yanoff 2009, finally, holds that models prove modal hypoth-eses, a view with which I have also toyed (Reiss 2008a: ch. 6). Grüne-Yanoff writes that folk wisdom is full of modal claims such as "Necessarily, segregation is a consequence of racist preferences" or "It is impossible that intelligent behaviour be produced without a 'vitalistic' element present in the organism" (2009: 96). We learn from models such as Schelling's 1978 model of racial segregation or Hull's psychic machines, Walter's tortoises and Newell and Simon's simulations, as discussed in Schlimm 2009, that there are possible worlds in which the held beliefs are not true. We learn a possibility result: that racial segregation can result from non-racist preferences; that machines can produce intelligent behavior. (See Reiss 2008a: ch. 6, where I discuss this function of economic models in some detail.)

Possibility hypotheses, as much as they might teach us about the world, do not explain economic phenomena. It may have been an enormously valuable insight that racial segregation does not have to be the result of outright racism. But this hypothesis at best shows us that actual segregation *can* result otherwise, not that it does so, even in a single case. Economic models therefore may well play the role Grüne-Yanoff ascribes to them, but that they do so does not advance our quest to find out why economic models explain.

All these views, then, ignore rather than resolve the problem. Clearly, economic models perform functions other than that of providing explanations. Conceptual explorations (Hausman), heuristics for constructing hypotheses (Alexandrova) and establishing modal hypotheses (Grüne-Yanoff, Reiss) are salient non-explanatory functions of models, and there may well be others. But some models also explain, and it is this function that the views discussed in this subsection cannot account for.

Explanation Doesn't Require Truth

The last premise of our explanation paradox was that genuine explanation requires truth. This is a widely held belief among philosophers. For most of its history, it was a condition on the logical positivists' D-N model of scientific explanation. It is, necessarily in my view, a condition on acceptable causal explanations. It is very intuitive: telling stories or out-and-out lies isn't giving explanations. The truth may not explain much, but without giving at least a slice of truth we haven't explained anything. Or so it seems.

When it became apparent that the D-N model of explanation is likely to be irretrievably flawed, philosophers of science sought alternatives, some of which made do without the truth requirement. I will discuss such an account of scientific explanation in detail shortly. First, however, let us examine one final view of models, given by a prominent economic theorist and experimentalist and methodologist.

Robert Sugden subscribes to the first two premises of our paradox, as indicated by the following statements:

> Economic theorists construct highly abstract models. If interpreted as representations of the real world, these models appear absurdly

unrealistic; yet economists claim to find them useful in understanding real economic phenomena.

(Sugden 2009: 3)

More recent work confirms that Sugden thinks economic models can be explanatory (Sugden 2011, especially p. 733). To dissolve the paradox, then, he must reject its third premiss. He does so by proposing an account of models as "credible worlds" (Sugden 2011, 2000). A credible world is a deliberate construction, by the modeler, of an abstract entity: a parallel or counterfactual world which, to a greater or lesser extent, resembles aspects of our own world. To learn about the latter, inductive inferences analogous to those from one instance of a type to another are needed. Thus, what we learn from studying Baltimore, Philadelphia, New York, Detroit, Toledo, Buffalo and Pittsburgh we infer to be true in Cleveland as well (Sugden 2000: 24). Analogously, we may infer a model result to hold true of a real-world phenomenon. But, according to Sugden, we do so only to the extent that the parallel world depicted by the model is "credible." Credibility is thus a key notion in this account. Sugden explains:

We perceive a model world as credible by being able to think of it as a world that *could* be real—not in the sense of assigning positive subjective probability to the event that it *is* real, but in the sense that it is compatible with what we know, or think we know, about the general laws governing events in the real world.

(Sugden 2009: 18; original emphasis)

Sugden explicitly rejects thesis three of our paradox: "Credibility is not the same thing as truth; it is closer to *verisimilitude* or *truthlikeness*" (Sugden 2009: 18; original emphasis). There is neither the space nor the need here to rehearse the notorious problems with verisimilitude (for an attempt to cash out the notion in an economics context, see Niiniluoto 2002). What we have to do instead is to consider whether "credibility" can act as a stand-in for explanatoriness.

I want to address that question at two levels: a descriptive level, which considers whether practicing economists hold that (only) credible models are explanatory, and a prescriptive level, which considers whether economists have good reason to do so. Anyone familiar with the way modeling proceeds in economics will agree that Sugden's account is largely descriptively adequate. There is something that characterizes good economic models in virtue of which they are acceptable by the economics community. Let us call that their credibility. And most economists definitely consider good models explanatory (these are all examples discussed by Sugden; emphases added):

The example of used cars captures the essence of the problem. From time to time one hears either mention of or surprise at the large price difference between new cars and those which have just left the show-room. The usual lunch table justification for this phenomenon is the pure joy of owning a "new" car. We offer a different *explanation*.

(Akerlof 1970: 489)

Models tend to be useful when they are simultaneously simple enough to fit a variety of behaviors and complex enough to fit behaviors that need the help of an *explanatory model*.

(Schelling 1978: 89)

A different *explanation* of herd behavior, which, like the present work is based on informational asymmetries, was suggested in an interesting recent paper by Scharfstein and Stein [1990]. The key difference between their *explanation* and the one suggested here is that their *explanation* is based on an agency problem; in their model the agents get rewards for convincing a principal that they are right. This distortion in incentives plays an important role in generating herd behavior in their model. By contrast, in our model agents capture all of the returns generated by their choice so that there is no distortion in incentives.

(Banerjee 1992)

However, we need to ask whether the fact that an economist (or the economics community) regards a model as credible is also a good reason for them to hold that it genuinely explains. Here is where I disagree with Sugden: the "credibility" of an account of a phenomenon of interest to an individual or a group of researchers is not *per se* a reason to accept it as an explanation of the phenomenon. Many factors affect judgments of credibility, most of which have no essential relationship with explanatoriness: the specific experiences and values of an individual; his or her upbringing and educational background; local customs and culture; social norms and etiquettes of a community of researchers; its theoretical preferences and history.

In Reiss 2008a: ch. 6 I argued that economists' subjective judgments of plausibility or credibility are strongly influenced by their theoretical preferences for models that are mathematized, employ the tools of rational-choice theory and solve problems using equilibrium concepts. Such preferences are no good reason for considering models with these characteristics as explanatory. Additional arguments would have to be given. One could hold with Galileo, for instance, that the world is Pythagorean, that the book of nature is written in the language of mathematics. (And then go on to argue that therefore genuine explanations have to be couched in mathematical language.) Many readers today will regard this particular claim as highly implausible, but an argument based on a claim *of that kind* is needed.

Resources for such an argument can be found in conceptions of scientific explanation that compete with the causal model. In particular, the view of explanation of successful unification of diverse phenomena is fruitful in this context. Let us examine in some detail Philip Kitcher's 1981 account of explanation (omitting some of its technical details for brevity) and then see whether we can supplement Sugden's proposal in such a way as to resolve our paradox.

Central to Kitcher's account is the notion of an *argument pattern*. Kitcher defines a general argument pattern as consisting of the following: a schematic argument, a set of sets of filling instructions containing one set of filling instructions for each term of the schematic argument and a classification for the schematic argument (1981: 516). A schematic argument is an argument in which some of the non-logical terms have been replaced by dummy letters; filling instructions are directions specifying how to substitute dummy letters with terms such that sentences obtain that are meaningful within the theory; a classification determines which sentences are premises and which are conclusions, and what rule of inference to use.

Argument patterns are meant to be stringent in that schematic sentences, filling instructions and classification jointly restrict the number of arguments that can be recovered from an argument pattern. An argument pattern that allows the generation of any argument is uninteresting from a scientific point of view. (As an aside: this is a version of Karl Popper's idea that the more conceivable empirical phenomena a scientific theory *excludes*, does *not* predict, the better the theory. See Popper 1959: ch. 6.)

Suppose K is the set of sentences accepted by some scientific community. A set of arguments which derives some members of K from other members is a *systematization* of K. Recall that argument patterns can be used to generate arguments. Kitcher calls sets of argument patterns such that every argument in a systematization of K is an instantiation of a pattern in that set a *generating set*. The *basis* of systematization is a generating set that is complete (in that every argument which is acceptable relative to K and which instantiates a pattern belongs to the systematization) and has the greatest unifying power. Finally, the unifying power of a basis (with respect to K) varies directly with (a) the number of conclusions that can be derived from the set of arguments it generates and (b) the stringency of its argument patterns, and it varies inversely with the number of its members (Kitcher 1981: 520).

Intuitively, the more conclusions that can be derived from using the same set of argument patterns again and again, the more stringent the argument patterns, and the smaller the set of argument patterns needed to derive the conclusions, the greater the unifying power of a basis. While the precise formulation is certainly something one can argue about, Kitcher's notion of unifying power expresses a desideratum many economists require of a good explanation (see for instance Mäki 2001; Lehtinen and Kuorikoski 2007; Reiss 2002).

Let us now address the lacuna Sugden's account of models left. In his view, a model that describes a world that is "credible" is one that is explanatory. Above I argued that the credibility of a model doesn't lend it explanatory power in itself. But what if economists regard models that are unifying as particularly credible? This would allow us to make sense of their demand to make models mathematical and use the principles of rational-choice theory and equilibrium concepts—all these form part of argument patterns from which descriptions of a large range of empirical phenomena can be derived. A credible model is one that is explanatory *because* it is unifying.

Why might unifying power be that which lends explanatoriness to a model? Why do we believe that a set of argument patterns that allows us to derive descriptions of a larger range of phenomena of interest is one that is more explanatory? Because to no small extent it is the business of science to achieve cognitive economy—or at least this is one way of thinking about what science tries to achieve. A social practice that told a different story about every phenomenon we ask questions about would not be called a science, because it would not *systematize* what we know about the world. It would not *reduce the number of brute facts* we need to know in order to understand phenomena of interest. It would not enable us to use what we know in order to make inferences about new, hitherto unobserved phenomena. Unifying power is surely not the only thing we might seek when we seek explanations of economic phenomena. But the idea that accounts are explanatory to the extent that they are unifying is certainly defensible.

It is unfortunate, therefore, that the argument patterns economics tends to produce are at best spuriously unifying. This is to say that they *look very much like* having been defined by a set of assumptions that could be instantiations of generating sets with high unifying power. But in fact they are not.

The problem lies with the notion of stringency. Recall that the unifying power of an argument pattern varies directly with its stringency and that the more arguments a pattern *disallows* to be recovered from it (by specifying highly restrictive schematic sentences, filling instructions and classifications), the more stringent it is. The argument patterns of economics are not at all stringent.

A notorious example is a schematic sentence such as "Consumers act so as to maximize utility" or, to use a dummy letter in place of a non-logical term, "Consumers act so as to maximize U." What are the restrictions on the filling instructions for U? Answer: very few, if any. Often enough people are modeled as deriving utility from some material gain but models do not cease to be economics models if they are more interested in immaterial goods such as reputation or fame, or world peace for that matter. The same is of course true of producers who are said to maximize "profits." "Profits" may be monetary but often they are not. Hotelling-like settings have often been used, for example, to model electoral competition (see for instance Osborne 2004: section 3.3). Political parties, of course, maximize votes, not profits.

What makes matters worse is that not only can "utility" be replaced by a dummy letter but also "consumer" (or "producer"), with similarly unrestrictive filling instructions. In particular Don Ross has been arguing not only that an "economic agent" does not have to be a human person, but that economics formalism is more likely to work in other species or at sub- or super-human scales (e.g., Ross 2009). People's preferences are sometimes time-inconsistent because of hyperbolic discounting, in apparent violation of economic theory. But, argues Ross, the mistake does not lie with economic theory. Rather, we should move beyond anthropocentric neoclassicism and cease to think of persons as the necessary bearers of economic agency. Consistency can be restored for instance by conceiving of human behavior as the result of a bargaining process between various subpersonal economic agents such as "short-term" and "long-term interests" (see also Ross 2005, especially ch. 8).

And the maximization principle is one of the few principles worth mentioning in economic theory. Schematic sentences and filling instructions thus do not restrict the range of arguments that can be generated very much. The same is true of the classification. The classification contains rules of inference. The most important inference rule in economics is "Solve the model using an equilibrium concept." But of course there are many equilibrium concepts. Especially in game theory there is an abundance: the (pure-strategy/mixed-strategy) Nash equilibrium and its various refinements: subgame-perfect equilibrium, trembling-hands equilibrium, Markov-perfect equilibrium, sequential equilibrium, perfect Bayesian equilibrium, evolutionary stable equilibrium and so on (see for instance Fudenberg and Tirole 1991). Equilibrium concepts do not restrict the range of arguments that can be generated much, either. To be sure, the inference rule "use a Nash equilibrium to solve a game" *does* restrict the solution space. But given that (a) there are normally many Nash equilibria; (b) there are no clear rules which among a set of Nash equilibria to select; (c) from the point of view of economic theory the justification for using the Nash equilibrium as solution concept is very thin, it would be hard to maintain that economic theory greatly restricts the number of arguments that can be generated from an argument pattern (see Chapter 4).

Friedman wrote that a theory worth its name consists of a language and a body of substantive hypotheses (M. Friedman 1953). Contemporary economics does well on the language (the language of logic and mathematics, of rational-choice theory and of equilibrium concepts) but lacks substantive hypotheses—schematic sentences that have genuine content in that they (in conjunction with filling instructions and a classification) restrict the number of sentences that can be generated from them. To claim that contemporary economics is unifying is therefore like saying that expressing economic ideas in Italian is unifying. Whatever economists think when they say they provide explanations of this or that phenomenon, the accounts they give are not explanatory *qua* the unifying power of the argument patterns from which they are derived.

Conclusions

The curious thing about genuine paradoxes is that they are not so easily resolved. True, one can always resolve a paradox by fiat—by rejecting one or more of the theses that make up the paradox—but this usually means to ignore the problem. Moreover it creates the need to explain why so many people believe the claim if it is so unmistakably and so recognizably wrong.

The paradox of economic modeling is genuine in this sense. I think that previous attempts to resolve it have failed, and I do not see many likely avenues for future attempts. Perhaps thinking about how models explain in ways different from the usual causal and unificationist paradigms is a way forward. But before such a new way of thinking about explanation is forthcoming and shown to fit contemporary economic modeling, the rational response to the paradox is to remain baffled.

Study Questions

1 Perhaps it is true that all models idealize in one way or another, but some models may be more approximately true than others. Does this suggestion help resolve the paradox?
2 Do you see other ways for resolving the paradox?
3 Compare economic models with physics models. Are physics models more constraining than economic models?
4 Why does successful causal explanation presuppose truth? Can a false causal account explain?
5 The reason why the unification view of explanation does not apply to economic models (as has been argued above) may have to do with Kitcher's specific formulation of the account. Is there an intuitive sense in which economic models are unifying?

Suggested Readings

There is a large literature on models now, to which Frigg and Hartmann 2012 provide a good introduction. A must-read is Morgan and Morrison 1999, which contains a number of articles specifically on models in economics. One of the first to discuss at some length the importance of models (rather than *theories*) for science was N. Cartwright 1983. Specifically on models in economics see Alexandrova 2006, 2008, Gibbard and Varian 1978, Gilboa *et al*. 2011, Hindriks 2008, Knuuttila 2009 and Morgan 2001, 2012. An important recent collection of articles on models and idealization is Suárez 2009.

A classic on idealization is McMullin 1985. Chapter 5 in N. Cartwright 1989 contains a very useful discussion. Weisberg 2007 is an important more recent article. Specifically for economics, see Hamminga and De Marchi 1994, and especially the chapter by Hoover.

This chapter discussed Philip Kitcher's unificationist account of explanation at some length. The other main defender of a unificationist view of explanation is Michael Friedman; see Michael Friedman 1974. Strevens 2004 develops an account of explanation that he claims has the virtues of both the causal and the unificationist account. Bokulich 2011 and Kennedy 2012 provide accounts of how false physics models can explain.

Part II

Methodology

8   Measurement

- **Overview**
- **Observation**
- **Consumer Price Inflation**
- **Unemployment and GDP**
- **Conclusions**
- **Study Questions**
- **Suggested Readings**

Overview

Part I of this book dealt with economic *theory*. Economists theorize for a variety of purposes, a prominent one being the scientific explanation of economic phenomena. But no matter what the pursued purpose is, theory is very unlikely to serve its purpose well unless it is supported by evidence. Part II therefore looks at the topic of evidence, the generation of empirical support or methodology. There are two main types of method for generating empirical support in economics: observational and experimental methods. Observational methods, as the term suggests, aim to draw conclusions about economic theories without the benefit of interventions designed by the economist. In practice, economists rely on the work of statistical offices and other data-supplying bodies, and analyze the data given to them by means of statistical and econometric models. Econometrics is the topic of Chapter 9. Experimental methods require a more active role in the data-generating process on the part of the economist. The economist designs and executes an intervention, observes and records the result and only then analyzes the data, often also using statistical techniques that are as elaborate as those of observational methods. Economic experiments will be considered in Chapters 10 and 11.

The present chapter looks at the hard work done by statistical offices such as the Bureau of Labor Statistics in the USA, the UK Office for National

Statistics, the Statistische Bundesamt in Germany, the Centraal Bureau voor de Statistiek in the Netherlands, the World Health Organization and the United Nations, and many non-governmental data providers such as Transparency International (an NGO that publishes the Corruption Perception Index, CPI) or the private US National Bureau of Economic Research (NBER) to inform policy-makers, scientific researchers and the population at large about the state of the economy by constructing economic indicators. Economic indicators are index numbers such as the Consumer Price Index (also abbreviated CPI) and industrial production that aim to represent some fact about the economy—in these cases the current inflation rate and changes in output for the industrial sector of the economy.

Most economists are aware of the fact that huge measurement issues lurk behind innocuous-sounding statements like "Consumer price inflation in the Netherlands has been +2.6 percent in the year to April 2011" or "45 percent of Spanish people below 35 are currently unemployed." But they rarely engage actively in the process of designing a measurement procedure, leaving that task to the "professionals"—the statistical officers. Later I will give some reasons to regard this as a regrettable state of affairs. It is important to understand the measurement issues associated with each economic indicator. This chapter looks at one indicator, consumer price inflation, at some length, and at gross domestic product and unemployment more briefly. All three are of enormous theoretical and practical importance. All three are highly problematic. First, however, I will make a number of general remarks concerning "observation."

Observation

Why does observation play such an important role in science? What are observation, data, evidence, and how do they relate? We can once more look to David Hume for an answer. As we saw in Chapter 1, Hume thought that genuine knowledge is of two kinds: it is either a truth of logic and mathematics, and as such true by definition (or self-evidently true), or it is a factual truth, and as such true by observation. What does not fall into either of these categories is simply not knowledge, it is at best an opinion. This bifurcation of all genuine knowledge into either logic and mathematics on the one hand and observable matters of fact on the other is called "Hume's fork" (see Hume 1999 [1748]).

The progress of science made the belief that all genuine knowledge is of either of these two kinds untenable. The invention of scientific instruments such as the telescope, microscope and thermometer made a whole world that is unobservable to the unaided human senses accessible to scientific investigation. Demanding that science deal only in what is observable would cripple science.

However, it is hard to overcome the intuition that scientific knowledge is different from other kinds of knowledge—artistic, literary, religious—that this differentness has to do with its claims being better supported by evidence and that being supported by evidence has something to do with observation. One way to reconcile the two conflicting ideas—that knowledge based on observations is more reliable than other kinds of knowledge and therefore plays a somewhat privileged role on the one hand, and that most things advanced science deals in are not observable on the other—is to show that the concept of observation or observability itself has changed with technical progress. And indeed this is what seems to be the case, both in natural and social science.

Scientists often apply terms like observe, observation and observable to phenomena that are clearly inaccessible to human sensation. Here is how astrophysicists describe their observations of the interior of the Sun (quoted from Shapere 1982: 486):

> [N]eutrinos originate in the very hot stellar core, in a volume less than a millionth of the total solar volume. This core region is so well shielded by the surrounding layers that neutrinos present the only way of directly observing it.
>
> (Weekes 1969: 161; quoted from Shapere 1982: 486)

> There is no way known other than by neutrinos to see into a stellar interior.
>
> (Clayton 1968: 388; quoted from Shapere 1982: 486)

Neutrinos are tiny, nearly massless and uncharged particles that because of their size, mass and neutral charge have a very low probability of interacting with other matter. To "observe" them, highly sophisticated detectors (a tank of the size an Olympic swimming pool filled with chlorine) have to be used, and even these devices capture them extremely infrequently. Human sensation is not even close to being sensitive to them.

Of course, a lot of background information is necessary to observe the interior of the Sun using bubble-chamber photographs, which indicate the presence of argon, which in turn indicates an interaction of chlorine with a neutrino, which is very unlikely to have originated elsewhere than in the interior of the Sun. Dudley Shapere distinguishes a theory of the source, a theory of the transmission and a theory of the receptor among the things required to make the inference from marks on bubble-chamber photographs to facts about the interior of the Sun (Shapere 1982). What is important for Shapere is (a) that astrophysicists have the appropriate theories at their disposal; and (b) that they have no reason to doubt the validity of these theories in the context of this application. It is for these reasons that the interior of the Sun is regarded as "observable," even directly so, despite the fact that it is not visible to humans without the aid of sophisticated instruments.

Economists have a similar concept of observability. Consider the following:

> Diewert … showed that the (unobservable) Pollak-Konüs true cost of living index was between the (observable) Paasche and Laspeyres price indexes.
>
> (Diewert 1998: 48)

> It is easy to theorize about the relationships among precisely defined variables; it is quite another to obtain accurate measures of these variables. For example, the difficulty of obtaining reasonable measures of profits, interest rates, capital stocks, or, worse yet, flows of services from capital stocks is a recurrent theme in the empirical literature. At the extreme, there may be no observable counterpart to the theoretical variable. The literature on the permanent income model of consumption … provides an interesting example.
>
> (Greene 2000: 211)

> In his *A Theory of the Consumption Function*, Friedman (1957) develops the concept of permanent income, $Y(P)$, as an explanatory variable for consumption. As an estimate of the unobservable $Y(P)$, he proposes the following:
>
> $$E[Y(P)] = \beta \int_{-\infty}^{T} e^{(\beta-\alpha)(-T+t)} Y(t) dt \qquad (1)$$
>
> where E denotes "estimate of," $Y(t)$ observable income in period t, β the coefficient of adjustment in the adaptive expectations model from which (1) is derived, and α a trend variable used in the weighing process.
>
> (Wright 1969: 845)

> The Kalman-filter technique (state-space modelling) offers a fruitful approach to estimating the Nairu because it is designed to identify an unobservable variable—like the Nairu—on the basis of assumptions made about the econometric properties of the variable and the economic interrelation between this variable and other observable variables [such as unemployment].
>
> (Logeay and Tober 2004: 2–3)

In each of these extracts, "observable" variables—the Paasche and Laspeyres price indices, income, unemployment—are contrasted with others that are considered "unobservable"—the "true" cost-of-living index, *permanent income*, the NAIRU (non-accelerating inflation rate of unemployment). The crucial difference between observable and unobservable in these cases has to do, as it has in physics, with the reliability of the background knowledge needed in order to learn about the phenomenon in question. As we will see in detail below, many, often contentious, assumptions have to be made in order to infer the value of a variable from the data, even for variables that count as observable. But these assumptions do not include any specific *economic theory*. This is different in the case of the unobservable variables. The true cost-of-living index is derived from rational-choice theory, permanent income from Friedman's consumption theory, and the NAIRU from "assumptions made about the economic interrelation between this variable and other observable variables." Economists, it thus seems, trust statistical offices but not their own theorizing. At any rate, they share with Shapere's astrophysicists a concept of observability that is very different from the concept of ordinary folk and that of philosophers. Philosophers and ordinary folk regard as observable that which is detectable with the unaided senses. Scientists, by contrast, regard as observable that which is reliably measurable (or, alternatively, that which is detectable by an appropriate apparatus and produced by a process that is well understood—cf. Shapere 1982). Changes in the price level (or national income or the rate of unemployment) are at best observable in the economist's sense but not in the ordinary sense of the word. Using nothing but your eyes you can see an individual price label but not the average rate of price changes across a whole economy.

A few more terminological remarks are necessary. *Data* are the immediate outcomes of measurements. Barometer readings, bubble-chamber photographs, price records or questionnaire results are all data. They are observable in the ordinary sense of the word. And they serve as evidence for (facts about) *phenomena*. Phenomena have been defined in Chapter 2 as (usually repeatable) events or processes of scientific interest. As James Bogen and James Woodward have observed, theories predict and explain (facts about) phenomena, not data (Bogen and Woodward 1988). Data are produced by factors too idiosyncratic to be the object of scientific theorizing. Take the record that an individual, John Doe, became unemployed last week as an example. Theories of unemployment describe the stickiness of wages, a fall in aggregate demand, negative external shocks, excessive unemployment benefits and friction as causes of unemployment. Perhaps some of these factors have contributed to John Doe's unemployment. But chances are that it is the outcome of myriad circumstances that are far too specific, far too peculiar to his individual case to be the object of an economic theory: perhaps he stole office supplies; perhaps his employer was arrested for financial fraud; perhaps he used an outside option as a bargaining tool in wage negotiations, his employer said "Take it, then!," but the option fell through. Thus, the record of John Doe's unemployment is used as a mere data point to infer a fact about a phenomenon—say, the current rate of change in the unemployment rate in some country—which is itself the object of scientific theorizing.

In what follows I will describe this process of using data to infer facts about an economic phenomenon—specifically, the value of an economic variable—for the three examples I mentioned above: consumer price inflation, gross domestic product (GDP, a measure of national income) and unemployment. Consumer price inflation will be my main case but I will briefly discuss GDP and unemployment as comparisons. All three variables are regarded as observable by economists. But, as we will see, measuring them requires making a large number of substantial, and often contentious, assumptions. Making these assumptions requires real commitment on the part of the investigator as regards certain *facts* relevant to the measurement procedure, the *measurement purpose* as well as *evaluative judgments*. A natural consequence of these points is that economists, who know best about these aspects of the measurement procedures relevant to them, should be more involved than they currently are in the design of the measurement procedure.

Consumer Price Inflation

The variable I will look at in this section is the US Consumer Price Index (CPI), which measures consumer price *inflation*. Measuring inflation is of immense significance for the wider public, both present and future generations. Since tax brackets and public spending programs as well as many private contracts are inflation-indexed, the measured inflation rate affects disposable incomes for most employees and recipients of government benefits and pensions, government receipts, expenditures and national debt. Measuring inflation is also of unrivaled importance for economic *analysis*. Many, if not most, empirical analyses of economic phenomena concern what economists call *real* variables, by which they mean variables that are deflated by an inflation index. Finding that our index seriously misrepresents the aspect of the phenomenon we are interested in potentially invalidates much of what we know about the economy, not only in terms of describing different economies and comparing them but also in terms of understanding the causal relationships responsible for the phenomena of interest. If we find a significant bias in the measured inflation rate many of our ideas and results regarding economic quantities such as income, growth, productivity, money and their interrelationships may have to be reconsidered (of course only to the extent that the CPI is indeed used as a deflator).

Measuring CPI: The Basics

As its name suggests, the CPI is a *price index*. A price index tracks the cost of purchasing a fixed basket of goods through time. If q_{i0} denotes the quantity good i in the base-period basket at time 0 and p_{i0}, p_{i1} denote its base- and current-period price at times 0 and 1, respectively, then $L_{01} = \Sigma q_{i0} p_{i1} / \Sigma q_{i0} p_{i0}$ is the price index for the current period relative to the base period or *Laspeyres price index*.

In the USA, the CPI is measured by the Bureau of Labor Statistics (BLS), which collects monthly price quotations on 71,000 individual goods and services at about 22,000 retail units in 88 regions throughout the country known as primary sampling units. In addition to that, the BLS collects information from about 40,000 tenants or landlords and 20,000 homeowners for the housing components of the CPI. These individual goods and services are aggregated in two steps. In the first step, the individual prices are aggregated into 9,108 strata, one for each of 207 *items* in 44 *areas*. An item stratum is a low-level index for groups and services such as "Men's suits, sports coats and outerwear" and "Gardening and lawncare services." Within each item stratum entry level items (ELIs) are defined. Some strata may have only one ELI (e.g., "Apples") while others can have a number of more or less heterogeneous ELIs (e.g., "Physicians' services"). An area is either an actual geographical region (32 areas correspond to locations in 29 cities) or a construct that represents smaller and mid-sized cities in several regions in the USA (that is, the remaining 12 areas are constructed from 56 primary sampling units).

Since a price index measures the cost of purchasing a *fixed basket of goods*, decisions have to be made how to treat cases where characteristics of goods change in one way or another. Here are some examples of relevant changes: some goods grow in their relative importance for consumers whereas others decline; the production of some goods discontinues and new goods are launched; the quality of goods improves or deteriorates; distribution channels change and new channels emerge; environmental factors of relevance for the consumer change.

The BLS employs an array of methods to deal with a changing world. Although the CPI is nominally a fixed-basket index, it is BLS practice to update its weights every few years. The weights themselves are obtained from the so-called Consumer Expenditure Survey (CES), which collects detailed information on all out-of-pocket expenditures from a national sample of households. Thus one could simultaneously tackle the substitution as well as the new goods problem, though somewhat crudely.

The weights obtained from the CES are used to aggregate higher-level price indices from indices for item strata. Below the level of the stratum, the weights used in the aggregation of individual prices stem from two sources. First, the Census Bureau conducts a so-called Point-of-Purchase Survey (POPS) which attempts to measure the distribution of expenditures across different retail outlets. Based on the results of the POPS the BLS selects a sample of outlets in a given area. The probability of being sampled is proportional to the share of that outlet in total expenditures in the area for the item selected. Second, BLS economists visit these stores and choose one or more specific items from which the broader category of items is to be priced. The probability to be selected for any given item is proportional to its estimated share in the outlet's revenue.

In this process, about 20 percent of all items undergo sample rotation every year, that is, they are replaced by other, not directly comparable items.

This means that full rotation takes place about every five years. For those items rotated into the sample, the BLS performs various quality-adjustment procedures.

Sample rotation is not the only source of item substitution. The BLS tries to make sure that each month exactly the same kind of item is repriced. This is, however, not always possible because an item may be temporarily or permanently unavailable. In this case the BLS representative can judge the new item to be comparable to the old one, following certain standardized guidelines. If the item is judged to be non-comparable, one of a number of adjustment procedures will be applied. Here is an overview:

1   *Overlap method.* If in the given period (say, t) both the new and the old item are available, the change in the index is calculated by using the change in the price of the old item between $t - 1$ and t, and that of the price of the new item between t and $t + 1$. This implicitly treats the price differential between the old and the new item as reflecting their quality difference and nothing else. Because old and new items are hardly ever available in the same period, this method is seldom used except in sample rotation.

2   *Mark-up method.* In some categories, producers are asked to estimate the cost of a given quality improvement. This cost (marked up to an estimated retail value) is then deducted from the price change to reflect the quality improvement. The widest application of this method is in the area of motor vehicles.

3   *Hedonic method.* The BLS makes limited use of hedonic estimation techniques, mainly in the area of housing and apparel. In hedonic estimations, the value of a good is broken down to various characteristics such as square feet, number of bathrooms and age of an apartment. Given estimates of the individual characteristics and observations of these characteristics in a good or service, a price change can be analyzed into change due to quality change and that due to other factors.

4   *Link method.* The link method exploits information on closely related items. If the old item is last observed in $t - 1$, and the new one is first observed in t, then the price change between $t - 1$ and t is calculated using the price change of the closely related item between $t-1$ and t, and thereafter, the change in the price of the new item. This is the most commonly used method outside sample rotation. It also implies a quality adjustment: in this case the price difference between the closely related good and the new good is treated as reflecting nothing but quality change.

The Index Number Problem

A price index measures the changes in the price level correctly only in the case where nothing changes except the prices. If prices and quantities change (i.e., when people decide to consume more of some goods and less of others), an ambiguity emerges: shall we use the (quantity) weights of the base period or those of the current period? Doing the former yields the Laspeyres index we have encountered above, doing the latter the Paasche index. Both have advantages and disadvantages. The Laspeyres index answers a precise question: what would I have to pay today if I were to buy the same basket of goods I bought last period again? But the Laspeyres index is outdated very fast. Suppose Engel's law (which says that people tend to buy proportionally less food as they get richer) were true and people's incomes increased rapidly. In the base period, being still relatively poor, consumers will spend most of their budgets on food. But the share of their income spent on food will decrease with increasing incomes. The Laspeyres index freezes people's tastes in the base period, which will become increasingly unrepresentative. The Paasche index, by contrast, is in a sense always up-to-date, using the weights of the current period. It can be interpreted analogously to the Laspeyres index: what would I have had to pay last period if I had bought the same basket of goods I bought this period? One disadvantage is that it is harder to measure. To measure the Laspeyres index, once the initial basket of goods has been established, one requires only price observations. The Paasche index requires quantity observations in addition because it uses current period weights. Both indices also have theoretical drawbacks. For example, an index number should have the following property: given three ordered periods t_1, t_2, t_3, the price index for periods t_1 and t_2 times the price index for periods t_2 and t_3 should be equivalent to the price index for periods t_1 and t_3. Neither the Laspeyres nor the Paasche index satisfies this property.

This ambiguity in choosing the right index has sometimes been referred to as the "Index Number Problem" (e.g., Samuelson and Nordhaus 1992: 590). It is sometimes suggested that the Laspeyres index overstates inflation whereas the Paasche index understates it. This claim is based on the idea that consumers, in order to maintain a constant level of well-being, substitute cheaper goods for those that have become more expensive. A Laspeyres index thus overrepresents expensive goods (as consumers have substituted away from them) and a Paasche index underrepresents them (in the base period people have bought these goods after all!).

A so-called "cost-of-living index" (COLI) estimates the amount of money required not to purchase a fixed basket of goods but a *fixed level of utility*. This concept has been developed by proponents of the "economic approach" to index numbers, which assumes that consumers are fully rational economic agents. One can show that under certain assumptions a Laspeyres index indeed overstates the COLI whereas the Paasche index understates it, but an index constructed by taking the geometric mean between the Laspeyres and Paasche indices approximates it well. This new index is called the "Fisher index" (after the economist Irving Fisher, one of the founding fathers of the theory of index numbers, among many other things) and is referred to as a "superlative index" because it approximates a true COLI.

There are two issues relating to the question whether the COLI is the right concept behind the CPI, one relating to a factual, the other to an evaluative question. The factual question is to what extent goods substitutions can actually be explained by the rational-choice model that assumes constant preference across different periods. It is certainly conceivable that people buy a new(ly weighted) basket of goods not because they maximize the satisfaction of constant preferences at changing prices but rather because their tastes changed. That those goods which now have a higher weight in the basket are also cheaper would then come as an additional boon. With changing preferences, the COLI framework is difficult to make sense of (though see Heien and Dunn 1985).

The evaluative question is to what extent substitution behavior that is due to price increases should guide economic policies. People who substitute away from goods that have become relatively more expensive (recall that it is well possible that the prices of all goods increase; people will, if the rational-choice model is correct, still substitute goods that are now relatively cheaper for those that are relatively more expensive) are, to a degree, forced to change the composition of their consumption baskets. Even if the changes are voluntary in a sense (because no one uses physical force to make people choose what they do) it is questionable whether they are fair. Perhaps people would like to continue making the same purchases they did in the base period but they can no longer afford to. If so, wouldn't it be more appropriate to use a base-weighted index rather than one that pretends people substitute some goods for others because they want to?

Substitutions are only one of several sources of potential bias in the CPI. I will discuss two further sources: quality changes and aggregation.

The "House-to-House Combat of Price Measurement": Quality Changes

The quality change problem has been referred to as the "house-to-house combat of price measurement" (Shapiro and Wilcox 1996) because of its highly contested nature. So far we have considered a world that is fairly static except that the prices of goods change and people react to these changes by adjusting their consumption bundles. In fact, many more things change: old product lines are discontinued and new lines are launched; the quality of existing goods changes; goods are traded in novel channels such as at discounters and over the internet; the range of available goods changes such as the varieties of breakfast cereals; environmental features change—for instance the amount of traffic on the way to the supermarket or the quality of the air in which the traded goods are consumed.

A traditional price index has no answer to the problem of quality changes. As it tracks the cost for purchasing a *given basket of goods* over time there is simply no room for new goods, changed goods or different distribution channels. Once more, one could freeze the basket in the base period but such a basket would soon become unrepresentative. Moreover, the index is unidentified when there are no prices for some goods—for instance because their production is discontinued.

As with quantity changes, in practice the basket is updated periodically. But how should one deal with the fact that a new good differs in quality from an old good? If the new good constitutes an improvement over the old one and it is treated as equivalent substitute, inflation would be over-estimated because consumers profit from better goods and a higher price is justified because companies invest in their development. On the other hand, if price changes are interpreted as reflecting nothing but quality changes (thus, if the new model of the car costs €25,000 versus €20,000 for the old model, inflation would be estimated as 0 percent because the 25 percent price increase reflects an identical increase in quality), inflation would be underestimated because price changes are often introduced at the same time as quality changes in order to hide them.

In principle the "economic approach" to index numbers has an answer to this problem. That approach regards goods not as ends in their own right but rather as vehicles to provide "utility" to the consumer. Thus, old models provide the consumer with level of utility U_{old} and new models with level U_{new}. The quality change could be estimated as (in percentages) $U_{new}/U_{old} - 1$. Price changes could then be discounted by the quality change: Net Inflation $= P_{new}/P_{old} - U_{new}/U_{old}$. Suppose for instance that our new model of the car yields 10 percent higher utility. The net inflation would then be estimated as 25% – 10% = 15%.

There are various problems with this procedure, though. First, utility is not measurable on a ratio scale as would be required. As saw in Chapter 3, utility expresses nothing but preference ordering, and a ratio between two utilities is a meaningless number. If consumers choose a new good over an old one, all we can infer is that they prefer it, not by how much they prefer it. The degree of quality change has to be estimated (or "imputed" as it is called) by the economist or statistician even if the rational-choice model were true.

Second, there are at least some reasons to doubt that the rational choice model can or should be employed here. Often when new goods enter the market old goods disappear. Consumers have to buy the new goods whether they like it or not. In such a context, choice cannot be used as an indicator of preference.

Third, economists tend to be highly theory-driven when they estimate the impact of quality changes on people's well-being. To give just one example, an increased variety of products is always interpreted as a good thing because consumers can satisfy their preferences more precisely. But greater variety is not necessarily a good thing as it increases the costs of decision-making, among other things. What is the true value of having yet another variety of Cheerios?

Whatever the best way to address these questions, it is important to notice that they cannot be answered without taking a substantive stance regarding certain factual and evaluative issues. If consumer choice is to be interpreted as indicating preference satisfaction there had better be evidence that consumers could have chosen otherwise and that their preferences satisfy the axioms of rational-choice theory. Any estimate of the degree of quality changes (i.e., whether the new MacBook Pro is 10 percent or 15 percent better than the old one or in fact 5 percent less good) must reflect value judgments about how far consumers actually benefit from new goods. There is no way to do so without a substantive concept of consumer well-being (see Chapter 13).

Aggregation

Thus far I have said little about the estimation of the quantities with which the prices are weighted in the index. As briefly mentioned above (see "Measuring CPI: The Basics"), in the USA they are estimated in a point-of-purchase survey, which attempts to measure the distribution of expenditures across different retail outlets. What is important here is that every good is weighted in proportion to its expenditure share in total expenditure. If 10 percent of national expenditures go into internet services, then internet services will have a 10 percent weight in the CPI.

This means that richer households—households that spend more on consumption—are overrepresented or, at any rate, that their spending is weighted by their share in expenditure and not by number of people living in a household or by household. The index is "plutocratic": governed by wealth (Schultze and Mackie 2002).

An alternative that has been proposed is a "democratic" index in which every household's expenditure receives the same weight. Since the consumption patterns change considerably with income (recall Engel's law), moving from the current index to a democratic index would have a significant impact on inflation estimates.

Households' consumption patterns differ across more dimensions than just income. Older people, for example, may be less able to benefit from new distribution channels such as discounters and online shops—if, say, they do not drive and are not technology-savvy. Single households can make less use of quantity discounts than large families and so on.

The adequacy of this or that weighting scheme depends on the purpose pursued by measuring the CPI. Now, prominent uses for the CPI are the following (Schultze and Mackie 2002: 192):

- as a compensation measure to calculate how much is needed to reimburse recipients of social security and other public transfer payments against changes in the cost of living and for formal or informal use in wage setting;

- for inflation indexation in private contracts;
- as a measure of inflation for inflation-indexed Treasury bonds;
- as a measure with which to index the income tax system to keep it in-flation-neutral;
- as an output deflator for separating changes in gross domestic product (GDP) and its components into changes in prices and changes in real output; and
- as an inflation yardstick for the Federal Reserve and other macroeco-nomic policy-makers.

Different purposes require different weights. If social security recipients are to be compensated for changes in the cost of living, it seems that *their* budgets are the relevant ones, not those of wealthy households or the popula-tion at large. If, by contrast, the index is used for macroeconomic purposes such as testing the quantity theory of money, it seems reasonable to weight households by their expenditure—as this is where the money goes. If the index is used to keep the income tax system inflation neutral, then the rele-vant expenditures should be those of taxpayers, and so on.

Now, perhaps it does not make a lot of sense to calculate a different index for all these groups. In fact, because calculating an index is costly, it might well be preferable to calculate fewer indices (or even just one), even if that means that these indices are (or this index is) less accurate. But this doesn't invalidate my more general points, namely that (a) the adequacy of an index number is to be judged in the light of the purpose for which the index is used (the "measurement purpose") and (b) normative or evaluative judgments play an important role in the construction of the measurement procedure.

Unemployment and GDP

CPI measurement is not an exception. Measuring any economic indicator is a complicated business and raises conceptual, factual and normative/evalu-ative issues. Take unemployment as a further example. The International Labour Organization (ILO) defines someone as unemployed when they are out of work, currently looking for work and available for work. This defi-nition is used around the world but is quite vague and therefore subject to different interpretations. Using US standards, for example, Canadian unemployment is about 1 percent lower than Canada's official rate says it is (Flaherty 2012: 35). The definition says "*someone* who is looking for work." This does not apply to teenagers under 16, to persons confined to institu-tions such as nursing homes and prisons or persons on active duty in the armed forces. Nor does it apply to people who are willing to work but are not currently looking because they have been discouraged. Should discouraged workers be counted as unemployed or as having left the labor force? Should military personnel count as employed (currently they are not part of the labor force)? How active does one have to be in order to count as "looking for work"? Moreover, in the USA the estimate comes from the so-called Current Population Survey, which interviews a sample of 60,000 households. This sample may be unrepresentative and people may not answer all questions truthfully (for example about how actively they were looking for work). In other countries, a person has to be registered with a government agency (such as a UK Jobcentre) in order to count as unemployed.

Gross domestic product (GDP) is defined as the market value of final goods and services produced within an economy in a given period of time. There are three basic approaches to measuring the quantity: the income method, the expenditure method and the product or output method. To give an example, the income method adds the incomes of all sectors of the economy. The US National Income and Expenditure Accounts divide incomes into five categories:

- wages, salaries and supplementary labor income;
- corporate profits;
- interest and miscellaneous investment income;
- farmers' income;
- income from non-farm unincorporated businesses.

These five income components sum to net domestic income at factor cost. To get to GDP, two adjustments must be made: indirect taxes minus subsidies must be added to get from factor cost to market prices, and depreciation must be added to get from net domestic product to gross domestic product.

GDP is used for many purposes, a prominent one being as an indicator of consumer value. But are market prices a good measure of value? Once more one would have to assume that consumers are rational (which is already questionable) but also that all markets are competitive (which is most certainly false). The production of many goods has externalities, which are, by their nature, not reflected in market prices. Many goods do not have market prices, for instance publicly provided services such as the military as well as non-marketed goods and services such as housework and childcare. Should an economy be regarded as poorer just because more of its goods and services are provided by the government and private households?

Conclusions

Economic indicators require substantial background assumptions about *facts* (e.g., whether or not consumers make their decisions according to the rational-choice model given by economic theory), *values* (e.g., whether or not a given quality change constitutes consumer benefit) and *measurement purpose* (e.g., whether an inflation indicator is used for indexing purposes or for macroeconomic analysis). Because of this, academic economists should take a more active stance in designing measurement procedures than they currently do. Most of the work is done by statistical offices, and academic economists tend to be mere consumers rather than producers and consumers of the data. But as users of the data economists should know best what procedure would be adequate to their purposes because they know their purposes best and, at least in principle, what background assumptions to make.

Take unemployment as an example. For theoretical reasons, what is important is that persons are willing to work *at the prevailing rate of pay*. The US Current Population Survey does not ask about rates of pay. Its definition of unemployment does not match up with the economists' definition. That this can't be good for applied econometric work such as testing theories against data is evident. Moreover, the measurement issues show that a neat dichotomy between "facts" on one side and "values" on the other cannot be upheld. To describe the facts about an economy, for instance facts about its rate of inflation, unemployment and growth, means to make substantial normative commitments. Facts and values are entangled.

Study Questions

1 Analyze an economic indicator other than CPI, GDP and unemployment. Does it make background assumptions about facts, value judgments and measurement purpose?
2 One of the important claims made in this chapter concerns fact and value entanglement. Are facts and values necessarily entangled in economic measurement?
3 If you were to design a measurement procedure for the CPI, how would you solve the quality change problem?
4 We have seen that slightly different CPIs should be measured for different segments of the population. How many indices should we ideally compute for a developed country?
5 How much effort should someone put into finding a job in order to be able to register as unemployed in your view? Justify your answer. On what kinds of grounds do you justify your answer?

Suggested Readings

The section on "Consumer Price Inflation" is basically a summary of chapters 2–4 of Reiss 2008a. For a more detailed discussion of measurement issues in the context of price indices and references, refer to these chapters. Reiss 2001 presents an earlier account of what makes a measurement procedure adequate.

The logical positivists inherited the observable/unobservable dichotomy from Hume, and it played a very important role in their philosophy of science initially. In the second half of the twentieth century it came under attack by philosophers such as Russell Hanson, Thomas Kuhn, Paul Feyerabend and others. Key references include Hanson 1958, Kuhn 1996 [1962], Feyerabend 1975, Maxwell 1962, Shapere 1982 and Hacking 1983: chs 10–11.

A really good and comprehensive discussion of measurement and normative issues in the construction of GDP is Stiglitz *et al.* 2010. Historically inclined readers will appreciate Tom Stapleford's history of CPI measurement in the United States (Stapleford 2007). A collection of papers on economic measurement also with historical focus is Morgan and Klein 2001.

9 Econometrics

Overview

Econometrics is the study of the economy using the methods of statistics. Its aim is to estimate economic relationships, to test theories and to evaluate policies. In other words, it provides economic theories with empirical content. Ragnar Frisch (1895–1973), a Norwegian economist and co-recipient with Jan Tinbergen of the first Nobel prize in economics in 1969, is sometimes credited with coining the term. In his editor's note to the first issue of the journal of the Econometric Society, *Econometrica*, he explains:

> [T]here are several aspects of the quantitative approach to economics, and no single one of these aspects, taken by itself, should be confounded with econometrics. Thus, econometrics is by no means the same as economic statistics. Nor is it identical with what we call general economic theory, although a considerable portion of this theory has a definitely quantitative character. Nor should econometrics be taken as synonymous with the application of mathematics to economics. Experience has shown that each of these three view-points, that of statistics, economic theory, and mathematics, is a necessary, but not by itself a sufficient, condition for a real understanding of the quantitative relations in modern economic life. It is the unification of all three that is powerful. And it is this unification that constitutes econometrics.
>
> (Frisch 1933: 2)

Econometrics does not only apply statistical methods to pre-existing economic theories. Rather, it transforms theoretical claims into testable empirical propositions that can be expressed in a precise mathematical form and statistically estimates their parameters.

From the philosopher's point of view, there are two related fundamental issues that make econometrics important and intriguing. The first is the *testing* or *confirmation* of scientific theories. In many ways this has been *the* issue in the philosophy of science in the twentieth century and beyond. It was certainly the most important issue for logical positivists, and a dividing issue between them and Karl Popper and his followers. The second is the issue of identifying causal relationships from data: *causal inference*. In what follows I will first introduce the topic of theory testing or confirmation in purely philosophical terms. I will then move on to econometrics, show that the major approaches to theory testing have econometric counterparts and discuss these econometric approaches. Issues of identifying causal relationships will be treated along the way

Induction, Deduction and All That

The testing or confirmation of scientific theories by observations is a special case of a mode of reasoning called inductive inference or simply *induction*. In most general terms, induction refers to the inference from a set of statements concerning observed particulars ("Swan 1 is white," "Swan 2 is white," "Swan 3 is white ...") to a statement concerning unobserved particulars. Very often these will be general statements ("All swans are white"; in this case there are some unobserved particulars because not all swans, born and unborn, could have been observed at this point). Inductive inferences are *ampliative*: they go beyond what is already known, enlarge our knowledge base. David Hume, once more the (anti-)hero in the story, argued forcefully that there is no guarantee that ampliative reasoning is reliable: even when all premises in an inductive argument are true, the conclusion might still be false—because a case that hitherto has not been observed may turn out to differ from all those cases that have been observed. The future might not resemble the past, and therefore all our inductive inferences may be false (see Hume 1999 [1748]: section 7).

To explain Hume's reasoning briefly, recall from Chapter 1 that Hume thought that all reasoning concerning matters of fact has to be based on observations. Generalizations such as "All swans are white" concerns a matter of fact—it is not a *logical* truth. We are not contradicting ourselves when we say "Not all swans are white" or "Some swans are black" while accepting our premises ("Swan 1 is white," "Swan 2 is white," "Swan 3 is white ..."). We may be *mistaken* to make these statements but we are *not* committing a *logical error*.

Now, the evidential base for any generalization can only contain a finite number of observations made in the past. Since the generalization concerns all cases, including future and hitherto unobserved cases, it is always possible that a new observation falsifies the generalization. Even though all swans that have been observed up to now may have been white, it might well be that the next swan to be observed turns out to be black. This is essentially the position Europeans were in before 1697 when Willem de Vlamingh, a Dutch sea captain who explored the coast of Australia in the late seventeenth century, discovered black swans in the Swan River in Western Australia. Pre-1697 the generalization "All swans are white" was based on the best evidence available in Europe. Nevertheless it turned out to be false, and like it all generalizations may share the same fate.

Perhaps, we might argue, before 1697 the generalization was based on the best evidence available to Europeans but not on all relevant or enough evidence. Evolutionary theory teaches us that populations can evolve very differently when they become spatially separated, and so we have to expect an Australian swan to look different from a European swan. Of course, this is anachronistic reasoning, as Darwin did not publish his *On the Origin of Species* until 1859. But more importantly, it doesn't undermine Hume's argument.

Even if, contrary to fact, every swan that has ever lived had been observed and found to be white, it is still possible that a hitherto unborn swan will turn out to be black. The future might just not be like the past. Thus, even if for all of human history, day has followed night there is no guarantee that it will continue to do so. Any reason to believe a generalization can only lie in the past, and the future might differ from the past. Higher-level principles such as "Nature is uniform" themselves have to be supported by evidence, and this evidence will again concern facts about the past. This is Hume's *problem of induction*.

Not everyone in the history of philosophy post-Hume has been equally impressed by Hume's inductive skepticism. Notably, John Stuart Mill, another of our philosopher-economist heroes, agreed with Hume that inductive inference can never achieve certainty. However, to him this did not mean that judgments concerning matters of fact that go beyond past experience are unreasonable. It just means that as humans we have to contend with knowledge that is fallible and uncertain.

Even if all human knowledge is fallible, there are better and less good inductive inferences. So-called "simple induction," the inference from (usually, a small number of) instances to a generalization is, by and large, a highly unreliable mode of reasoning. The swans story is one example of a bad inference. Such stories can be multiplied at will. From "Erasmus University has more than 15,000 students," "Leiden University has more than 15,000 students" and "Delft University has more than 15,000 students" we cannot infer "All universities have more than 15,000 students." From "These samples of wax melt at 93°C" we cannot infer "All samples of wax melt at 93°C," and so on.

There are more reliable forms of inductive inference. One of Mill's greatest contributions to logic and philosophy of science was to formalize some of these into what he called a "Canon of Inductive Methods," some kind of inductive logic. It comprises four methods:

- Method of Agreement
- Method of Difference
- Method of Residues
- Method of Concomitant Variation.

For our purposes the Method of Difference is most important. Mill describes it as follows:

> If an instance in which the phenomenon under investigation occurs, and an instance in which it does not occur, have every circumstance in common save one, that one occurring only in the former; the circumstance in which alone the two instances differ, is the effect, or the cause, or an indispensable part of the cause, of the phenomenon.
>
> (Mill 1874 [1843]: 280)

Causal inference, in other words, can proceed by comparing two situations that are exactly alike except that in one the phenomenon is present and in the other it is absent. If the two situations differ with respect to some factor, then that factor is judged to be an effect or a cause or indispensable part of the cause of the phenomenon. Causal claims generalize to all situations that are identical in all causal factors ("Same causes—same effects").

Mill regarded the Method of Difference as a generally reliable inductive principle but did not think it worked in economics. His reason to reject it was that economic phenomena are too complex to ever occur naturally in a form that would allow applying the Method of Difference, and experimentation—the artificial creation of the right circumstances—is not usually an option. As we will see below, there are prominent economists who do not accept Mill's reasons for rejecting inductive causal inference. In the next section I will discuss a movement in contemporary econometrics that aims to exploit *natural experiments*, which essentially are situations of the kind Mill envisaged. And in Chapter 10 I will discuss *laboratory experiments*, which have gained popularity in economics since the 1950s.

First, however, let us consider Mill's alternative to inductive causal inference. Among the scientists Mill distinguishes two kinds of reasoners: practical men and theorists, and explains:

> But, although both classes of inquirers do nothing but theorize, and both of them consult no other guide than experience, there is this difference between them, and a most important difference it is: that those who are called practical men require *specific* experience, and argue

wholly *upwards* from particular facts to a general conclusion; while those who are called theorists aim at embracing a wider field of experience, and, having argued upwards from particular facts to a general principle including a much wider range than that of the question under discussion, then argue *downwards* from that general principle to a variety of specific conclusions.

(Mill 1844: 142; original emphasis)

Mill's practical men employ the inductive method as I've described it above. The theorists, by contrast, first—inductively—establish highly general principles about human behavior, and then, in order to arrive at a prediction about a specific phenomenon, apply the general principles by concretizing them (saying what they means in the specific circumstance) and adding other relevant factors.

An example Mill briefly discusses concerns the question whether absolute kings are likely to employ the powers of government for the welfare or rather for the oppression of their subjects. Practical men would collect cases of absolute monarchies, observe what kings do and generalize from their observations. Theorists, by contrast, regard absolute monarchs as mere instances of the more general kind human being, whose major behavioral tendencies they already know. Thus, from our experience with humans in other situations we can predict that a human being in the situation of a despotic king will make a bad use of power (Mill 1844: 143).

The general principles are the tendency laws (for a discussion of this term, see Chapter 5) of human behavior such as Engel's law or the laws of supply and demand. How, finally, are we using this idea for testing or confirming economic theories? Daniel Hausman nicely summarizes Mill's account of theory testing as follows:

1 *Borrow* proven [tendency] laws concerning the operation of relevant causal factors [such as people's desire to have more wealth, to avoid labor and so on].
2 *Deduce* from these laws and statements of initial conditions, simplifications, etc., predictions concerning relevant phenomena.
3 *Test* the predictions.
4 If the predictions are correct, then regard the whole amalgam as confirmed. If the predictions are not correct, then *judge* (a) whether there is any mistake in the deduction, (b) what sort of interferences [i.e., disturbing factors] occurred, (c) how central the borrowed laws are (how major the causal factors they identify are, and whether the set of borrowed laws should be expanded or contracted).

(Hausman 1992a: 147–8)

The reason to discuss Mill's position here at quite some length is that in my view (as in Dan Hausman's) theory testing in contemporary economics basically follows Mill's schema with slight modifications. Economists today rarely use the notion of law, but their principles that people have stable preferences that satisfy certain axioms, that people generally prefer more to less and so on are the contemporary equivalents of Mill's laws.

There are, then, two ways to furnish economic hypotheses with empirical content. The *inductive method* proceeds bottom-up by collecting specific instances of the hypothesis and generalizing from those instances. The *deductive method* proceeds top-down by using general principles established elsewhere, deducing concrete predictions from these principles together with initial conditions and then testing the predictions against data.

As mentioned above, Mill thought that the inductive method was inapplicable to economics. Many economists still share his views on this matter. But in recent years there has been an intense debate in econometrics about methods, with two camps that resemble quite closely Mill's "practical men" and "theorists." Thus in what follows I introduce the contemporary debate in econometrics and show how it can be regarded as a debate between "practical men" and "theorists."

Mostly Harmless Econometrics?

Regression Analysis

The main tool of econometrics is regression analysis. In regression analysis, a *dependent variable y* is expressed as a function of *independent variables X* = $\{x_1, x_2, ..., x_n\}$ and an error term ε: $y = f(X) + \varepsilon$. "Dependence" for now means only functional, not causal dependence. The dependent variable is also sometimes called output or explained variable or regressand, and the independent variables input or explanatory variables or regressors. Regressand and regressor are in fact the least misleading terms but they are ugly and easy to confuse, so I will stick with the usual language of dependent and independent variables here.

In order to do regression analysis, a functional form for f must be specified. The simplest and most common specification of f is a linear additive function:

$$y = \beta_0 + \beta_1 x_1 + ... + \beta_n x_n + \varepsilon,$$

where the βs are unknown parameters. Under a number of assumptions, the βs can be estimated from observations on y and X using a variety of estimation methods. One such method, ordinary least squares, makes the following assumptions:

- *Exogeneity*: errors have mean zero: $E[\varepsilon] = 0$, and independent variables are uncorrelated with the errors: $E[X'\varepsilon] = 0$.
- *Linear independence*: the independent variables are linearly independent. That is, no variable is a linear function of the other variables.

- *Homoscedasticity*: $E[\varepsilon^2|X] = \sigma^2$, which means that the error term has the same variance σ^2 in each observation.
- *Nonautocorrelation*: the errors are uncorrelated between observations: $E[\varepsilon_i\varepsilon_j|X] = 0$ for $i \neq j$.

Suppose now that we are interested in the question whether schoolchildren do better in smaller classes. A precondition for using regression analysis to help answer this question is to measure the variables of interest, in this case "doing well at school" and "class size." The latter is straightforwardly measurable by counting the number of students in class. The "doing well at school" variable is usually called educational or academic achievement, and there are standard tests for it. To make things easier, let us suppose that both variables have been measured satisfactorily.

We might now be tempted to run a simple regression such as:

$$educational\ achievement = \beta_0 + \beta_1 class\ size + \varepsilon,$$

and judge that class size contributes positively to educational achievement whenever β_1 is significantly greater than zero. The problem with this procedure is that the exogeneity condition is most likely not fulfilled. There could be many reasons for this, one of the more important ones being that unobservable factors such as parents' educational backgrounds affect both independent and dependent variables. Thus, better-educated parents might be likely to send their kids to schools that have small classes, and provide them with more learning opportunities outside school, affecting their educational achievement. In this case the error would be correlated with the independent variable in violation of the exogeneity condition.

Instrumental Variables

In a highly original contribution, the econometricians Joshua Angrist and Victor Lavy have exploited a feature about determining students' allocation to classes in Israel to solve this problem: Maimonides' rule (Angrist and Lavy 1999). Many countries set their class sizes to conform to some version of Maimonides' rule, which sets a maximum class size, beyond which additional teachers must be found. In Israel, the maximum class size is set at 40. (This is the original "Maimonides' rule." Maimonides was a rabbi in the twelfth century who interpreted what the Talmud says about class size as follows: "Twenty-five children may be put in charge of one teacher. If the number in the class exceeds twenty-five but is not more than forty, he should have an assistant to help with the instruction. If there are more than forty, two teachers must be appointed" (Hyamson 1937: 58b; quoted in Angrist and Lavy 1999: 534.) If there are fewer than 40 children enrolled, they will all be in the same class. If there are 41, there will be two classes, one of 20, and one of 21. If there are 81 or more children, the first two classes will be full, and more must be set up, and so on for higher numbers. Angrist and Lavy's Figure 1a, which demonstrates the efficacy of the rule in Israel, appears here as Figure 9.1.

The graph starts off running along the 45-degree line, and then falls discontinuously to 20 when enrolment is 40, increasing with slope of 0.5 to 80, falling to 27.7 (80 divided by 3) at 80, rising again with a slope of 0.25, and so on. They show that actual class sizes, while not exactly conforming to the rule, are strongly influenced by it, and exhibit the same saw-tooth pattern.

Maimonides' rule creates a *natural experiment*. This is due to the fact that there is no reason to suspect any systematic differences between students relevant to educational attainment around the points of discontinuity. Students and their parents have no way of knowing ahead of time whether they will be member of a cohort of, say, 80 students, in which case there will be two classes of 40, or 81 students, in which case there will be three classes of 27. Any variation induced by the rule will therefore be independent of confounding factors such as parents' educational background: "Since it seems unlikely that enrollment effects other than those working through class size would generate such a pattern, Maimonides' rule provides an unusually credible source of exogenous variation for class size research" (Angrist and Lavy 1999: 536).

Angrist and Lavy analyze the natural experiment created by Maimonides' rule constituted by interpreting it as a valid *instrumental variable*. One (somewhat non-standard) way to define an instrumental variable Z is the following (cf. Reiss 2008a: ch. 7):

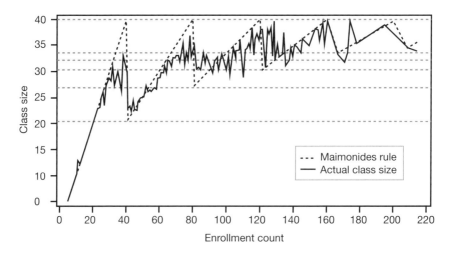

Figure 9.1 Maimonides' Rule in Action

Source: Angrist and Lavy 1999: 541.

a Z causes the independent variable (in this case, class size);
b Z affects the dependent variable, if at all, only through the independent variable;
c Z is not itself caused by the dependent variable or by a factor that also affects the dependent variable.

That Z is effective in determining class size is shown in Figure 9.1. It is highly unlikely that the rule affects educational achievement in any other way but class size. And the rule is itself not caused by background factors such as parents' educational achievements.

   Studies like Angrist and Lavy's have become increasingly popular in recent econometrics. A country dummy for Egypt has been used as instrument to determine the efficacy of foreign aid, because Egypt gets a great deal of American aid as part of the Camp David accords (see Deaton 2010a). "Random sequence numbers" (which were used to determine draft status for serving in the Vietnam war) have been used as instrument to show that serving in the army negatively affects civil earnings later in life (Angrist 1990). Rainfall has been used as instrument for economic growth in explaining civil war (Miguel *et al.* 2004).

Practical Men versus Theorists

Proponents of these kinds of studies are akin to Mill's "practical men": they aim to establish generalizations ("Class size causes educational achievement"; "Foreign aid promotes economic growth"; "Being a Vietnam veteran reduces civil earnings" and so on) on the basis of specific experience. They are well aware of the methodological problems Mill pointed out. Mill thought that the method of specific experience—the inductive method—couldn't successfully be applied in economics because of the complexity of economic phenomena (which in the present context means that regressions are likely to be confounded) and because of the impossibility of experimentation.

   As mentioned above, we will look at economic laboratory experiments in Chapter 10. If controlled manipulation is unavailable, the problem of confounding can still be tackled: by exploiting *natural* experiments using instrumental variables. Mill thought that natural experiments were supremely unlikely because of the complexity of economic phenomena. But Mill was mainly concerned with macro-social phenomena. And indeed it seems unlikely to successfully test a theory about the effects of free trade by examining two countries that are identical in all respects except for their trade policy. Contemporary "practical-men"-type econometricians agree with Mill's general sentiment but think that there are situations—usually micro situations—where we are lucky enough to find a quasi-experimental set-up—such as the determination of class size by Maimonides' rule—that can successfully be exploited econometrically.

But can it? Mill's "theorists" also have their contemporary counterparts. They argue, essentially, that unless supported by a theoretical model, any instrument is likely to be invalid. An explicit claim along these lines has been made by Angus Deaton, who distinguishes between "external" and "exogenous" variables (2010a). An external variable is one that is caused independently of the phenomenon of interest. An exogenous variable is one that satisfies the exogeneity condition described above. For an instrument to be valid it has to be truly exogenous (the three conditions [a]–[c] defining an instrument entail exogeneity!). The evidence (inductivist) econometricians give for an instrument to be valid often shows only that it is external. Theoreticians claim that in many cases there are reasons to doubt that it is exogenous.

Thus, it has been argued that Maimonides' rule (though "external") is an invalid instrument because parents can and will anticipate its operation. Parents who care more about education (say, because they have themselves a higher educational achievement) will make sure that their kids end up in smaller classes (Urquiola and Verhoogen 2009). Similarly, James Heckman has argued that the random sequence number is an invalid instrument because employers will take note of the number and make their decisions concerning training investment dependent on the number (i.e., if the employee's number is high and he therefore has a low probability of being drafted, they will invest more in his training than into the training of an otherwise identical employee with a low number). In turn, employees with more training have higher wages (Heckman 1996a: 461). Lastly, a country's being Egypt surely affects its economic growth by many more routes than just through foreign aid. This last one is indeed a particularly dumb choice of an instrument.

None of this shows, however, that the instrumental variables technique is generally faulty. It only shows that choices of instruments have to be supported in a more principled, more systematic fashion. One way to support the choice of instrument in a more principled way is to derive it from theory. This is what the contemporary counterpart of Mill's "theorists" demand: derive your instrument from a theoretical model. More specifically, they recommend that an econometric specification be deduced from general economic principles and assumptions about initial conditions, simplifications and so on. I will use an example due to Angus Deaton because it shows what the idea is in an extremely simple model (Deaton 2010a).

The model is the Keynesian macroeconomic model of national income determination taken from once-standard econometrics textbooks. There are two equations which together comprise a complete macroeconomic system. The first equation is a consumption function, in which aggregate consumption is a linear function of aggregate national income, while the second is the national income accounting identity that says that income is the sum of consumption and investment. The system can be written in standard notation as:

$$C = \alpha + \beta Y + u \qquad\qquad (1)$$
$$Y \equiv C + I \qquad\qquad (2)$$

According to (1), consumers choose the level of aggregate consumption with reference to their income, while in (2), investment is set by the "animal spirits" of entrepreneurs in a way that is outside of the model.

In this model, consumption and income are simultaneously determined so that, in particular, a stochastic realization of u—consumers displaying animal spirits of their own—will affect not only C, but also Y through equation (2), so that there is a positive correlation between C and Y. As a result, ordinary least squares estimation of (1) will lead to upwardly biased and inconsistent estimates of the parameter β.

However, our knowledge of equation (2) tells us that investment is an instrumental variable for income: it affects income, it affects consumption if at all only through income, and it doesn't have causes in common with consumption as it is determined outside the model by the "animal spirits" of entrepreneurs. In the instrumental variable regression, there is a first-stage regression in which income is regressed on investment. In the second stage, consumption is regressed on the predicted value of income.

This is an admittedly crude form of theoretical derivation of a regression equation as the theoretical principles already almost look like regression equations. But more realistic models are essentially similar. In their critique of Maimonides' rule as instrumental variable, for instance, Miguel Urquiola and Eric Verhoogen build a highly complex microeconomic model in which households make optimal decisions concerning school choice conditional on their willingness to pay for quality and on the qualities and tuition fees of schools, schools produce "quality" (of education) as sole good and maximize profit over the choice of tuition, enrollment and the number of classrooms (Urquiola and Verhoogen 2009). They derive the following two "testable implications" of this model:

> Testable Implication 1: In equilibrium, there is an approximately inverted-U relationship between class size and average household income.

> Testable Implication 2: In equilibrium, schools may stack at enrollments that are multiples of 45 [Chile's version of Maimonides' rule has an upper limit of 45], implying discontinuous changes in average household income with respect to enrollment at those points.
>
> (Urquiola and Verhoogen 2009: 192–3)

Both implications are then tested against Chilean data and found to be consistent with it.

The "practical-men" econometricians rebut that it is the implausible assumptions from economic theory, which go into a model such as Urquiola and Verhoogen's, that make much of this kind of econometrics incredible.

Indeed, it seems hard to think of parents being fully informed and rational and schools being profit-maximizing entities in the way the authors portray. Against the theoreticians they argue that their exploitation of natural experiments constitutes "mostly harmless econometrics" (Angrist and Pischke 2008), which has induced a "credibility revolution" in empirical economics (Angrist and Pischke 2010), which in turn has "has greatly improved the standards of empirical work" (Imbens 2009). The debate between practical men and theoreticians is alive and well.

Conclusions

Econometrics is too vast and complex a field to provide a comprehensive review of all methodological issues in a short introductory text, so in this chapter I have focused on one issue that is important and alive but has at the same time some philosophical pedigree: Should learning about economic phenomena proceed essentially inductively or deductively? John Stuart Mill was, despite all the work he did on formalizing inductive inference, an early proponent of the deductive approach because he thought that the economic world was too complex and could not be controlled experimentally. Nor did Mill think that inductive learning was necessary, because the most fundamental principles of economics were already well understood in his view. Mill's "theory-first" view has dominated economics ever since. But from time to time, inductivists have offered alternatives and engaged theorists in methodological debates.

An early example of such a debate was the so-called *Methodenstreit* between the German Historical School and the Austrian economist Carl Menger at the beginning of the twentieth century (see Caldwell 2004: part 1). Gustav Schmoller and his fellow historical economists tried to defend their vision of an evidence-based, inductive model of economic learning against the deductive mainstream exemplified by Menger. But they lost. Schmoller's thought influenced American economics through his student Thorstein Veblen, and through the latter what has come to be known as American institutionalism. At some point in its history, the National Bureau of Economic Research (NBER) in Boston was a stronghold of institutionalism. Arthur Burns and Wesley Clair Mitchell, two NBER institutionalists, defended an inductivist, relatively theory-free approach to business-cycle measurement nearly 50 years later. Tjalling Koopmans criticized them with arguments that mirrored the first *Methodenstreit*, and the "Measurement without Theory" controversy ensued (see Koopmans 1947). Burns and Mitchell lost it. In fact, their whole institutionalist school has practically disappeared from the planet. Today, the "Mostly Harmless Econometrics" movement represents an inductivist approach and their critics such as James Heckman and Angus Deaton a deductivist approach. Let me predict that the latter will once more win and that a new school of inductivist econometrics will arise in about 50 years.

Study Questions

1 Was Hume right to be a skeptic about inductive generalizations?
2 Mill thought that inductive causal inference was impossible in economics. Do you concur?
3 The characterization of an instrumental variable given in this chapter differs from the standard econometrics textbook presentation. What are the main differences? Do they matter?
4 Do you side with the contemporary version of Mill's practical men or the theorists? Defend your answer.
5 What role, in your view, can and should theory play in econometric investigations?

Suggested Readings

A wonderful and philosophically informed history of econometrics is Morgan 1990. Many of the classic papers can be found in Hendry and Morgan 1995. Hoover's 2006 overview of methodological issues in econometrics is a lot more comprehensive than I could be here. I defend my causal reading of instrumental variables in Reiss 2005 and Reiss 2008a: ch. 7. A highly sophisticated discussion of causality in econometrics can be found in Hoover 2001. In that book Hoover develops some ideas of Herbert Simon's (Simon 1953). An alternative account of Simon's ideas can be found in N. Cartwright 2007b: ch. 14. Recent exchanges between "practical men" and "theorists" are in the *Journal of Economic Perspectives* 24:2 (2010) and the *Journal of Economic Literature* 48:2 (2010).

10 Experiments

- Overview
- Speaking to Theorists
- Searching for Facts
- Whispering into the Ears of Princes
- Methodological Issues
- Conclusions
- Study Questions
- Suggested Readings

Overview

Simplifying somewhat, we can say that there are four kinds of experiments in economics. There are, first, *thought* experiments in both macroeconomics (see Chapter 6 on Hume's monetary thought experiment) and microeconomics (see Chapter 7 on Galilean thought experiments and models). Thought experiments abstract a situation from the real world, simplify it to a greater or lesser degree, manipulate a variable and contemplate what would happen in the idealized situation. There are, second, *natural* experiments. In a natural experiment there is no manipulation by the experimenter. Rather, the experimenter finds a natural situation that resembles an experiment and uses statistical methods to analyze it. In the previous chapter we have seen that the econometricians' instrumental-variables technique is often employed to that effect. There are, third, randomized field evaluations that have become popular in development economics in very recent years. In a randomized field evaluation, experimental subjects are divided into two groups, an experimental treatment is applied to one and a control treatment to the other. The treatment is judged to be effective if there is a difference in outcome between the two groups. These experiments we will examine in the following chapter.

The final category is that of the laboratory experiment. When there is talk of experiments in economics or experimental economics, it is usually laboratory experiments that are referred to. These started in about the 1950s, and thus are a relatively recent phenomenon. Only randomized field evaluations are younger. That this book treats the different types of experiments in their historical order of appearance is pure chance.

Laboratory experiments in economics test hypotheses drawn from economic theory in the "lab," which usually means a specially prepared classroom or other university environment. That is, *real people* (unlike the idealized agents of economic models and thought experiments) are brought into an *artificial environment* (unlike in randomized field evaluations, where agents are observed in their natural habitat) and subjected to *interventions controlled by the experimenter* (unlike in natural experiments, where variation is not under experimental control). When I say "experiment" or "economic experiment" in this chapter, I mean this kind of experiment: a controlled, laboratory experiment.

I said that experiments test hypotheses from economic theory. This is too narrow a focus. According to one practitioner, economists pursue at least three purposes with experiments, which he describes metaphorically as follows (Roth 1986):

- *speaking to theorists* ("testing and modifying formal economic theories");
- *searching for facts* ("collect data on interesting phenomena and important institutions"); and
- *whispering into the ears of princes* ("providing input into the policy-making process").

In what follows I will give one or a few examples of each category and describe some of the things economists have learned from performing this type of experiment. I will then take a step back and examine some of the methodological issues involved in economic experimentation in general.

Speaking to Theorists

Experimental economists examine two main economic theories: individual rational-choice theory and game theory. Some of the results we have already encountered in Chapters 3 and 4. Economists and methodologists of economics usually cite Lichtenstein and Slovic 1971 as the seminal paper on "preference reversals," which sparked a whole industry of contributions to the topic (e.g., Hausman 1992a; Cox 2008), but in psychology the phenomenon of intransitive preferences was already well known at the time. Here is the description of an experiment conducted in reaction to a series of findings in the early 1950s:

> We presented a paired comparisons schedule of nine stimuli to 47 undergraduate male students in an elementary psychology course. Our stimuli

were verbal descriptions of girls. These verbal descriptions were typed on lantern slides and shown to the students with a slide projector. Each girl was described by three adjectives. The descriptions of the girls were as follows: (1) plain, very charming, wealthy; (2) pretty, average charm, wealthy; (3) pretty, very charming, average income; (4) pretty, charming, well-to-do; (5) average "looks", charming, wealthy; (6) average "looks", very charming, well-to-do; (7) beautiful, very charming, poor; (8) beautiful, average charm, well-to-do; (9) beautiful, charming, average income. Each stimulus was compared with every other stimulus. Thus there was a total of 36 comparisons. The students were asked to indicate which of the two girls in each comparison they would rather marry. The study was repeated with the same students using the same stimuli six weeks after the original presentation.

The students took considerable time making their choices and seemed to be making their choices carefully and honestly.

(Davis 1958: 29)

A triad is a series of preference rankings such as [(9) > (8); (8) > (7); (9) > (7)], which is transitive, or [(9) > (8); (8) > (7); (7) > (9)], which is intransitive or "circular." The results were that of 3,948 possible triads on the two presentations, 487, a little over 12 percent, were intransitive; 22.8 percent of the preferences changed from the first to the second presentation; and 28 were circular on both presentations. It seems that we did much better constructing our "love lists" at school (see Chapter 4), but perhaps that was due to the fact that we ranked real girls rather than descriptions.

Davis' findings arguably should not worry economists too much given that they are not primarily interested in dating. Lichtenstein and Slovic 1971 was brought to the attention of economists as evidence for systematic and economically significant preference reversals (Grether and Plott 1979). As we saw in Chapter 3, the preference-reversal experiments are subject to more than one interpretation because, given the set-up, reversals can be understood as evidence for intransitive preferences but also, among other things, as the result of individuals responding differently to choice problems on the one hand and valuation problems on the other. Graham Loomes, Chris Starmer and Robert Sugden have proposed an experimental set-up intended to control for known alternative explanations (Loomes *et al.* 1991). More specifically, they ran an experiment that was designed to (a) show that intransitive preferences are a genuine phenomenon (rather than an artifact of the chosen experimental procedure); and (b) show that the kind of intransitivity found can be better explained by "regret theory" (an alternative to expected-utility theory due to Loomes and Sugden 1982) than by alternative possible explanations.

Here is, in brief, their experimental set-up. Loomes *et al.* constructed 20 pairwise choice problems such as that shown in Figure 10.1.

	1...	...30	31...	...60	61...	...100
A	£8.00		£8.00		£0	
B	£18.00		$0		$0	
%	30		30		40	

Figure 10.1 An Example Choice Problem
Source: Loomes *et al.* 1991: 434.

The subjects were asked to pick a sealed envelope from a box of 100 such envelopes, and to keep the envelope sealed until the end of the experiment. The envelopes contained the numbers 1–100, with each envelope containing just one number; the subjects knew about the set-up but not what number was in the envelope. The subjects also knew that at the end of the experiment, they would be asked to roll a 20-sided die to determine which of the questions would be played out for real. If, say, the question from Figure 10.1 was selected, the experimenter would then check which option the subject chose. If she chose "A," she would receive £8 if the number was between 1 and 30, the same amount if it was between 31 and 60, and nothing if it was between 61 and 100. If she chose "B," she would receive £18 if the number was between 1 and 30 and nothing otherwise. Two hundred subjects took part in the experiment and were randomized into two subgroups of 100 subjects each. The two subgroups received slightly different choice problems (the main difference was the expected value of the lotteries). At the beginning of the experiment, the subjects received a booklet containing all 20 choice problems and explanatory notes. Thus they could look at all the problems before answering any of them.

Not too surprisingly, Loomes *et al.* found systematic violations of the transitivity axiom. Cyclical (non-transitive) responses accounted for 14 to 29 percent of observations. More interesting for them was the fact that there were substantially more "predicted" than "unpredicted" violations of transitivity, in line with regret theory but inconsistent with the idea that people should frequently make mistakes for whatever reason (if violations were due to error, all kinds of violations should roughly be equally probable).

As we saw in Chapter 3, evidence of systematic violations of the transitivity axiom (and other axioms) is very important if rational-choice theory is used as a predictive or explanatory theory. The experimental findings are therefore of enormous theoretical significance.

Searching for Facts

Game theory too has of course been tested "in the laboratory." One of the more striking results comes from experimental applications of the Ultimatum

Game (see Chapter 4, Figure 4.4). Recall that in an Ultimatum Game a proposer has an initial endowment of x which he may or may not split with a respondent. The respondent has the choice of either accepting, in which case the parties receive the amounts offered by the proposer, or rejecting, in which case both receive nothing. Game theory is taken to predict that proposers offer the minimum amount possible (e.g., $1 or $0.01), and that responders accept any positive offer.

Alas, this is not what is observed in experiments. Instead of keeping the maximum amount to themselves, proposers offer respondents a substantial share of the endowment, in developed countries typically about 30–40 percent on average, with 50:50 splits being quite common. Notable also is that low offers often get rejected. That is, respondents appear to punish proposers for offers they regard as inadequate at a cost to themselves.

These, then, are examples of experimental "facts": proponents in Ultimatum Games offer about 30–40 percent of the total stakes on average; respondents often reject low offers. The notion of a "fact" is not standardized in experimental economics or philosophy of economics. I take it that in experimental economics a "fact" is a kind of phenomenon in the philosophy of science sense (see Chapters 2 and 8): a behavioral pattern that is repeatable and noteworthy. The facts reported here are repeatable in that they have been reproduced in countless experiments, and there is little doubt that they would be reproduced if a new experiment was conducted under similar conditions. They are noteworthy in that they are taken to constitute violations of game-theoretic predictions. In what follows I will therefore use the technical philosophy of science term "phenomenon," even though economists might be more familiar with the notion of "fact."

As an aside, let me note that experimental economics is quite theory-driven even in its search for phenomena (Reiss 2008a: ch. 5). Outside of theory, there isn't much particularly remarkable in the fact that many people split an endowment they've been given by an experimenter with another person half-and-half. It is only against the backdrop of the prediction derived from game theory and other assumptions that such behavior appears noteworthy. It constitutes a violation of a theoretical prediction and is therefore significant from an economist's point of view.

New experimental phenomena often come to the fore in the course of seeking explanations for already established phenomena. Out-of-equilibrium offers in Ultimatum Games may, for instance, be explained by appealing to the proposers' fear that low offers might be rejected (which isn't an unfounded fear, as we have seen). To test this hypothesis a related game can be played: the Dictator Game. A Dictator Game is essentially the same as an Ultimatum Game except that the responder has no choice. He cannot reject low offers—which turns the proposer into a "dictator," as she will decide about the amount both parties take home. In Dictator Games, however, proposers continue to offer positive amounts (in experimental tests in developed countries). With about 20 percent of the endowment, offers are lower to be sure, but they are much higher than what game theory predicts. Fifty–fifty splits also continue to be significant. These, then, are some new phenomena.

Another set of phenomena comes from experimental tests of public-goods (PG) games. PG games are n-person Prisoner's Dilemmas. Each of the n players can contribute an amount c_i of their endowment that is the same for each player. The total amount of contributions is then multiplied by some factor m and divided equally among all players regardless of their contribution. Each player's monetary payoff is thus given by $m\Sigma c_i - c_i$. If players care only about monetary payoffs, their maximizing strategy is to contribute nothing; that is, to free ride on the others' contributions. Since players are completely symmetric, the same reasoning applies to each player, so that in equilibrium no one makes a contribution.

Once more, this is not what is being observed in experimental implementations. In one-shot PG games subjects contribute about half of their endowment. In repeated games, subjects initially contribute a substantial amount, which decreases as more rounds are played. This fact has come to be known as "overcontribution and decay." Results from two PG games are illustrated in Figure 10.2.

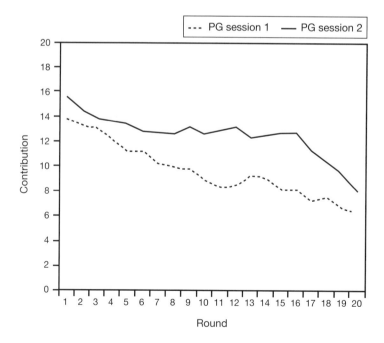

Figure 10.2 "Overcontribution and Decay" in Public-Goods Games

Source: Guala and Burlando 2002.

A remarkable fact about the phenomena of experimental economics is that they tend to be very sensitive to the precise setting in which the experiment is conducted. Almost any variation in setting can lead to a variation in outcome. Important factors that have frequently affected results are for instance the size of the "stake"; the subjects' experience; the information players have and how it is distributed among players; culture and environment (for details, see Reiss 2008a: ch. 5). About monetary incentives I will say more below. Here let me briefly report some fascinating results of experimental tests of the Ultimatum Game in developing countries.

I suggested above that offers in Ultimatum Games are fairly robust in developed countries, but this is actually somewhat misleading as there are systematic differences even there. For instance, in the USA offers are higher than in Japan, and higher in Japan than in Israel (Roth *et al.* 1991). Within the USA students appear to be more generous than workers (Carpenter *et al.* 2005). Variation increases when one leaves the developed world. A remarkable study conducted by an interdisciplinary group of researchers has investigated to what extent economic and social environments shape behavior in 15 small-scale societies in 12 countries on 5 continents (Henrich *et al.* 2001). There is great cultural variation among the societies studied. For example, the sample consisted of three foraging societies, six that practice slash-and-burn horticulture, four nomadic herding groups, and three sedentary, small-scale agriculturalist societies. Behavior in games such as the Ultimatum Game was found to co-vary systematically and quite dramatically with cultural differences. Thus, there is extensive variation in the mean offer in Ultimatum Games, ranging from about a quarter (for instance, 27 percent among the Hadza in Tanzania, with very high rejection rates) to over a half (for instance, 58 percent among the Lamalara in Indonesia, with rejection rates near zero). Importantly, these differences can be much better explained by group-level differences in economic organization and the degree of market integration than by individual differences (Henrich *et al.* 2001). Table 10.1 reproduces Henrich *et al.*'s table 1, which summarizes their most important results.

Whispering into the Ears of Princes

Even though I haven't investigated the matter systematically, I think it is safe to say that economic experiments conducted in the preparation of the US Federal Communications Commission (FCC) spectrum auctions in the early 1990s are the experiments that have received the greatest attention in the methodological literature. One of the reasons why these experiments have received so much attention is that they had a clear and immediate policy goal. An auction is but one of several allocation mechanisms for licenses to use the electromagnetic spectrum. Alternatives such as administrative processes or lotteries were used in the 1970s and 1980s but they are fraught with difficulties and fell out of favor. Auctions, however, come

Table 10.1 The Ultimatum Game in 15 Small-Scale Societies

Group	Country	Mean offer[a]	Modes[b]	Rejection rate[c]	Low-offer rejection rate[d]
Machiguenga	Peru	0.26	0.15/0.25 (72)	0.048 (1/21)	0.10 (1/10)
Hadza (big camp)	Tanzania	0.40	0.50 (28)	0.19 (5/26)	0.80 (4/5)
Hadza (small camp)	Tanzania	0.27 (38)	0.20 (8/29)	0.28 (5/16)	0.31
Tsimané	Bolivia	0.37	0.5/0.3/0.25 (65)	0.00 (0/70)	0.00 (0/5)
Quichua	Ecuador	0.27	0.25 (47)	0.15 (2/13)	0.50 (1/2)
Torguud	Mongolia	0.35	0.25 (30)	0.05 (1/20)	0.00 (0/1)
Khazax	Mongolia	0.36	0.25		
Mapuche	chile	0.34	0.50/0.33 (46)	0.067 (2/30)	0.2 (2/10)
Au	PNG	0.43	0.3 (33)	0.27 (8/30)	1.00 (1/1)
Gnau	PNG	0.38	0.4 (32)	0.4 (10/25)	0.50 (3/6)
Sangu farmers	Tanzania	0.41	0.50 (35)	0.25 (5/20)	1.00 (1/1)
Sangu herders	Tanzania	0.42	0.50 (40)	0.05 (1/20)	1.00 (1/1)
Unresettled villagers	Zimbabwe	0.41	0.50 (56)	0.1 (3/31)	0.33 (2/5)
Resettled villagers	Zimbabwe	0.45	0.50 (70)	0.07 (12/86)	0.57 (4/7)
Achuar	Ecuador	0.42	0.50 (36)	0.00(0/16)	0.00 (0/1)
Orma	Kenya	0.44	0.50 (54)	0.04 (2/56)	0.00 (0/0)
Aché	Paraguay	0.51	0.50/0.40 (75)	0.00 (0/51)	0.00 (0/8)
Lameiara[e]	Indonesia	0.58	0.50 (63)	0.00 (3/8)	0.00 (4/20)

Notes: PNG = Papua New Guinea.
a This column shows the mean offer (as a proportion) in the ultimatum game for each society.
b This column shows the modal offer(s), with the percentage of subjects who make modal offers (in parenthesis.
c The rejection rate (as a proportion), with the actual numers given in parenthesis.
d The rejection rate for offers of 20 percent or less, with the actual numbers given in parenthesis.
e Includes experiementer-generated low offers.

Source: Henrich *et al.* 2001: 74.

with problems of their own. One well-known example is the possibility of the "winner's curse." A winner's curse may arise in a common-value auction with incomplete information. Suppose the different bidders are on average correct in their estimation of the value of the auctioned item. But since it is the highest bidder who wins the auction, she is likely to have overestimated the item's value. So the winner is "cursed" in that she receives an item at too high a price.

Changing the rules of the auction can help ameliorate problems such as the winner's curse. For instance, if the highest bidder wins but pays only the minimum necessary to win (i.e., second-highest bid plus a penny), the chances that a winner's curse obtains are smaller. The task for the FCC then was to find an auction design that would allocate licenses efficiently, without creating undesirable phenomena such as the winner's curse, and in accordance with the goals set by Congress.

Economists soon entered the stage (often as consultants to telecoms firms)—"auction theory" is one of the more important branches of applied economics, after all. Initially, it was theorists who tried to model the auction with a view to maximizing the government's revenues (among them, Paul Milgrom, Robert Wilson and Preston McAfee). But it turned out that an auction of the degree of complexity required for the FCC resisted mathematical modeling. Individual mechanisms could well be modeled, but not the auction in its entirety (Guala 2001). To examine how the different mechanisms interact, a group of economists from Caltech, led by Charles Plott, conducted a series of experiments. In March 1994, the FCC announced the chosen auction structure, which was essentially simultaneous multiple-round bidding (for high-value licenses), where bidders can withdraw their bids, albeit with penalties. The decision was made at least in part on the basis of the experimental results.

There aren't always princes involved in cases such as the FCC auctions but the meaning of Roth's analogy is clear: one goal of economic experimentation is the preparation of and assistance in policy-making decisions. This goal is clearly different from the other two. On the one hand, if auction mechanisms of certain types cannot be modeled theoretically, then observing how these mechanisms perform in an experiment cannot aim at testing theoretical predictions. On the other, these "testbeds for policy" (Plott 1997) do not aim to establish robust facts as such. The experiments that were run in the course of preparing the FCC auctions were so specific that their results were from the outset unlikely to travel far beyond the setting relevant to these auctions. I will come back to this point later on.

Methodological Issues

How good are experiments in each of these three roles? Let us first note that there is a sense in which the second role ("establishing phenomena") is prior to the first ("testing theory"). The Bogen–Woodward distinction between data and phenomena has already been introduced in Chapter 8. Data are the observable but idiosyncratic outcomes of individual experimental procedures. Phenomena are unobservable but systematic effects of theoretical (or otherwise scientific) interest. In the first instance, experiments produce data. Often data can be used to reliably infer a phenomenon, but phenomena do not automatically fall out of an experiment. It requires a good experimental design, usually statistical analysis, and always a good deal of interpretation and idealization to extract a phenomenon from experimental data. But it is phenomena against which theories are tested, not data. Thus, we need to establish first that the experimental result is a genuine phenomenon rather than an artifact of the experiment. We can then decide whether we use that experimental phenomenon for testing theories or instead for examining its robustness, searching for explanations, etc. In what follows, I will, consequently, first examine some general methodological issues concerning the establishment of experimental phenomena, then talk about issues surrounding theory-testing and finally ask how one can extrapolate knowledge gained in an experiment to a setting relevant for policy.

Establishing Experimental Phenomena

We've already noted that phenomena of potential theoretical or otherwise scientific interest to economists do not sit around like a flower in the meadow, just waiting to be plucked by any economist who wants it and happens to pass by. This remains true of laboratory situations. For a variety of reasons most economic experiments involve university students at computer terminals, and experimental "manipulations" are implemented via on-screen instructions. The observable outcomes of these experiments are, typically, strings of numbers such as that in Figure 10.3.

```
0:1:10:10:34:::1:2:20:0:38:::2:3:20:0:40:::3:4:3:
17:41:::4:1:20:0:24:::5:2:20:0:38:::6:3:20:
0:40:::7:4:3:17:41:::8:1:20:0:24:::9:2:15:5:43:::
10:3:20:0:40:::11:4:20:0:24:::12:1:0:20:44:::13:2:
20:0:38:::14:3:20:0:40:::15:4:20:0:24:::
```

Figure 10.3 The Observable Outcome of an Economic Experiment

Source: Guala 2005: 41.

Whether an experimental output such as that of Figure 10.3 can be interpreted as a phenomenon of scientific interest depends on the (pre-experimental) *design* of the experiment as well as on the (post-experimental) *data analysis*.

Pre-experimentally, the experiment should be designed so as to minimize the chance that the data are produced by anything but the phenomenon of interest. It is a simple fact of experimental life that countless things can go wrong, often in unforeseeable ways. To begin with, we prefer the data to be the result of the subjects' input, and not of a malfunctioning software code or a terminal gone crazy. It is therefore a good idea to investigate the equipment for proper functioning beforehand. We also prefer the data to result from an experimental subject's own reflections about the task, and not from one person copying another person's answers, and so we screen the subjects off from one another. Further, a subject's decisions should result from his or her *reflections* on the task and not from error and chance, and so we provide very clear instructions before the experiment begins, allow for time to think during the experiment and make the on-screen prompts as unambiguous as possible. And so on.

Bogen and Woodward call these endeavors "empirical investigation of equipment" (e.g., verification of the software code, testing of the terminals) and "control of possible confounders" (e.g., suppressing communication between subjects, providing clear instructions), respectively (Bogen and Woodward 1988: section VI). The aim is the same: to separate signal from noise, or phenomenon from artifact.

Even a perfectly designed experiment will not immediately reveal a phenomenon of scientific interest. As we have seen, an experiment, whether well or ill designed, produces data, not phenomena. Thus, post-experimentally, the resulting data have to be aggregated and (statistically) analyzed in order to allow the drawing of inferences about the phenomenon of interest. For example, the decisions of an individual experimental subject are not normally of scientific interest but rather the behavior of *populations* of subjects. Often, therefore, averages over the test population are calculated and reported, rather than the decisions of individual subjects. Moreover, frequently the effect of some manipulation is a subject of the investigation, and therefore the *difference* between an outcome in one set-up and the outcome in another set-up is of interest. But given chance variation between subjects, a difference between the average outcomes of two test populations may be systematic or due to chance, and statistical tests can be employed to discern which is which. A "statistically significant" difference between two treatments is usually interpreted as being systematic, and one that is insignificant as being due to chance. For instance, the difference between the two schedules in Figure 10.2 is that in PG Session 1 (bottom schedule) the game was played with heterogeneous players (that is, groups were composed of some subjects who always free ride on the contributions of others, some who always contribute, some who contribute when others do and so on), whereas in PG Session 2 (top schedule) only the same types were allowed to play each other. The authors observe that "in the second PG game the average level of contribution is *significantly* higher than in the first one" (Guala and Burlando 2002: 44; emphasis added), and go on to infer that representative-agent models are of limited usefulness in this context because they are "likely to lack explanatory depth and will fail to capture the important mechanisms that sustain cooperation" (Guala and Burlando 2005: 49). Agent heterogeneity matters. There is a fascinating story to be told about the adequacy of inferring the reality of an effect from its statistical significance but sadly this story is beyond the scope of this book.

In the recent literature on scientific experiments, especially in the social and biomedical sciences, methodologists often speak of the "internal" and "external" validity of an experimental result (e.g., Guala 2005). The former is very closely related to the notion of a phenomenon but is mainly used when the phenomenon of interest is some causal effect. Suppose we are interested, as Burlando and Guala were, in whether agent heterogeneity has a systematic effect on the level of contribution in public-goods games. An experimental result—say, a measured difference (of size *d*, say) in average contributions between heterogeneous and homogeneous groups of players—can then be said to be "internally valid" if (and only if) it correctly indicates that a causal effect (of size *d*) of agent heterogeneity on contribution levels exists *in the experimental population*. (The internal validity of an experimental result implies thus the existence of a phenomenon.) A result is said to be "externally valid" if it correctly indicates that the causal effect exists *in other populations*. I will say more about external validity in the section on that topic later in this chapter and in Chapter 11 below.

Testing Economic Hypotheses

The nineteenth-century French physicist Pierre Duhem argued that theoretical hypotheses are never tested individually but only against the backdrop of auxiliary assumptions about the details of the experimental procedure (Duhem 1991 [1914]). This is certainly the case in economic experiments. If, for example, we would like to test whether people's preferences are indeed transitive (as rational-choice theory would have it), and people reverse their choices between two apparently equivalent tasks in an experiment, the experimental result does not automatically refute the theoretical hypothesis. It may be the case that the experiment is flawed in myriad ways, as we have just seen. But even if we can be reasonably certain that some experimental result is a genuine phenomenon and not an artifact of the specific experimental procedure, the result does not normally entail the truth or falsity of the theoretical hypothesis at hand. Rather, by and large, an experimental phenomenon allows more than one theoretical interpretation.

We've already encountered one example above. Suppose that in certain kinds of experiments subjects often value one of a pair of options more highly but later choose the other option. Such experimental results do not necessarily indicate intransitive preferences, and even less any specific explanation why preferences might be intransitive. To begin with, it has to be assumed that preferences are stable over time. This is a frequently made assumption but it is not part of economic theory as such (see Chapter 3). It is an auxiliary assumption. It further has to be assumed that there are no relevant differences between the valuation- and the choice-task, an assumption which happens to be controversial.

Whether a difference between two decision tasks is relevant or not is difficult to determine outside a theoretical framework. Conventional expected-utility theory (EUT) is usually taken to imply that presenting a decision problem as choice- or as valuation-task should not make a difference to a rational decision-maker, and so the preference reversals revealed in these series of tasks violates EUT. Slovic and Lichtenstein 1983 suggest that preference reversals are the result of information-processing effects, and occur because the mental processes brought to bear on valuation-tasks are different from those brought to bear on choice-tasks.

Thus, one explanation of the reversal phenomenon holds that people have (at least) two different sets of preferences which are activated in different decision situations. Another explanation holds that there is something wrong with the experimental procedure. Many of the preference-reversal experiments use the so-called Becker–DeGroot–Marschak (BDM) elicitation procedure in which subjects are given lotteries they can sell back to the experimenter. It can be shown that if subjects' preferences satisfy the axioms of EUT they will use their certainty equivalent as minimum selling price. If, conversely, the independence axiom does not hold, the BDM procedure cannot be guaranteed to elicit true certainty equivalents (Karni and Safra 1987). Under this interpretation, the reversal phenomenon conflicts with EUT, but with the independence axiom and not with transitivity.

Yet another explanation is offered by regret theory. Regret theory is a theory of choice under uncertainty, developed by Graham Loomes and Robert Sugden, which models choice as the minimizing of a function of the regret vector, defined as the difference between the outcome yielded by a given choice and the best outcome that could have been achieved in that state of nature. Preference cycles are an implication of regret theory (Loomes *et al.* 1991: 429–30).

The phenomenon of preference reversals is therefore consistent with at least three theoretical interpretations. This is a general fact about hypothesis-testing: because theoretical hypotheses are never tested in isolation, and there is always *some* uncertainty concerning auxiliary assumptions, an apparent conflict between an experimentally established phenomenon and a theoretical hypothesis can always be interpreted in more than one way— as refutation of the hypothesis at stake, as refutation of another theoretical claim made in the derivation of the prediction or as violation of an assumption about the experimental set-up.

I mentioned above that Loomes *et al.* 1991 designed their experiment with a view to ruling out all alternative explanations. Thus, they believe that their experiment not only demonstrates that preference reversals are a genuine phenomenon, they also believe that their specific results cannot be explained by problems with the elicitation procedure or subjects' switching between "valuation preferences" and "choice preferences." I cannot discuss here whether they are right. But what is clear is that at best only alternative explanations that are *known* can be ruled out (cf. Guala 2005). The possibility that there is an alternative, even an empirically more successful alternative, always remains.

One often hears that (good) experiments prove their results. There is a sense in which this piece of popular lore is true. *Conditional* on an assumed background of theoretical alternatives, it is sometimes possible to design experiments that are able to rule out all but one candidate. This form of induction is called *demonstrative induction* or *deduction from the phenomena* (Worrall 2000). How powerful this method is depends on how certain we can be that the known alternatives exhaust the space of possible alternatives. In economics it would probably be wise not to be too optimistic.

External Validity

When the aim is to "whisper into the ears of princes," whether or not an experimentally established phenomenon can be theoretically explained is of secondary importance. Of primary importance is whether the experimental knowledge is of the right kind to underwrite a policy intervention. If, as is often the case, the experimentally established phenomenon is some causal relation between variables X and Y, and policy-makers would like to affect Y, the question is whether what can be learned in an experiment about the relation between X and Y is a reliable guide to what will happen to Y when X is intervened on. X might be a variable whose values are different auction designs and Y government revenue. Experimental economists can test which auction design maximizes revenues under laboratory conditions. But will that knowledge carry forward to actual auctions performed by the government?

There is some reason for skepticism. We saw above that the experiment has to be tightly controlled in order for it to generate valid results. But the more experimenters control an environment, the less natural and more artificial it becomes. Are people likely to behave the same under artificial laboratory conditions as they would if the policy was implemented—under whatever conditions that prevail then? W. Allen Wallis and Milton Friedman thought not. They wrote, albeit at a time when experimental economics wasn't considered to be economics proper (Wallis and Friedman 1942: 179–80): "It is questionable whether a subject in so artificial an experimental situation could know what choices he would make in an economic situation; not knowing, it is almost inevitable that he would, in entire good faith, systematize his answers in such a way as to produce plausible but spurious results."

The problem of judging whether an inference from an experimental situation to another situation (which may but does not have to be a policy situation) is well founded has come to be known as the "problem of external validity" (Shadish *et al.* 2002; Guala 2005: ch. 7; Reiss 2008a: ch. 5; Steel 2008). The problem is, essentially, to decide under what conditions an experimental result can be projected onto a hitherto unobserved situation of interest. This is a genuine problem, because experimental situations differ by their very nature more or less dramatically from those situations about which we would ultimately like to learn. One reason for this we have already encountered: experimental control makes experimental situations artificial to some extent, and people's behavior may differ between these artificial laboratory and more "natural" policy situations. There is another reason. By and large, experiments are conducted on "models," that is, on substitute systems that act as stand-ins for the systems of ultimate interest. As mentioned above, most economic experiments use university students as subjects. But few economists are interested specifically in the behavior of university students. University students are cheap, available and relatively reliable. They are used in economic experiments because it is convenient to do so, not for any good epistemic reason. And there is a good chance that their behavior differs from the behavior of others, be they the population at large or specific target populations such as "managers of companies interested in buying licenses for the use of the electromagnetic spectrum."

Experimental and target situation differ, then. But do they differ in *relevant* ways? Do they differ in ways that potentially invalidate the inference from an experiment to a target? The problem is that for the most part we cannot answer this question for specific cases at hand. All we know is that all humans are alike in some respects but differ in others. We don't have to conduct further experiments to find out whether the causal relation "holding a person's head under water for five minutes causes their death" continues to hold in new, hitherto unobserved human populations. By contrast, people's behavior in economic experiments appears to vary with factors such as level of monetary incentives, culture and social norms, experience, the distribution of information, social status and what have you. It is therefore difficult to predict whether an experimental result will still hold when some of these factors differ between experiment and target situation—as is invariably the case.

The problem of external validity has received considerable attention in recent philosophy of science, partly because it is ubiquitous in the special sciences. Especially in the biological and biomedical sciences researchers often encounter the problem because in those sciences, too, experiments are usually conducted on models. The fact that some substance has been shown to be toxic (safe) in some animal species, say, is on its own no good reason to believe that it will also be toxic (safe) for humans. One of the problems for a researcher trying to draw inferences about humans is that the toxicity of substances often varies considerably between different animal species, and it is not clear which species is the best model for humans (Shanks and Greek 2009). As far as I can see, the attempts at solutions philosophers of science have developed can be organized into four groups: solutions based on causal mechanisms, on causal tendencies, on engineering and on field experiments.

External validity by causal mechanisms. As we saw in Chapter 6, causes don't normally influence their effects across spatio-temporal gaps. Rather, when some C causes some E, there will normally be a mechanism that mediates the causal influence of C on E. The mechanistic theory of external validity makes the reasonable assumption that if C causes E in experimental population P_e via the set of mechanisms M, and M is known to operate also in target population P_t, then one can infer that C causes E in P_t. An immediate problem with this mode of reasoning is that it is entirely uninformative, as that which we wish to infer—the causal relation between C and E—follows immediately from what we have to assume at the outset—the mechanisms between C and E. That is, if we know what mechanisms M operate in the target population, there is no need to run an experiment on another population, because the causal relation is known already. In order to turn this kind of mechanistic reasoning into a more fruitful inferential strategy Daniel Steel makes an additional assumption (Steel 2008). The additional assumption is that only downstream differences at relevant stages of the mechanisms matter. Suppose (this is Steel's example, see Steel 2008: 90) that a cause C causes an effect E through the mechanism $C \rightarrow X \rightarrow Y \rightarrow A \rightarrow Z \rightarrow B \rightarrow E$. X, Y and Z signify points at which the mechanisms are likely to differ whereas A and B are likely to be similar in model and target. Then, if upstream differences must result in downstream differences, it is necessary to compare only the mechanisms at Z. This reduces the amount of information about the mechanism in the target that is necessary for the inference. Thus, even if the mechanisms in the target are not perfectly well understood, successful inferences from experimental to target population can sometimes be made.

This form of mechanistic reasoning (called "comparative process tracing" by Steel) works only when three conditions are met. First, the mechanisms responsible for experimental phenomena have to be well understood. That it is sometimes possible to establish an explanation for an experimental phenomenon has been shown above. But, arguably, to do so successfully is very difficult, and consequently this happens rarely. An indication of this difficulty is the lack of consensus among economists regarding the explanation of experimental phenomena. Preference reversals are a case in point. While most economists seem to accept the phenomenon as such, there is a large variety of opinions regarding its correct interpretation (see for instance Cox 2008). Obviously, if the mechanism responsible for the phenomenon of interest isn't well understood, knowledge about the mechanism can hardly be used for assessing external validity. Second, to the extent that "whispering into the ears of princes" is the goal of experimentation, a successful extrapolation from experiment to policy situation presupposes that the policy does not affect the mechanisms prevailing in the population where the policy is implemented. That policies sometimes, or perhaps as a rule, change the mechanisms responsible for phenomena of interest has been understood in economics since at least the Lucas critique (Lucas 1976; Steel 2008: 154–60 discusses the relevance of the Lucas critique for comparative process tracing). These are complications for the mechanistic account of external validity, but there is no reason to believe that they cannot at least sometimes be overcome.

External validity by causal tendencies. In Chapter 5 we saw that some economists and philosophers interpret causal claims such as "C causes E" as implying that C *tends to* bring about E, even in the presence of factors that disturb the operation of C. Nancy Cartwright's account of external validity builds on this understanding of causation (e.g., N. Cartwright 2009a, b). The basic idea is simple. To assert that a factor C has a tendency to produce E is to assert that the causal relation is to some extent independent of the causal background. So if we learn that C causes E in situation X (an experiment, say), and we have reason to believe that C has a stable tendency to produce E, then we can infer that C will also cause E in situation Y (a policy situation, say). To illustrate, if some specific auction design causes revenue to be maximal in the experimental situation, then it will still try to maximize revenue in the policy situation, which in this case means that it will affect revenue positively.

The tendency account helps with judgments of external validity only to the extent that factors do have stable tendencies to affect outcomes and that we can learn about these tendencies. Currently, the balance of the evidence seems to indicate that most factors experimental economists consider do not have stable tendencies. Rather, these factors act "holistically"; that is, what these factors do depends on the complex arrangement of other factors within which they operate. Examples of such context dependence were given above. But perhaps the reason for the lack of evidence for factors with stable tendencies is that economists haven't looked hard enough (I suggest this explanation in Reiss 2008b). Unfortunately, there are no off-the-shelf methods to establish tendencies (for a discussion, see Reiss 2008b; N. Cartwright 2009a). Most methods of causal inference establish that one factor causes another in the experiment but are silent about the extent to which the result is dependent on the specifics of the experiment. N. Cartwright 2009b suggests that the inference from "C causes E" to "C has a stable tendency to affect E" can sometimes be made on the basis of *theory*. John List, a prominent experimental economist, makes the same point (List 2007: 2): "Indeed, theory is the tool that permits us to take results from one environment to predict in another, and laboratory generalizability should be no exception." As we have seen, however, theory is a tool experimental economists rely on only at their own peril.

External validity by engineering. This proposal seeks to establish external validity not by modifying the experiment or the inference from an experimental result but by modifying the target system about which the inference is made. Theories can be tested only under tightly controlled conditions, as we have seen, and to tightly control conditions means to make the experiment less like the policy situation to which the experimental result is supposed to apply. But if the experiment cannot be like the policy situation, why not make the policy situation like the experiment? If the mountain won't come to Mohammed, Mohammed must go to the mountain, as they say. Francesco Guala has argued that this strategy was used in the FCC auctions, partly explaining their success (Guala 2005: ch. 8).

The main scientific problem in the FCC auctions case was a *mechanism design* problem. In Chapter 6 we discussed the notion of a mechanism in some detail, but the mechanisms design literature has an entirely different understanding of the term. In mechanism design, a branch of game theory (sometimes called "reverse game theory"), "mechanism" refers to a system of rules regulating the behavior of agents with the aim of achieving certain goals or outcomes. The goal of mechanism design is therefore not to analyze and explain existing phenomena (such as institutions) but rather to create blueprints for new institutions with certain desirable features. Charles Plott explains it as follows:

> Designs are motivated by a mechanism (a mathematical model, a body of theory) that is perhaps completely devoid of operational detail. The task is to find a system of institutions—the rules for individual expression, information transmittal, and social choice—a "process" that mirrors the behavioral features of the mechanism. The theory suggests the existence of processes that perform in certain (desirable) ways, and the task is to find them. This is a pure form of institutional engineering.
>
> (Plott 1981: 134)

The FCC auctions were such an engineered institution. The US Congress commissioned the FCC to design and test alternative forms of competitive bidding, and the FCC asked economic theorists and experimentalists for help. Theory could provide some insight into what plausible candidate auction designs should look like. The "winner's curse" phenomenon, for instance, was theoretically fairly well understood and, importantly, theory offered strategies for how to avoid it. But the auctions the FCC required were too complicated to be modeled in their entirety by game-theoretic means. It is at this point that experimental economists came in, because the behavior of alternative designs could be tested by experimental means. Importantly, experiments could help not only to understand differences between different basic designs but also of the details of their implementation.

Armed with this theoretical and experimental understanding of the auction design, the FCC knew precisely how to organize the actual auctioning of the spectrum licenses such that an efficient outcome would result. The auctions were subsequently hailed as a great success (Cramton 1997). Indeed, the auctions generated some $23 billion in government revenue between 1994 and 1997.

The engineering strategy is thus: build your institution in such a way as to mimic the experimental conditions as closely as possible. Obviously, mechanism design is a quite special case—as is indicated by the alternate name "*reverse* game theory." It is not the case that existing phenomena are analyzed and explained but rather new phenomena (or institutions) are created, following the recommendations derived from theory and experiments. This approach works, at best, only when the latter and not the former is the aim. And there are other problems. Guided by economic theory, economists reinterpreted the goals of the auctions as set by Congress (see Reiss 2008a: ch. 5; Nik-Khah 2005: ch. 5). Economic theory is often useful when the goal is to improve efficiency or to maximize profits but not usually when the goals are different. Finally, the approach works only to the extent that an institution that closely mirrors the experiment can be created. This seems to have been the case in the FCC auctions, but that this is possible is not guaranteed.

External validity by field experiments. John List and his co-authors have argued that field experiments can help with ascertaining the external validity of laboratory results (Harrison and List 2004; Levitt and List 2007; List 2007). List distinguished lab and field experiments as follows:

> Similar to laboratory experiments, field experiments use randomiza-
> tion to achieve identification. Different from laboratory experiments,
> however, field experiments occur in the *natural environment* of the agent
> being observed and cannot be reasonably distinguished from the tasks
> the agent has entered the marketplace to complete.
>
> (List 2007: 7; original emphasis)

Harrison and List 2004 offer a classification of different types of field experiments. To that end they propose six characteristics aimed at describing all
kinds of experiments: the nature of the subject pool, the nature of the information that the subjects bring to the task, the nature of the commodity, the
nature of the task or trading rules applied, the nature of the stakes and the
environment in which the subjects operate. An "artifactual field experiment"
(AFE), then, is one that is just like a laboratory experiment, except that the
subject pool is more representative of the target population of interest. As
discussed above, most lab experiments use university students as subjects. But
university students' behavior may not be a strong indicator of what market
participants do. An AFE uses subject pools that are more "realistic," such as
businesspeople or fishermen or policy-makers. A "framed field experiment"
(FFE) is also tightly controlled but uses a field context in the commodity,
task, stakes or information set of the subjects. Instead of trading "tokens"
(currency units that may or may not be converted into real money at a predetermined exchange rate after the experiment), say, real goods are traded for
real money, the stakes are higher, the distribution of information is more
realistic. A "natural field experiment" (NFE), finally, moves the environment from the lab to the field. That is, subjects are observed in their natural
habitat rather than in a university laboratory. The only difference between
NFEs and naturally occurring situations is that subjects are randomized into
treatment and control groups (usually, unwittingly).

   List believes that field experiments thus build "a bridge between lab and
naturally occurring data" (this is the title of List 2007). Indeed, economists have made interesting observations using field experiments. Here are
some examples. The so-called "endowment effect," the (positive) difference
between a person's willingness to accept (WTA) and their willingness to pay
(WTP) for it once their property right to it has been established, (Kahneman
et al. 1990), is an experimental phenomenon in violation of neoclassical
economic theory that is across a wide variety of laboratory settings. In a
series of field experiments, List (2003, 2004) shows, by contrast, that individual behavior converges to the neoclassical prediction as market experience
increases. Another example concerns so-called "social preferences," that is,
preferences expressing altruism, fairness, reciprocity, inequity aversion and
such. Social preferences, too, have been observed in countless laboratory
contexts (though the results have not always been consistent; see Woodward
2009). List 2006 carried out different kinds of field experiments in which
buyers make price offers to sellers, and in return sellers select the quality level

of the good provided to the buyer. Higher-quality goods are more costly to produce but more valuable to the buyer. Now, artifactual and framed field experimental results replicate the laboratory experiments: evidence for social preferences in the form of positively correlated prices and qualities. However, in a natural field experiment where subjects were observed in the market but unaware of the observation, no strong statistical relationship between price and quality could be found. Finally, another study (Carpenter and Seki 2006) tried to replicate behavior in a public-goods experiment (see above) with different types of members of the fishing industry in one particular Japanese community. What has been found is that individuals who perceive more competition in the workplace contribute significantly less to the public good, conditional on their job type. Such a result could hardly emerge from a lab or artifactual field experiment.

The bridge metaphor is a powerful one, but field experiments are reliable tools for judging external validity only to the extent that the effect of factors that are varied between the different kinds of experiment on the outcome of interest behaves regularly and is reliably measurable in the experiments, and that the experimental results are free of artifacts to begin with. There might be, say, a quasi-linear and stable relationship between market experience and the WTA–WTP gap, or between perceived competitiveness and contributions to a public good, which can be used to predict hitherto unobserved factor–outcome combinations. But this will work only if these relationships are indeed stable and do not depend on the exact background of other factors. That typical economic factors are not that well behaved but rather vary with background has been argued above in the context of the causal tendency account. Moreover, the closer one gets to an actual field setting, the more likely it is that the experimental result is invalidated by confounders that affect treatment and control group differently, simply because confounders cannot be controlled to the same extent as in laboratory experiments.

Conclusions

This chapter has looked at the role experiments may play in establishing phenomena, testing economic theories and giving policy advice. Experiments are a powerful tool of scientific investigation because they allow the control of background factors in a way that makes causal inferences very reliable. But the reliability comes at the cost of increased unrealisticness with respect to the situations economists are ultimately interested in: "natural" market or policy situations. The problem of drawing inferences from the lab to the situation of ultimate interest is now recognized by economists and philosophers of science, who have developed a number of solutions in response. Each of these solutions "works," but only under conditions that tend to be restrictive. Experiments thus constitute a valuable addition to the economist's methodological toolbox, but certainly not a panacea for all problems surrounding reliable causal inference.

Study Questions

1 The chapter discusses three roles experiments play in economics. Can you think of other functions?
2 It is sometimes suggested that there is a trade-off between internal and external validity of an experiment. What is behind this claim? Do you agree?
3 Are there *always* alternative explanations of phenomena, as Duhem's problem suggests?
4 The chapter looks at four ways to deal with the problem of external validity. Which approach do you think is most promising? Defend your answer.
5 Does the existence of experimental economics turn economics into an "experimental science"?

Suggested Readings

Guala 2005 is the canonical source for philosophical work on experimental economics. Look at Santos 2010 for a social epistemology perspective. Reiss 2008a: ch. 5 takes a critical look at the FCC auction case and economic experimentation in general. A very comprehensive bibliography of "the philosophy of experimental economics" can be found on Francesco Guala's website: http://users.unimi.it/guala/MEE_Bibliography.htm.

All these discussions of experimental economics follow in one way or another the so-called experimental philosophy of science, a movement within philosophy of science away from the exclusive focus on theory that characterized earlier philosophy of science and towards greater emphasis on scientific practice. "Classics" in experimentalist philosophy of science are Hacking 1983, Franklin 1986, Galison 1987 and the essays in Gooding *et al.* 1989.

For detailed surveys of work in experimental economics, see Kagel and Roth 1997. A more recent book on experimental methodology, written by economists, is Bardsley *et al.* 2010. The FCC auctions have also been discussed by Alexandrova 2006, Alexandrova and Northcott 2009, Callon and Muniesa 2007, Guala 2001, Nik-Khah 2005, 2006 and Mirowski and Nik-Khah 2007.

For an elementary introduction to significance tests from a philosopher's perspective, see Hacking 1999: ch. 18. For a critical discussion of the school of statistics on which significance tests are built, see Royall 1997: chs 2–3.

11 Evidence-Based Policy

- Overview
- What Is Evidence-Based Policy?
- What Is an RCT, and What Are Its Virtues?
- What, Then, Is Wrong with Evidence-Based Policy?
- Conclusions
- Study Questions
- Suggested Readings

Overview

Evidence-based policy is currently a highly influential movement. Though it originated in the field of medicine, in the UK, the USA and other (mostly Anglo-Saxon) countries, there is an increasing drive to use evidence to inform, develop and refine policy and practice. This push to improve how research and analysis informs policy and practice is increasingly being felt in a wide range of areas: in addition to evidence-based health and social care, we now hear of evidence-based housing policy, transport policy, education and criminal justice.

An example of an evidence-based approach to policy-making is the UK Sure Start program. Initiated in 2001, the aim of the program is to break the cycle of poverty by providing children and families with childcare, health and educational support. The Sure Start program has been evidence-based from the start, using extensive reviews of research findings on what approaches and early interventions are most likely to work; its execution and continuing evaluation and refinement have also been evidence-based. Another notable example in the UK is the National Institute for Health and Clinical Excellence (NICE), which provides regulatory guidelines for the National Health Service (NHS) on particular treatments. These guidelines are based on reviews on the effectiveness and cost-effectiveness of various treatments.

In the USA, the Department of Education (USDE) is actively committed to furthering evidence-based approaches to education policy and practice. The Department's Institute of Education Sciences established the "What Works Clearinghouse" in 2002 "to provide educators, policymakers, researchers, and the public with a central and trusted source of scientific evidence of what works in education" (Department of Education 2005). Furthermore, the Department in 2005 implemented a recommendation by the Coalition for Evidence-Based Policy (CEBP) that projects that include a randomized evaluation should have priority in its grant process.

Its most prominent implementation was in connection with the US *No Child Left Behind* policy. The CEBP describes it as follows:

> The recent enactment of *No Child Left Behind*, and its central principle that federal funds should support educational activities backed by "scientifically-based research," offers an opportunity to bring rapid, evidence-driven progress—for the first time—to U.S. elementary and secondary education. Education is a field in which a vast number of interventions, such as ability grouping and grade retention, have gone in or out of fashion over time with little regard to rigorous evidence. As a result, over the past 30 years the United States has made almost no progress in raising the achievement of elementary and secondary school students, according to the National Assessment of Educational Progress, despite a 90 percent increase in real public spending per student. Our nation's extraordinary inability to raise educational achievement stands in stark contrast to our remarkable progress in improving human health over the same time period—progress which, as discussed in this report, is largely the result of evidence-based government policies in the field of medicine.
> (CEBP 2002: iii)

Social policy is not the only area in which a move towards more "scientifically based research" has taken place in recent years. The other main field is development economics. In this field proponents of evidence-based approaches promise a "radical rethinking of the way to fight global poverty" (the subtitle of Banerjee and Duflo's 2011 book *Poor Economics*) and a cutting-edge approach to "Making Aid Work" (the title of Banerjee's 2007 book).

There is no doubt that a new thinking concerning social and development aid policy is needed. Our knowledge of "what works" in both areas is lamentable. With respect to development, Angus Deaton expresses the situation as follows (Deaton 2010a: 425): "I shall have very little to say about what actually works and what does not—but [since?] it is clear from the literature that we do not know."

Moreover, it never seems a bad idea to urge that our policies should be "evidence-based." Imagine someone tells you that there is a new movement in social science whose proponents call for a more "faith-based approach" to social policy or a more "story-telling-based foreign aid policy." Advocates of evidence-based policy have the rhetorical advantage on their side.

Looking behind the rhetoric of new beginnings and revolutions in the making, we see that these movements do not merely demand that policies be based on evidence, but rather on a very specific kind of evidence: randomized controlled trials (RCTs). The debate whether randomization is necessary, or, more generally speaking, useful, is in fact quite old, going back to at least the 1980s (e.g., Urbach 1985). Then as now proponents and opponents of RCTs have fought about the virtues and vices of randomization.

In this chapter I will first introduce the evidence-based policy movement and show how it arose out of medicine, then describe what an RCT is and why we might think that it is a highly reliable tool of causal inference and finally list the drawbacks critics have pointed out. I will finish with a dilemma regarding the role of theory in establishing policy claims.

What Is Evidence-Based Policy?

The evidence-based policy movement can be understood as a reaction to what was perceived as over-reliance on expertise and related sources of knowledge such as folklore and tradition. These unreliable guides to practice, in the eyes of proponents of the movement, should be replaced by rigorously established scientific evidence, and many regard the randomized controlled trial (RCT) as the "gold standard" of evidence. The movement became prominent first in medicine where practitioners announced the beginning of a "new paradigm" in the early 1990s. One of the first formulations is the following by the Evidence-Based Medicine Working Group:

> Evidence-based medicine de-emphasizes intuition, unsystematic clinical experience, and pathophysiological rationale as sufficient grounds for clinical decision making and stresses the examination of evidence from clinical research.
>
> (Guyatt *et al.* 1992: 2420)

The canonical statement stems from a widely cited article by Sackett *et al.*:

> Evidence based medicine is the conscientious, explicit and judicious use of current best evidence in making decisions about the care of the individual patient. It means integrating individual clinical expertise with the best available external clinical evidence from systematic research.
>
> (Sackett *et al.* 1996: 71)

Evidence-based medicine is thought to have revolutionized medical research by downplaying what are regarded as "soft" kinds of evidence such as intuition, clinical experience and knowledge about the biological mechanisms, and emphasizing what is regarded as "hard" evidence, namely, systematic clinical research.

Proponents of evidence-based approaches in economics and other social science often appeal to this (alleged) success story of medicine when they defend the special role RCTs should play. One of the major figures in the movement, MIT economist Esther Duflo, for instance, says the following: "Creating a culture in which rigorous randomized evaluations are promoted, encouraged, and financed has the potential to revolutionize social policy during the 21st century, just as randomized trials revolutionized medicine during the 20th" (Duflo *et al.* 2004: 28).

Evidence-based approaches are now gaining popularity in social and public policy in the United States and many other, mostly Anglo-Saxon, countries as well as in the field of development economics. RCTs have been conducted to study questions as diverse as the effect of CCTV surveillance on crime, class size on academic achievement, cognitive-behavioral treatment on anti-social behavior, correctional boot camps on offending, whether deworming provides effective incentives to go to school and many more.

One of the definitions for the term "evidence" is "something that tends to prove, ground for belief" (e.g., *Webster's New World Dictionary*, 2nd College Edition, third entry under "evidence"). Strictly speaking, a policy can be called "evidence-based" whether it is grounded in intuition, experience, econometric models, theory, laboratory (animal, in vitro) experiments or randomized trials. The main difference between traditional approaches and the recent evidence-based approaches is an organization of kinds of evidence, or kinds of methods that produce evidence, into hierarchies.

Figure 11.1 shows an example of such a hierarchy of *levels of evidence* and the associated *recommendation grades*, which is taken from a clinical guideline of the UK National Institute for Clinical Excellence.

Only RCTs and systematic reviews thereof are in the highest evidence category. Observational studies appear as second-lowest category, expert judgment as lowest. Knowledge of the "pathophysiological rationale" by which, essentially, the biological mechanism is meant, does not even appear here. (Nor, in fact, does theory; but this particular "hierarchy of evidence" is meant to apply to biomedical research, and there aren't really any theories like economic theory in most areas of medicine. There is now a new development in medicine called "evolutionary medicine," and the theory of evolution *is* a theory, but I suspect it hasn't reached the proponents of evidence-based medicine yet.)

This is in stark contrast to traditional ways of thinking about assessing causal claims in medicine. Traditionally, Austin Bradford Hill's criteria played an important role (Hill 1965):

Recommendation grade	Evidence
A	Directly based on category I evidence
B	Directly based on • category II evidence, or • extrapolated recommendation from category I evidence
C	Directly based on • category III evidence, or • extrapolated recommendation from category I or II evidence
D	Directly based on • category IV evidence, or • extrapolated recommendation from category I, II or III evidence
Good practice point	The view of the Guideline Development Group
NICE 2002	Recommendation taken from the NICE technology appraisal

Evidence category	Source
Ia	Systematic review and meta-analysis of randomised controlled trials
Ib	At least one randomised controlled trial
IIa	At least one well-designed controlled study without randomisation
IIb	At least one other type of well-designed quasi-experimental study
III	Well-designed non-experimental descriptive studies, such as comparative studies, correlation studies or case studies
IV	Expert committee reports or opinions and/or clinical experience of respected authorities

Adapted from Eccles M, Mason J (2001) How to develop cost-conscious guidelines. Health Technology Assessment 5 (16).

Figure 11.1 Grading Scheme and Hierarchy of Evidence

Source: NICE 2003: 23.

- *Strength*: a small association does not mean that there is not a causal effect, though the larger the association, the more likely that it is causal.
- *Consistency*: consistent findings observed by different persons in different places with different samples strengthen the likelihood of an effect.
- *Specificity*: causation is likely if there is a very specific population at a specific site and disease with no other likely explanation. The more specific the association between a factor and an effect is, the bigger the probability of a causal relationship.
- *Temporality*: the effect has to occur after the cause (and if there is an expected delay between the cause and expected effect, then the effect must occur after that delay).
- *Biological gradient*: greater exposure should generally lead to greater incidence of the effect. However, in some cases, the mere presence of the factor can trigger the effect. In other cases, an inverse proportion is observed: greater exposure leads to lower incidence.
- *Plausibility*: a plausible mechanism between cause and effect is helpful.
- *Coherence*: coherence between epidemiological and laboratory findings increases the likelihood of an effect.
- *Experiment*: "Occasionally it is possible to appeal to experimental evidence."
- *Analogy*: the effect of similar factors may be considered.

Two things are worth noting about Hill's criteria for assessing causal claims. First, Hill himself did not think that any single one of these criteria was necessary to determine causality—or that the whole set or a subset was sufficient: "None of my nine viewpoints can bring indisputable evidence for or against the cause-and-effect hypothesis and none can be required as a *sine qua non*" (Hill 1965: 11; his emphasis). These are to be understood more like dimensions along which to assess the quality of a causal claim such as clarity, carat, color and cut are the dimensions along which to assess the quality of a diamond. Second, experimental evidence is mentioned as only one type of evidence among others, and explicitly as an "occasional possibility." I will come back to this later.

Evidence-based medicine differs significantly from Hill's view of evidence, which used to be dominant. While evidence-based medicine does not have an explicit concept of evidence, an account that tells us what evidence is, it has the understanding that different methods generate evidence of different quality and that RCTs produce—independent of context, hypothesis under test, purpose of the investigation and so on—evidence of higher quality than all other methods.

I have spent some time talking about evidence-based medicine because the evidence-based approaches in social science (and particularly, in economics) share this understanding of evidence and in fact try to build on the perceived successes in medicine. Let us now examine the central pillar of the "evidence base," the randomized trial.

What Is an RCT, and What Are Its Virtues?

In an RCT eligible subjects are divided into two groups using a random number generator. The aim of randomization is to create two groups that are "exchangeable" from a statistical point of view; that is, identical in all respects relevant for the assessment of the treatment effect (see R. Fisher 1935). One group is assigned a treatment while the other figures as control group (and either remains untreated, receives an alternative treatment or is given a placebo). In a double-blind trial neither the participating subjects nor the treatment administrators know which is the treatment and which the control group. There are also multiple-blind trials in which the statistician who analyzes the data and other researchers are also blinded.

RCTs aim to implement a probabilistic version of Mill's method of difference (see Chapter 9). Recall that that method compares two situations that are exactly identical except for some factor of interest and, perhaps, a further factor (which, in this case, is an outcome). In an RCT the factor of interest is the treatment—receiving the active drug, the bed net, the social policy or what have you. If the treatment makes a difference to an outcome of difference, the treatment is judged to be effective. In the biomedical and social sciences it is very unlikely that we will find two situations that are exactly alike with respect to all relevant factors. So what an RCT aims to create is a comparison of two situations such that the *probability distributions* over all factors that are causally relevant to the outcome are identical.

RCTs are regarded as the gold standard of evidence in the evidence-based movements in social science because they are, if implemented successfully, highly reliable sources of evidence for causal claims. If implemented successfully, they solve the problem of confounders, because any difference in outcome between treatment and control group is attributable to the treatment when all other causal factors are distributed equally between the two groups.

There is another reason why RCTs have been endorsed by many researchers in economics and other social sciences in recent years. Standard econometric methods require a great deal of background knowledge. This is true of standard regression analysis, which is invalid, for example, when there is reverse causation from dependent to independent variable or when factors that affect both dependent and independent variables are not modeled. This means in turn that a lot of causal background knowledge is needed. The same is true of instrumental variables (see the characterization in Chapter 9) and, most obviously, of structural (theory-driven) approaches to econometrics.

Econometricians often find one another's identification assumptions incredible. Here is a description of the situation in the growth-regression literature in development economics:

> The pessimism surrounding big pushes [for specific development aid policies] intensified as the credibility of the cross-country growth

literature declined, with its endless claims for some new "key to growth" (regularly found to be "significant") and probably well-deserved reputation for rampant data mining. As the Easterly comment on Banerjee notes [Easterly 2009], the number of variables claimed to be significant right-hand-side (RHS) determinants approached 145, which is probably an undercount. Having a long list of possible controls to play with, researchers found it easy enough to arrive at significant results, and using the abundant heuristic biases that make it possible to see patterns in randomness, convinced themselves that the significant results were from the "right" specification, and that the others (usually unreported) were from the "wrong" ones.

> (Cohen and Easterly 2009: 3; footnotes suppressed)

RCTs are in this respect easier to handle because they do not require "incredible" background assumptions. True, causal conclusions from RCTs are based on assumptions, too. But they are of a very general nature, for example, about the connection between probability and causation and that randomization has been successful (in balancing the probability of causal factors between treatment and control group). They do not require specific assumptions, say, about what other factors might be responsible for an outcome or whether there is reverse causation (as the treatment is allocated randomly, it can't be caused by the outcome). For these reasons, defenders of evidence-based approaches claim that RCT results are more credible, and more easily agreed upon by different researchers.

A third advantage that is claimed for RCTs, especially in medicine, is that they help in blinding both researchers who administer the treatment and experimental subjects (cf. Worrall 2002). Blinding is useful because it reduces the "experimenter's bias," which can be created, for example, when a treatment is given to patients a researcher expects to benefit more from it. Blinding the experimental subject helps to control the placebo effect.

What, Then, Is Wrong with Evidence-Based Policy?

Evidence-based approaches have come under severe attack by philosophers (Worrall 2002, 2007a), economists and other scientists, both in their original area, biomedical research (Vandenbroucke 2008), and in more recent evidence-based social policy (N. Cartwright and Munro 2010). The main thrust of the criticisms is that randomized trials should not be regarded as a gold standard because they in no way *guarantee* the validity of their causal conclusions and these conclusions are often hard to generalize or apply to situations that have not been experimentally tested. Policy conclusions, however, always have this characteristic: they concern novel situations that have not been investigated yet. If randomized trials fare badly at establishing these, and there are reasons to believe that other methods might do better, the criticism should indeed be taken seriously.

The first important qualification one must make when describing the epistemic power of RCTs is captured by the phrase I used above: "if implemented successfully." RCT results are certain only under highly stringent, and indeed unrealistic conditions. These conditions include that the set of all other factors that affect the outcome are distributed identically between the two groups and that correlations always have a causal explanation (see for instance N. Cartwright 2007a).

However, randomization in no way *guarantees* that treatment and control group are identical with respect to all confounders (see for instance Worrall 2002), and especially in social science applications, correlations may have a variety of non-causal sources (Reiss 2007b). Let us focus on the first point here.

Randomization ensures that treatment and control groups are balanced only in the limit. That is, the probability that the groups are balanced approximates one as the size of the groups goes to infinity. Of course, the groups in actual trials always have a finite size, and often, especially in the social sciences, they are quite small. This means in turn that in practice treatment and control groups may always be unbalanced. For example, it might be the case that researchers suspect that gender influences an outcome of interest and that despite randomization all women end up in the treatment group and all men in the control group. In such an obvious case, one might try to solve the problem by re-randomizing but this is only possible with respect to known factors, and randomization is thought to control for all confounders, known and unknown.

One consequence of this is that RCT data are usually analyzed using models that look quite like ordinary econometric models—and are therefore subject to the same criticisms. One researcher might believe that we should control for age, gender and socio-economic background, another that the relevant variables are health status, gender and education. The precise choice of covariates will influence the results. More importantly, however, this procedure invites data mining. Since, by and large, social science trials do not follow a standardized and pre-specified protocol, researchers can, as in standard regression models, use a set of covariates such that they get a significant result and ignore other specifications (Cohen and Easterly 2009; cf. Deaton 2010a):

> If the randomization is successful, the inclusion of covariates should not change the coefficient but only increase precision. In the presence of budget and administrative constraints, however, RE [randomized evaluations] samples are often small, which means that it is more difficult to achieve a balance across treatment groups, and covariates can change the estimated treatment effect. Data mining is most likely to occur in the search for a significant program impact among different subpopulations. After all the expense and time of a randomized trial … it is very hard to conclude "we found nothing."
>
> (Cohen and Easterly 2009: 14)

Second, unlike in medical trials, in the social sciences neither subjects nor experimenters can typically be blinded. You can't hide the fact that you're giving someone a bed net, for example. Moreover, social science trials typically require the collaboration of the experimental subjects. A bed net can be effective for preventing malaria only when it is used as such, not when it is used as a fishing net. Unlike in medicine, in most social science contexts, compliance cannot usually be forced, and often it is hard to monitor.

Third, randomized trials may actually introduce new confounders relative to observational studies. Risk-averse people might not like to be part of a lottery and therefore not participate, or they participate but undermine group allocation by getting the treatment elsewhere if they've been assigned to the control group or refuse to take it up when being assigned to the treatment group (cf. Heckman 1992). Both kinds of problems can be addressed by defining narrower treatment effects (the "effect of the treatment on the treated," etc.) but these tend to be even less useful for applications than the more general "average treatment effect," which I will introduce now.

Fourth, the questions that can be addressed with RCTs are very narrow in a variety of ways. At best (that is, even when the groups are balanced, etc.), an RCT is able to successfully identify an "average treatment effect" (ATE), which measures the mean difference of outcomes between treatment and control group. However, by and large, the ATE is not the quantity researchers are interested in. In the medical case, physicians do not want to know whether a new drug works "on average," "for the population at large" but rather whether it works for an individual patient, John Doe. Similarly, when investigating whether handing out bed nets for free or selling them at a small price is more effective in preventing malaria by using different policies in different, randomly allocated, villages, researchers want to know what policy is better for a specific village where they think about implementing this or that policy, not what policy is better "on average."

Another problem is that the ATE may mask the fact that a treatment is highly effective for some subpopulations but not at all effective or outright harmful for others. Especially in these cases it is necessary to know what background factors matter when applying the treatment to an individual.

Another way in which RCT evidence is "narrow" is that RCTs can be used only to address efficacy questions: questions about "what works" (N. Cartwright 2009a). Especially in the social sciences we often want to know many other things besides efficacy: cost–benefit ratios, side effects, what other effects implementing a policy has and how to deal with moral, cultural and political issues.

Fifth, external validity (see Chapter 10) is a big problem for RCTs and potentially bigger than for other methods. There is no guarantee that RCT results generalize to other settings. Even in the ideal case, when randomization is successful and the test population (the population that takes part in the RCT) is a representative sample of the underlying population, it is possible that the causal effect of interest differs between populations. Providing bed nets free of charge may be the best policy in Uganda but selling them at a nominal fee more effective in India.

In general, every study is subject to external validity issues, observational and experimental, and among the experimental studies randomized or not randomized. If one measures the causal effect of growth in money supply on inflation or changes in nominal income using US data between 1960 and 1990, the result might not hold for the USA of the 2000s or for the Netherlands in the same period. External validity is a problem for everyone, and it would be a mistake to criticize RCTs for that reason.

But there are some peculiarities that make the external validity problem more pressing for RCTs than for other methods. As explained above, RCTs, when implemented successfully, give us knowledge "cheaply" in the sense that they require no specific background knowledge in order to identify a causal effect from the data. But this does come at an eventual cost: if the understanding of the causal structure that is being experimented on in the RCT is very limited, there are no good grounds for believing that a result will also hold in this or that population that differs from the test population.

In a sense an RCT is a "black-box" method of causal inference. A treatment is administered, an outcome observed, with no need for any understanding of what is going on in between and *why* a treatment produces its outcome. But if there is no knowledge of why a treatment produces a given outcome, the basis for drawing inferences beyond the immediate test population is very narrow.

This is different, for example, with respect to alternative methods such as structural or other theory-driven forms of econometrics. Consider the example discussed in Chapter 9 regarding Maimonides' rule as an instrument for class size. The paper by Miguel Urquiola and Eric Verhoogen criticized the choice of Maimonides' rule as an instrument on the basis of a detailed model about how parents choose schools for their kids and schools make decisions about the quality of education they offer (Urquiola and Verhoogen 2009). Such a model, if correct, gives us a lot of information about why a causal relation holds when it does. Having this information then allows us to make reasonable guesses about where else outside the experimental study it might hold.

Another problem related to that of external validity is the possible existence of so-called "general equilibrium effects" (Morgan and Winship 2007). General equilibrium effects obtain when an intervention changes the causal structure of a population not because of the intervention as such but rather because the intervention is extended from a small sample to the population at large. For instance, a new schooling program that aims to improve test scores by reducing class size might work for a small sample of schools that receive the experimental treatment. When extended to all schools, however, it ceases to work because there aren't enough well-qualified teachers to take charge of all the new classes. The program works "holding fixed" other determinants of educational achievement such as the quality of teachers but not when the program itself has an influence on the other determinants.

The problem of external validity has received a great deal of attention in recent philosophy of science, and now there exist a variety of approaches to confront it (see Chapter 10). But none of these has the logical stringency of the ideal RCT. Therefore, the certainty associated with testing a policy proposition using RCTs is at least to some extent illusory.

Conclusions

Although this last section has adopted a critical tone toward RCTs, I do not maintain here that randomization is always a bad idea or that there is no virtue in evidence-based policy. Quite to the contrary. Evidence-based movements have brought to the fore a number of methodological issues that are important for practice—for using evidence to learn about causal relationships—and that had been neglected in the literature. The problem of external validity is one among several examples of an obstacle to learning about policy from experience, and it is quite an embarrassment that philosophers of science and other professional methodologists only recently discovered it. Francesco Guala aptly refers to it as a "minor scandal in the philosophy of science" (Guala 2010: 1070).

I want to end with a dilemma and call for future research. The dilemma is the following. We can either let theory guide us in our attempts to estimate causal relationships from data (and other causal inferences such as generalizing a known causal relationship to a new setting) or we don't let theory guide us. If we let theory guide us, our causal inferences will be "incredible" because our theoretical knowledge is itself not certain. It is often easy to build a number of theoretical models with conflicting conclusions, and quite generally theoreticians do not really trust one another's assumptions. If we do not let theory guide us, we have no good reasons to believe that our causal conclusions are true either of the experimental population or of other populations because we have no understanding of the mechanisms that are responsible for a causal relationship to hold in the first place, and it is difficult to see how we could generalize an experimental result to other settings if this understanding doesn't exist.

Either way, then, causal inference seems to be a cul-de-sac. More methodological research is needed on the question how precisely to integrate theoretical knowledge with empirical studies for successful policy applications, of what nature the theoretical knowledge should be and what to do about the problem that theoretical conclusions are often sensitive to changes in the assumptions made but different sets of such assumptions are equally plausible. This pretty much mirrors Angus Deaton's conclusion on the matter:

> It is certainly not always obvious how to combine theory with experiments. Indeed, much of the interest in RCTs—and in instrumental

variables and other econometric techniques that mimic random allocation—comes from a deep skepticism of economic theory, and impa-
tience with its ability to deliver structures that seem at all helpful in
interpreting reality. Applied and theoretical economists seem to be
further apart now than at any period in the last quarter century. Yet
failure to reintegrate is hardly an option because without it there is no
chance of long-term scientific progress or of maintaining and extending
the results of experimentation. RCTs that are not theoretically guided
are unlikely to have more than local validity, a warning that applies
equally to nonexperimental work.

(Deaton 2010a: 450)

My only qualification would be that RCTs that are not theoretically guided
are unlikely to have even local validity.

Study Questions

1   The chapter criticized the evidence-based movements for regarding
     RCTs as the only source of reliable evidence. What other reliable
     sources are there? Can you order different sources in terms of their
     reliability?
2   What do all kinds of evidence have in common? Is there a prop-
     erty in virtue of which a body of data becomes evidence?
3   Phrase the debate concerning RCTs in terms of Mill's practical
     men and theorists, whom we first met in Chapter 9.
4   Identify an area in economics where RCTs are most likely to be
     very useful.
5   Apply the four theories of external validity you know from
     Chapter 10 to RCTs. Which account is most promising?

Suggested Readings

Prominent defenders of the use of RCTs in development aid are Abhijit
Banerjee and Esther Duflo; see for instance their book Banerjee and Duflo
2011 or Banerjee 2007. The issue is critically discussed in Cohen and
Easterly 2009. The introduction to that book is very informative, and there
is a chapter by Banerjee with comments.

To a great extent the debate concerning RCTs overlaps with that about
instruments discussed in Chapter 8—because randomization is in fact an
instrumental variable (Heckman 1996b). Therefore many of the papers
mentioned in the readings to that chapter continue to be relevant. I'd especially look at the papers by Angus Deaton again (Deaton 2010a, b).

Philosophers of science have practically ignored evidence-based social policy so far. A notable exception is Nancy Cartwright, whose "evidence page" is a useful source of published and unpublished papers on the topic: https://www.dur.ac.uk/philosophy/nancycartwright/ncpapersonevidence/

By contrast, evidence-based *medicine* (EBM) has received much attention from philosophers of science. Insofar as the lessons carry over, which I think is true to a large extent, the literature on EBM is relevant. A thorough discussion of the advantages and pitfalls of randomization is Worrall 2002; see also Worrall 2007a, b. On hierarchies of evidence, see Borgerson 2009, in particular.

Part III

Ethics

12 Welfare and Well-Being

Overview

This chapter will introduce welfare economics, look at its normative foundation and discuss alternative proposals for one of its core ideas: its conception of well-being. (This is a philosophers' term. Economists usually refer to the same thing as "welfare." "Welfare," however, also means "social support," so I will use the philosophers' term in what follows.) Theories of well-being are highly controversial. That this should be so is not hard to see. Well-being measures, roughly speaking, how well a life is going for the person leading it. That different people, coming from different social and cultural backgrounds, should have different ideas of what that means is not surprising. Nor is it surprising that philosophers, who value abstract and universal theories, do not easily find a fully adequate theory.

And yet, we cannot avoid theorizing about well-being. Normative economics cannot do without the concept, nor can moral and political philosophy. Below I will sketch an understanding of the various theories of well-being on offer that minimizes the substantial commitments the normative economist has to make. But minimal is not none, and to get there we have to get an idea of what is at stake in the debate about well-being.

Welfare Economics

Welfare economics uses microeconomic techniques to evaluate the consequences of economic institutions for individuals' well-being. What most former students of economics will remember from welfare economics is that its crowning achievement is the proving of two "fundamental theorems." The "First Fundamental Theorem of Welfare Economics" states that any Walrasian equilibrium is Pareto-efficient. The "Second Theorem" states that any Pareto-efficient allocation can be realized as a Walrasian equilibrium as long as transfers of initial endowments are possible. Walrasian equilibrium and Pareto-efficiency are the key terms here. They are defined as follows (cf. Varian 1992: ch. 17; Mas-Colell *et al.* 1995: ch. 10): a Walrasian equilibrium is an allocation of goods and a vector of prices at which all consumers maximize utility (firms maximize profits) and all markets clear—that is, that there is no excess supply or excess demand. A Pareto improvement is a change from a given allocation to a new one such that the new allocation is preferred by at least one agent and no one prefers the old allocation. An allocation is Pareto-efficient if there are no possible Pareto improvements.

One important condition for the theorem to hold is that preferences are locally non-satiated. That is, for any consumer and any bundle of goods, there is always another bundle of goods arbitrarily close to the first, which is preferred by the consumer. This assumption is similar to the assumption of monotonic preferences—preferences are monotonic if more of a good is always preferred—but weaker and therefore better.

Put this way, the first fundamental theorem is trivial. If people choose the consumption bundles they prefer most given their budget constraints (they are utility maximizers), if there is always some bundle of commodities in the economy they would prefer (they are locally non-satiable) and all goods have been allocated already (markets clear), then it must indeed be the case that one cannot reallocate the goods in a way that there is not at least one consumer who would prefer the current allocation (the current allocation is Pareto-efficient).

The theorem gets some bite, and with that, notoriety, only when two amendments are made. First, Pareto-efficiency is equated with some kind of "optimality." Specifically, it is assumed that a Pareto improvement is a (morally and politically) good thing. Daniel Hausman and Michael McPherson call this assumption the "Pareto principle" (Hausman and McPherson 2006: 136, 218). Value judgments have thereby entered the argument: preference satisfaction is identified with well-being, and to increase people's well-being is judged a morally and politically good thing. Second, it is shown that under some—this time, far more restrictive—conditions, free markets lead to an equilibrium allocation of goods. The conditions under which a free market leads to an equilibrium allocation include price-taking behavior by everyone (which has some plausibility when there are many firms and many consumers), perfect information and that there are markets for all goods. Both amendments are highly controversial. Figure 12.1 summarizes the structure of the argument.

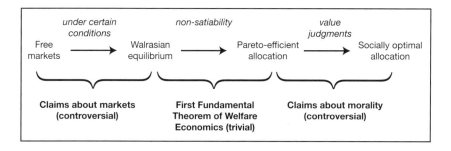

Figure 12.1 Arguing from Free Markets to Social Benefit

The first fundamental theorem of welfare economics is often alleged to be a version of Adam Smith's "invisible-hand" argument. In *The Wealth of Nations*, Smith (1904 [1776]: book IV, ch. 2) wrote: "Every individual necessarily labours to render the annual revenue of the society as great as he can. He generally, indeed, neither intends to promote the public interest, nor knows how much he is promoting it … He intends only his own gain, and he is in this, as in many other cases, led by an invisible hand to promote an end which was no part of his intention." That end, of course, was some sort of socially (rather than merely individually) desirable outcome.

Another way to put Smith's claim is that *if* people pursue their self-interest, then free markets will lead to a socially desirable outcome. Let us call this claim the "invisible-hand hypothesis." We see here that the invisible-hand hypothesis contains the fundamental theorem only as a small part. The more interesting and controversial elements are claims about how free markets operate and how to evaluate market outcomes. This chapter is concerned with whether to satisfy someone's preferences means to make him or her better off, that is, whether it promotes the individual's well-being. Markets will be examined in more detail in Chapter 13. Whether the promotion of well-being is the *only* moral and political good will be the subject of Chapter 14. Finally, to what extent people really pursue what is in their self-interest will be discussed in Chapter 15.

Well-Being

General Remarks

The invisible-hand hypothesis assumes that the satisfaction of an individual's preferences makes the individual better off. To make someone better off means to enhance her *well-being*. In ordinary language, when we talk about a person's well-being we talk about her health, her happiness or her "milk and honey." These are related to the philosopher's concept, but the philosopher's concept is technical and abstract. According to the latter, a person's well-being is that which is *ultimately good for her* (see for instance Crisp 2008). All three aspects: "ultimately," "good" and "for her" are essential to that concept.

"That which is *ultimately* good for her" expresses that theories of well-being focus on what is intrinsically, not what is instrumentally good for a person. A "wealth theory of well-being" would be a contradiction in terms because wealth is always at best instrumentally good. A person's wealth enables him to purchase and consume more goods and services, to be more autonomous, to have a greater influence on the world around him, to live a healthier life and, perhaps, to be happier. But it is these latter things we care about, not wealth as such.

What is true of wealth is in fact true of most things economists talk about. If wealth enables us to buy goods and services, many of these goods and services are themselves not intrinsically but rather instrumentally valuable. We do not buy and consume an apple for the apple's sake but because it nourishes us and makes us happy and satisfied. As there is no wealth theory of well-being, there is no apple theory of well-being. Well-being is something we *ultimately* care about.

Another aspect of this dimension of the concept of well-being is that it is evaluated over a person's entire lifetime, not as a momentary glimpse. Eating lots of *foie gras* may be good for me for every point in time but not for my life as a whole because it will eventually make me sick. We will see later that various paradoxes and counterexamples to theories of well-being hinge on this aspect. But that this should be so is clear from the role well-being plays in various ethical theories. If the rightness or wrongness of actions depends on its consequences on people's well-being (utilitarians think that *only* the consequences on well-being matter for moral evaluation) and the consequences unfold over time, it is certainly important to look at all the consequences of an action, and not only those pertaining to a single point in time. Similarly, if the rightness or wrongness of a socio-economic policy is evaluated with respect to its effects on people's well-being, the evaluation should not be myopic.

"That which is ultimately *good* for her" expresses that well-being is an evaluative term. There is no descriptive theory of well-being. We cannot talk about well-being without making value judgments. We will see below that economists subscribe to a formal as opposed to substantive theory of well-being. That is, they tell us how to go about finding out what is good for people, but not what this good ultimately is (Hausman and McPherson 2006: 119). Economists are inclined to believe that only individuals know what is best for them. Therefore, economists should not have substantive views about the conception of the good. But this is of course to make a moral judgment and to subscribe to a particular theory of well-being: namely, well-being is what people desire. One can have an alternative theory of well-being—for instance, that health is good for people independently of whether they desire it or not—but one cannot have a theory of well-being and abstain from value judgments.

"That which is ultimately good *for her*" expresses that well-being concerns an individual's *personal* good and not what is good for others or animals or nature or deity. Most of us care deeply about other people's well-being. We care about our children and future generations, about relatives and spouses, countrymen and supporters of our values, about the human race, about animals, nature, God and abstract ideas. But these considerations count towards our well-being only insofar as they affect us, for instance, through the joy experienced by seeing one's children doing well.

So much for the general conceptual remarks. Substantially, there are three families of theories of well-being. The first is the one we have already encountered. It is endorsed by many economists and by a number of contemporary philosophers; the second, by contemporary psychologists (as well as some dead philosophers and living economists); the third, by other contemporary philosophers. There is no satisfactory theory, and this area of philosophy is a highly disputed one where agreement is largely lacking. The problem for a philosopher of economics is that one cannot just leave the formation of a conception of well-being to the individual because well-being matters for moral evaluation and political decision-making. As we will see in Chapter 14, there is a view in moral philosophy which holds that well-being is all that matters morally (and politically): welfarism. This is probably an extreme view, but to hold the opposite view—that well-being does not matter at all—is probably just as extreme. So we should know what theories there are, what makes them plausible and what their drawbacks are.

Well-Being and the Satisfaction of Preferences

In Part I we saw that rational-choice theories play a double role in economics: a descriptive role in explaining and predicting choices and a prescriptive role in vindicating certain choices as rational. In welfare economics and moral philosophy, these theories play a third role: they give an account of a person's well-being. The preference-satisfaction theory of well-being simply identifies well-being with the satisfaction of preferences. There are several versions of this theory. Here I will consider an actual preference and a laundered preference view of well-being.

Actual Preferences

If we take, as many economists do, the satisfaction of actual preferences as constitutive of well-being, we can cash in on a virtue of this theory: well-being in this sense is measurable relatively unproblematically. If people choose what they prefer and they prefer what is better for them, then well-being can be measured by observing people's choices. But as we saw in Chapter 4 and will discuss at greater length in Chapter 15, people do not always choose what they prefer. Let us focus here on whether what people prefer is good for them.

It is quite clear that people sometimes make bad choices. Two-thirds of Americans aged 20 years and older are overweight or obese. Many of these cases would be preventable by a healthier diet and more exercise. Obesity is associated with many of the leading causes of death in the USA, including heart disease, several kinds of cancer, stroke and diabetes. About 12 million French people, a fifth of the population, are smokers, and more than 70,000 people die in France every year from smoking-related illnesses (Sciolino 2008). Many of these deaths may be premature in the sense that had people known better, thought things through more thoroughly or exerted more willpower, they would have chosen differently.

Bad choices are made for at least three reasons. First, people are misinformed about the objects of their preferences. In the afternoon, I prefer black coffee with no sugar when it's quite good coffee, white coffee with no sugar when it's so-so, and white coffee with sugar when it's really bad coffee. There have been occasions where I mistakenly assumed coffee was good and (literally) bitterly regretted my choice once I had tried it. I may have had perfectly "rational" preferences (in the sense of being able to rank available options in a way which tracks my well-being, and I chose the highest-ranking option) but I was ill-informed and thus chose badly on these occasions. Second, I may have a perfectly well-informed preference but for whatever reason fail to act on it. One source of such a failure to act on one's preferences is weakness of will, called *akrasia* by the Greeks. Third, I might prefer states of affairs that do not affect my well-being or that make me worse rather than better off. If I was a bodyguard and threw myself in the line of fire to protect my client, I may do so entirely deliberately and fully informedly but without promoting *my* well-being.

If people do not always choose in ways that are good for them, there must be more to well-being than actual preferences. It is important to see that it is not even necessary to have evidence that actual people sometimes make bad choices. For the actual-preference theory of well-being precludes the conceptual possibility of people preferring what is not good for them. But that is quite implausible. Some philosophers have therefore proposed that preferences undergo a process of cleansing before they are counted as advancing well-being. Ill-informed and inconsistent preferences are meant to be ruled out in this way. The result is called an "informed," "rational" or "laundered" preference ordering (e.g., Arneson 1990; Gauthier 1986: ch. 2; Goodin 1986; Griffin 1986).

Laundered Preferences

To conceive of well-being as the satisfaction of laundered preferences of course eliminates a major advantage of the actual-preference theory: the relatively straightforward measurability of the concept. We can observe only how people actually choose, not how they would choose if they were fully informed, rational and possessed infinite amounts of strength of will. At the same time this move away from an operationalizable concept brings with it increased plausibility. That people sometimes make bad choices is allowed by the theory, for instance because they do not know everything that is relevant for making welfare-enhancing choices.

There remain three problems, however. One has to do with the fact that (fully informed and rational) people do not always prefer what is good *for them*; another, with the fact that they do not choose what is *ultimately* good for them; and a third, with doubts that even fully informed people choose what is *good* for them.

Most people have other-regarding preferences alongside their self-regarding preferences, even when fully informed and upon reflection. We have preferences concerning our families, neighbors and society at large, about our elders and generations to come. People's decisions to donate money to earthquake victims do not directly benefit them. Leonard Sumner (1996: 132ff.) pointed out that the identification of well-being with the satisfaction of (laundered) other-regarding preferences involves a conundrum that is similar to one discussed above: self-sacrifice is conceptually impossible. On November 21, 2011, Jenni Lake, a teenager from Idaho, died of cancer just days before her eighteenth birthday. She had stopped chemotherapy and radiation treatments to avoid terminating her pregnancy, and gave birth to a healthy baby 12 days before she died (ABC News 2011). Whatever is true of this particular case, it would be odd if we could not describe the teenager's decision to forgo treatment as one of self-sacrifice for her child. But on the (laundered) preference-satisfaction view, the satisfaction of her preference of no treatment/premature death/delivery of a healthy child over treatment/ deferred death/no child would necessarily constitute an enhancement of *her* life, which is implausible.

Preference *changes* also induce problems. Someone may make a clear-headed decision to take a highly addictive drug for the first time but thereby practically enslave his future selves. That the satisfaction of these preferences should be well-being promoting is at least dubious (cf. Crisp 2008). The problem manifests itself particularly when decisions have externalities (as in the drug-addiction case or when preferences are sadistic).

That conflicts can arise when earlier selves try to commit later selves is easy to see. Carolus Van Cleef, hero of Kyril Bonfiglioli's novel *All the Tea in China*, had a bad hangover after an overdose of opium. Once he felt better he told his servant-boy, "You":

> Do you see these two sixpences? Now, hold, one of them is for you, to spend on nourishing food. The other you are to hide, "You," and the next time I bid you go out and buy me opium, either tincture or the lump, you are to take that sixpence into the street and hire a hulking carter, drayman or vegetable porter from the market and bid him come in here and beat me about the head until I fall unconscious. This will be both cheaper and better for my health. Is that clear?
>
> (Bonfiglioli 2008: 57)

Suppose after a passage of time our hero indeed sends "You" out to buy opium for him. Which preference should he satisfy, the current or the earlier?

In the present case we are inclined to give the earlier preference priority. But many commitments we make may later sound foolish to us. Suppose a friend of yours, at age 50, paid a hired gun to kill her or him in 10 years (after careful deliberation and being informed comprehensively about all the options, of course). If your friend, upon turning 60, truly desires to live for another 10 years, it is not at all clear that the satisfaction of the earlier preference would have made her or him better off.

When the reason for evaluating people's well-being is economic policy, the problem of changing preferences and, more specifically, endogenous preferences becomes particularly acute. Policies often influence people's preferences. Though probably no amount of confrontation with pictures of the cancerous lungs of hapless smokers will suffice to make everyone stop smoking, one of the aims of this campaign is to change smokers' preferences. But if social policy aims to promote people's well-being and that consists of satisfying their post-policy preferences, many successful policies will justify themselves because they will make it true that people prefer the state of affairs the policies bring about (such as being a non-smoker). Consequences of a policy will often unfold over time. If they do, and people's preferences change over the course of their unfolding, we have three sets of preferences to choose from: the initial pre-policy preferences, the intermediate preferences and the long-run preferences.

Finally, there are some doubts that people prefer what is good for them. One potential counterexample comes from John Rawls. He considers someone whose only (perfectly informed and thought-through) desire is "to count blades of grass in various geometrically shaped areas such as park squares and well-trimmed lawns" (Rawls 1971: 432). One might want to argue that the grass-counter's life could be improved by frustrating her preference and forcing her to pursue the greater things in life such as playing the piano, becoming an art collector and a connoisseuse of fine dining and old wine. But is it clear that frustrating a person's preferences can be a good thing for the person?

In an episode of the TV series *Frasier* the radio psychologist faces just this dilemma. One day he notices that a tape from his precious collection of recordings of his past shows is missing. He asks on air whether one of his listeners recorded the missing show, and, lo and behold, someone calls in. Visiting the caller to pick up the tape, Frasier finds out that his fan, Tom, is completely obsessed with him. Not only has Tom listened to every show from day one, he records all shows to listen to them a second time, he transcribes the shows, and he boarded up the sole window of his apartment just so he could hang up more autographed pictures of the radio personality. After hearing that Tom quit his job in order to be able to fully devote himself to his passion, and following an exchange in which Frasier explains that the purpose of his show is to help people live better lives, to which Tom rebuts that he is fulfilled as it is, Frasier says: "Tom, what I'm getting at here is I think that there could be more to your life than just my tapes and pictures. Now, if you'd be interested in exploring those issues further, I can recommend someone who'd be glad to talk with you." Tom replies: "Why? I have you!"

Some of us might find it difficult to tell Tom and Rawls' grass-counter that their lives are going badly for them. Many people devote much of their lives to a cause. When they are a Mother Teresa or cancer researcher, we admire them; Tom and the grass-counter, on the other hand, are supposedly lacking something. Some of us might think such an attitude patronizing.

A more convincing objection is that it seems implausible that the satis-faction of preferences about which the owner of the preference does not know and that does not affect him in any way should constitute a well-being enhancement for that person. We have many preferences of that kind. Most people will prefer that the global mean surface temperature in 2100 will be the same as today's to it being five degrees higher—but few people who have the preference will see that day. Some of us prefer God to exist and others that racism be false. Somewhat more concretely, we may wish that a stranger recover from an illness but lose touch and never find out if he did (Parfit 1984: 494). According to the preference-satisfaction view a low temperature in 2100, an existing God, the falsity of racism and the stranger's recovery are all things that make our life go better, but it is hard to see how this should be so if we do not or cannot learn about the satisfaction of our preference.

Preference Satisfaction, Morality and Policy

Thus far I have considered the preference-satisfaction theory mostly inde-pendently of context. When we examine the theory in the contexts of moral evaluation and social policy, additional difficulties arise. Sadistic and other anti-social or perverse preferences pose problems in these contexts. Let us call any preference whose satisfaction harms other individuals "malevolent." Suppose Rawls' grass-counter by and by becomes bored with his grass-counting and develops a taste for cutting wings off butterflies. One might say that satisfying this preference promotes his well-being. But actions that promote well-being in this sense are hardly praiseworthy from a moral point of view. Nor does it seem that policies should be evaluated on the basis of their effects on well-being in this sense. We will discuss welfarism, the moral theory which holds that well-being is the only source of justification for moral claims, in Chapter 14. But it is clear that welfarism is a non-starter if well-being is understood as preference satisfaction, and preferences may be malevolent. Thus, to the extent that the concept of well-being is to be used for moral and political evaluation, the existence of such preferences counts against the view of well-being as preference satisfaction. The process of laun-dering preferences may get rid of some malevolent preferences but it would be utopian to assume no one would hold malevolent preferences after being informed about the consequences and thinking hard.

The so-called problem of expensive tastes (e.g., Keller 2002) is similar. Someone who is "desperate without pre-phylloxera clarets and plovers' eggs" requires many more resources than someone who is "satisfied with water and soy flour" (Arrow 1973: 254). There is surely nothing intrinsically bad about having or cultivating expensive tastes. But if social policies are to be evaluated in terms of their consequences on well-being, it would seem unfair to regard all preferences on an equal footing, especially when people are to some extent responsible for their tastes. To the extent, then, that policy evaluation uses exclusively information about well-being, a different concept is needed.

These difficulties for a preference-satisfaction theory of well-being—changing, endogenous and other-regarding preferences, and states of affairs we wish obtained but whose obtaining does not affect us, malevolent and expensive preferences—are often regarded as quite damaging (see for instance Sumner 1996; Hausman and McPherson 2006, 2009). This does not mean that they are necessarily insurmountable. But they cast doubt on the idea that preference satisfaction should be *constitutive* of well-being. We will later see that this is not the end of welfare economics as we know it because there are views that see preference satisfaction and well-being as related, albeit not as closely as by the relation of identity. First, however, let us examine the main contenders in the preference-satisfaction view: hedonism and objective-list theories.

Hedonism

Hedonism is the theory that well-being consists in a mental state such as pleasure or happiness. Hedonism is a truly ancient theory of well-being, having been discussed in Plato's *Protagoras* first. It is the view of well-being that underlies the classical utilitarianism (see Chapter 14) of Jeremy Bentham (1907 [1789]), James Mill (1986 [1823]) and John Stuart Mill (1963b [1861]) and Henry Sidgwick (1874), though the four had different views of what mental states are regarded as constitutive of well-being. The view has recently undergone a small rejuvenation in economics (Layard 2005; Kahnemann and Krueger 2006); it has been experimental psychologists' conception of well-being for quite a while (see Angner 2009).

Jeremy Bentham's is the simplest and best-known account. It holds that well-being is the balance of pleasure over pain (1907 [1789]). All pleasures are of a kind, no matter what they are derived from—riding a motorcycle, swallowing an oyster, admiring a painting, reading a thriller. Pain is simply negative pleasure.

Hedonism is an initially plausible theory of well-being: pleasure is surely something that is good for us, even ultimately so. Many of the counter-examples to the preference-satisfaction view are easily accommodated by hedonism. If Parfit's stranger recovers but I don't know about it, I will not experience pleasure, and my well-being will not be enhanced. By contrast, the satisfaction of many other-regarding preferences may well affect one's well-being *qua* the pleasure the satisfaction of the preference yields. Thus, if I prefer my grandchildren to do well at school and my grandchildren do well at school, my well-being may be enhanced. If it is, according to hedonism this must be because I learn about my grandchildren's doing well, and that gives me pleasurable feelings. As we will see in a moment, this theory's catch is that the pleasurable feelings improve my well-being independently of whether my grandchildren are indeed doing well.

There are difficulties, of course. One set of issues has to do with the idea that all pleasures are regarded as on equal footing. Our experiences of riding a motorcycle, swallowing an oyster, admiring a painting, reading a thriller are all very different. Perhaps it is the case that with every pleasurable experience another mental sensation is associated, and that's what we call "pleasure." Thus, when looking at a painting, I don't only experience the painting; I have a second experience, namely of pleasure of a certain degree. That secondary experience is what is common to all pleasurable primary experiences.

From a moral point of view, different pleasurable experiences should count differently. Crisp makes the point with a thought experiment:

> Imagine that you are given the choice of living a very fulfilling human life, or that of a barely sentient oyster, which experiences some very low-level pleasure. Imagine also that the life of the oyster can be as long as you like, whereas the human life will be of eighty years only. If Bentham were right, there would have to be a length of oyster life such that you would choose it in preference to the human. And yet many say that they would choose the human life in preference to an oyster life of any length.
>
> (Crisp 2008)

John Stuart Mill tried to get around that problem by distinguishing lower- and higher-level pleasures (1963b [1861]: ch. 2). But, arguably, this is a move away from hedonism. At any rate, there is a more decisive objection to hedonism: Robert Nozick's "experience machine" (Nozick 1974: 43).

Nozick imagines an individual living in a Matrix-like world. This individual has all the experiences one may wish to have: to ride an Aprilia across the Italian Riviera, to swallow a Bélon oyster in the company of Chloë Sevigny or George Clooney (you choose), to admire a Gustave Courbet painting, to read a Robert Wilson thriller. However, these experiences aren't the product of your life circumstances and choices but those of the Matrix. Would you opt into such a life?

There are further issues. Amartya Sen (1999b: 162) mentions the problem of mental adaptation. Individuals who have grown up into living a certain kind of life may experience pleasure rather than pain even though viewed from outside their lives appear miserable. Happy slaves, suppressed women and members of lower castes may be cases in point. There is also the converse possibility that one adapts to circumstances of affluence and thereby fails to appreciate one's privilege. Sen's main point about mental adaptation is that other considerations apart from pleasure seem to matter for evaluating how well someone's life is going. Nozick's and Sen's arguments therefore point in the same direction: we can live impoverished lives even though we're quite happy about it (or unhappy in spite of affluence). The bottom line is that there is more to well-being than pleasure.

This might not be the end of the story: perhaps the hedonist has ways to avoid these criticisms (Crisp 2008 raises this possibility). We also have to make sense of the fact that contemporary experimental psychologists subscribe to a hedonist theory of well-being. Perhaps we should respond the same way as to the preference-satisfaction theory: pleasure or happiness and well-being are related, albeit not identical. Pleasure is probably a way in which our lives can go well for us, but not the only way, and we can sometimes experience pleasure even though our lives are not going so well for us.

Objective-List Theories

Many things seem to be good for people quite independently of whether they give pleasure or people want them. Health is a good and obvious example. Someone who has never been sick will hardly enjoy being healthy. And yet it is highly plausible to say that that person's health contributes to her wellbeing. Likewise, chronically ill persons may adapt to their circumstances and, some time after the illness has first set in, are not less happy than healthy persons (Frederick and Loewenstein 1999). It is at least plausible to say that a happy chronically ill person lacks something that a happy healthy person does not lack.

The main idea behind so-called "objective-list theories of well-being" is: there are certain things everyone values, or ought to value, because they are good for him or her. Objective-list theorists then list these things without trying to find a single common element among them.

There are two main sets of issues for an objective-list theory: one having to do with "objective," the other with "list." How are we justified in drawing up such a list? Specifically, what are reasons to believe that philosophers know better what's good for people than those people whose well-being they theorize about? Further, what are the items that should be on the list? How are we justified in including this particular item on the list?

To give a flavor of what a list can look like, consider Martha Nussbaum's (2000: 78–80):

- *Life.* Being able to live to the end of a human life of normal length; not dying prematurely or before one's life is so reduced as to be not worth living.
- *Bodily health.* Being able to have good health, including reproductive health; to be adequately nourished; to have adequate shelter.

- *Bodily integrity.* Being able to move freely from place to place; having one's bodily boundaries treated as sovereign, i.e. being able to be secure against assault, including sexual assault, child sexual abuse, and domestic violence; having opportunities for sexual satisfaction and for choice in matters of reproduction.
- *Senses, imagination and thought.* Being able to use the senses, to imagine, think and reason—and to do these things in a "truly human" way, a way informed and cultivated by an adequate education, including, but by no means limited to, literacy and basic mathematical and scientific training. Being able to use imagination and thought in connection with experiencing and producing self-expressive works and events of one's own choice, religious, literary, musical and so forth. Being able to use one's mind in ways protected by guarantees of freedom of expression with respect to both political and artistic speech, and freedom of religious exercise. Being able to search for the ultimate meaning of life in one's own way. Being able to have pleasurable experiences, and to avoid non-necessary pain.
- *Emotions.* Being able to have attachments to things and people outside ourselves; to love those who love and care for us, to grieve at their absence; in general, to love, to grieve, to experience longing, gratitude, and justified anger, or by traumatic events of abuse or neglect. Not having one's emotional development blighted by fear and anxiety. (Supporting this capability means supporting forms of human association that can be shown to be crucial in their development.)
- *Practical reason.* Being able to form a conception of the good and to engage in critical reflection about the planning of one's life. (This entails protection for the liberty of conscience.)
- *Affiliation*:
  - Being able to live with and toward others, to recognize and show concern for other humans, to engage in various forms of social interaction; to be able to imagine the situation of another. (Protecting this capability means protecting institutions that constitute and nourish such forms of affiliation, and also protecting the freedom of assembly and political speech.)
  - Having the social bases of self-respect and non-humiliation; being able to be treated as a dignified being whose worth is equal to that of others. This entails, at a minimum, protections against discrimination on the basis of race, sex, sexual orientation, ethnicity, caste, religion, national origin and species. In work, being able to work as a human being, exercising practical reason and entering into meaningful relationships of mutual recognition with other workers.
- *Other species.* Being able to live with concern for and in relation to animals, plants and the world of nature.
- *Play.* Being able to laugh, to play, to enjoy recreational activities.

- *Control over one's environment*:
  - *Political*. Being able to participate effectively in political choices that govern one's life; having the right of political participation, protections of free speech and association.
  - *Material*. Being able to hold property (both land and movable goods), not just formally but in terms of real opportunity; and having property rights on an equal basis with others; having the right to seek employment on an equal basis with others; having the freedom from unwarranted search and seizure.

The only thing the different items on this list—or any other—have in common is that they all advance a person's well-being, and all in their own way. This is an advantage of objective-list theories: they do not seek to reduce well-being to a single characteristic. Whatever that characteristic may be, chances are that it is possible to construct cases in which someone who lacks that characteristic nevertheless enjoys well-being, and converse cases in which someone has the characteristic but lacks well-being. These counterexamples are much less likely to obtain when the list is longer.

However, a list with two or more items also creates a significant problem. How do we rank the well-being of people who fare differently with respect to the different items on the list? There may be practical problems in measuring people's pleasure but at least conceptually every person's pleasure is commensurable. This is not so with respect to lists: if one person fares better on one criterion and another on a different criterion, there is no way to compare their levels of well-being unless one has a scheme that assigns weights to the different criteria. Using such a scheme, however, undermines the greatest advantage of objective-list theories, namely their relatively open and pluralistic approach to well-being. It is surely more plausible to say that we all value "play" than to say that we all value "play" to the same extent.

A case discussed by Amartya Sen illustrates the issue (Sen 1999b: ch. 4). Extreme poverty is heavily concentrated in two regions of the world: South Asia and sub-Saharan Africa. In terms of income, infant mortality and adult literacy rates the two regions are quite comparable. However, there are sharp differences when one looks at mortality and nourishment. For instance, the median age at death in India is 37 years compared to a shocking 5 years in sub-Saharan Africa; by contrast, 40–60 percent of children in India are undernourished, compared to a "mere" 20–40 percent in sub-Saharan Africa.

Sen uses this case as an illustration of his point that well-being is a multidimensional concept, and that to come to an adequate assessment for policy we do have to look at all morally relevant aspects of the situation. But it is easy to hijack the case to draw attention to a problem of any multidimensional account. For moral evaluation and especially policy analysis we require a basis for ranking two individuals, situations or policies. Suppose as the US government we have a certain amount of money to spend on development aid. Shall we invest it in India or sub-Saharan Africa? An account that regards life, bodily health (including nourishment) and literacy all on a par will not be very useful for making a decision. But trying to construct an index out of the various dimensions will reintroduce problems the pluralist account sought to overcome.

Problems about measuring and weighting the items on the list aside, how do we decide what is on the list in the first place? There are in principle two ways: participatory or philosophically-reflectively, both of which are problematic. To have representatives of the population participate in the decision-making is obviously impractical at the global level. By limiting the decisions to the national or subnational level we would lose the ability to criticize other cultures for failing to respect dimensions of well-being we consider important. Other cultures might, for example, not regard choice in matters of sexual reproduction as valuable. If lists are "objective" only within the confines of a culture, there would be no basis for criticizing that culture.

Proceeding by philosophical reflection faces an obvious legitimacy problem: how can we make plausible to anyone, including members of cultures that subscribe to very different sets of values, that the reflecting philosopher knows more about their well-being than they do themselves? But we must not ignore the fact that the democratic procedure faces a similar problem: why should I accept the values of the majority of my own culture, not to mention every other human being on the planet? Unanimity would in theory be a way out, but the chances of reaching consensus are, given the realities of cultural diversity, quite slim.

The Evidential View of Preferences

It may seem as though we've come to a dead end. There are three families of theories of well-being and all three have serious difficulties. Does that mean that we should stop thinking about well-being and therefore leave many important issues unsettled? There is a way out of muddle, but it requires us to make two changes in the question we are asking. First, rather than asking "What is well-being?" we could ask "What source(s) of information should we consider to evaluate (or measure) people's well-being?" Even if preference satisfaction, happiness and the items on the objective lists that have been drawn up by philosophers are problematic in their function as theories of what well-being is, information about preference satisfaction, happiness and the items on objective lists may well be useful in order to assess people's well-being. Thus, we should stop thinking that preference satisfaction, happiness and items on an objective list *constitute* well-being and rather think of them as *evidence for* well-being (Hausman and McPherson 2009). Second, we should ask about the sources of information about well-being in the context of concrete applications rather than in the abstract. On the one hand, in a concrete application there may be good contextual reasons for preferring one measure over another. On the other, concrete applications might allow us to assess the likelihood of a counterexample actually occurring. A case that speaks against an account as general theory of well-being will not be relevant in the context of a concrete application if it is exceedingly unlikely to occur.

Cost–benefit analysis (CBA) seeks to evaluate socio-economic projects in terms of the net benefit the realization of the project would provide. Net benefit here is understood as the total amount the supporters of a project would be *willing to pay* to realize the project minus the total amount that those who are against the project would require in compensation for agreeing to it. CBA assumes that willingness to pay indicates preference satisfaction. Therefore, the project with the greatest net benefit is regarded as the most efficient at satisfying preferences, and on the preference-satisfaction theory of well-being, the same project is the one that has the greatest capacity to make people better off. CBA is one of the main applications of welfare economics.

Hausman and McPherson 2009 argue that while preference satisfaction is untenable as a theory of well-being, under certain conditions preference satisfaction can provide good evidence for well-being in the context of CBA. The main conditions they discuss are that people are good judges of the consequences of the project for their well-being and that their preferences are self-interested. People are good judges when they are well informed about the consequences of a project and free of biases. People's preferences are self-interested if they prefer states of affairs that promote their well-being. The notion of a self-interested preference thus presupposes a notion of well-being, which would make a preference-satisfaction theory of well-being circular. But since Hausman and McPherson are not after a theory of well-being this is not a problem as long as one can assume that people sometimes know what is good for them. They argue that this is an assumption that can safely be made (Hausman and McPherson 2009: 18).

Do we have reason to believe that the two conditions are sometimes met? Let us consider the question whether people's preferences can be assumed to be self-interested. Hausman and McPherson discuss a case where it is unlikely that people prefer what is good for them: the protection of endangered species. They write:

> The survival of Siberian tigers and whooping cranes bear to some extent on the welfare of individuals because people take pleasure in seeing these magnificent creatures or in merely contemplating their survival from the edge of extinction. But for most people, these pleasures are modest, and there are other non-self-interested reasons why one would prefer that these creatures not become extinct. In the case of endangered species, preferences are a poor measure of benefit.
>
> (Hausman and McPherson 2009: 17)

Thus, people's willingness to pay for policies that protect endangered species is likely to be guided by considerations other than what is good for them, perhaps moral and aesthetic considerations or concern for non-human animals. In such cases, willingness to pay is a bad indicator of well-being. In other cases (perhaps the building of infrastructure such as roads and power supplies) people's willingness to pay may track well-being more accurately.

The other condition was that people do not make mistakes in assessing the consequences of implementing projects. There is considerable work in contemporary psychology that identifies areas where people are biased and likely to make mistakes, and policy-makers can build on this work in order to assess the chances of willingness to pay being an accurate guide to well-being (Hausman and McPherson 2009: 22–3).

There is another partial defense of CBA. In cases where people are likely to be self-interested and good judges of the consequences of a project, willingness to pay seems to be a *better* guide to well-being than alternatives. Self-reported happiness is unlikely to be reliable. There is evidence that such reports are heavily biased by information that is entirely irrelevant. Indeed, how *would* one answer a question such as "Generally speaking, how happy would you be with your life if the bridge were to be built?" Especially when the scales on which happiness is measured are very coarse (for instance, "very happy, pretty happy, or not too happy" in the US General Social Surveys), it is not plausible to assume that the impact of a project on self-reported happiness can reliably be estimated.

Similarly for objective measures. It is unlikely that the potential impact on any of the aspects of an objective-list theory of well-being—mortality and morbidity, mobility and political participation, say—can reliably be estimated. Moreover, here we would also face the weighting/aggregation problem discussed above.

The upshot is, when preference satisfaction is not understood as constitutive of well-being but rather as providing evidence for well-being, there may well be contexts where there are reasons to believe that a CBA based on willingness to pay can provide valuable information. When people's preferences are self-interested and people are good judges of the consequences of a policy, willingness to pay can be a good indicator of well-being. There are a multitude of difficulties concerning the measurement of willingness to pay, and since willingness to pay depends not only on preferences but also on wealth, policies should not be evaluated using "net benefit" as sole criterion. Nevertheless the discussion has shown that preferences are sometimes a defensible source of information for the evaluation of projects in terms of their consequences for well-being.

Conclusions

This chapter has surveyed the three main kinds of account of well-being that are currently being discussed in the philosophical literature: preference-satisfaction, hedonist and objective-list accounts. They all face serious objections. But we have also seen that there is a possible way out. If we understand information about preferences as characterizing *evidence for* well-being rather than what constitutes well-being itself, standard welfare economics can be made more plausible in the context of a limited application.

Welfare economics is therefore not impossible, even if there is no common understanding of its core notion, welfare or well-being. But there is an important implication for the invisible-hand hypothesis with which we began this chapter. Even ignoring the difficulties market imperfections cause (these will be examined in Chapter 13) and the fact that for an outcome to be regarded as socially optimal we may have to look to factors other than well-being alone (this will be examined in Chapter 14), self-interested choices will be transformed into a social good only when people are good judges of what is good for them and make no mistakes in their choices. Assuming that people are always good judges of what is good for them and make no mistake is not an innocuous idealization. When people aren't good judges or make mistakes in their choices or both, and we will see in Chapter 15 that there is at least some evidence that this is not infrequently the case, then the invisible-hand hypothesis is false and self-interested choices do not automatically lead to social benefit.

Study Questions

1   Is welfare economics necessarily a value-laden subject?
2   What theory of well-being do you find most convincing? Defend your answer.
3   The section on "Well-Being and the Satisfaction of Preferences" in this chapter presented a number of fixes to the actual preference-satisfaction theory of well-being. Can you think of further amendments to the theory that overcome the remaining problems?
4   What are the consequences of the criticisms of the preference-satisfaction view of well-being discussed in the section on "Well-Being" in this chapter for welfare economics?
5   Could one also construct evidential accounts of well-being that take information about happiness or items on objective lists such as health and education as evidence for well-being? What would be the differences between such accounts and that presented in the section on "The Evidential View of Preferences" in this chapter?

Suggested Readings

The most important general text on ethical aspects of economics is Hausman and McPherson 2006, which can serve as further reading for all chapters of Part III of this book. Hausman and McPherson treat all ethical topics discussed here, except market failure, in greater detail. Specifically on well-being, Crisp 2006 is a very good introduction. Book-length treatments include Sumner 1996, which defends a view of well-being based on the idea of "life-satisfaction," and Griffin 1986, which defends an objective-list view. On the general topic of "ethics within economics," see Dasgupta 2005. Dasgupta defends a version of what one might call the "standard" position in economics. See also Hilary Putnam and Vivian Walsh's comments (Putnam and Walsh 2007) as well as Dasgupta's rejoinder (Dasgupta 2007).

13 Markets and Morals

Overview

Economists often justify their advocacy of free markets by the invisible-hand hypothesis. Recall from Chapter 12 that the hypothesis holds that if people pursue their self-interest, then free markets will lead to a socially desirable outcome. It implies that organizing goods exchanges by free markets is (not necessarily the only but) one effective strategy to reach a socially desirable outcome.

But what are "free markets"? Pre-analytically, one might understand the term as referring to markets involving no or a minimum of government intervention. Whatever the virtues of that understanding, it is not what is required for the invisible-hand hypothesis. The first fundamental theorem of welfare economics (the analytical part of the hypothesis) assumes, among other things, that producers and consumers behave competitively and are perfectly informed, and that markets are complete. Producers and consumers behave competitively when they are price takers; they are perfectly informed when they possess all information relevant to their transactions; and markets are complete when everything people value has a price at which it can be exchanged without transaction costs. In many existing markets producers or consumers have considerable market power, information is not perfect and markets for many goods are non-existent. A better term for what is required for the invisible-hand hypothesis would be an "ideal market system." An ideal market system is, quite obviously, not the same as "free markets," pre-analytically understood.

This chapter looks at some of the ethical implications of mixing up free markets and the ideal market system. It will ask two main questions. First, are the moral implications of the invisible-hand hypothesis still valid when markets operate "freely"—that is, with no intervention by the government or other regulatory agency—but the assumptions of the ideal market system are false? Second, are certain interventions that make actual markets more like an ideal market system morally justified?

The two questions are closely related. If a market imperfection that leads to a morally undesirable outcome occurs, then interventions that eliminate the market imperfection seem justified (at least as long as the regulated market does not produce a morally inferior outcome). But as we will see, it is guaranteed neither that the moral implications of market failure are easily evaluated nor that interventions with a view to making actual markets more ideal are always desirable. Markets, then, are moral minefields.

Market Failure

Markets fail for numerous reasons. This is hard to deny. The interesting issues are how to respond to what kinds of market failure, and on what moral grounds. In this section I will go through the most common kinds of market failure—market power, informational asymmetries and externalities—and very briefly discuss some of the responses that have been given. This will be a boring section to readers with an economics background, but it is important to know the kinds of market failure that may obtain in order to see what is at stake in the discussion of the cases concerning moral challenges to the market that will follow. So please bear with me (or skip ahead).

Monopoly and Market Power

Western philosophy is often said to begin with Thales of Miletus, who thought that everything was made of water. Aristotle said so, and so did Bertrand Russell (Aristotle, *Metaphysics A*: 983b18; Russell 1967). The beginning of Western philosophy has a date, too: 585 BC, the year in which a solar eclipse occurred that Thales had predicted. Thales was, however, known for more than his mythology-free explanations of natural phenomena. According to one anecdote, Thales became tired of people poking fun at him for his poverty, which was supposedly due to the practical uselessness of philosophy. To demonstrate that philosophy wasn't necessarily an unprofitable enterprise, one winter he bought, at small value, all the olive presses in Miletus after predicting a particularly good harvest on the basis of his knowledge of astronomy. When harvest came presses were in enormous demand, and Thales could charge any price he wanted. Aristotle concluded: "He is supposed to have given a striking proof of his wisdom, but, as I was saying, his device for getting wealth is of universal application, and is nothing but the creation of a monopoly. It is an art often practiced by cities when they are in want of money; they make a monopoly of provisions" (*Politics*, book I, part XI). At the beginning of Western philosophy, then, stands an exercise of market power.

The invisible-hand hypothesis assumes that both producers and consumers behave competitively. There are a variety of reasons why they might not do so. A so-called "natural monopoly" arises when a producer faces high fixed costs and increasing returns to scale in the relevant range. If that is the case the average cost of production declines as the quantity produced increases, and it is always cheaper for one large instead of many small companies to supply the quantity demanded. An example that is often given is utilities. The production of electricity and the supply of water require enormous initial investments in infrastructure but the production of an additional unit of the good is practically negligible. In addition to natural monopolies there are government-granted monopolies where the lack of competition does not stem from production technologies but government enforcement.

Economies of scale and government grants are two kinds of barriers to entry that enable companies already in the market to exert market power. There are numerous others. A situation analogous to that of the natural monopoly can arise when the value of a good to a user increases with the number of other users; that is, when there are network effects. Think of the position Microsoft occupies in the market for PC operating systems. When there are network effects, the first company in the market (or the company whose product is adopted as standard) can have an enormous advantage quite independently of the quality of the good. Other barriers to entry include the control of natural resources (for instance, OPEC's control over oil in the 1970s) and the technological superiority of a large firm that is better able to acquire, integrate and use the best possible technology in producing its goods.

Though everyone who has received some economics tuition knows how to calculate the deadweight loss created by monopoly price-setting, it is not guaranteed that monopolies or other forms of market power are welfare-decreasing or morally undesirable in other ways. The standard model compares consumer and producer surpluses under monopoly pricing versus competitive pricing *in the same good*. But one important way to create temporary monopolies is by innovation. An innovating firm creates a new product and is able to charge higher prices until imitators have come up with substitutes that are good enough. The monopoly profit an innovator makes in the period he can charge a higher price is an important incentive to innovate in the first place. Without such monopolies there might be less innovation. Now, while it is not the case that consumers benefit from *all* innovation

(Reiss 2008a: ch. 3), it does not require an enormous stretch of the imagination to see that consumers do, by and large, profit from highly innovative industries. This, in turn, means that whether the existence of market power is morally desirable or undesirable cannot be answered in abstraction from the details of the concrete markets where the market power is exercised.

Informational Asymmetries

Another reason why producers and consumers do not always behave competitively is that they are not perfectly informed about aspects of the traded good, and, in particular, that relevant information is asymmetrically distributed between two traders. The seminal paper to introduce considerations about information distribution into mainstream economics was George Akerlof's "Market for 'Lemons'" (Akerlof 1970). This paper showed how asymmetric information can lead to a complete market breakdown.

Akerlof's reasoning was essentially this. When traders are asymmetrically informed about the quality of a good such as a second-hand car, an individual's labor or a person's health, and sellers know more than buyers, those who know that their good is of low quality (i.e., those who own a "lemon" or whose labor or health is of bad quality) will be incentivized to sell their good, while those in possession of a high-quality good will have an incentive to keep theirs. This is because the market will offer at best an average price across all qualities, as buyers cannot observe the quality. But rational buyers will predict this behavior on the sellers' part and offer a price below the average (because they know that the chances of getting a high-quality good are very low). This only strengthens the incentives to keep high-quality goods out of the market until only the lowest-quality goods remain. His lesson is thus: Markets in which the quality of goods matters but is not observable by buyers are thin, and prices and qualities low.

One mechanism to overcome this type of market failure is the signaling of the good's quality by the seller. For instance, firms may invest in brand names consumers can use to determine quality. The consumer knows that particular brands have supplied high-quality goods in the past and that the producer has an incentive to maintain the quality in order not to destroy the value of the brand name. Given the initial investment in the brand name is very costly and the cost of producing an additional unit of the good relatively low, information asymmetries provide another source of market power from barriers to entry.

A special kind of information asymmetry leads to principal–agent problems. These can arise in situations in which one individual, called the principal, hires another individual, called the agent, in order to perform a specific task. The principal cannot observe the effort the agent puts into the fulfilling of the task, and the result is in part due to chance. Examples are employer–employee contracts, contracts between insurers and insured persons, shareholder–manager or doctor–patient relations.

Take the latter as an example. Patients normally do not know, or not as well as their doctors, about the relative efficiency and effectiveness of treatment options. Moreover, there is always a large element of chance involved in any treatment, so an adverse treatment result cannot easily be blamed on poor doctor performance. A purely self-interested doctor will exploit this situation and recommend treatments that are good for him and not necessarily in the patient's best interest (especially when the patient is insured and therefore bears the cost only indirectly). Rational patients will, in turn, predict this behavior and seek a suboptimally low level of doctors' services (or, in a system where insurance is mandatory, costs will be inefficiently high).

Two further concepts may be of use here: *adverse selection* and *moral hazard*. Akerlof's lemons model, when applied to the insurance market, is a model of adverse selection. The "quality" at stake here is not the quality of a used car but rather an insured person's health (which may be expressed in probabilities of contracting all kinds of diseases). Insurers will not as a matter of principle be able to observe the health status of those seeking insurance. When patients know their health status better (because they know whether they are smokers and drinkers and whether they engage in dangerous hobbies such as parachuting and eating *foie gras*), the situation is analogous to Akerlof's lemons market. In a free market, only the lowest-quality risks will be insured, which most certainly is not a good thing.

Another aspect of the contract between insurance provider and buyer is the fact that the buyer can influence the probability of occurrence of the insured event. Will I lock my bike if it is fully insured for theft? Will I accept a generic instead of a branded drug if I'm fully insured for treatments? Will I turn off the gas if my flat is fully insured for fire? Will I stop smoking if I am fully insured for cancer treatments? No? Then I'm subject to moral hazard. Moral hazard refers to the incentives insurance and other similar contracts provide for the buyer not to take every possible precaution in avoiding the payment of insurance claims. Moral hazard, too, causes inefficiently low levels of insurance.

Public Goods and Externalities

Many goods in the economy are such that when one consumer has it or consumes it, the ability of others to also enjoy it are diminished or nil. I cannot both eat and share a cherry. To the extent that I have a cherry, you can't have it. But not all goods are that way. I'm currently listening to the Dave Matthews Band's *Busted Stuff*, and whether you do so too does not affect me in the least. Goods like cherries economists call "rival in consumption" and goods like listening to music, "non-rival."

There is a second dimension. Some goods are such that their producers can make sure that those who benefit from the production of the good actually pay for it. Short of illegal activities, producers of cherries or CDs can make their customers pay. But this is not the case for the producer of clean air, national defense or, at least in the old days, radio and television. Once the air is clean, everyone will benefit from it independently of whether they've paid for it. The same is true for national defense and was true for public broadcasting before the advent of encryption technologies. Economists call cherries and CDs goods that are "excludable" and clean air, national defense and broadcasting "non-excludable."

Public goods are goods that are non-rival and non-excludable. Clean air, national defense and radio broadcasts are examples of goods that have both characteristics. It is important to note that it is a good's physical characteristics and technological possibilities that make it public or private, not, or not so much, the institutional setting in which it is traded. Before the encryption technologies were available, radio and television broadcasting was a public good. With the new technology users can be excluded. These public goods were thereby transformed into club (non-rival, excludable) goods. This is independent of whether it was (prior to encryption) legal for the public to watch television or listen to the radio without paying a fee. Music (and other media, such as films, books, magazines, etc.) experienced a transformation in the other direction. Before digital computers made high-quality sharing extremely cheap, these goods were so-called "club goods" (non-rival and excludable) because a consumer had to buy a record in order to enjoy the music. The digital revolution turned these into public goods, as it is very hard for producers to control who listens (or reads, watches …). Once more, whether or not the producer is protected by a copyright does not affect these characterizations.

Public goods are underproduced in free markets because individuals have incentives to free ride. The decision to invest in a public good can be modeled as an *n*-person Prisoner's Dilemma, and in equilibrium contributions are zero for all individuals, which means that the public good does not get produced (see Chapter 10). People's actual behavior doesn't quite conform to the game-theoretic prediction, but it is clear that to the extent that people free ride, public goods are provided at inefficiently low levels.

Various solutions have been proposed, including assurance contracts in which participants make a binding pledge to contribute to building a public good, contingent on a quorum of a predetermined size being reached, government provision and government subsidies, all of which require a great deal of coordination among the contracting partners.

An *externality* is a cost or benefit of a transaction on individuals who are not a party to the transaction. A producer sells his goods to customers at marginal costs. But his production technology involves pollution. He, the consumers and others will suffer from the pollution but this "cost" is not reflected in the price the producer charges. Externalities can be positive or negative. If I play the piano during lunch hour, and my neighbors overhear it, this is a positive externality. If I were to play Lady Gaga on the radio, this would be a negative externality. Examples for positive externalities include education (which benefits the individual but also society), beekeeping (through pollination), vaccination, painting one's house in an attractive color. Examples for negative externalities include pollution and climate change, the systemic risk some large banks incur, the use of antibiotics if it contributes to antibiotic resistance, drug abuse.

Public goods and positive externalities are in fact the opposite sides of the same coin. If a private radio station were to be set up in a neighborhood, paid for by the neighbors, others could profit from it free of charge. The transaction between radio station and neighbors thus has positive externalities. Conversely, pollution can be regarded as a negative public good or "public bad." If it is produced, it affects people if they want it to or not. And by affecting one person, another person's ability to be affected is not diminished. Negative externalities are therefore overproduced, positive externalities underproduced.

The solutions are also analogous. Public solutions include government taxes (in this case called "Pigouvian taxes," after the British economist Arthur Cecil Pigou) and subsidies aimed to bring production up or down to efficient levels. Private solutions include neighborhood associations where neighbors regulate precisely what kinds of externality-laden actions (playing the piano, painting one's house, mowing one's lawn) are permissible and under what conditions.

Transaction Costs and the Coase Theorem

At first sight, one would think that the allocation of property rights should play an important role in markets with externalities. If, say, the inhabitants of a region have the right to clean air or water or soil, companies intending to use dirty production technologies will either (inefficiently) have to refrain from using these technologies or agree with their "victims" on a compensation scheme that enables efficient trades in externalities. Therefore, under well-defined property rights, it is possible that private parties find efficient solutions to externalities problems. The economist Ronald Coase has shown that if there are well-defined property rights and trade in an externality is possible and there are no transaction costs, bargaining will lead to an efficient outcome *regardless of the initial allocation of property rights*. Discussing the theorem named after Coase provides an opportunity to demonstrate how the various market imperfections introduced so far—such as public goods, externalities and information asymmetries and property rights—are interrelated.

Explaining the Theorem

The first thing Coase claims is that externalities are a joint product of two parties (Coase 1960). Neither pollution nor beautification would constitute an externality unless there was, next to the producer, another party on the receiving end. From an efficiency point of view, it is not guaranteed that interventions (such as Pigouvian taxes) affecting only the producer are always best. If my neighbors are disturbed by my piano-playing after all, I could stop altogether or not play when they're in or soundproof my flat, but they could also soundproof theirs or move out. From an efficiency point of view, it does not matter who changes behavior but what the cheapest solution is, and that might be on the side of the "victim" of the externality.

Suppose my piano-playing is so bad that my neighbors, after having to listen to me for three months, find it so nerve-racking that they could go on living in their apartment only if they undergo intense counseling, at a monthly cost of €500. They were planning to live in their apartment for another 10 years, so the total cost would come to €60,000. (These costs are meant to be all-encompassing; that is, my neighbors are assumed to be indifferent between living in their flat without noise and continuing to endure the noise with €60,000 in hand for medical and other expenses.) Moving to a new place would cost only €40,000. Soundproofing either flat would cost €80,000, and let us suppose that my stopping playing the piano or moving out would cost me €100,000. The Coase theorem now says that the allocation of property rights is ignorable, provided there are no transaction costs. To see this, first assume that I have the right to make any noise I want (because, say, I own the apartment building, or because I've lived there for longer, or because the culture we live in values piano-playing more highly than peace and quiet). In this case, my neighbors would make a simple calculation, see that their moving out is the lowest-cost solution to them and move out. But (nearly) the same would happen if my neighbors had a right to peace and quiet. Assuming as we did that they'd be indifferent between staying in the flat, now quiet, and moving out plus cash payment of €40,000, I can give my neighbors that money plus a little extra for their troubles, and they'd happily accept and move out. Apart from an extra €40,000 in my neighbor's pockets (and corresponding loss in mine), the outcome is the same.

Now suppose that the "polluter" is not facing one "victim" but many. The "polluter" might be a company using a dirty industry and the "victims" the entire population of the region affected by by-products of the production process. Given the affected population is large, it is likely that the most efficient solution requires the firm to install emission controls. But if the firm has the right to pollute, the individuals living in the affected area face a collective-action problem analogous to contributing to a public good. Everyone has an incentive to free ride, and it is unlikely that the public good—clean air in this case—will be produced. The converse is true when people in the region have the right to live pollution-free. The firm could offer compensation, but since each individual has a veto right, everyone has an incentive to use his or her bargaining power to extract more money and negotiations will break down.

Coase regards these adverse incentive structures as creating transaction costs. In the absence of transaction costs, efficient solutions can be found, and the allocation of property rights does not matter. With transaction costs, the free market is unlikely to supply efficient solutions, and the allocation of property rights matters a great deal. In the last example, the firm using a dirty production process will produce an inefficiently high amount of pollution unless the affected individuals are able to solve the collective-action problem *if it has the right to pollute*; if people have the right to clean air, an inefficiently low amount of pollution will be produced.

The discussion of the Coase theorem nicely illustrates how different kinds of market imperfections interrelate. More importantly, it makes plain that it is not normally possible to ignore moral considerations when one thinks about how best to organize or regulate production processes. In the next subsection I will look at some of the relevant considerations.

The Moral Limits of Coase's Theorem

Coase's essay is titled "The Problem of Social Cost." Let us focus on the idealized case in which there are no transaction costs first. The "social costs" Coase considers are measured exclusively in terms of efficiency. As we saw in the previous chapter, an allocation is Pareto-efficient if and only if there is no alternative allocation that makes at least one individual better off without making at least one individual worse off. "Better off" and "worse off" are understood in terms of (actual) preference satisfaction. An individual is thus regarded to be better off in social state S' than in the status quo S if and only if that individual prefers S' to S (and vice versa for "worse off").

Coase's reasoning thus depends on measuring social costs and benefits in terms of their consequences:

- on the *welfare*
- of *individuals*
- as measured by (actual) *preference satisfaction*
- irrespective of *distributional considerations*.

All these assumptions are problematic. That more matters in the moral assessments of economic transactions than just the consequences of the transaction on the welfare of the affected individuals can easily be seen if we consider exchanges that are, albeit welfare-enhancing, extremely unfair. Suppose for instance that the dirty producer from the last subsection is a multinational setting up its plant in an area characterized by abject poverty. Even if the inhabitants living in the area have the right to clean air, chances are that they will agree to a compensation scheme that, while making them better off, is exploitative. The multinational has vastly more bargaining power. If the deal falls through, it will simply move to another region. The area's inhabitants do not have this option. Their lives might well improve with new business in the area, but nevertheless the exchange can be considered exploitative (cf. Hausman and McPherson 2006: 20). This might not be a compelling reason against exchanges of this kind but it does cast doubt on the idea that evaluating economic transactions should be done in terms of consequences on welfare alone.

Of course, the point about the fairness of exchanges goes both ways. In the piano-playing example, a mischievous neighbor who has the right to enjoy his flat in peace and quiet might exploit my situation if I really need to practice the piano and, because of the architecture of our apartments (say), soundproofing mine costs four times as much as soundproofing hers. If there are no other alternatives, she can get me to pay nearly four times the cost of soundproofing her apartment, which would still result in a Pareto-improving exchange.

The outcome of exchanges, then, will crucially depend on the relative bargaining power of the parties to the exchange and that will depend on their outside options. By and large, people or institutions with more wealth and political power have more outside options. But it seems unfair that their preferences should matter much more in negotiations concerning compensation for externalities. Adam Smith, in *The Wealth of Nations*, describes an analogous situation in a different context as follows:

> It is not, however, difficult to foresee which of the two parties must, upon all ordinary occasions, have the advantage in the dispute, and force the other into a compliance with their terms. The masters, being fewer in number, can combine much more easily; and the law, besides, author-ises, or at least does not prohibit their combinations, while it prohibits those of the workmen. We have no acts of parliament against combining to lower the price of work; but many against combining to raise it. In all such disputes the masters can hold out much longer. A landlord, a farmer, a master manufacturer, a merchant, though they did not employ a single workman, could generally live a year or two upon the stocks which they have already acquired. Many workmen could not subsist a week, few could subsist a month, and scarce any a year without employ-ment. In the long run the workman may be as necessary to his master as his master is to him; but the necessity is not so immediate.
>
> (Smith 1904 [1776]: book I, ch. 8)

Second, it is not uncontroversial that only the consequences for individual human beings should matter. Perhaps we should be concerned also with the environment and animal welfare. Perhaps pollution is an ill that is to be avoided at a greater cost than economic efficiency.

Third, we saw in the previous chapter that the preference-satisfaction theory of well-being is mistaken. In the context of Coase's theorem, the problems of the theory come to the forefront. People will often engage in exchanges even though they are bad for them. Incomplete information is one important reason, and asymmetrically distributed information might be an additional reason for considering certain kinds of exchanges as morally problematic.

Who could quantify precisely the consequences of noise or other kinds of pollution for his or her well-being? Even if one does, it is important that this information is common knowledge. Otherwise the parties have incentives to overstate costs or harms. Asymmetrically distributed information can therefore lead to asymmetric bargaining power in much the same way as outside options. Just consider a situation in which a "polluter" knows both the cost of reducing emissions as well as the likely harm pollution incurs whereas the "victim" has only a very imprecise estimation of the harm (see Hahnel and Sheeran 2009 for a detailed discussion of the informational requirements behind the Coase theorem).

The last issue is that Coase's bargaining solutions ignore distributional issues. If compensations for externalities exacerbate existing inequalities, as is likely to be the case when the negotiating parties have different bargaining power, exchanges may be considered to be morally undesirable even if they are welfare-enhancing. This is closely related to the first point about fairness but not the same. Often we may consider an exchange to be unfair because it arises from harsh inequalities (as in the example above) or because it creates them. But we can imagine cases where an exchange is unfair not because it creates distributional inequalities but because one of the parties has been tricked or misled by the other party. And we can imagine cases where an exchange is fair in many ways except that it creates inequality.

We will examine distributional issues in greater detail in the next chapter. For now, let us move on to a fascinating case where it is likely that current government regulation moves actual markets further away from the ideal system of the invisible-hand hypothesis rather than closer to it.

Intellectual Property Rights

Intellectual property rights are, as their name suggests, kinds of property rights. Property rights are often considered to be the key to economic activity and prosperity, especially by economists with libertarian leanings (e.g., Hayek 1960; M. Friedman 1962; D. Friedman 1989 [1973]). In philosophical discussions, property rights are usually understood as relating to land and other natural resources, and their essence as the exclusion of others from the use of the resource (e.g., Wolff 2006: ch. 5). In the ideal-typical case, the holder of a property right has a claim to a plot of land, say, and the main content of the claim is his ability to stop others from trespassing by building a fence around it. But things aren't quite so simple, as the following passage from Friedman's *Capitalism and Freedom* suggests:

> A still more basic economic area in which the answer is both difficult and important is the definition of property rights. The notion of property, as it has developed over centuries and as it is embodied in our legal codes, has become so much a part of us that we tend to take it for granted, and fail to recognize the extent to which just what constitutes

property and what rights the ownership of property confers are complex social creations rather than self-evident propositions. Does my having title to land, for example, and my freedom to use my property as I wish, permit me to deny to someone else the right to fly over my land in his airplane? Or does his right to use his airplane take precedence? Or does this depend on how high he flies? Or how much noise he makes? Does voluntary exchange require that he pay me for the privilege of flying over my land? Or that I must pay him to refrain from flying over it? The mere mention of royalties, copyrights, patents; shares of stock in corporations; riparian rights, and the like, may perhaps emphasize the role of generally accepted social rules in the very definition of property. It may suggest also that, in many cases, the existence of a well specified and generally accepted definition of property is far more important than just what the definition is.

(M. Friedman 1962: 26–7)

Property, then, is usually thought of as pertaining to physical things. Not all economic goods are physical things, however. We encountered earlier in the chapter a selection of non-physical goods: music, radio and TV broadcasting, education and many kinds of services. Some of these goods have the property of non-rivalry. Can and should we have property rights in non-rivalrous goods? Defenders of *intellectual* property rights think so.

Intellectual property rights come in two main forms: patents and copyright. Patents provide the right to exclude others from making, using, selling and importing an invention for the term of the patent in exchange for making the invention public. A copyright gives the holder the exclusive "right to copy," which also includes the right to be credited for the work, to determine who may adapt the work to other forms, who may perform the work, who may financially benefit from it and so on. In their modern form, both patents and copyright date back to at least the Renaissance. Inventors were granted monopolies in Venice and Florence in the fifteenth century. Copyright was introduced after the invention of the printing press, which took place in the Holy Roman Empire in around 1440.

The "property" nature of patents and copyright is evident. Like ordinary property, intellectual property gives the holder a right to exclude others from using his or her property. Like the first American settlers claiming a plot of land and building a fence around it, the inventor of a new process or contraption or song or story claims the process, contraption, song or story to be his or hers and stops others from using it without purchasing the right to do so. Unlike ordinary property, intellectual property does not pertain to a physical thing, however, but to an idea.

Ideas are not only non-rivalrous but also non-excludable. That is, they are public goods. If I invent a contraption that helps me transfer ground coffee from its vacuum pack to the coffee tin without much spillage and you hear about it, your rebuilding my gadget does not in any way diminish the usefulness of my gadget for me. Moreover, I cannot protect my idea by physical means (such as building a fence around it). In a free market, once an idea is out, it's out.

As we saw above, in a free market public goods are undersupplied. Who on earth would bother racking his brains to come up with a contraption for pouring coffee into a tin if he could just sit there and wait until his neighbor invented it? Standard wisdom is therefore that just as people have to be *dis*couraged from polluting because of its negative externalities, they have to be *en*couraged to create ideas because of the positive externalities they come along with.

But there is a downside to providing state-sponsored incentives to generate ideas: intellectual property gives the creator of an idea monopoly rights over the use of the idea for a period of time, and market power is not always a good thing. To see when it is bad, we first have to understand an important difference between ordinary property rights and intellectual property rights. Ordinary property rights, too, give the holder the exclusive right over her property. But in the case of physical things, the right is over a *token*: this apple, that plot of land and so on. In the case of intellectual property, the claim is over a *type*: the design of a contraption (rather than its physical instantiation in a machine, say), the words of a novel (rather than its physical instantiation in a book), the composition of a music piece (rather than its physical instantiation in a CD or computer code). If I own a plot of land and am entitled to its fruit, I can stop you from eating my apples but I cannot prevent you from copying me by claiming your own land, growing your own apples and even selling them as my competitor. If I own the copyright to this book (as I do) I can well prevent you from making your own copies and especially from selling them. Ordinary property rights therefore tend to encourage competitive behavior (presumably, if I didn't own my apples, you'd just take them rather than growing your own), while intellectual property rights tend to prevent competition because they create monopolies over types of things.

So there seems to be a trade-off: on the one hand, we need incentives to encourage the creation of ideas; but on the other, we do not want to encourage anti-competitive behavior on the part of monopolists in ideas. This trade-off is well appreciated in the economic literature:

> The basic problem is that the creation of a new idea or design … is costly … It would be efficient, ex post, to make the existing discoveries freely available to all producers, but this practice fails to provide the ex ante incentives for further inventions. A tradeoff arises … between restrictions on the use of existing ideas and the rewards to inventive activity.
> (Barro and Sala-i-Martin 1999: 290; quoted from
> Boldrin and Levine 2008: 158)

Theoretically, we seem to be at an impasse, then. How else might we justify the existence and protection of intellectual property rights? The literature provides three answers: an argument from natural rights, an argument from personality and a utilitarian argument (De George 2009).

The argument from natural rights is an application of Locke's defense of (ordinary) property rights, which will be discussed in the next chapter. In essence, Locke argues that people can acquire property rights over land and other natural resources, subject to certain provisos, because they own themselves, thus have the right to preserve themselves, and they own the fruits of their labor. Further, by mixing their labor with a (previously unowned) physical thing they acquire ownership over that thing. We will see in the next chapter how successful these arguments are in defense of ordinary property rights. Here we should ask whether the analogous arguments work for intellectual property rights.

Land and its fruit on the one hand and ideas on the other are quite different kettles of fish. Unlike food, clothing and shelter, ideas, especially of the kind that fall under intellectual property protection, are not needed for survival. To be able to appropriate something if it is necessary to ensure one's survival seems fair enough. But an invention will help me in my struggle for survival whether or not someone copies it from me. If I have leisure enough to write a novel, why should I be empowered to stop others from reading it?

Further, land and natural resources can be regarded as "commons," owned by everyone prior to acquisition. Ideas, by contrast, do not exist prior to their invention. By mixing one's physical labor with a physical resource, one enhances the value of the resource. So perhaps one should benefit from increasing its value. If others were to take the fruit of one's labor, one would lose that benefit. In the case of creating ideas, however, one can benefit whether or not another also benefits. Stopping others from also benefiting seems much less justifiable in case of a non-rivalrous good.

The argument from personality builds on the Hegelian idea that property is the outward symbol of one's personality. Thus, one owns one's attainments and talents as something internal to one, but expresses them in something embodied, external. But just as one cannot give up one's freedom, one cannot give up one's right to externally express one's personality in, say, a book or record. So one maintains ownership of the idea.

No matter how successful this argument is where it applies (apparently this Hegel-inspired view is very prominent among legal scholars in continental Europe; see De George 2009: 417–18), it underwrites at best a very limited form of copyright such as the right to have one's name listed as author when the work is published and no one else's, the right to protection from defamation or maltreatment of the work and so on. The Hegelian argument does not seem to provide a reason to prevent others from copying one's idea.

The final argument in favor of intellectual property is a utilitarian one, and the most important of the three. The utilitarian has to address the question: What would the world be like if there was no intellectual property? Defenders of intellectual property might say, "Just look to the Soviet Union and other communist regimes and compare their standard of living with ours!" But of course, there are many differences between these and capitalist countries, and so the difference in standard of living cannot be attributed to differences in intellectual property regimes. Historically, it seems that in the nineteenth century the US patent system was regarded as successful in stimulating innovation and technological progress and therefore adopted by many other nations: "U.S. institutions performed well in stimulating inventive activity. Not only did they enhance the material incentives to inventors of even humble devices with grants of monopoly privileges for limited duration, but they also encouraged the development of a market for technology and the diffusion of technological knowledge" (Khan and Sokoloff 2001: 234–5). But once more, it is clear that there are other differences between the USA and other nations than rate of innovation and patent system.

There is in fact quite substantial evidence that intellectual property stifles rather than encourages innovation. Some theoretical considerations point in that direction. On the one hand, by patenting certain processes or contrivances, the development of others is hindered. New ideas always build on old ideas. By preventing the creator of a new idea using an old one, new products can often not be developed. To give just one example, James Watt's first steam engines were less efficient than they could have been because he was prohibited from using a method to efficiently transform reciprocating motion into rotary motion he had developed by a patent held by the inventor James Pickard (Boldrin and Levine 2008: 2). Such "innovation chains" are common to all areas of technological research and development. Especially in biomedical research, scientists are often hindered in their efforts to develop new medical therapies because competing researcher teams or pharmaceutical companies hold important patents on compounds, genes, microorganisms and the like.

On the other hand, patents create monopolies and thereby encourage rent-seeking behavior. James Watt is again a case in point. During the term of the patent of Watt's steam engine, few steam engines were built. Watt really started to manufacture steam engines only after his patents expired. Before then, he devoted his efforts primarily to extracting hefty monopolistic royalties through licensing as well as legal action targeted at fending off competitors and protecting his monopoly (Boldrin and Levine 2008: 2).

Moreover, it does not seem to be true that there would not be innovation without patents, copyright and the monopolies created by them. In Watt's case, the development of new steam engines and wide adoption happened only after his patent expired. There are many examples for creative activity that makes do without IP protection: open source software, the distribution of news on the internet, the creation of music and literature before copyright was invented (i.e., during most of its existence), financial innovation prior to 1998 (for these and more examples, see Boldrin and Levine 2008: chs 2, 3).

In case of the market for ideas (inventions, books, music, etc.) the regulation of one type of market failure (the undersupply of a public good) creates another type of market failure, namely the monopoly power of the creator of the good. We seem to be stuck between a rock and a hard place. Personally I find the evidence and arguments provided by Michele Boldrin, David Levine and others to the effect that intellectual property rights are harmful persuasive. But whatever the result of the utilitarian calculation of their harms and benefits, it is clear that there is a large and growing segment of the economy for which a straightforward application of the invisible-hand hypothesis is simply impossible.

Commodification: What Money Can't Buy

Another way of trying to make actual markets resemble more closely the ideal market system is by introducing markets where formerly there were none; that is, by making the market system more complete. Allegedly, there is a tendency for market economies to extend the reach of the market to more and more spheres of life. Indeed, today you can pay for dating services, to skip ahead of the queue, to sit in an acceptable seat on a plane, to have your book displayed prominently in a bookshop (such as in the window), to send your kid to a school in which she stands a lower risk of being victim to a fellow pupil running amok; you can be paid for donating your blood, kidney, egg or sperm or offering "reproductive services," for your good grades or losing weight, for your right to immigrate to the USA, for your right to pollute.

The invisible-hand hypothesis assumes that there are markets in everything. But is that a good thing? Should we, perhaps, forgo efficiency for the sake of some other good? Some philosophers have argued that there are things that *should* not be for sale. At least three arguments can be identified in the literature. A premiss of the first argument, the argument from fairness, we have already encountered above: not all exchanges that are voluntary are also fair. If the market exchange of a certain kind of good necessarily, or usually, involves unfairness for one of the parties involved (especially when it's always the same party, or if the disadvantaged parties are always members of the same segment of society), then there might be a good reason to proscribe market exchange in that good. The second argument, the argument from degradation, has to do with the kind of valuation specific forms of exchange allow. It says that market exchange may corrupt the exchanged good if markets are not the appropriate place to trade that good. The third argument is a utilitarian one. It says that substituting markets for other forms of exchange may sometimes be welfare-diminishing. Let's consider the three arguments in turn.

The Argument from Fairness

To understand this argument, suppose that in some faraway town there is only one employer, Monohire. Monohire employs everyone in the faraway town who seeks work, but only for in-kind payment in the form of a bed and two meals a day. The firm allows exchanging one of the meals for a small cash payment. As it happens, Monohire controls the sole railway from the faraway town. People are free to leave whenever they want, but they have to purchase tickets from Monohire which cost the equivalent of a year's worth of second daily meals.

Those who work for Monohire are assumed to do so voluntarily. The exchanges are most likely to be welfare-increasing—without Monohire, its workers would starve. But the exchanges are certainly exploitative on the part of Monohire. Monohire is not only a monopsonist concerning labor, it is also a monopolist concerning exit options. This allows the firm to pay very low wages and charge very high prices for the company railway. These circumstances, in turn, make alternative options for the inhabitants of the faraway town very unattractive. But exchanges are fair only to the extent that not entering the exchange is a feasible, realistic option.

What this example highlights is that considerations other than "effects on the well-being of the parties involved" matter for the moral evaluation of market transactions. Many actual exchanges may be voluntary but unfair in this sense. A single mum selling her secretarial services to a multinational at a wage far below the market rate may be one case in point, and a teenage prostitute selling sexual labor to fashion designers in support of his drug addiction another. If outside options are rare, voluntary exchanges may well be unfair.

It is important to see that what matters is not only whether the market participant has an actual range of outside options but also what he or she knows. Exploitative exchanges can occur even though the inferior party actually has attractive outside options but does not know about it, and the dominant party capitalizes on this fact.

Now add to this the empirical claim that certain markets almost always involve unfair exchanges understood in this way. Then we would have a good argument for not allowing the sale of goods or services in that market. Some argue that prostitution is such a market: prostitution is rarely if ever "fair" because those who sell their bodies for money are forced to do so "by poverty, drug addiction, or other unfortunate life circumstances" (Sandel 1998: 95).

Two comments on the argument from fairness. First, whether a market, be it that for sexual services or any other, is fair depends in part on empirical facts that cannot be settled by *a priori* argument alone: What outside options do participants have? Are these outside options attractive enough to constitute genuine alternatives? Would participants continue to engage in exchange of this kind if they were fully informed?

Second, it is not at all clear that prohibiting markets in these areas is the best strategy to solve the ethical problems associated with them. Obvious alternatives include improving people's informedness and enhancing their outside options. If coercion is the problem, coercion can be tackled by means other than prohibiting markets in certain goods. It can be tackled by stopping the "forced" of "forced exchange" rather than the "exchange."

The Argument from Degradation

The second argument is more powerful if it is successful. Perhaps the problem is not that prostitutes tend to be forced into selling their bodies but rather that the activity is intrinsically degrading. If the activity is intrinsically degrading, then the improvement of participants' living conditions cannot help. Then market exchange is bad *per se*. In essence, the argument says that exchanging certain goods on a market cannot provide the kind of valuation adequate to this good, and engaging in market exchanges of the good undermines its proper valuation. A forceful proponent of this argument is Elizabeth Anderson (e.g., E. Anderson 1993), so here I shall examine a number of examples she discusses. Anderson thinks that market relations can be characterized by the following norms:

1   they are impersonal;
2   everyone is free to pursue his personal advantage;
3   the goods traded are exclusive and rivals in consumption (i.e., they are private goods);
4   valuations are purely subjective or want-related (rather than deriving from need or objective quality);
5   in case of dissatisfaction one replies by "exiting" rather than "voicing" one's complaint.

   To give a stereotypical example of what she means, consider someone buying a new laptop computer. The purchasing act or relation is characterized as follows:

1   *Impersonality*. These days, most of us will go to the Apple store and buy the preferred model quite independently of who is selling it to us; we don't have personal relations with the vendor that make us buy the computer or this rather than that model.
2   *Personal advantage*. One buys the computer out of self-interest, not for the fulfilling of so-called "higher goals" such as world peace and justice; and there's nothing wrong with that.
3   *Private goods*. A computer is a private good: if I work on it, no one else can; Apple controls who the company is selling computers to. (There are obvious network externalities involved in the use of computers but we'll ignore these here.)
4   *Subjective valuation*. My having the computer might make me better off in some objective sense but what counts is that I wanted the computer; that's what makes the purchase one that is good for me.
5   *Complaints are made by exiting*. If the Mac turns out to be too easy to use after all, if one enjoys working around the bugs Microsoft builds into its applications and their slow, aesthetically unpleasing and convoluted user interfaces, one simply reverts back to a Windows-operated machine: one does not complain to Steve Jobs, God bless him.

Economic goods are simply goods whose exchange is properly governed by these norms. Anderson now simply but very insightfully argues that there are goods that, when traded in a setting characterized by (1)–(5), do not fully realize their value. That is, there are goods whose value cannot be fully realized through market exchange: there are goods that are not economic goods. She considers two kinds of goods in particular: gift goods and shared goods.

Gift goods are characterized by features that contrast with the first two norms of market exchange: intimacy and commitment. Typically, economic goods are produced for "the market," not in response to an individual's needs or personality traits. Even when goods are "customized," as many are today, this happens for the sake of increasing sales, not primarily in order to respond to someone's needs and characteristics. Gifts, by contrast, are supposed to do just that. Even though we all know that gifts often tell us at least as much about the gift-giver as they tell about the receiver, it is clear that a goal pursued by gift-giving is to respond to the receiver's needs and characteristics. Impersonal gifts aren't very nice gifts.

Moreover, gift-giving is an expression of a more long-term relationship. Typically, one does not give gifts to strangers, but if one does one is met with suspicion. I, for one, never accept offers of drinks from strange women in bars—what if they have less than perfectly honorable intentions? Both gift and market exchanges are reciprocal, but reciprocity is of a one-shot, immediate nature in market exchanges and of a repeated and long-term nature in gift exchanges. Misunderstanding the long-term nature of the reciprocity involved in gift exchanges is met with incomprehension and feeling offended. In another episode of the series *Frasier*, Daphne, the healthcare worker, gives Martin, Frasier's father, a cardigan for no apparent reason—she thought he might like it and uses the gift as a means to express her caring for him. Martin understands the reciprocal nature of gift-giving but thinks reciprocity is immediate. So he's hardly tried on the cardigan when he goes off to the shop to get Daphne a basket full of her favorite toiletries. Daphne hesitates and the following dialogue ensues:

MARTIN: Daphne, will you please just take the damn basket?
DAPHNE: Well, what are you getting so cross about?
MARTIN: Well, what? You can give me a gift but I'm not allowed to give you one back?
DAPHNE: Oh, so that's the only reason you gave me this?
MARTIN: Yeah, that's the way it works.
DAPHNE: Well, where I come from you don't just give someone a gift because you have to. Here, take your silly basket.

Gifts lose their character if they are not exchanged in a way compatible with the norms of intimacy and commitment. On the basis of these considerations, Anderson criticizes a range of social practices that involve market exchanges for goods that should properly be exchanged by gift relations:

prostitution, exploitative manipulation of gift relations in commercial trans-actions, marriage contracts and loans between friends.

Anderson also addresses what she calls "shared goods." Apart from market and gift relations, people have also fraternal relations. These obtain when individuals agree to refrain from making claims to certain goods that come at the expense of those less well off than themselves and when they regard that achievement as part of their own good. Political goods are an example. These are characterized by norms of exchange that contrast with market norms (3)–(5): they involve important (usually, positive) externalities, they are distributed in accordance with principles and needs rather than wants, and freedom is exercised through voicing one's complaint rather than exiting.

It is harder to find unequivocal examples in this area but national defense might constitute one. National defense is clearly a public good: once produced, it is impossible to exclude any citizen from benefiting, whether she wants it or not; and any one citizen's "enjoying" of the good does not stop any other from doing the same. It would be quite peculiar to argue that the decision to introduce, maintain or give up national defense, and to deter-mine its goals and operative assignments, is a matter of citizens' personal tastes; rather, it should be a matter of well-reasoned principle. And if, as a citizen, we do not accord with the adopted principle, we should voice our disagreement through the political process or public protest. "Exit" is not usually an option, and when it is, it constitutes an inadequate response.

As before, Anderson criticizes certain social practices on the basis of the preceding considerations. Certain goods such as the provision of public roads and spaces, the provision of welfare benefits and of primary education are more like national defense than like computers. If all roads and public spaces were privately owned, we'd lose spaces for expressing our political views in demonstrations and campaigns; certain forms of welfare provision should be made in kind rather than in cash because we, as a community, value them highly: thus, a benefits recipient should not be given the oppor-tunity to opt out of health insurance and get the equivalent in cash because health is too important a good; school vouchers are generally a bad idea because they encourage the formation of specialized schools and lead to parents "choosing" the school they deem appropriate for their children rather than exercising their democratic right and duty to contribute to values and curricula taught at schools.

Now, we certainly did not need Elizabeth Anderson to remind us that prostitution is different from matrimonial sex (and a one-nighter different from sex as an expression of "intimacy and commitment," for that matter). But she points to an important phenomenon which should make us worry about tendencies we currently find in many Western societies. The phenom-enon is that there is more than one way to enjoy a good, and our ability to enjoy a good in a given form depends in part on the way in which it is exchanged. A gift that does not respond to its recipients' needs and person-ality traits, and that expects immediate reciprocation ceases to be a gift. A society in which the school system is balkanized and parents express their political views only through choice has a harder time building a democratic tradition than one in which every pupil attends public school and parents decide about values and curricula in common.

The tendency we find in many Western societies is that more and more spheres of our lives are subject to market principles. I began by giving a number of examples, so let me end this discussion of the argument from corruption with a final example. University education used to be free or come at a symbolic "registration fee" in many countries. More and more governments now make public universities charge tuition fees which are often considerable. There is an economic argument behind this practice: university graduates have, on average, higher salaries, and it is only fair that they should pay for the cost of the investment in their human capital. Education has some externalities, to be sure, but that only means that the public should subsidize education, not that it bears the full cost.

Tuition fees affect students' expectations about university education. They're paying for it, so they expect to be treated like customers. For the same reason they treat their educators as service providers. They also expect to get good grades: "I paid a lot of money for my grades, so they had better be really good!" But students are no customers and university teachers no service providers. Grades should not reflect the amount of money paid for the tuition but the quality of the student's performance. The content of curricula should not respond to student preferences but be determined on the basis of principles such as academic excellence and students' needs. Tuition fees corrupt students.

Everything said so far should be fairly uncontroversial. The real question is what to do about it. Where do we put a stop to the tendency for more and more spheres of our lives to be characterized by market relations? Shall we prohibit the sale of some goods altogether? These are hard questions, and there is no space here for me to try to provide an answer. Let me just say this much: the argument from corruption does not, by itself, provide a good reason to prohibit trade in some good. It is true that exchanging gifts using the norms of the market corrupts the nature of the gift good. We can't enjoy something as a gift if it is impersonal and comes with a call for immediate reciprocation. But that doesn't mean that there is anything wrong with a good exchanged in that way. Think of the British practice of buying drinks in rounds rather than individually. Here the reciprocation is pretty immediate: you buy your round when it's your turn. And the buyer of the round hardly responds to the needs and traits of the other drinkers—at least not to a degree characteristic of gift exchange. According to Anderson's schema, "rounds" are an economic good in British pub culture. And yet I fail to see what is wrong with it, or what could be gained by organizing it such that it more closely resembles typical gift goods.

My core point is that exchanging goods via market principles is not harmful as long as there are avenues for other kinds of exchanges (cf. Wolff 2004).

We'd live in an impoverished world without gifts and common goods. But of course it is also true that we'd live in a literally much impoverished world if there were no economic goods. And other than extreme conservatism I don't see a reason to believe that all goods should come with an *a priori* knowable, unique "proper" or "adequate" form of exchange. Luckily for the critics, there is an arrow left in their quiver.

The Utilitarian Argument

The utilitarian argument says that replacing other forms of exchange by market exchange can be welfare-decreasing. It is closely related to the second argument and can therefore be discussed quite briefly. The story is this. Take a good for which there is a shortage of supply: organ and blood donations, punctuality, quiet on the part of students during classes. Think like an economist and introduce monetary incentives in order to stimulate supply. Observe that the opposite happens: supply actually goes down. Ask yourself, what has happened? Answer: the existence of monetary incentives crowds out certain forms of intrinsic motivation. Since market exchange may corrupt a good (see above), people are less inclined to supply it. Then, when monetary incentives are not strong enough to fully replace or surpass the original motivation, supply will go down.

This argument is based on a famous study by Richard Titmuss (1970). Titmuss compared the US and UK systems for procuring blood and argued that the UK system of donated blood was superior not only in quality but also in efficiency to the US system, which allowed blood to be bought. He argued that unlike the UK's altruistic donors, the US sellers have a reason to conceal illnesses, and so the quality of marketed blood should be inferior. He further claimed that the introduction of markets "represses the expression of altruism [and] erodes the sense of community" (Titmuss 1970: 314). Actions formerly based on "higher motives" now have a price tag. "Higher motives" often provide a better incentive than money, and therefore the willingness to donate decreases.

The beauty and strength of the argument lies in its claim that it is the pure existence of a market exchange that crowds out intrinsic motivations; it does not depend on the market taking over other forms of exchange completely. But it is also an *a priori* argument whose significance relies on it actually being the case that the introduction of markets decreases welfare by crowding out intrinsic motivations.

There is some evidence that the mechanism Titmuss describes is sometimes in place. Debra Satz describes one famous experiment:

> Faced with parents who habitually arrived late to pick up their children at the end of the day, six Haifa day care centers imposed a fine for such parental lateness. They hoped that the fines would give these parents a self-interested reason to arrive on time. The parents responded to the fine

by doubling the amount of time they were late. Even when the fine was revoked three months later the enhanced lateness continued. One plausible interpretation of this result is that the fine undermined the parents' sense that they were morally obligated not to take advantage of the day care workers; instead they now saw their lateness as a commodity that could be purchased.

(Satz 2010: 193)

But, as Satz also observes, whether the introduction of markets actually does crowd out intrinsic motivation, thereby reduces the supply of important goods and thus decreases welfare or whether financial incentives provide the expected stimulus is an empirical one that has to be addressed on a case-by-case basis. Once it mattered, from grade 10 or so onwards, my parents gave me money for good grades. That was the only way to get me to try to improve my academic performance and it worked. I am eternally grateful to my parents for not having known about Titmuss *et al.*

In sum, the utilitarian argument is inconclusive. It simply depends on empirical facts that cannot be settled by philosophical argument. I do not get the feeling that the existence of prostitution has a negative effect on the exchange of sex according to the norms of gift exchange, that the existence of private or confessional schools crowds out parents' motivations to contribute to the life of public schools or that paying some kids to perform better at school eliminates all nerds. But one should certainly introduce markets for "goods" such as kidneys if at all only after a careful study of the relevant empirical facts (which of course also include facts about the outside options of potential donors/sellers; see above) and consideration of the moral issues involved.

Study Questions

1   Think about the things you consume in the course of a normal day. How many of them are purely private goods? How many are public goods?
2   What solutions are there to the problem of externalities? Which one do you find most convincing?
3   Should there be property rights and how strong should they be? Justify your answer.
4   Are there goods the market exchange of which is always unfair?
5   How convincing do you find the utilitarian argument against market exchange? Defend your answer.

Suggested Readings

Four books that are absolute "must-reads" for the moral limits of markets are E. Anderson 1993, Sandel 2012, Satz 2010 and Walzer 1983. A detailed justification of intellectual property rights is Merges 2011; Boldrin and Levine 2008 is a scathing critique. On the commercialization of biomedical research, see Krimsky 2003 and Angell 2004. Proposals for reforming biomedical research, with a focus on intellectual property, are Baker 2005, Reiss and Kitcher 2009, Reiss 2010 and Stiglitz 2006. One of the few philosophical texts that looks at market imperfections is Graafland 2007. That book contains a variety of applications on parenting, pensions, globalization, development and other topics.

14 Inequality and Distributive Justice

Overview

The second fundamental theorem of welfare economics (Chapter 12) is sometimes held to show that questions of *distribution* can be separated from those of *allocation*. As any Pareto-efficient outcome can be reached as a competitive equilibrium, the proper role for the government is merely to redistribute wealth; other than that it should just "let the market work" (Mas-Colell *et al.* 1995: 308).

The previous chapter showed that in actual markets allocation may raise fairness issues. So, unless the market system is "ideal," questions of allocation cannot be fully separated from questions of distribution. Either way, we want more than brute intuition to guide our thinking about fairness and distribution. This chapter discusses a number of principles that help us evaluate economic outcomes, policies and institutions with respect to distributive fairness or justice. Is inequality necessarily unfair? Should we buy additional economic efficiency at the cost of allowing some people to be treated unfairly? To what extent can government efforts to "correct" market outcomes by redistribution be justified? I begin by reviewing some facts and figures giving evidence that actual markets often produce a high degree of inequality.

Inequality

The world we live in today is characterized by an enormous and increasing degree of economic inequality. This is as true between countries as it is within countries. According to the International Monetary Fund (World Economic Outlook), in 2011, Qatar had the highest per capita income with $102,943, and Congo the lowest with a shockingly low $348 (per annum!). In OECD countries today, the average income of the richest 10 percent of the population is about nine times that of the poorest 10 percent (OECD 2011). But inequalities in developed countries are in fact relatively benign. Thus, the Gini coefficient, a measure of inequality that expresses perfect equality as zero and perfect inequality (if, say, one person has all the income) as 100, is 28 for Germany, for the Netherlands 31, for the UK 36 and for the USA 41. The most unequal countries, according to the Gini coefficient, are Namibia (74), South Africa (67), the Seychelles (66) and the Comoros (64), the most unequal OECD country being Mexico (52). (The data are from the World Bank Gini Index.)

Inequality is also on the rise in most countries. In traditionally egalitarian countries—such as Germany, Denmark and Sweden—the income gap between rich and poor is widening—from 5 to 1 in the 1980s to 6 to 1 today. In all OECD countries, the Gini coefficient stood at an average of 29 in the mid-1980s but had increased to 32 by the late 2000s. It rose in 17 of the 22 OECD countries, climbing by more than 4 percentage points in Finland, Germany, Israel, Luxembourg, New Zealand, Sweden and the United States (OECD 2011).

And inequalities do not only concern income. A study by the World Institute for Development Economics Research at United Nations University reports that the richest 1 percent of adults owned 40 percent of global assets in the year 2000 (Davies *et al.* 2006). The three richest people in the world possess more financial assets than everyone who lives in the poorest 48 nations combined. North America and Europe together have not even 15 percent of the world population but control over half of the world's net worth. Along with these inequalities, of course, go inequalities in access to health, education, freedom, political influence and many more expressions of a flourishing life.

Many people find great economic inequalities as such unjust. In 2007, CEOs in the American stock index S&P 500 had an average salary of $10.5 million annually, 344 times that of typical American workers (Maloney and Lindenman 2008). Now, some income inequality may be deserved. Perhaps CEOs work harder and longer hours, they probably have a better education and carry greater responsibility. But does that justify a 344-fold increase in salary? One should also note that in 1980, the ratio was "only" 42 to 1 (Maloney and Lindenman 2008). Moreover, most people would regard inequalities due to factors that are completely accidental from a moral point of view, such as having wealthy parents or being born in a developed country, as unfair. The fact that inequalities systematically correlate with social variables that have nothing to do with desert is exacerbating: practically all countries that have a per capita GDP above world average are in the North and the far South whereas all those with a below-average income are close to the equator; in many countries women earn systematically less than men; in the USA and other countries, people of African descent have considerably lower incomes than Caucasians and the gap is widening.

Principles of Distributive Justice

How can we tell whether most people's intuitions that inequalities such as those mentioned above are indeed unjust? Countless principles have been offered in the literature. Here I will consider four main theoretical frameworks that are important in the context of economic justice: utilitarianism, libertarianism, social-contract theories and the capabilities approach.

Some preliminaries first. There are three fundamentally different kinds of theories of justice: consequentialist, deontological and virtue theories. Consequentialist theories maintain that acts, policies and institutions are just to the extent that they produce good consequences. Utilitarianism is an example. Consequentialist theories contrast with deontological theories, which determine the rightness of an action, policy or institution on the basis of its compliance with an abstract principle (such as the principle "Do unto others as they do to you" or the Ten Commandments). Both libertarianism and social-contract theories are examples of deontological theories. Virtue theories focus on the character and flourishing of the individual rather than her acts or the principles she follows. The capabilities approach can be given a virtue-ethical reading.

Utilitarianism

Roughly speaking, utilitarianism holds that the distribution of goods is just if and only if it maximizes aggregate utility. According to one slogan, utilitarianism seeks the "the greatest amount of good for the greatest number," and principles of distributive justice have to accord with this maxim.

As Amartya Sen explains, utilitarianism has three ingredients: consequentialism, welfarism and sum-ranking (Sen 1999b: ch. 3). We've already seen what consequentialism is. Welfarism holds that the relevant consequences are those for individuals' well-being. And sum-ranking, finally, says that what matters is the sum total of well-being (perhaps divided by the number of people) and not its distribution.

A straightforward implication of utilitarianism is that the enormous degree of inequality we currently observe in most countries in the world is probably unjust. Here is the simple explanation. The marginal utility in most goods (as well as resources such as money) is decreasing for most people. If you have nothing, a single meal will make a huge difference to your well-being.

If you've had four meals already today, an additional meal will not make you much better off. Consuming it might actually make you worse off. The principle also applies to money. Give a few dollars to a beggar, you can make a great difference to his life; give it to a millionaire, she will hardly notice. Thus, redistributing goods or money from society's wealthiest to its poorest will probably increase aggregate utility:

> Nevertheless, it is evident that any transference of income from a relatively rich man to a relatively poor man of similar temperament, since it enables more intense wants, to be satisfied at the expense of less intense wants, must increase the aggregate sum of satisfaction. The old "law of diminishing utility" thus leads securely to the proposition: Any cause which increases the absolute share of real income in the hands of the poor, provided that it does not lead to a contraction in the size of the national dividend from any point of view, will, in general, increase economic welfare.
>
> (Pigou 1932 [1920]: I.VIII.3)

I said above that redistribution will *probably* increase aggregate utility because there are two assumptions in the argument that might be challenged. The first is the principle of decreasing marginal utility. Pigou calls it a law but it is hardly a strict law and it will not be true for some people. I take the principle to be a relatively uncontroversial idealization, but given that utility is not straightforwardly observable it will not be easy to support it with good evidence. The second assumption is more serious. It is that redistribution does not have a significant effect on the amount of goods there are to be redistributed; redistribution doesn't substantially affect the size of the pie. Now, it is probably false that redistribution does not affect the size of the pie at all, but it is difficult to know how large the effect is.

Suppose everyone had the same utility function and that was marginally decreasing. In this case, an equal distribution of goods would maximize aggregate utility. But if I knew that I'd end up with my equal share of the pie no matter how much effort I put in, I have a strong disincentive to put in effort. That does not mean that I won't put in any effort. I might simply enjoy doing so; I might think that it is my duty to do what I can; I might not reflect about the matter at all and simply do as I am told. But many people will expect some kind of positive relationship between effort and reward, and they will be put off by a strict egalitarian distribution of goods.

There are also considerations that go the other way. If one lives in a very unequal society and particularly if inequality is not only due to differential amounts of effort but also due to accidental factors such as luck one might not feel motivated to try very hard, even if doing so would come with some reward. Suppose for instance that entering the labor market increases everybody's income to some extent, and there are a few lucky people who get incredibly rich. Now even though not entering the labor market gives them a lower income, some people will prefer that because of the regret they would feel if they did enter but did not luck out. Things get worse of course if the inequalities aren't only due to effort and luck in the process but other factors one has little chance of influencing, such as family background and ancestry, sex, race and so on.

What precisely utilitarianism entails about the redistribution of resources in a society depends on many concrete facts about that society. It is likely, however, that utilitarianism justifies *some* degree of redistribution from the richest to the poorest. But considerations such as the above will only convince someone who is already a utilitarian. We should therefore ask how plausible and justifiable utilitarianism itself is.

The term "utility" is ambiguous. The classical utilitarians Bentham, Mill and Sidgwick (and other so-called "hedonists") meant by it happiness or the balance of pleasure over pain or some other mental quality with it. Most contemporary utilitarians mean preference satisfaction. The criticisms discussed below pertain by and large to either understanding of "utility." I will therefore disambiguate only when necessary.

There are a number of considerations that count in favor of utilitarianism. It is clear that people care very deeply about utility, and so it should play some role in evaluations of social outcomes, policies or institutions. Suppose there was a policy proposal (e.g., "Ban the production, distribution and consumption of *foie gras*") that made nearly everyone concerned very unhappy. It would be madness to enact the proposal just because some small minority of activists argue that the ban is justified by some abstract principle they have concocted.

It is also clear that in the actual evaluations of outcomes, policies and institutions, consequences for individuals' well-being matter a great deal. Think again of the financial crisis. For years now, governments have broken every imaginable rule and principle in order to save banks and states that were risking failure, in view of expected consequences for future well-being: "The Greek economy will collapse!"; "Germany's exports will break down!", "There will be years of global depression!" If there were good reasons to believe that such consequences would ensue, breaking rules such as "The primary objective of the European Central Bank's monetary policy to maintain price stability has overriding importance" would indeed seem to be the smaller evil.

Utilitarianism, however, holds not only that consequences matter but that consequences for people's utilities are all that matters. This is implausible, because people also have rights and it does not always seem morally permissible to violate someone's rights just because doing so would result in greater aggregate utility. Consider a situation in which person A suffers from a predicament that makes her need a kidney and person B has two healthy kidneys. The two people are unrelated, but by some fateful twist of genetics, person B's kidney is the only one that could save person A's life. Person B prefers to keep her kidney, but as she would not suffer very much from giving it up, her preference is less intense than person A's preference to receive the kidney (life is at stake, after all). Perhaps it is clear what would be the nice thing to do in this situation. But if you are a utilitarian, you think that it is right to force B to give up her kidney without having a say in it. This will not sound appealing to everyone.

Utilitarianism, then, completely ignores people's rights (except of course insofar as the violation of someone's right has consequences for her well-being). Policies based on utilitarian calculations will therefore often appear to result in the production of unfair harm for those individuals the violation of whose rights maximizes aggregate utility. While this is not a conclusive objection to utilitarianism, it certainly casts some doubt on the notion that consequences for people's well-being should be all that matters for moral evaluation.

Just as utilitarians care about people's rights only indirectly, distribution matters only indirectly. *If* people's utility functions are decreasing, then utilitarianism favors a redistribution from affluent to poor. But it is at least conceivable that the situation that maximizes aggregate utility is one that is radically unequal, simply because some people are better at converting resources into utility than others (Sen 1970). For instance, if two people A and B would like to go to the Glastonbury music festival and both would derive the same utility from it if they were to go, but A is in a wheelchair and B isn't, A requires more resources (such as a specially designed vehicle or a helping hand) to get to the festival. If B has more resources to begin with, utilitarianism might underwrite a redistribution from A to B because B is more efficient at converting resources into well-being. In such cases, utilitarianism seems to justify the exacerbation of existing inequalities.

Most contemporary utilitarians think of utility as preference satisfaction. This leads to a problem concerning interpersonal comparisons of utility. Obviously, to compute the sum total of utility requires comparing person A's level of utility with that of person B. But what does it mean to compare the satisfaction of person A's preference of apples over bananas with the satisfaction of person B's preference of cherries over strawberries? Many economists would deny that such interpersonal comparisons can be done. Others have suggested that the conceptual problem can be solved by asking someone (the social planner?) to imagine himself in the position of both A and B and ask whether *he'd* prefer to get apples as person A or cherries as person B (see Binmore 2009; Dasgupta 2005). It is doubtful whether this works in principle (cf. Hausman and McPherson 2006), and certainly it won't do as a practical approach to measuring preferences.

In order to avoid the problem of interpersonal comparisons of utility, economists have developed the idea of Pareto-superiority. An outcome *X* is said to be Pareto-superior to outcome Y if and only if no individual prefers *Y* to *X* and at least one individual prefers *X* to *Y*. But this criterion is extremely thin for judging policies. Most policies create winners *and* losers, and can therefore not be Pareto-ordered.

In sum, these are the main conceptual difficulties that beset utilitarianism:

- utilitarianism ignores people's rights;
- utilitarianism ignores the distribution of resources;
- interpersonal comparisons of utility are perplexing if utility is understood as preference satisfaction;
- Pareto-optimality as a substitute criterion is rarely applicable.

Property Rights and Libertarianism

One, admittedly very crude, way to justify existing inequalities would be to claim that they are the outcome of free people making voluntary decisions about the use of their resources. Outcomes, whatever they are, are justified because people have property rights over their resources and are entitled to the holdings that spring from these rights. We then may ask: Are property rights themselves justified?

Libertarianism is the theory that asserts that states of affairs are just to the extent that they are the outcome of a process in which individuals act voluntarily and their rights are not being violated. It is a deontological theory. Actions are right as long as they do not violate anyone's freedoms or liberties.

Suppose that in some hypothetical original state, previously unowned territory gets divided equally among the members of society. Its members are free and have property rights over the land allocated to them. Everyone can therefore make use of their land as they please. In order to survive, they have to use the land to produce food, clothes and shelter. Not everyone will produce the same amounts of everything. Some might be better at growing vegetables, others at turning hides into clothes. They are free to contract with each other and exchange the fruits of their land. Some might be more successful than others and perhaps cleverer in specifying the terms of trade. Some people's land might not produce enough to feed them. They can use their land as collateral in debt contracts. If they do not produce sufficiently next year, they will lose their land. They will seek to work on farms owned by more successful individuals. They enter into labor contracts, once more in a voluntary act. After some time, chances are that there will be inequality in income, wealth or whatever. Some people will own a lot of land and produce far more than they can consume themselves. Others own nothing except their own bodies and depend on labor income. If all the acts responsible for the new situation were voluntary, libertarians consider the situation just. On what grounds do they do so?

Any resource to which an individual may obtain the property rights was either previously unowned or owned. If it was previously unowned, for the resulting state to be just the resource must be justly acquired. If it was previously owned, for the resulting state to be just the resource must be justly transferred. If acquisition or transfer were unjust, for the resulting state to be just there must be some rectification of injustice. Robert Nozick, the most prominent defender of libertarianism in the twentieth century, lays out three principles that jointly describe his so-called "entitlement theory of justice" (Nozick 1974):

a   the Principle of Justice in Acquisitions;
b   the Principle of Justice in Transfers;
c   the Principle of Rectification of Injustice.

Can people ever be justified in appropriating a previously unowned resource? In his *Two Treatises of Government* (1988 [1689]), Locke argued that they could, under certain conditions. Locke's arguments are ultimately unsuccessful (Wolff 2006: ch. 5), and Nozick himself presents a number of worries. One of Locke's arguments, for instance, is that individuals acquire ownership over a resource by mixing their labor with it. But, as Nozick argues,

> why isn't mixing what I own with what I don't own a way of losing what I own rather than a way of gaining what I don't? If I own a can of tomato juice and spill it in the sea so its molecules ... mingle evenly throughout the sea, do I thereby come to own the sea, or have I foolishly dissipated my tomato juice?
>
> (Nozick 1974: 174)

Thus, Nozick does not present a fundamental defense of property rights (Nozick 1974: xiv). Instead, he elaborates a little on Locke's understanding of the conditions under which unowned resources could be appropriated. Locke argued that in order to justly acquire a resource, there had to be "enough and as good left in common for others" (Locke 1988 [1689]). Nozick interprets this proviso as saying that no one should be made worse off by the initial acquisition of property rights (Nozick 1974: 178–83). The proviso implies, for instance, that no one could appropriate all of a resource others need (such as all the drinkable water in the world). It does not imply, on the other hand, that someone can't legitimately appropriate a resource in order to enter into competition with someone else whose position is thereby "worsened."

The justification of property rights is certainly a lacuna Nozick left. Others have offered defenses, for instance based on the idea that government-sponsored property rights are essential for human development and well-being (de Soto 2000) or that they guarantee freedom (Hayek 1944). It is important to notice, however, that property rights remain difficult to defend within the deontological system Nozick proposes.

Supposing that property rights are defensible under certain conditions, how would a libertarian evaluate any given income distribution as just or unjust? According to Nozick, "a distribution is just if everyone is entitled to the holdings they possess under the distribution" (Nozick 1974: 151). Following the three-part entitlement theory described above, individuals can be entitled to their holdings only if either (a) they were justly acquired; (b) they were justly transferred; or (c) they constitute a rectification of prior injustice. It is clear that in order to evaluate a given outcome (such as an income distribution) *historical information* is required according to the entitlement theory. Nozick consequently distinguishes between historical and end-result principles of distributive justice (Nozick 1974: 153ff.) and explains that the former hold that "whether a distribution is just depends upon how it came about. In contrast, current *time-slice principles* of justice hold that the justice of a distribution is determined by how things are distributed (who has what) as judged by some *structural* principle(s) of just distribution" (Nozick 1974: 153; original emphasis). End-state principles comprise all unhistorical principles of distributive justice such as current time-slice principles.

Nozick further distinguishes between patterned and unpatterned principles (which can themselves be historical or end-state). Patterned principles require that distributive shares vary directly with some (combination of) natural dimension(s) such as moral merit or usefulness to society. Most principles of distributive justice are patterned. But the requirement that a distribution be patterned (a patterned distribution is simply one that accords with a patterned principle), argues Nozick, will result in constant violations of people's liberties. He asks us to contemplate the following thought experiment. Suppose that the holdings in a society are indeed in complete accordance with some favored patterned principle of distributive justice D_1. Suppose also that in that society, a famous basketball player, Wilt Chamberlain (an American player for the Los Angeles Lakers at the time of Nozick's writing), signs a contract with his team according to which 25 cents of the price of each ticket of each home game goes to Chamberlain. Nozick further supposes that during one year no transfers occur except those from 1 million persons attending the games, making Chamberlain $250,000 richer. Call the new distribution D_2. But if D_1 was just and people voluntarily moved from D_1 to D_2, how could D_2 not be just? More importantly, if D_1 is regarded as the solely just distribution under the favored principle, in order to preserve justice either Wilt Chamberlain's rights have to be violated by taking the $250,000 away from him or by proscribing contracts such as that between Chamberlain and his team and between team and fans. Neither option seems particularly attractive.

In the novel *Life and Fate*, written in 1950s Stalinist Russia, Vasily Grossman describes what could happen when individuals are not guaranteed property rights and rights to exchange goods:

> I wanted since childhood to open a shop, so that any folk could come in and buy. Along with it would be a snack-bar, so that the customers could have a bit of roast meat, if they like, or a drink. I would serve them cheap, too. I'd let them have real village food. Baked potato! Bacon-fat with garlic! Sauerkraut! I'd give them bone-marrow as a starter, a measure of vodka, a marrow bone, and black bread of course, and salt.

Leather chairs, so that the lice don't breed. The Customer could sit and rest and be served. If I were to say this out loud, I'd have been sent straight to Siberia. And yet, say I, what harm would I do to people?

(quoted from Wolff 2006: 147)

Nozick cuts right to the chase: "The socialist society would have to forbid capitalist acts between consenting adults" (Nozick 1974: 163). He goes even further. In principle one could uphold any patterned distribution, at least approximately, by a system of (progressive) taxes. Capitalist acts between consenting adults would not be banned, only their consequences cushioned. Against this idea Nozick argues that taxation is (on par with) forced labor (Nozick 1974: 169). If the income tax is, say, 25 percent, a person working 40 hours a week works 10 hours for other people. These 10 hours are forced labor, akin to slavery.

It is important to notice that despite his taxation/forced labor analogy, Nozick is not opposed to all taxation. Thus, he supports a minimal state: "limited, to the narrow functions of protection against force, theft, fraud, enforcement of contracts, and so on" (Nozick 1974: ix), and the level of taxation necessary to uphold it. But by allowing the state to play these roles (and there is no reason why he shouldn't), Nozick might open the door to a much greater degree of state involvement than he would like. For what is "protection against force, theft, fraud, enforcement of contracts, and so on" other than a public good, and aren't there other public goods for whose supply the state might be justified? More generally, aren't there many kinds of market imperfection that require state interventions or at least make them sensible?

Nozick bites the bullet in this respect. If some individuals voluntarily produce a good that has positive externalities—public entertainment, say—its recipients who have not agreed to take part are under no obligation to contribute (Nozick 1974: 90ff.). The negative consequences one would expect—undersupply of these goods—is something the libertarian will have to live with. The case of negative externalities is even worse. Suppose, as Nozick does, that the public entertainment comes in the form of a powerful public-address system in my vicinity I have no choice but to overhear. On some occasions I might enjoy it, but when I don't, my rights to a peaceful afternoon reading a book on my front porch are violated. Most productive activities involve at least some negative externalities (pollution, noise, depletion of resources, overuse of antibiotics, etc.), and thus engaging in these activities will come along with violations of someone's rights.

Nozick has two ways out. He could, first, extend the role of the state to protect its citizens from all negative externalities. This would be extremely expensive because of the direct costs of enforcement and the indirect costs of lost opportunities to produce. It would also mean that the state interferes a great deal more than Nozick would like. He could, second, in principle allow productive activities involving negative externalities but demand that rights violations are rectified in accordance with his third principle. But

Nozick says very little about that third principle except that it "presumably will make use of its best estimate of subjunctive information about what would have occurred (or a probability distribution over what might have occurred, using the expected value) if the injustice had not taken place" (Nozick 1974: 153). But in the absence of markets (and externalities only arise when certain markets are absent) such calculations are bound to be very difficult if not impossible to make. Externalities pose a problem to Nozick's theory (cf. Hausman 1992b).

There is another serious problem. Even supposing that people have exclusive property rights, given that there is overwhelming evidence that in the past many violations of people's rights have occurred, it is not clear why *today's* holdings should be protected by the state. It is overwhelmingly likely that today's distribution of property and other resources is not just according to Nozick's entitlement theory. But since an enormous amount of historical information is needed in order to determine the just state, information we don't have and most likely cannot have, there is no way to move from the current state to one that is just. Within the Nozickean system it is very hard to see, however, why an unjust distribution of property rights should be defended.

In sum, Nozick's libertarian proposal raises the following problems:

- Property rights are hard to justify within Nozick's system; at any rate, he doesn't offer a defense.
- Externalities pose a serious threat to all libertarian proposals; Nozick simply ignores this issue.
- Nozick's theory cannot justify *present* inequalities because they are likely to have arisen in part from past injustices; this poses a problem because:
  - it is difficult to identify the sources of current outcomes in the past;
  - Nozick doesn't offer a theory of rectifying past injustices.

Rawls and the Veil of Ignorance

John Rawls was a prominent American political philosopher, and his magnum opus, *A Theory of Justice* (Rawls 1971), is arguably the most important book in political philosophy of the twentieth century. In this book, he presents his account of "justice as fairness," which has important implications concerning principles of distributive justice. It is easiest to begin by stating the two principles Rawls defends in *A Theory of Justice* (and repeats in later work such as Rawls 1993, 2001):

1 Each person has an equal right to the most extensive scheme of equal basic liberties compatible with a similar scheme of liberties for all.
2 Social and economic inequalities are to satisfy two conditions: they must be (a) to the greatest benefit of the least advantaged members of society;

and (b) attached to offices and positions open to all under conditions of fair equality of opportunity.

The first principle concerns the political institutions of a society, and the second principle its socio-economic institutions. Rawls understands these principles to be "lexicographically ordered," with the first principle being prior to the second. This means that departures from the most extensive possible scheme of basic liberties cannot be justified or compensated for by greater socio-economic opportunities. Trade-offs are not allowed. For this reason, the first principle has also come to be known as the "Priority of Liberty" principle. It implies, for instance, that slavery can under no circumstances be justified, no matter what additional economic benefit a slaveholder economy would bear relative to alternative regimes in which people live in individual freedom. Rawls requires equality of the *fair value of political liberties*, not just formal equality. That is, citizens should have the same opportunities to hold office, to influence elections, etc., regardless of their income and social standing.

The first part of the second principle is also called the "Difference Principle." It requires that the socio-economic institution must be arranged in such a way as to benefit the worst off in society relative to a situation of greater equality. Table 14.1 describes four different imaginary institutional arrangements, the corresponding gross products and the products for different strata of society.

Provided that these are the only possible institutional arrangements, and interpreting the numbers as representing the value of "primary goods" rather than money income (see below), the difference principle would pick out the third arrangement as just. Inequalities exist—the least advantaged group has 20,000 on average, the richest group 45,000, but compared to other arrangements, the least advantaged benefit the most. The principle thus aims to trade off equality and efficiency considerations. Under the assumption that people tend to work harder when they have more allowing some degree of inequality can lead to a greater total income. Therefore, the completely

Table 14.1 Four Economic Systems

Society	Least advantaged	Middle class	The rich	Gross product
Egalitarianism (North Korea)	2,000	2,000	2,000	6,000
Social market economy (Germany)	15,000	20,000	65,000	100,000
Market economy, Scandinavian model	20,000	35,000	45,000	100,000
Hong Kong capitalism	5,000	30,000	115,000	150,000

egalitarian arrangement with very small gross product is rejected. But the poor should benefit from inequality. Economic growth cannot be bought at any cost. The highly unequal fourth arrangement is therefore rejected. Between the two societies with identical mid-range products, the more equal arrangement is preferred.

The second part of the second principle, fair equality of opportunity, requires that citizens with the same talents and willingness to put in effort have the same cultural, political and economic opportunities independently of whether they were born rich or poor. This calls for a much higher degree of social mobility than we currently observe in most societies. According to Rawls, fair equality of opportunity has priority over the difference principle. That is, even those inequalities that benefit the least advantaged in society are admissible only to the extent that everyone has the same degree of access to socio-economic goods.

To understand the significance of the two principles it is useful to explain in some detail how Rawls derives them. (I will focus on Rawls 1971 here, ignoring his later work, which keeps the principles but argues for them in different ways.) Rawls' main philosophical tool is a thought experiment about a hypothetical social contract we are invited to imagine forming. Justifying political institutions by means of a social contract has a long tradition in political philosophy, going back to Hobbes, Locke and Rousseau. Hobbes, Locke and Rousseau, each in his own way, have us imagine a situation in which all political institutions are absent, a "state of nature." Living in the state of nature is, according to these writers, not fun. In Hobbes' (1994 [1651]) words, the life of individuals in the state of nature would be "solitary, poor, nasty, brutish and short" (*Leviathan*, ch. 13, section 9), and there would be "warre of every one against every one" (ch. 14). For someone who agrees that the state of nature is undesirable (not everyone does!), it is easy to see that political institutions such as the state can help to overcome the downsides of anarchy. Social-contract theories all build in one way or another on this idea.

Rawls' theory stands firmly in the social-contract tradition but the philosopher adds a Kantian twist to it. With Kant Rawls thinks that people have the capacity for reasoning from a universal point of view, which for him means that they can judge principles from an impartial standpoint. The Rawlsian thought experiment, therefore, does not involve a state of nature but rather what he calls an "original position." In the original position we are placed behind a "veil of ignorance" that lets us forget everything about ourselves that is irrelevant, according to Rawls, from the point of view of justice. Thus, we don't know our race and class, gender and possessions, our natural talents, abilities and willingness to work. The selection of principles of justice is meant to be *disinterested*. Factors such as race and class, etc. are, however, likely to bias one's point of view. Being very talented, say, might incline us to regard arrangements in which the talented receive a large share as fair. Another thing we do not know is our conception of the good. We do not know, for instance, whether we are religious or whether we value freedom higher than equality or the other way around.

However, we are not completely ignorant. Quite to the contrary. We do know a great deal about general psychological tendencies, about human behavior, how markets work, biological evolution and the capacity of humans to develop ideas of justice and rationality. We also know a particular fact: that they are in a situation Hume described as "the circumstances of justice."

Hume famously said in his *Treatise of Human Nature* (Hume 1960 [1739]: 495): "that 'tis only from the selfishness and confin'd generosity of men, along with the scanty provision nature has made for his wants, that justice derives its origin." Only when resources are scarce, is there a point in competing for them; and only when we are not fully altruistic, when our interests sometimes conflict, would we compete for them. And only under these circumstances can something be gained from cooperation (Rawls 1971: 126). Conversely, it is important that resources not be *too* scarce. When people are fighting for their lives, proposals for acting justly and with consideration of others are likely to die away unheard. The circumstances of justice, according to Rawls, are such that cooperation is not only necessary but also possible.

Moreover, while we do not have a specific conception of the good, Rawls assumes that we all share some desires and lack others. What we all desire are what Rawls calls "primary goods": all-purpose means necessary to exercise morality and to pursue a wide variety of conceptions of the good. Specifically, primary goods are: rights and liberties, powers and opportunities, income and wealth and the social bases of self-respect. Rawls thinks that these are goods that any rational person should want, whatever his or her rational plan of life, whatever his or her conception of the good. While we all want primary goods (and the more of them, the better), Rawls assumes that in the original position we do not have other-regarding preferences; that people are mutually disinterested.

It is now easy to see how Rawls' first principle would be chosen by agents in the original position. Granting liberties to individuals is not immediately costly for other individuals. Rational and impartial agents with a desire for primary goods would therefore choose the maximum possible schema of liberties for everyone. But since the liberty of some individuals may conflict with that of others—my liberty to play my out-of-tune piano late at night conflicts with my neighbors' liberty to enjoy their peace and quiet at night—the extensiveness of liberties that can be granted is limited by requirement to grant the same liberties to everyone. The liberty to play music at night is not something that can be granted to everyone if there is a possibility that some members of society have a preference for peace and quiet at night. But since I don't know whether I'll be on one or the other side of the divide I will demand only such liberties everyone can enjoy. These are familiar examples: liberty of conscience and freedom of association, freedom of speech and liberty of the person, the rights to vote, to hold public office, to be treated in accordance with the rule of law and so on.

Would one always choose extensive liberties over advances in well-being, as is required by the lexicographic ordering of the two principles? This is where Rawls' assumption that people are in the "circumstances of justice" matters. There might well be situations in which it would be rational to curb freedoms in exchange for economic progress—who wouldn't rather have something to eat than the freedom of speech? But Rawls assumes away extreme situations such as wars and famines, and focuses on the, in his view, more common circumstances in which abject poverty and emergency are absent. (We will see below that this is one of the major criticisms of Rawls' position by Amartya Sen, who is greatly interested in poverty and development.)

As to the second principle, we first have to observe that we are in a situation of uncertainty (rather than risk; see Chapter 3). In the original position we simply don't know in what positions we will end up, and there are no probabilities attached to outcomes. We do not even know what the possible outcomes are. What would it be reasonable to do in such a situation? Of all possible answers, Rawls considers two in some detail: the utilitarian response—maximize expected utility!—and a principle called maximin.

As the name suggests, maximin picks out that alternative that *maximizes* the decision-maker's payoff among the states of the world that result in a *minimum* payoff for each strategy. The principle thus ignores all information except that about the worst-case scenarios for each alternative strategy.

Suppose now that our available "strategies" are the four institutional arrangements of Table 14.1. What decision principle would one choose behind the veil of ignorance? That situation is both one-off and final. That is, the choice is made just once, and once it is made, one will have to stick with it come what may. To maximize expected utility gives one a higher average payoff, if the choice is repeated. But the one-off situation choosing according to the maximin principle it is certainly plausible. If you don't know where you will be in society and you can choose only once, it makes sense to choose such that you'll be reasonably well off even if fate lets you end up at the bottom of society. The difference principle is a version of maximin, applied to the choice between socio-economic institutions.

Let us now turn to Rawls' method as such. Can the question "What is fair?" be addressed by asking "What would be fair in ideal conditions X?" Many social scientists do not hold this kind of speculation in high regard. This is not because they are generally opposed to speculation about "what would have been"—to some extent such speculation is an inevitable feature of life—but rather because their extreme remoteness from our everyday experiences is likely to make the results of such speculations unreliable. How *could* we know what we'd think if we were radically different people? In social science, this way of thinking goes back to at least Max Weber: "Max Weber insisted that plausible counterfactuals should make as few historical changes as possible on the grounds that the more we disturb the values, goals, and contexts in which actors operate, the less predictable their behavior becomes" (Lebow 2010: 55).

Even if we could agree on the outcome of the speculation, the question arises how binding it is. Not very much, thinks Ronald Dworkin (R. Dworkin 1978: 151): "A hypothetical contract is not simply a pale form of an actual contract; it is no contract at all." He illustrates his worry with a—hypothetical—poker game in which, after the cards have been dealt, it is discovered that a card is missing from the deck (R. Dworkin 1978: 151). You propose to throw in the cards and deal anew. If I refuse, because I was about to win, you might try to persuade me by saying that I would certainly have agreed to the procedure "behind the veil of ignorance," if the possibility of a missing card was raised before we knew what our hands were. However, argues Dworkin, this argument works only because "the solution recommended is so obviously fair and sensible that only someone with an immediate contrary interest could disagree" (R. Dworkin 1978: 151). It is therefore the fairness of a procedure that makes the thought-experimental result seem credible and not vice versa. The point is that we'd need an independent argument to show that Rawls' two principles are fair. Wouldn't it be much more convincing to show that it is in an agent's own best interest to agree to an institutional setting characterized by Rawls' principles than to argue that an agent would agree if he did not have any interests whatsoever?

We might also ask if the particular ingredients of the original position are as compelling as Rawls makes it seem. He assumes, as we have seen, that behind the veil of ignorance everyone will continue to want primary goods, and more of them is always better. But who is to say that this is true for every human being? Liberty, income, wealth and the "social bases for self-respect" may well be important in contemporary developed societies but not necessarily in every society (Wolff 2006: 170).

Finally, Rawls' principles themselves can be challenged. Many of us would agree that people who work harder than others, and those who have talents and use them intelligently, deserve more than those who are lazy, untalented or both. Even if I don't know whether I'll be hard-working or lazy, talented or klutzy, I might agree to a principle that rewards the hard-working and talented, simply because I believe that social outcomes should roughly be proportional to individuals' inputs. Moreover, from a libertarian point of view redistribution of the extent suggested by Rawls would be considered grossly unjust anyway (see previous section).

In sum, Rawls' principles of justice raise the following difficulties:

- The principles are established using a method that doesn't have the best credentials and whose results aren't regarded as binding by everyone.
- Rawls' "veil of ignorance" makes peculiar assumptions about what people know and do not know that do not seem compelling and that, arguably, are designed just so as to yield Rawls' principles as a result.
- The principles will not be convincing to those who come from radically different starting points, such as proponents of desert-based theories of justice or libertarians.

Capabilities

Amartya Sen is, in most of his work, less concerned with the fundamental justification of his preferred principle(s) of justice than with the day-to-day concerns of a working economist interested in existing poverty and deprivation and how to overcome them. His contributions to theories of justice and inequality are best regarded as being conceptual in nature and having in view the measurement of inequality, poverty and deprivation, rather than foundational issues. (I should add: probably rightly so—can the foundational issues ever be addressed convincingly?)

A central question Sen asks is (e.g., Sen 1999b: ch. 3): what is the kind of information we have to look for when addressing matters of justice? The different theories we have looked at so far give different answers, all of which are severely flawed in Sen's view.

Take utilitarianism first. Utilitarianism is a consequentialist theory, and as such it assesses the justice of acts, policies and institutions exclusively in terms of their consequences for the well-being of individuals. But not all situations where people are well off appear to be just. Sen is mainly concerned about phenomena such as adaptive preferences, where people's preferences are satisfied and yet, according to Sen, there is lack or deprivation of justice. Because of misinformation, destitution, oppression or personality, persons who lack even the most basic amenities of a flourishing life may not desire any of these amenities because they lost them in a process of coming to terms with the situation they find themselves in which is characterized by lack of realistic opportunities of change. They adapt to their situation because not doing so would result in enduring frustration and pain. Under utilitarianism, a person who's adapted to his or her situation would, in a way, be doubly deprived: first, by the lack of the amenities leading to a good life and, second, by the lack of recognition of their plight.

Another problem of utilitarianism we have considered is that people's utilities are not observable. Applied economists therefore often take income as a proxy for utility, which, at least under a preference-satisfaction view of utility and well-being, is sensible: the more income one has, the more preferences one can satisfy. But income, Sen argues, is a resource, and different people have differential abilities to convert resources into well-being. Suppose "being warm" and "being able to get around" are things that contribute to a person's well-being. If two people have the same income, this is a bad indicator of equivalent levels of well-being if one, say, lives in a hot country and another in a cold country, or if one is paraplegic and the other isn't. A person living in a cold country requires more resources than a person living in a hot country if she wants to be warm—she'll require more clothes, better insulation in her dwelling, heating in the winter. The paraplegic will require a wheelchair and the community to provide for ramps, lifts and other means to make places accessible in order to "get around." Their ability to convert resources into well-being differ therefore in numerous respects (Sen 1999b: 70–1):

- in personal heterogeneities;
- in environmental diversities;
- in variations in social climate;
- in differences in relational perspectives; and
- in the distribution within the family.

This point about heterogeneities Sen also uses to criticize Rawls' theory of justice. As we have seen, in Rawls' theory primary goods—rights and liberties, powers and opportunities, income and wealth, and the social bases of self-respect—play a central role. But, Sen argues, primary goods are resources, and their usefulness to an individual depends on his or her personal characteristics and environment. What is true for income and wealth is true also for rights and liberties. An individual may, for instance, be granted the freedom of movement, but if he or she needs a wheelchair and does not have the financial resources or is not covered by a health insurance policy, he or she will nevertheless not be mobile. Freedoms an individual has but cannot use to achieve well-being because of the lack of some other resource or natural talent or ability Sen calls "formal freedoms." And this is the core of Sen's critique of primary goods: formal freedoms may in many cases not be enough for people to achieve the kind of life they would value. Something else is needed, and Sen thinks that his notion of a "capability" captures what this is.

Before turning to capabilities, however, let us briefly consider Sen's other criticisms of liberal theories such as Rawls' and libertarian theories such as Nozick's. Sen acknowledges that rights and liberties should have a special status in political theory, because of their importance in political judgments, but he disputes that they should be given uncompromising priority over other considerations. Specifically, he asks, "Why should the status of intense economic needs, which can be matters of life and death, be lower than that of political liberties?" (Sen 1999b: 64). (As we know, Rawls is aware of this limitation of his theory. He explicitly restricts its application to the societies in the "circumstances of justice," i.e., when economic issues are not "matters of life and death." Unlike Rawls, Sen is interested in development, poverty and destitution, however, and therefore has to build a theory that applies to *these* circumstances.)

Sen's criticism of Nozick's libertarian theory is a simple appeal to our intuitions. He notes that he has shown in his book *Poverty and Famines* (Sen 1983b) that even grave famines can result without anyone's libertarian rights being violated. This he takes to show that the satisfaction of formal freedoms cannot be all that matters in a theory of justice.

Two concepts are at the core of Sen's alternative account: functionings and capabilities. *Functionings* are people's doings and beings. People like to *do* things: read, move about, have fun with their friends, voice their agreement or disagreement with the government; and they like to *be* things: healthy, fed, clad, respected. Capabilities are alternative combinations of functionings that are feasible for a person to achieve. As I understand it, the idea is best illustrated mathematically (see Figure 14.1).

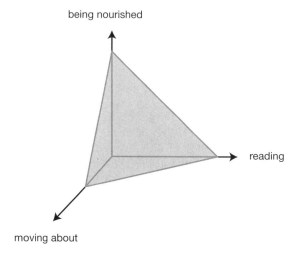

being nourished

reading

moving about

Figure 14.1 Representation of a Capabilities Set

Suppose an individual, Marina, values only three things in her life: she wants to be fed, move about and read. These are her functionings. Now, given her resources (including her natural talents and the willingness to use them), she can achieve a certain level of functioning along each of the three dimensions. For instance, she could invest most of her money in food and read only the free paper on the Underground. Or she could, instead, fast and invest every penny in highbrow literature. Or she can learn how to ride a Harley, save all her money for it and eventually buy one. And so on. Marina's capabilities set is the set of alternative combinations of functionings she is able to achieve, given her situation. The triangle in Figure 14.1 represents this set.

In order to compare levels of development or poverty between different social groups according to the capabilities approach, we have to know what the relevant functionings are, how to weigh and aggregate them, and how to measure capabilities. Unfortunately, Sen is very unspecific in all three respects. With regard to the question of how to determine the core functionings and their weights, two alternative proposals have been made. Sen himself argues in favor of a deliberative-democratic approach. At the level of the individual, persons can arrive at a list of the things they value most and an estimation of how much they value each functioning through reflection. For policy purposes, something else is needed:

> However, in arriving at an "agreed" range for *social evaluation* (for example in social studies of poverty), there has to be some kind of a reasoned "consensus" on [functionings]. This is a "social choice" exercise, and it requires public discussion and a democratic understanding

and acceptance. It is not a special problem that is associated only with the use of the functioning space.

(Sen 1999b: 78–9; original emphasis, footnote suppressed)

Martha Nussbaum, the classicist, political philosopher and public intellectual mentioned in Chapter 12, by contrast, endorses a well-defined objective list of core functionings: life, health, bodily integrity, being able to think and imagine, being able to have emotions, being able to form a conception of the good, being able to live with and toward others, having the social bases of self-respect, being able to live with concern for animals, being able to laugh and play and having control over one's material and political environment. Nussbaum thinks that each of these functionings is needed in order for a human life to be "not so impoverished that it is not worthy of the dignity of a human being" (Nussbaum 2000: 72) and argues that every human being on earth is entitled to them. While the list is formulated at an abstract level, she advocates implementation and policies at a local level which take into account local differences.

Both views have obvious and complementary drawbacks. If one were to follow Sen to the letter, one could not even do social science without a prior democratic deliberation on the list of functionings that matter. This would not only hobble social science as we know it, we can also expect that for most cases, democratic deliberation of the kind Sen envisages remains an unattainable ideal. Nussbaum does not have these problems, but she has to respond to the charge of being patronizing (see Chapter 12). Why should anyone accept that her preferred set of functionings are what he or she ought to value?

Even when there is agreement on the list of core functionings, there are serious practical obstacles to implementing the approach. In order to provide a basis for social evaluation, capabilities have to be measured. Sen says very little about practical implementation, save that one might try to *directly* measure capabilities, *supplement* current measures of well-being (such as GDP) with information about capabilities, or *adjust* current measures using information about capabilities (Sen 1999b: 82–5). The basic problem is, however, that capabilities are not directly observable. Central to the idea of capabilities is the distinction between achievements (or outcomes) and real freedoms (or what one could have achieved). The capabilities set refers to the set of combinations of functionings that a person could have achieved. Obviously, at best what a person achieves is directly observable and not what he or she could have achieved. But this does not mean that it is impossible to give the capabilities idea some empirical content. Data on, say, mortality and morbidity, on literacy and educational attainment are all plausibly relevant for the assessment of people's capabilities.

The Human Development Index (HDI) is an example of what Sen would call an income-adjusted measure that has been computed and published by the United Nations Development Programme since 1990. It combines measures of life expectancy at birth, schooling and gross national income.

Specifically, the HDI is calculated as the geometric mean of a life-expectancy index:

LEI = (life expectancy at birth – 20)/(83.4 – 20),

an education index:

EI = √(MYSI × EYSI)/0.951,

where the mean years of schooling index (MYSI), a calculation of the average number of years of education received by people aged 25 and older in their lifetime, is computed as (mean years of schooling)/13.4 and the expected years of schooling index (EYSI), a calculation of the number of years a child of school-entrance age is expected to spend at school or university, as (expected years of schooling)/20.6, and an income index:

II = (ln(GNP per capita) – ln(100))/(ln(107,712) – ln(100)).

HDI = ³√(LEI × EI × II).

While Sen was instrumental in devising and launching the index, he has always remained at a critical distance from it because he doubts that a complex idea such as human development can be expressed by a single number (Sen 1999a). In 2010, the Oxford Poverty and Human Development Initiative (OPHI) developed the Multidimensional Poverty Index (MPI), which measures poverty in these 10 dimensions: child mortality, nutrition, years of schooling, child school attendance, electricity, sanitation, drinking water, floor, cooking fuel and assets. A household is regarded as deprived if, for instance, it has no electricity, a dirt, sand or dung floor, or if it cooks with dung, wood or charcoal. While including more information than the HDI, the MPI also aggregates it into a single index. A true multidimensional index would abstain from the aggregation, as Sen seems to suggest, but that would come at the expense of making comparisons across countries, regions or times much harder.

These practical obstacles aside, it is important to note that the capabilities approach is not a full-fledged theory of justice. It helps the social analyst to think about how to evaluate matters of social justice but it does not in itself provide resources for justifying interventions (or justifying not intervening). Ingrid Robeyns argues that the approach needs fixing in these seven areas (Robeyns 2011):

1   it needs to explain on what basis it justifies its principles or claims of justice;
2   it has to decide whether it wants to be an outcome or an opportunity theory (i.e., whether the focus should be on functionings or capabilities);

3   [as explained above,] it has to address the issue of selecting, quantifying and aggregating of dimensions;
4   it may need to address other "metrics of justice" (such as Rawlsian primary goods);
5   it needs to take a position on the principle of distribution that it will endorse: will it argue for plain equality, or for sufficiency, or for prioritarianism or for some other (mixed) distributive rule?
6   it needs to specify where the line between individual and collective responsibility is drawn;
7   it will have to address the question who should bear the duties for the expansion of the selected capabilities.

The capabilities approach has been enormously successful in drawing economists', philosophers' and political and other social scientists' attention to it in recent years but much work needs to be done before it can be accepted as a viable alternative to utilitarianism, libertarianism or Rawls' theory of justice.

Conclusions

Theories of justice are meant to help justify institutions and policy interventions. Depending on some empirical facts, one can probably justify a relatively free market economy with some welfare state on utilitarian grounds, a much higher degree of redistribution on Rawlsian grounds, abstaining from almost all redistribution on libertarian grounds and (depending on specifications in various dimensions) redistribution aimed at securing a threshold level of capabilities for everyone on capability theory grounds. But each of these theories is itself hard to justify. It is certainly plausible that in deciding whether and how to build institutions and implement policies the consequences of these institutions and policies for people's levels of well-being should count, but why should that be all that counts? It is also plausible to assume that people have certain rights, but why should these include strong property rights, especially when using one's rights almost always results in externalities? We can also plausibly assume that people would agree to Rawls' principles of justice if they were in the original position, but why should just that context be relevant to considerations of justice, and anyway why should we care, if we haven't actually agreed to anything? And it would be nice if we lived in a world where states guarantee a threshold level of capabilities to everyone, as Martha Nussbaum demands, but if we don't, how can we persuade people to give their money away so that less fortunate people's capabilities can be increased?

These are all serious foundational problems philosophers, economists and other social scientists are debating with more or less success. All available theories of justice might have their flaws but they certainly help raise important normative issues and help make us think clearly about income distribution and other matters of social justice. The inexistence of easy solutions doesn't give us a reason not to try.

Study Questions

1   Can the utilitarian provide a defense for the criticism that he ignores people's rights?
2   Develop a utilitarian justification of property rights. How convincing could such a defense be?
3   What would be an alternative justification of Rawls' social contract that does not make use of his hypothetical thought experiment?
4   Do you find Nussbaum's universalist or Sen's public-reasoning approach to capabilities more convincing? Defend your answer.
5   All the theories of justice discussed suffer from a lack of ultimate justification. What would be an alternative form of justification that makes this or that theory more palatable?

Suggested Readings

A good introduction to the *history* of utilitarianism is Driver 2009. The most prominent contemporary utilitarian is probably Peter Singer; see for instance Singer 1979. Among many other things, Singer defends the view that the principle "the greatest good to the greatest number" should also apply to non-human animals. A staunch critic was Bernard Williams (e.g., Williams 2011). The collection Sen and Williams 1982 contains defenses and criticisms of utilitarianism and some essays on utilitarianism and economics.

Lomasky 1987 presents a forceful rights-based approach to morality. Otsuka 2003 and Steiner 1994 defend so-called left-libertarianism. In contrast to right-libertarianism (of which Nozick 1974 was a proponent) left-libertarianism holds that unappropriated natural resources belong to everyone in some egalitarian manner, which provides a justification for redistribution. See Vallentyne 2012 for the distinction. Among economists, right-wing libertarianism is not uncommon. One of the more radical defenders is Milton Friedman's son David; see D. Friedman 1989 [1973]. A near-contemporary critic of the idea that capitalism can be derived from self-ownership and defender of socialism is Cohen 1995.

Social-contract theories originate in the political thought of Hobbes, Locke, Kant and Rousseau. Contemporary social-contract ideas come in two guises: contractarianism and contractualism. The former derives from Hobbes and holds that persons are self-interested; cooperation and moral action are a result of a rational self-interested analysis of the situation. The latter derives from Kant and holds that rationality requires that we respect persons; moral principles must therefore be such that they are publicly justifiable. The most prominent contemporary defender of contractarianism is David Gauthier; see Gauthier 1986. A prominent contemporary defender of contractualism apart from Rawls 1971 is Thomas Scanlon; see Scanlon 1998.

A good recent collection of essays on the capabilities approach is Brighouse and Robeyns 2010. In his 2009, Sen criticizes what he calls "transcendental" approaches to political philosophy that understand their task to be the identification of the perfectly just society. He argues that we need instead *comparative* approaches that tell us how to make the world less unjust; knowing the nature of perfect justice he thinks is neither necessary nor particularly helpful for this task.

15 Behavioral Economics and Nudge

- Overview
- Behavioral Economics
- Libertarian Paternalism
- Philosophical Issues in Libertarian Paternalism
- Conclusions
- Study Questions
- Suggested Readings

Overview

The book *Nudge: Improving Decisions about Health, Wealth, and Happiness* by Richard Thaler and Cass Sunstein (Thaler and Sunstein 2008; henceforth T&S) has received much critical and wider attention. According to Google Scholar, it has been cited 1,760 times (June 2012); even *Freakonomics* (Levitt and Dubner 2005) achieves only 943 citations, despite being a couple of years longer on the market. It has been reviewed countless times, including in daily newspapers such as the *New York Times*, the *Guardian* and the German *Handelsblatt*, as well as magazines such as the *New Yorker* and *Newsweek*. *The Economist* named it a "Best Book of the Year" in 2008. Richard Thaler, the Ralph and Dorothy Keller Distinguished Service Professor of Behavioral Science and Economics at the University of Chicago Booth School of Business, is the founder of an asset management firm, Fuller & Thaler Asset Management, that enables investors to exploit numerous cognitive biases. Cass Sunstein, a legal scholar who taught for 27 years at the University of Chicago Law School, is now Administrator of the White House Office of Information and Regulatory Affairs and has exerted a notable influence in the Obama administration. The latter has brought him a recognition of being "seventh-ranked Global Thinker" in *Foreign Policy* magazine. If you want to do philosophy of economics in a practically relevant and influential way, write a book like *Nudge*.

The reason for ending this book with a discussion of *Nudge* is not so much to add to its praise (though I do quite like it, unlike many of my philosophy of economics colleagues) but to discuss a policy proposal that nicely brings together many of the themes that have been touched upon in this book: rationality, experimental economics, evidence, theories of well-being and justice and market failure. In my view it is hard to fully appreciate T&S's policy proposal "libertarian paternalism" without a good understanding of all these areas within the philosophy of economics. And so it's most appropriate to end this book with a discussion of *Nudge*.

Behavioral Economics

T&S's policy recommendations are based on various experimental findings concerning the effects of cognitive, emotional and social factors on decision-making, and their consequences for market outcomes, which are loosely united under the label "behavioral economics." Behavioral economics is now a thriving subdiscipline within economics, and has sometimes been described as the "combination of psychology and economics" (Mullainathan and Thaler 2001). One way to portray its achievements is to say that behavioral economics makes economic theory somewhat more realistic by relaxing (relative to mainstream neoclassical economics) a number of core idealizations concerning agents' rationality, willpower and selfishness. Let us go through failures of each of these in turn. (All findings discussed below have to be taken with caution as they are potentially subject to problems of internal and external validity, see Chapters 10 and 11. Focusing on ethical and policy related issues I will ignore the methodological complications here. A full-fledged appraisal of Nudge would, of course, have to include their assessment.)

Failures of Rationality

In the chapters on rational-choice theory, game theory and experimental economics we've already encountered some of the experimental findings showing that ordinary humans do not always display full rationality as described by rational-choice and game theory in their behavior. Here are some examples of failures that will be relevant later in the chapter.

Loss Aversion/Framing

Loss aversion refers to people's tendency to strongly prefer avoiding losses to acquiring gains. People, for example, can be shown to have a certain willingness to pay for a good they could buy; but they often demand a higher price after they've owned the good for a short period of time. Some studies suggest that losses are twice as powerful as gains in terms of psychological experience.

This is related to an issue called "framing." There is some evidence that people will make different decisions depending on whether the transaction is framed as a gain or a loss. This explains the widespread practice of describing credit-card surcharges as "cash discounts": people prefer to avoid a loss to making an identical gain. To give a numerical example, consider the following choices (Tversky and Kahneman 1981):

Choice 1
Program A: Saves 200 people;
Program B: Saves 600 people with p = 1/3; saves no one with p = 2/3;

Choice 2
Program C: 400 people die;
Program D: No one dies with p = 1/3; 600 people die with p = 2/3.

Studies have shown that about three-quarters of respondents prefer option A to B in choice 1; in choice 2, about three-quarters prefer option D to C. But options A and C, and B and D, respectively, say exactly the same.

Time-Inconsistent Choices

People often make more reasonable choices when planning ahead of time but relatively shortsighted decisions when some costs or benefits are immediate. It is much easier, for instance, to prefer doing what one considers to be the right thing when the alternatives occur far into the future than when they occur very soon. I can form a preference for working rather than drinking on November 1, 2017 relatively easily (and even commit to this preference!), but my willpower concerning the same decision for this evening is fading as we speak. People, thus, discount the immediate future much more heavily than periods that occur later in time. In one study Indian farmers made several choices between amounts of rice that would be delivered either sooner or later. The discount rate was estimated by fixing the earlier rice ration and varying the amount of rice delivered later. None of the choices was delivered immediately. Per-period discount rates declined with the increasing horizon: the mean estimated discount rate was 0.46 for 7 months and 0.33 for 5 years (Pender 1996).

Now, the fact that people discount in one way or the other does not as such constitute an irrationality. The problem is that time-varying discount rates induce preference changes. Jon Elster illustrates this in what he calls the "dentist puzzle," as follows:

On March 1 I make an appointment with the dentist for April 1. On March 30 I call her to say that because of a (fictitious) funeral in the family I cannot keep it. Except for the sheer passage of time, no change has occurred in the interval. In particular, the pain from toothache is the same.
(Elster 2007: 218)

The situation is illustrated in Figure 15.1. The subjective value of option O_2 is higher than alternative option O_1 if the decision is made at T_1. At time T_2, the preference has changed, and O_1 is now valued higher than O_2.

The endowment effect, loss aversion, framing and hyperbolic discounting induce preference changes. Subjects prefer having $2 to having a mug if they don't own it already, but they prefer having the mug to as much as $5 once they own it; they prefer saving 200 people for sure to a lottery in which on average 200 people are saved but the lottery to the certain outcome when the outcome is described in terms of "killings" rather than "savings"; they prefer a dentist's appointment to an increased chance of a toothache when the appointment is in three weeks but the increased chance of a toothache to seeing the dentist if it is tomorrow. Since all these factors—ownership, framing, time—are ones that should be irrelevant to someone's preferences, these data show that people's preferences violate the stability assumption, the invariance assumption or both. (See Chapter 3 for statements of these assumptions.)

Anchoring

For expected-utility theory one also needs beliefs concerning probabilities, and further results show that subjects often misjudge probabilities in ways that conflict with the axioms of probability theory. For instance, one study shows that when subjects are given the choice of betting on one of two events where each event is of the following kind:

- *simple event*—drawing a red marble from an urn containing 50 percent red and 50 percent white marbles;

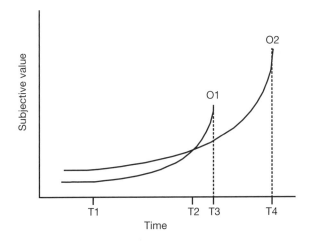

Figure 15.1 Discounting-Induced Preference Changes

- *conjunctive event*— drawing a red marble (with replacement) seven times in succession from an urn containing 90 percent red and 10 percent white marbles;
- *disjunctive event*—drawing a red marble (with replacement) at least once in seven draws from an urn containing 10 percent red and 90 percent white marbles;

people tend to prefer the conjunctive event (probability = 0.48) to the simple event (probability = 0.5) and the simple event to the disjunctive event (probability = 0.52) (Bar-Hillel 1973). Amos Tversky and Daniel Kahneman explain this phenomenon by "anchoring" (Tversky and Kahneman 1974). The probability of the simple event provides a natural starting point for estimating the conjunctive and disjunctive events. Adjustments are made but they typically remain insufficient, so that estimates of the complex events are too close to the probability of the simple event which in this case provides the "anchor."

Failing Willpower

Whereas violations of the assumptions of rational-choice theory such as those discussed in the previous subsection also constitute problems for the theory as predictive and explanatory theory, the fact that people don't always do what they would like to if they had complete self-control is mainly a problem for that theory as a normative theory of choice and for the preference-satisfaction theory of well-being (see Chapter 12). People who behave in ways that do not correspond to their preference ordering can be hardly said to act rationally, and it is unlikely that in so doing they promote their well-being. I can be as resolved as I want to stay home, have tea and read a good book though in fact I end up going out drinking and doing silly things anyway. Resolve doesn't promote well-being, action does.

An early study on willpower was the Stanford marshmallow experiment, conducted by the psychologist Walter Mischel in 1972 (Shoda *et al.* 1990). In the experiment, children aged four to six were led into a room where a treat of their choice (such as an Oreo cookie, marshmallow or pretzel stick) was placed on a table. The children could have the treat immediately, but were told that if they waited for 15 minutes without giving in to the temptation they would be rewarded with a second treat of the same kind. Only about a third of the children could hold out, most of them waiting for some time but eventually giving in. The experiment does not provide conclusive evidence that most of the children in the experiment lack willpower. Perhaps they genuinely prefer one marshmallow sooner to two marshmallows minutes later. But the fact that only a minority of the children had theirs immediately while most of them waited for some time (on average about three minutes) strongly suggests that they would have liked to wait but weren't able to. An interesting follow-up finding was that those children who were able to delay gratification were, years later, significantly more likely to be described by their parents as "competent adolescents" and had higher SAT scores (Shoda *et al.* 1990).

Similarly, a more recent study finds that, following a cohort of 1,000 individuals from birth to age 32, childhood self-control predicts physical health, substance dependence, personal finance and criminal-offending outcomes, controlling for intelligence and social class (Moffitt *et al.* 2011). Other findings suggest that willpower (or lack thereof) explains the degree of self-control individuals are able to exert, and that willpower comes in cycles and can deplete and replenish (Burger *et al.* 2009).

Failures of Selfishness

People clearly care about more than their own bellies and often decide in ways that benefit others at a cost to themselves. People also *punish* others at a cost to themselves. To call such behavior irrational would be disingenuous. Our species would not be able to survive if there was no altruism, and even in economic transactions some degree of altruism seems necessary in order not to create transaction costs that would make most exchange prohibitively expensive (Arrow 1973). Nevertheless, it would be as mistaken to regard altruistic decisions generally as ones that promote the decision-maker's well-being. A father's decision to share the small bowl of rice that constitutes his only meal of the day with his son may well be for the benefit of the species but it is most probably not good for him; a vegan activist's decision to punish the Big John Steak & Onion customer at a cost to herself may well benefit Milwaukee cows but it is not good for her. Altruistic acts therefore constitute another reason why the satisfaction of actual preferences cannot be identified with well-being.

We have seen many examples of evidence for non-selfish behavior in previous chapters: people give up almost half of their endowments in ultimatum games; they still transfer money to the other player in dictator games, even though there is no risk of punishment; some individuals reject unfair and sometimes even hyper-fair offers in ultimatum games in order to uphold social norms; people contribute significant amounts to public goods and cooperate in many other Prisoner's Dilemma-type situations and so on. But since T&S do not consider nudges towards more self-interested behavior, I will not further discuss altruistic preferences here.

The Behavioral Alternative

As mentioned above, behavioral economics is more an umbrella term referring to approaches that seek to account for observed anomalies of human behavior (relative to mainstream economics) than a theoretical framework in its own right. One cannot therefore summarize the essence of what the alternative amounts to in a few sentences. So instead of providing such a summary, let me briefly introduce a couple of examples of theoretical achievements within behavioral economics.

Prospect Theory

Prospect theory is thought to explain certain phenomena more accurately than expected-utility theory (Kahneman and Tversky 1979). The theory distinguishes two phases in the choice process: editing and evaluation. The editing phase organizes and reformulates the offered prospects into a simplified form. For example, using an operation Kahneman and Tversky call "Coding," outcomes are transformed into gains and losses, using a neutral reference point such as the subject's current asset position. The second phase evaluates the simplified prospects and chooses the highest-valued prospect. This is done using a function with two main components: a probability-weighting function and a value function. The weighting function $w(p)$ combines two elements: (1) the level of probability weight is a way of expressing risk tastes (a risk-averse person places a low weight on any chance of winning anything, etc.); and (2) the curvature in $w(p)$ captures how sensitive people are to differences in probabilities. If people are more sensitive in extreme probabilities, then their $w(p)$ curve will overweight low probabilities and underweight high ones. The value function v reflects the fact that people value losses differently from gains. In Kahneman and Tversky's formulation, the overall or expected utility of a prospect is given by the following formula:

$$U = \sum w(p_i)v(x_i),$$

where the x_i's are the outcomes and the p_i's their probabilities. The shape v takes is shown in Figure 15.2.

Prospect theory thus builds various anomalies of EUT right into the theory. For example, the two programs A/C (as well as B/D) of the example

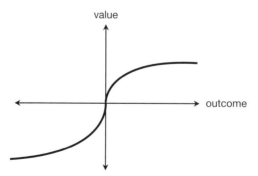

Figure 15.2 The Utility Function According to Prospect Theory

in the section on "Failures of Rationality" earlier in this chapter are not conceptualized as equivalent in the first phase of applying the theory but as involving a loss and a gain, respectively. Since losses are regarded as more important than corresponding gains (as can be seen from the shape of the valuation function), A/C (and B/D) are *not* equivalent, and the theory correctly predicts that subjects choose A in choice 1 and D in choice 2. The theory predicts anomalies such as the endowment effect, loss aversion, the status-quo bias and various puzzles in finance such as the equity premium puzzle, the excess returns puzzle and long swings/PPP puzzle of exchange rates.

Hyperbolic Discounting

A standard assumption economists make is that people weight future utilities by an exponentially declining discount factor $d(t) = \delta^t$, with δ strictly between 0 and 1. The discount factor δ can also be expressed as $1/(1 + r)$, where r is a discount *rate*. However, simple hyperbolic discounting functions of the form $d(t) = 1/(1 + kt)$ tend to fit experimental data much better than the exponential discounting model. An individual who discounts utilities exponentially would, if faced with the same choice and the same information, make the same decision prospectively as he would when the time for a decision actually arrived. In contrast, somebody with time-inconsistent hyperbolic discounting will wish prospectively that in the future he would take farsighted actions; but when the future arrives he will behave against his earlier wishes, pursuing immediate gratification rather than long-run well-being.

Hyperbolic discounting thus explains the dentist puzzle Elster described but also various other self-control problems involved in decisions concerning savings, educational investments, labor supply, health and diet, crime and drug use, as well as the commitment devices people use such as Christmas clubs and investment in illiquid assets (Laibson *et al.* 1998).

Behavioral Game Theory

The behavior of human subjects in experimental conditions violates the predictions of rational-choice theory also in strategic situations in numerous ways, as we have seen. Behavioral game theory builds on these findings, making a number of amendments to standard game theory. One of the amendments is the assumption of *social preferences*. People are thought not only to care about their own payoffs but also those of other players. We considered Fehr and Schmidt's theory of fairness above in Chapter 4. To repeat, their utility function for two-person games has the following form (Fehr and Schmidt 1999: 822):

$$U_i(x) = x_i - \alpha_i \max\{x_j - x_i, 0\} - \beta_i \max\{x_i - x_j, 0\}, \ i \neq j,$$

where the x's are player i's and j's monetary payoffs and α and β are parameters measuring how disadvantageous and advantageous inequality affects a player's utility. If players' α's and β's can be measured, the utility function can be used to predict choices in strategic settings.

Another amendment behavioral game theory makes is to give up the assumption of mutual consistency which is implied by the Nash equilibrium solution concept. Take the Beauty-Contest Game as an example. Players choose a number between 0 and 100, and the player whose number is closest in absolute value to 2/3 times the average wins a prize. The Nash equilibrium in this game is zero. Suppose a player believes that other players choose randomly so that the average guess among other players should be 50. She will therefore choose 33. If other players reason the same way, the best response to that strategy would be to choose 22. That reasoning continues all the way down to zero. In experimental tests of this game, most subjects choose either 33 or 22 but do not continue the stepwise reasoning further. Decision rules have been proposed to make sense of such choices in one-shot games or the first stage of repeated games (see for instance Stahl and Wilson 1995; Costa-Gomes *et al.* 2001; Camerer *et al.* 2003). There is also a great deal of work on theories of learning in games (for an overview, see Camerer 2003: ch. 6).

Libertarian Paternalism

The Theory

We learn from behavioral economics, then, that people often make bad choices—because they fail to get their preference ordering straight or misjudge probabilities or because of defective willpower. The simple idea of libertarian paternalism is that people's choices can be subtly manipulated in ways that make them better off, without limiting the range of options available to them. On the one hand, the policies T&S advocate are said to be *paternalistic* in that these authors "argue for self-conscious efforts, by institutions in the private sector and also by government, to steer people's choices in directions that will improve their lives." In their understanding, "a policy is 'paternalistic' if it tries to influence choices in a way that will make choosers better off, *as judged by themselves*" (T&S 2008: 5; original emphasis). The policies they advocate are, on the other hand, said to be libertarian in their "insistence that, in general, people should be free to do what they like—and to opt out of undesirable arrangements if they want to do so" (T&S 2008: 5).

How can people be free to do what they like and their choices at the same time be influenced by benevolent policy-makers and managers of private enterprises? To argue their case T&S invoke the notion of a choice *architecture*. Choices are necessarily made in a context or environment. If you choose strawberries over bananas you don't do so in an otherwise empty space (and even that would constitute a special environment!) but rather in a supermarket where the fruit is laid out in a certain way or from a restaurant menu where it appears somewhere in a list; if you don't choose a certain presumption will be made (for instance you'll be getting the standard desert—chocolate cake—in a three-course meal which you could have substituted, but did not, by your choice of fruit); in each case the options will be described or "advertised" in certain ways and so on.

T&S now observe that the choice context matters for the decision at hand. Items that are placed at eye level or near the cash desks in a supermarket are more likely to be chosen than items in less conspicuous locations, independently of what these items are. People's actions often display inertia and a status-quo bias so that whatever is the default option has an important influence on what alternative people end up with. An example of how framing effects influence people's choices has been given above. Now suppose you are not an experimental subject having to make a choice between policies described in terms of lives saved or humans killed, respectively, but rather a patient who is given treatment options by a physician:

> The doctor says, "Of one hundred patients who have this operation, ninety are alive after five years." What will you do? If we fill in the facts in a certain way, the doctor's statement will be pretty comforting, and you'll probably have the operation.
>
> But suppose the doctor frames his answer in a somewhat different way. Suppose that he says, "Of one hundred patients who have this operation, ten are dead after five years." If you're like most people, the doctor's statement will sound pretty alarming, and you might not have the operation.
>
> (T&S 2008: 36)

The first step in T&S's argument is, then, that choice context or environment influences the choices people actually make. The second step is their view that people do not always choose in ways that benefit them. There are in fact two sides to this step. T&S, first, assume some sort of "laundered preference" theory of well-being (see Chapter 12). This much is clear from their definition of a paternalistic intervention that was cited above: it aims to make choosers better off *as judged by themselves*. One can interpret that as saying that a choice is welfare-enhancing if and only if an individual would make that choice if she were fully informed and attentive, acted in accordance with her farsighted preferences, free of biases and so on. T&S thus reject alternative theories of well-being such as hedonism (a theory espoused by other behavioral economists, most notably Daniel Kahneman and his associates) as well as objective-list theories. This is important, as it seems to be a lot more difficult to provide evidence for a claim that holds that a policy improves a person's well-being when that well-being is constituted by what that person would choose if she were fully informed and so forth than when well-being is constituted by, say, health and other objective functionings.

That strawberries are better for a person's health than chocolate cake is pretty clear, but less clear is what that person would choose under somewhat idealized conditions if she in fact chooses chocolate cake.

Second is T&S's belief that there is evidence that people choose in ways they would not had they been better informed, possessed better strength of will and so on. Evidence is hardly ever conclusive but one can adduce considerations in favor of the claim. For instance, in their discussion of the Save More Tomorrow policy (which we will look at in more detail below) T&S argue that (T&S 2008: ch. 6):

- Americans save *little*, absolutely speaking (the personal savings rate has been declining since the 1970s and reached negative levels in the 2000s).
- The costs of saving too little are greater than the costs of saving too much (it is for instance easier to retire early than to find work after reaching retirement age).
- There are some people who *do not participate at all* in a retirement plan.
- Some people *say* they save too little: e.g., in one study, 68 percent of 401(k) participants said that their savings rate is too low.

The third step is, finally, the idea that the choice context or environment can be subtly manipulated such that people choose in a way they would have chosen if they hadn't been subject to decision-making flaws. These manipulations T&S call "nudges." Specifically, a nudge is "any aspect of the choice architecture that alters people's behavior in a predictable way without forbidding any options or significantly changing their economic incentives" (T&S 2008: 6). When an environment can be manipulated in ways that influence people's choices, the environment is called a "choice architecture" and the person doing the manipulation a "choice architect."

The "paternalism" part of their thought is that nudges should (a) interfere with choices; and (b) aim to improve the chooser's well-being. The "libertarian" part is that nudges are mere "nudges" and not "shoves" or outright "holdups": they (c) do not decrease the number of available options, nor do they dramatically alter the costs associated with the alternatives. In what follows, I will call only manipulations of choice environments that satisfy (a)–(c) "nudges" (possibly against T&S's use of the term; see below). Let us see how this is meant to work in practice by means of a few paradigmatic examples T&S give.

Examples

Carolyn's Cafeterias

T&S ask their readers to consider an imaginary friend, Carolyn, who runs the food services for a large city school system and has to decide whether to give directors of school cafeterias specific instructions about how to display food items, and if so, what directions to give. She knows that by rearranging the cafeteria, she is able to increase or decrease the consumption of food items by as much as 25 percent. Should she intervene? If so, how? She contemplates the following options (T&S 2008: 2):

1   Arrange the food to make the students best off, all things considered.
2   Choose the food order at random.
3   Try to arrange the food to get the kids to pick the same foods they would choose on their own.
4   Maximize the sales of the items from the suppliers that are willing to offer the largest bribes.
5   Maximize profits, period.

Carolyn is thus a choice architect. She'd act in accordance with the precepts of libertarian paternalism if she chose (1) without constraining the number of options available to the children. If, say, eating fruit rather than sweets makes them better off, she'd ask directors to place fruit at eye level and near the cash desks, but sweets could still be bought in the cafeteria. They'd just be slightly less convenient to find.

There are three important features of paradigmatic nudge cases I'd like to draw attention to. First, in cases such as *Carolyn's Cafeterias*, there is no clear sense of what it might mean *not* to intervene. She could of course abstain from giving the cafeteria directors any instructions. But in this case inaction would also be an intervention because the cafeterias will display food items in ways that might affect children's well-being. Second, the exact layout in which food items are displayed does in fact affect children's well-being. In an ideal world, it would not matter to an individual's choice whether the item is placed at eye level or slightly above or below that. But here it does matter, and significantly so. Third, the school cafeteria is likely to be a monopolist in food supply to school children. Though this aspect is not explicitly discussed by T&S, it does make a difference whether consumers in principle have a choice between different retail outlets. Given how schools normally operate, there will be one cafeteria, so students will have to take its food or not eat at all.

Under these circumstances it seems indeed that option (1) is a reasonable choice. Option (2) might disadvantage students who happen to go to a school where the food items are arranged such that the least healthy items are more likely to be chosen. Option (3) would be a good one in principle, but given that cafeteria layout does affect choice, it is hard to know what children would "choose on their own." Options (4) and (5) seem unfair, given that the cafeteria has a food supply monopoly. Option (4) in particular has a ring of illegitimacy around it, but in fact so-called "slotting fees"—payments made by food producers to purchase (specific kinds of) shelf space in retail stores—are now standard practice.

401(k) Savings Plans

A 401(k) is a type of retirement savings account in the United States. Specifically, they are defined contribution plans with annual contributions limited to (currently [2012]) $17,000. Saving in a 401(k) is attractive: contributions are tax deductible, accumulations are tax deferred, and in many plans the employer matches at least part of the contributions of the employee. Even though enrolling in a 401(k) plan seems to be very beneficial for the employee, about 30 percent of those eligible fail to sign up. For some types of employees, not to join means literally to throw away money: under certain conditions, employees can join, immediately withdraw their contributions without penalty and keep the employer match; still, a study finds that up to 40 percent of eligible employees either do not join the plan at all or do not save enough to get the full match (T&S 2008: 108).

We saw above that there are some reasons to believe that people do not save enough by their own lights. T&S's answer is that the default rule should be changed. Currently, the default is non-enrollment. When employees are first eligible to join, they receive a form to fill in. Those who want to join must decide how much to put aside, and how to allocate their investments among the funds offered in the plan. But because of inertia or status-quo bias, many who do want to join fail to fill in the required forms. T&S propose instead that, once eligible, the employee receives a notification that she will be enrolled unless she fills in a form asking her to explicitly opt out. Automatic enrollment has proved to be an effective way to increase enrollment in defined-contribution plans in the States (T&S 2008: 109).

Once more, then, we have an intervention (change the default from no enrollment to enrollment) that aims to improve the decision–makers' well-being (because most people do want to save but fail because of inertia and status-quo bias) without reducing the number of available options or making the alternative prohibitively costly: employees can still opt out, and that is easily done.

Save More Tomorrow

Save More Tomorrow is a related nudge that aims to increase contribution rates rather than enrollment. Enrolled employees tend to stick with the low default contribution rate. Save More Tomorrow is designed to increase contribution rates, based on the following principles (T&S 2008: 112):

- Many participants say that they think they should be saving more, and plan to save more, but never follow through.
- Self-control restrictions are easier to adopt if they take place sometime in the future. (Many of us are planning to start diets soon, but not today.)
- Loss aversion: people hate to see their paychecks go down.

- Money illusion: losses are felt in nominal dollars (that is, not adjusted for inflation, so a dollar in 1995 is seen as worth the same as a dollar in 2005).
- Inertia plays a powerful role.

The program's main idea is that contribution increases are timed so as to coincide with pay raises. This way participants never see their take-home amounts go down, and they don't view their increased retirement contributions as losses. Once an employee joins the program, her saving increases are automatic; inertia is thus used to increase savings instead of preventing savings. But should she later decide to opt out, she can always do so at low cost.

A Nudge or Not a Nudge?

T&S's preferred welfare-enhancing interventions should be distinguished from a number of obvious alternative attempts to influence behavior that are not nudges. In particular, let us consider rational persuasion through social advertising, direct mandates or prohibitions and subliminal advertising.

Social Advertising

Many governments spend money on advertising campaigns aiming to influence people's choices. After the 2006 heat wave across Europe, for instance, posters could be found on the London Tube network advising that passengers carry a bottle of water to help keep cool. Are such cases of social advertising nudges? The answer is: it depends. T&S discuss a number of campaigns approvingly and call specific signs or slogans nudges. One example is the "Don't Mess with Texas" campaign that originally sought to reduce littering on highways. Why is the latter slogan a nudge (see T&S 2008: 60) but not (necessarily) the posters recommending that people take a bottle of water with them on the Tube? The "Don't Mess with Texas" campaign had been preceded by other highly publicized advertising campaigns which attempted to persuade people that it was their civic duty to stop littering. But those didn't work. Apparently, typical litterers were not exactly impressed by the idea that some bureaucratic elite wanted them to change behavior. So an alternative was sought, one that would talk to the litterers by sounding tough and appealing to their pride in being Texans.

Nudges, then, are different from forms of social advertising that aim to *rationally persuade* their addressees in that they always exploit some bias or irrationality. The slogan, and its initial advertisement, which featured members of the Dallas Cowboys football team, made not-littering appear to be the "cool" option. This, and not the rational appeal to civic duty, carried the day.

By contrast, the London Tube campaign is largely one that tries to persuade. The large A0 poster is full of text giving various recommendations for what to do when it is hot and explaining why. This isn't a nudge, it's an appeal to reason.

Direct Mandates and Prohibitions

Wearing seat belts is mandatory in most countries, which is probably a good thing. It is very widely accepted that seat belts save lives. Most drivers are probably not suicidal, so saving their live improves their well-being. And yet, do seat-belt laws constitute a nudge? Answering that question is somewhat more involved than might seem at first sight because few policies close off alternatives in an absolute sense. Seat-belt legislation makes failure to comply illegal, but being fined or punished in other ways can be regarded as a cost imposed on choosing the illegal alternative. So is the so-called "war on drugs" just a massive concerted effort to nudge people into using fewer drugs?

Boundaries are somewhat fluid here, but policies that comply with libertarian paternalism cannot *significantly* alter economic incentives. That is one reason why seat-belt laws and other direct mandates or prohibitions do not constitute nudges. They greatly increase the cost associated with certain kinds of behavior. There is no sharp line between the cost of having to fill in a form to opt out of a savings plan and the $10 fines charged in Missouri, Pennsylvania and Wisconsin for not wearing a seat belt, but there are paradigmatic cases on both sides, so some policies are clearly nudges while others are clearly something else. Moreover, in the cases discussed here there is another difference in that direct mandates and prohibitions do not exploit a bias or irrationality on the chooser's part. They prescribe or proscribe behavior without attending to the psychology of those who fall under the law.

Subliminal Advertising

Subliminal advertising is a form of advertising consumers are not aware of. In a movie, say, suggestions such as "eat popcorn" or "drink Coca-Cola" can be projected on the screen for periods that are too short to be consciously noticed by the movie-goers. Whether such advertising can affect behavior is controversial (Pratkanis and Greenwald 1988), but let's assume that it can. Would libertarian paternalism condone subliminal advertising? According to T&S, clearly not. They endorse two principles subliminal advertising would violate: transparency and publicity. On the one hand, a nudge should be conspicuous to the individual being nudged if he looks for it. But the whole point of subliminal advertising is that the viewer is not conscious of the message he receives. On the other hand, T&S advocate adherence to John Rawls' "publicity principle," which bans government from selecting a policy that it would not be able or willing to defend publicly to its own citizens. Few governments would publicly defend the use of subliminal advertising to change consumer behavior.

Philosophical Issues in Libertarian Paternalism

Most philosophical commentaries on libertarian paternalism I've had a chance to see are very critical. In what follows I try to give a fair account of a number of objections one can find in the literature and discuss them.

Is It Really Paternalism?

Several authors have questioned whether the approach T&S advocate does indeed constitute a species of paternalism. Gerald Dworkin defines the notion as follows (G. Dworkin 2010): "Paternalism is the interference of a state or an individual with another person, against their will, and defended or motivated by a claim that the person interfered with will be better off or protected from harm." Three characteristics are salient in this definition: the existence of an *interference*, that the interference is implemented *against the will* of the person interfered with and that it *aims to make the person better off*. A paradigmatic example for a paternalistic act is to forcibly prevent someone from crossing an unsafe bridge. The example is due to John Stuart Mill, a harsh critic of paternalism (Mill 2003 [1859]: 80). Mill did not think that someone's freedom could, in general, be traded off against his well-being:

> His own good, either physical or moral, is not a sufficient warrant. He cannot rightfully be compelled to do or forbear because it will be better for him to do so, because it will make him happier, because, in the opinions of others, to do so would be wise, or even right.
>
> (Mill 2003 [1859]: 73)

Coercion is often seen to be an essential characteristic of paternalism. The nudges T&S describe do not ostensibly involve coercion, however. Both Joel Anderson and Dan Hausman and Brynn Welch therefore think that nudges that do not involve coercion are more appropriately called acts of *beneficence* rather than paternalism (J. Anderson 2010; Hausman and Welch 2010; neither denies that nudges can be paternalistic, however).

Perhaps calling the proposal a species of paternalism is somewhat misleading to a philosopher, but the fact that Thaler (a behavioral economist) and Sunstein (a legal scholar) don't use terms in precisely the same way as philosophers do should not speak against their proposal. There is more to this point than a mere dispute about words, though. Paternalism appears to some to be morally problematic *because* it involves coercion. Mill, for one, thought that all instances of paternalism were illegitimate except when the person whose choices are interfered with is not a competent decision-maker (because she is a child or drunk) or when the person is not fully informed (as in the bridge example—Mill presumes that the person who is about to step on the unsafe bridge desires to reach the other end safely). Taking out coercion, does this mean that nudges are not morally problematic? As we will see in the next subsection, while nudges are designed not to constrain a decision-maker's liberty in the sense that they do not close off alternative options or make them prohibitively expensive, it has been argued that nudges might well interfere with liberties more broadly construed.

Liberty and Autonomy

If the "paternalism" part of T&S's proposal is problematic, the "libertarianism" part is a true minefield. Most philosophers commenting on the proposal do not think that it is successful in its promise not to constrain decision-makers' liberties. While not limiting the range of available options or significantly increasing the costs associated with any of them, it is argued that nudges do interfere with liberties people are presumed to have. There are two main arguments. One is that nudges interfere with people's autonomy, even if they do not decrease their freedom to choose, narrowly construed. The other is that the proposal is likely to increase the government's influence on individuals and thereby limit their liberty. Let us consider these in turn.

There must be *something* fishy about T&S's claims. If nudges do not interfere with someone's exercise of her freedom, how can they affect someone's choices? Hausman and Welch argue that the supposed compatibility stems from a narrow understanding of the term "liberty" as the "absence of obstacles that close off possible choices or make them more costly in time, inconvenience, unpleasantness, and so forth" (Hausman and Welch 2010: 124). But there is another aspect of liberty, more broadly understood, which focuses on the control a person has over her desires, choices, characteristics and so on—her *autonomy*. A nudge at least risks interfering with someone's autonomy because a choice, formerly under the individual's control is, when nudged, at least in part a product of the nudger's will. Hausman and Welch write:

> The paternalistic policies espoused by [T&S] … may threaten the individual's control over her own choosing. To the extent that they are attempts to undermine that individual's control over her own deliberation, as well as her ability to assess for herself her alternatives, they are *prima facie* as threatening to liberty, broadly understood, as is overt coercion.
>
> (Hausman and Welch 2010: 130)

Given that T&S nowhere say that the nudges they espouse aim to "to undermine [an] individual's control over her own deliberation" and that, quite to the contrary, most examples concern situations where individuals do not seem under full control of their choices anyway (how else *could* it matter whether one finds the chocolate cake at eye level or slightly above it or below?), this passage must be taken with a grain of salt. A single nudge is unlikely to reduce individuals' autonomy in ways that matter morally.

There are, however, two ways in which nudging might affect autonomy significantly after all. First, suppose that nudging aimed at improving decision-makers' well-being became the norm (cf. Bovens 2009). At the end of a long process of manufacturing choice situations, most of them will be cleverly designed, and on average improve decision-makers' well-being. If that happens, decision-makers might, rather than try hard to make good decisions themselves, start to rely on external agencies (be it the government, their employers or whoever) to form a conception of the good for them and thus lose autonomy. It is clear, however, that if this were the case, libertarian paternalism would have undermined itself. A core characteristic of the approach is that nudges improve decision-makers' well-being as *judged by themselves*. If there is no standard against which to judge—the decision-maker's own conception of the good—there would be no sense in which a manipulation of the choice architecture could improve someone's well-being. In other words, these manipulations would cease to be nudges. We might still want to caution against overusing the approach, because it incentivizes people to think less about what is good for themselves and rely on others instead, but in the limit libertarian paternalism ceases to exist along with individuals' autonomy.

Second, nudges might reduce autonomy relative to alternative policies that aim to increase people's autonomy by improving their informedness, control over decisions and so forth. I think this is what Hausman and Welch really have in mind. They suggest, for instance, that Carolyn, instead of manipulating the layout in which food is presented, could provide placards containing information about the nutritional value of each food item (Hausman and Welch 2010: 129). Cafeteria-goers could then make more informed, and arguably more autonomous decisions about what to eat. This alternative strategy to influence people's choices they call "rational persuasion" and say about it:

> [R]ational persuasion respects both individual liberty and the agent's control over her own decision-making, while, in contrast, deception, limiting what choices are available or shaping choices risks circumventing the individual's will.
>
> …
>
> [R]ational persuasion is the ideal way for government to influence the behavior of citizens.
>
> (Hausman and Welch 2010: 130 and 135)

I agree that rational persuasion is *an* alternative to nudging which may often be a good strategy to influence other people, if one so wishes. I also agree with Hausman and Welch in worrying about possible threats to autonomy. But I think that they ignore an important premiss in T&S's argument. T&S begin from the behavioral economists' view that humans are *boundedly* rational, have *bounded* willpower and are *boundedly* selfish. Of course, one could challenge that premiss. But if we don't, and I don't think Hausman and Welch would, rational persuasion is a much less attractive strategy than they make it seem.

Since limited self-interest is less of a concern to T&S, let us consider the other two limitations here. Humans who have limited cognitive capacities and willpower cannot make every decision with the same care. Moreover, they would be ill-advised if they did. To see why, I want to go through both limitations in turn, beginning with limited willpower.

In the behavioral economists' image of human psychology, willpower acts like the charge in rechargeable batteries. One initially has much of it, but using it depletes one's "batteries" until they are completely flat. One can then recharge them and a new cycle begins. Many decisions are hard ones to make, and hard decisions deplete one's willpower. If people put the same effort into every decision they made, they'd probably end up minimally improving their day-to-day decisions at the cost of failing the big ones. Most people therefore, quite reasonably, navigate on autopilot a lot of the time. Rational persuasion in these cases does not help very much, because the problem in these cases isn't only one of knowing what the right thing to do (relative to one's underlying values and desires) really is but one of doing what one perceives as right. Rational persuasion targets those underlying values and desires. But most people already desire to eat more healthily, exercise more, drink less, send in their tax declarations and travel reimbursement forms on time, watch fewer sitcoms and send more Christmas cards (I certainly do). The question is often not to convince people of what the right thing is but rather to convert intention into action. And *this* is where nudges are supposed to help.

The matter is different with respect to bad decisions whose source is lack of information. But here too limited cognitive abilities play an important role. One cannot find out everything there is to know about all alternatives one is facing, often not even what alternatives there are in fact. People invest in information-gathering up until a point where they can make a decision that is "good enough." Herbert Simon calls this "satisficing," in analogy to "maximizing" (Simon 1959). Suppose Carolyn placed placards containing nutritional information about every food item close to the item. Would that strategy be likely to improve her customers' decisions? For them it would mean that there is an additional parameter—next to, say, expected taste, presentation, ease of availability—nutritional value, which is multidimensional—protein, carbohydrate, fat and fibre content, vitamins, say—and each of whose parameters is itself multidimensional—how much protein, is it animal or vegetable and so on. To have preferences over all these dimension is itself no small feat, not to mention calculating what would be the optimal choice. It is no surprise, then, that actual people tend to use heuristics when making food choices. And there was a time when taste would be a good indicator of nutritional value. Today, with many foods being industrially produced there is too much fat and sugar in almost everything. What tastes good is therefore no longer a good indicator of what is good for you. And so far, there are no good and simple strategies for dealing with highly processed foods. To provide some nudges for those who do not want to become experts in nutrition science might, from that point of view, not be such a bad idea.

There is also a justice aspect. Poorer people tend to be worse decision-makers than the relatively affluent because they tend to face more difficult trade-offs. An affluent person's decision about where to have dinner might consist in the choice between Italian, Chinese and diner. A poor person has to decide that, plus whether to have dinner out at all, which of the alternative uses of money would be best and many others. Given the cognitive limitations we all have, the more complex a decision, the worse the expected performance. Poverty might therefore cause suboptimal decision-making (Spears 2010). Nudges, then, might help everyone but be of particular value for disadvantaged people, who tend to have more difficult decisions to make.

Till Grüne-Yanoff raises a different issue. He worries about government extending its reach beyond what would be good for its citizens. Specifically, he argues the following:

> A government employing such policies therefore increases its arbitrary power over its citizens. An increase in arbitrary power, implying an increase in citizens' "defenceless susceptibility to interference" (Pettit 1996, 577), is a sufficient condition for a decrease in these citizens' liberty (for more details on this republican account of liberty, see Pettit 1996, 579). Thus the mere mandate to enact these policies decreases liberty, according to an influential liberal position.
>
> (Grüne-Yanoff 2012: 638)

At first sight this worry might seem odd since none of the paradigm nudge cases involves an increase in the government's "arbitrary power over its citizens." Carolyn is responsible for government-run cafeterias where the children are "defenselessly susceptible to interferences" anyway. In the other two examples I discussed the choice architects are employers, many of whom are private enterprises and not the government. Of course, the government might mandate cafeteria directors, whether they are government employees or not, to design the cafeteria layout in certain ways, and similarly force all employers to change defaults. But T&S seldom advocate new legislation, and when they do their proposals seem to be even more consistent with libertarian principles, for instance in that they require certain information to be disclosed in certain ways (see T&S 2008: 93–4.).

Now, one *could* understand T&S's project to be one of making recommendations primarily to government to mandate most or all choice architects in certain arenas to design choice environments in ways consistent with T&S's precepts. Would this be as worrisome as Grüne-Yanoff suggests?

Once more I feel that a crucial premiss is being ignored here. When choice architecture is unavoidable we do not face the choice between the government interfering or abstaining from it, but rather the choice between government interfering or someone else. And more often than not, it seems that actual choice architects have company profits and not consumer welfare in mind. There are many examples of course. Let me discuss one in particular.

Much of this chapter was written during the North Sea Jazz Festival in Rotterdam. I love the festival for the quality of its artists and their performances, but the way the catering is organized can only be described as one gigantic anti-nudge aimed at making festival-goers eat and drink more than they really want. The sole accepted means of payment for food and drink are tokens one has to buy from booths or machines. Even though one can, in principle, convert one's tokens back into cash immediately or at the end of the festival, loss aversion makes one feel as though the money is gone once one has the tokens, so one might as well exchange the tokens for food and drink. At any rate, the cash one gets back later is valued less than the initial expense.

The festival organizers might want to justify the token system by claiming that it facilitates consumption purchases because food stalls do not have to handle cash and return change, and so the consumers benefit from shorter queues and getting their food and drink faster. But the same effect could be reached if a "no-change" policy was introduced and change booths and machines were provided instead of the token booths and machines. Some public buses in the USA have such a no-change policy for exactly that reason. Moreover, the organizers could ask vendors to price items as multiples of 50 cents. Currently, all prices are multiples of €1.25.

A related anti-nudge is the sale of tokens in multiples of four. Again, it would, in theory, be possible to buy a single cup of water for one token—by purchasing four tokens, getting a refund for three of them and the glass of water for the fourth. But who would do that?

Next is the lack of transparency of the prices. One isn't told anywhere what a single token costs. This particular year the price wasn't difficult to determine because four tokens sold for €10. If I remember correctly, the price for four tokens last year was €9.60—at that price, can you tell me what a dish costs that sells for five and a half tokens and still enjoy the music?

And the prices are, of course, advertised exclusively in tokens. Even though tokens are the only currency of exchange, it would be easy to include euro equivalents on the menus as there is a fixed exchange rate. So keeping prices obscure is another way to make people consume more.

As we know from Chapter 13, there are a number of philosophers and social scientists who lament the tendency for more and more aspects of our lives to be commercialized. The North Sea Jazz Festival is an instance of that tendency. Some years back, when it still took place in The Hague, it was all about the music. Today one gets the feeling that the music is an excuse to eat anything from oysters to Swiss fondue to Vietnamese spring rolls to Dutch pannekoeken, washing it down with a drink from the champagne bar or, if one must, a Grolsch beer (at least they don't sell Heineken, I should add).

None of this is a problem, of course. But if it is true that our lives do get more commercialized as time goes on, if commercial suppliers do have a tendency to design choice architectures in ways that are good for them and not for their customers and if, moreover, suppliers have considerable market power, government-mandated nudges in the other direction do not seem quite as atrocious as Grüne-Yanoff makes them out to be. My own image of most markets is not the Nozickean one where absent the state happy people engage in "voluntary exchanges between consenting adults" that can only be disrupted by government action. Rather, humans with bounded rationality and willpower are subject to myriad influences anyway, and most of them do not aim to improve consumer well-being. If the government actually did mandate more "nudging," this would likely constitute a corrective rather than a liberty-diminishing interference.

How Typical Are the Paradigm Cases?

A final issue I want to consider is whether the paradigmatic examples T&S offer and which I discuss here are likely to be representative for other kinds of manipulations of choice situations. A conspicuous problem is that many of the proposals T&S make aren't in fact nudges as they characterize them. Indeed, even *Carolyn's Cafeterias* is likely not to involve a nudge proper. This is because nudges are meant to improve choosers' well-being *as judged by the choosers themselves* but, arguably, children are likely to be bad judges of their own well-being. The laundered-preference theory of well-being is problematic in general, as we saw in Chapter 12. Applied to children, it is hopeless. But if there are no underlying, laundered preferences, a manipulation of a choice situation cannot aim to improve the chooser's well-being as understood by T&S, and so the manipulation does not constitute a nudge. In fact, then, in *Carolyn's Cafeterias* the choice architect not only aims to improve the choosers' well-being but also knows better what is good for them than the choosers themselves. Now, paternalism is a lot less worrisome when the target is a child or someone else who is unlikely to make good decisions for him- or herself. Consequently (and, in my view, rightly) T&S here defend a more forthrightly paternalistic policy. I nevertheless included the example as one of the "paradigm" nudge cases because one can easily imagine the cafeterias to serve university students or employees in a large enterprise. All the points made above should be applied to such cafeterias, not ones serving children.

The original version of *Carolyn's Cafeterias* is, thus, paternalist but not libertarian paternalist. Other examples T&S discuss are consistent with libertarian principles but are not paternalist, because the policy involves providing information and giving advice. Hausman and Welch list the following as falling into this category (Hausman and Welch 2010: 127): "educational campaigns ([T&S 2008:] p. 68/69), warning labels on cigarettes (p. 189/191), requirements that firms notify employees of hazards (p. 189/191), and signs warning people on a hot day to drink more water (p. 244/247)." Cost-disclosure regulations T&S propose for mobile-phone companies should also be listed here (T&S 2008: 93–4).

Yet other policies they propose are libertarian in that they enlarge the range of available options. Thus, T&S argue that patients should be given the choice to opt out of their right to sue physicians for malpractice (T&S 2002: ch. 14). Their libertarian argument for their proposal is that having the right bears costs, and patients should decide for themselves whether the right is worth buying. They also adduce a consequentialist argument: the system in place does not provide significant deterrence against medical negligence, few patients who suffered malpractice file a claim and those who do sue and end up with favorable settlements often do not deserve the money. And much of that money goes to lawyers anyway. T&S argue that the system is very inefficient and patients should be given the right to opt out of it. One might question whether permitting people to opt out of their right to sue truly increases freedom, for instance because physicians might stop seeing patients who refuse to opt out. Be that as it may, nothing in this particular proposal is paternalist.

There is another category of proposals T&S make that also differs from paradigmatic nudges. In their chapter 11 T&S promote a policy of "presumed consent" to increase organ donations. The proposal is parallel to that for increasing retirement savings: shifting the default rule while preserving freedom of choice. Those who are unwilling to donate can register easily, for instance by a single click on the appropriate website.

There is an important difference between being nudged into saving more for one's retirement and being nudged into donating one's organs. In both cases there will be some people who do not want to be part of the scheme but, because of inertia or what have you, fail to opt out. However, giving someone a less desired alternative seems a lot less problematic if the beneficiary of that alternative is the decision-maker himself (even if it is a later self) than if it is someone else. Moreover, the choice concerning organ donation is a lot more weighty than that concerning retirement savings. Some Jehovah's Witnesses consider organ donation acts of cannibalism. Taking the organs of a deceased member of the creed who failed to register as non-donor certainly constitutes a greater ill than making someone save too much.

Given that only a small minority of the policy proposals T&S make are nudges proper according to their own understanding of the term, one might worry that this type of manipulation of a choice situation is in fact quite rare. I cannot pursue the issue any further here, but I do want to end with the cautionary remark that manipulations do have to fulfill quite a number of conditions in order to count as genuine nudges, conditions that may well be very difficult to meet.

Conclusions

Nudge makes an exciting public-policy proposal. Unlike many more traditional policy proposals, it is thought to be based on behavioral *science* rather
than economic or normative *theory*. It exploits experimentally established
flaws of human decision-making for the purported benefit of the human
decision-maker. In so doing it aims to square the circle: to make the libertarian concern for freedom of choice compatible with the paternalist concern
for people's well-being. This chapter has tried to provide a partial defense of
the proposal from some criticisms philosophers have raised for three main
reasons. First, I believe that it is an original and provocative new proposal
that should be taken seriously simply because it adds to the existing range
of policy options. Second, I regard it as highly laudable that an attempt is
made to design policies for humans rather than the highly idealized models
of man we find in much of philosophy and mainstream economics. Third,
it is one of the few policy proposals that focus on *institutions*, in this case
choice architecture. Most policy recommendations that are proposed and
taken up by philosophers focus on either outcomes (such as income distribution) or highly abstract principles (such as Rawls' principles of justice or
libertarian deontological principles). But outcomes are produced by institutions and principles can be effective only through them, and the precise ways
in which institutions are and can be implemented affect the desirability of
outcomes and adequacy of principles. *Nudge* focuses directly on one institution type and for that reason too presents a policy proposal that is a great
deal more concrete and realistic. Even if some details remain problematic,
Nudge presents the kind of proposal I believe advances the policy debate
much better than the traditional abstract proposals philosophers are good
at making.

Study Questions

1 "Behavioral economics is not a theory; it is a mere collection of
   empirical findings with no theoretical underpinnings." Discuss.
2 Is "libertarian paternalism" an oxymoron?
3 How promising is "rational persuasion" as a political strategy to
   improve people's well-being?
4 Think about the choice situations you are in in the course of a
   typical day. How often are you nudged in a way that is good for
   you? How often in a way that is bad for you?
5 Suppose you heard that your government is now pursuing nudge
   policies in all sorts of areas. Would you feel threatened by increased
   government interference? Defend your answer.

Suggested Readings

Angner 2012, Wilkinson and Klaes 2012 and E. Cartwright 2011 are useful and non-technical introductions to behavioral economics. For an introduction to its psychological foundations, see Kahneman 2011. There aren't many discussions of libertarian paternalism, and what I've found I have included above. Thaler and Sunstein 2003 offer a brief defense of libertarian paternalism. Bovens 2009 offers a classification of different types of nudges and asks what types of nudges are ethically justifiable. Heilmann forthcoming uses the dual process theory that is sometimes offered as theoretical framework to characterize nudges and formulates a success criterion. Sugden 2009 is a critical review of the initial book by Thaler and Sunstein.

References

ABC News (2011). "Teen Gives Birth, Loses Cancer Fight," December 29. Online. Available HTTP: <http://abcnews.go.com/blogs/health/2011/12/29/teen-gives-birth-loses-cancer-fight/>, accessed November 21, 2012.

Akerlof, G. (1970). "The Market for 'Lemons': Quality Uncertainty and the Market Mechanism." *Quarterly Journal of Economics* 84(3): 488–500.

Alexandrova, A. (2006). "Connecting Economic Models to the Real World: Game Theory and the FCC Spectrum Auctions." *Philosophy of the Social Sciences* 36(2): 173–92.

Alexandrova, A. (2008). "Making Models Count." *Philosophy of Science* 75(3): 383–404.

Alexandrova, A. and R. Northcott (2009). "Progress in Economics: Lessons from the Spectrum Auctions." In H. Kincaid and D. Ross (eds.) *The Oxford Handbook of Philosophy of Economics*. Oxford: Oxford University Press, 306–36.

Allais, M. (1953). "Le comportement de l'homme rationnel devant le risque: critique des postulats et axiomes de l'école Americaine." *Econometrica* 21(4): 503–46.

Anand, P. (1993). "The Philosophy of Intransitive Preference." *Economic Journal* 103(417): 337–46.

Anderson, E. (1993). *Value in Ethics and in Economics*. Cambridge, MA: Harvard University Press.

Anderson, J. (2010). "Review of *Nudge: Improving Decisions about Health, Wealth, and Happiness*." *Economics and Philosophy* 26(3): 369–76.

Andreoni, J. and L. K. Gee (2011). "The Hired Gun Mechanism." *NBER Report* 17032. Cambridge, MA: National Bureau of Economic Research.

Angell, M. (2004). *The Truth about the Drug Companies*. New York: Random House.

Angner, E. (2009). "Subjective Measures of Well-Being: Philosophical Perspectives." In H. Kincaid and D. Ross (eds.) *The Oxford Handbook of Philosophy of Economics*. Oxford: Oxford University Press, 560–79.

Angner, E. (2012). *A Course in Behavioral Economics*. Basingstoke: Palgrave Macmillan.

Angrist, J. D. (1990). "Lifetime Earnings and the Vietnam Era Draft Lottery: Evidence from Social Security Administrative Records." *American Economic Review* 80(3): 313–36.

Angrist, J. D. and V. Lavy (1999). "Using Maimonides' Rule to Estimate the Effect of Class Size on Scholastic Achievement." *Quarterly Journal of Economics* 114(2): 533–75.

Angrist, J. D. and J.-S. Pischke (2008). *Mostly Harmless Econometrics: An Empiricist's Companion*. Princeton, NJ: Princeton University Press.

Angrist, J. D. and J.-S. Pischke (2010). "The Credibility Revolution in Empirical Economics: How Better Research Design is Taking the Con out of Econometrics." Cambridge, MA: National Bureau of Economic Research. 15794.

Anscombe, E. (1992 [1971]). *Causality and Determination*. Cambridge: Cambridge University Press.

Arneson, R. J. (1990). "Liberalism, Distributive Subjectivism, and Equal Opportunity for Welfare." *Philosophy & Public Affairs* 19(2): 158–94.

Arnold, R. A. (2008). *Macroeconomics*. Mason, OH: Cengage Learning.

Arrow, K. J. (1973). "Some Ordinalist-Utilitarian Notes on Rawls's Theory of Justice." *Journal of Philosophy* 70(9): 245–63.

Aumann, R. J. (1959). "Acceptable Points in General Cooperative n-Person Games." In A. W. Tucker and R. D. Luce (eds.) *Contributions to the Theory of Games IV*. Annals of Mathematics Study 40. Princeton, NJ: Princeton University Press, 287–324.

Aumann, R. J. (1962). "Utility Theory without the Completeness Axiom." *Econometrica* 30(3): 445–62.

Backhouse, R. E. (2008). "Methodology of Economics." In S. N. Durlauf and L. E. Blume (eds.) *The New Palgrave Dictionary of Economics*. Basingstoke: Palgrave Macmillan.

Baker, D. (2005). "The Reform of Intellectual Property." *post-autistic economics review* 32, July 5, article 1. Online. Available HTTP: <http://www.paecon.net/PAEReview/issue32/Baker32.htm>, accessed November 21, 2012.

Banerjee, A. V. (1992). "A Simple Model of Herd Behavior." *Quarterly Journal of Economics* 107(3): 797–817.

Banerjee, A. V. (2007). *Making Aid Work*. Cambridge, MA: MIT Press.

Banerjee, A. V. and E. Duflo (2011). *Poor Economics: A Radical Rethinking of the Way to Fight Global Poverty*. New York: Public Affairs.

Bar-Hillel, M. (1973). "On the Subjective Probability of Compound Events." *Organizational Behavior and Human Performance* 9(3): 396–406.

Bardsley, N., R. Cubitt, G. Loomes *et al.* (2010). *Experimental Economics: Rethinking the Rules*. Princeton, NJ: Princeton University Press.

Barro, R. J. and X. Sala-i-Martin (1999). *Economic Growth*. Cambridge, MA: MIT Press.

Baumgartner, M. (2008). "Regularity Theories Reassessed." *Philosophia* 36: 327–54.

Becker, G. S. and Y. Rubinstein (2011). "Fear and the Response to Terrorism: An Economic Analysis." *CEP Discussion Paper* 1079. London: London School of Economics.

Bentham, J. (1907 [1789]). *An Introduction to the Principles of Morals and Legislation*. Oxford: Clarendon Press.

Bicchieri, C. (2006). *The Grammar of Society. The Nature and Dynamics of Social Norms*. Cambridge: Cambridge University Press.

Binmore, K. (1987). "Modeling Rational Players: Part I." *Economics and Philosophy* 3(2): 179–214.

Binmore, K. (2007). *Playing for Real: A Text on Game Theory*. Oxford: Oxford University Press.

Binmore, K. (2009). *Rational Decisions. The Gorman Lectures in Economics*. Princeton, NJ: Princeton University Press.

Binmore, K. and P. Klemperer (2002). "The Biggest Auction Ever: The Sale of the British 3G Telecom Licences." *Economic Journal* 112(478): C74–C96.

Blaug, M. (1992). *The Methodology of Economics or How Economists Explain*. Cambridge: Cambridge University Press.

Bogen, J. and J. Woodward (1988). "Saving the Phenomena." *Philosophical Review* 97: 302–52.

Bokulich, A. (2011). "How Scientific Models Can Explain." *Synthese* 180(1): 33–45.

Boldrin, M. and D. K. Levine (2008). *Against Intellectual Monopoly*. Cambridge: Cambridge University Press.

Bonfiglioli, K. (2008). *All the Tea in China*: New York: Overlook.

Borgerson, K. (2009). "Valuing Evidence: Bias and the Evidence Hierarchy of Evidence-Based Medicine." *Perspectives in Biology and Medicine* 52(2): 218–33.

Boumans, M. and J. Davis (2010). *Economic Methodology: Understanding Economics as a Science*. Basingstoke: Palgrave Macmillan.

Bovens, L. (2009). "The Ethics of Nudge." In T. Grüne-Yanoff and S. O. Hansson (eds.) *Preference Change*. Dordrecht, Netherlands: Springer, 207–19.

Box, G. and N. Draper (1987). *Empirical Model-Building and Response Surfaces*. New York: John Wiley & Sons.

Brenner, S. (2001). "Determinants of Product Differentiation: A Survey." Berlin: Institute of Management, Humboldt University.

Brighouse, H. and I. Robeyns, eds. (2010). *Measuring Justice: Primary Goods and Capabilities*. Cambridge: Cambridge University Press.

Broome, J. (1991). *Weighing Goods: Equality, Uncertainty and Time*. Oxford: Blackwell.

Bunge, M. (1997). "Mechanism and Explanation." *Philosophy of the Social Sciences* 27(4): 410–65.

Burger, N., G. Charness and J. Lynham (2009). "Three Field Experiments on Procrastination and Willpower." *Levine's Working Paper Archive*. Los Angeles: Department of Economics, UCLA.

Caldwell, B. (1982). *Beyond Positivism*. London: Allen and Unwin.

Caldwell, B. (2004). *Hayek's Challenge. An Intellectual Biography of F. A. Hayek*. Chicago: University of Chicago Press.

Callon, M. and F. Muniesa. (2007). "Economic Experiments and the Construction of Markets." In D. MacKenzie, F. Muniesa and L. Siu (eds.) *Do Economists Make Markets? On the Performativity of Economics*. Princeton, NJ: Princeton University Press, 163–89.

Camerer, C. F. (2003). *Behavioral Game Theory: Experiments in Strategic Interaction*. Princeton, NJ: Princeton University Press.

Camerer, C. F., T. Ho and K. Chong (2003). "Models of Thinking, Learning, and Teaching in Games." *American Economic Review* 93(2): 192–5.

Card, D. and A. Krueger (1995). *Myth and Measurement: The New Economics of the Minimum Wage*. Princeton, NJ: Princeton University Press.

Carpenter, J. and E. Seki (2006). "Competitive Work Environments and Social Preferences: Field Experimental Evidence from a Japanese Fishing Community." *B.E. Journal of Economic Analysis & Policy* 5(2): Contributions in Economic Analysis & Policy, Article 2. Online, December 31.

Carpenter, J., S. Burks and E. Verhoogen (2005). "Comparing Students to Workers: The Effect of Social Framing in Distribution Games." In J. Carpenter, G. Harrison and J. List (eds.) *Field Experiments in Economics*. Amsterdam: Elsevier, 261–90.

Cartwright, E. (2011). *Behavioral Economics*. Abingdon and New York: Routledge.

Cartwright, N. (1979). "Causal Laws and Effective Strategies." *Noûs* 13: 419–37.

Cartwright, N. (1983). *How the Laws of Physics Lie*. Oxford: Oxford University Press.

Cartwright, N. (1989). *Nature's Capacities and Their Measurement*. Oxford: Clarendon Press.

Cartwright, N. (1999a). *The Dappled World*. Cambridge: Cambridge University Press.

Cartwright, N. (1999b). "The Vanity of Rigor in Economics: Theoretical Models and Galilean Experiments." *CPNSS Discussion Papers* 43/99. London: Centre for Philosophy of Natural and Social Sciences, London School of Economics.

Cartwright, N. (2007a). "Are RCTs the Gold Standard?" *BioSocieties* 2(1): 11–20.

Cartwright, N. (2007b). *Hunting Causes and Using Them*. Cambridge: Cambridge University Press.

Cartwright, N. (2009a). "Evidence-Based Policy: What's to Be Done about Relevance?" *Philosophical Studies* 143(1): 127–36.

Cartwright, N. (2009b). "What Is This Thing Called 'Efficacy'?" In C. Mantzavinos (ed.) *Philosophy of the Social Sciences. Philosophical Theory and Scientific Practice*. Cambridge: Cambridge University Press, 185–206.

Cartwright, N. and E. Munro (2010). "The Limitations of Randomized Controlled Trials in Predicting Effectiveness." *Journal of Evaluation in Clinical Practice* 16(2): 260–6.

Coalition for Evidence-Based Policy (CEBP) (2002). *Bringing Evidence-Driven Progress to Education: A Recommended Strategy for the U.S. Department of Education*. Washington, DC: CEBP.

Coase, R. H. (1960). "The Problem of Social Cost." *Journal of Law and Economics* 3: 1–44.

Cohen, G. A. (1995). *Self-Ownership, Freedom, and Equality*. Cambridge: Cambridge University Press.

Cohen, J. and W. Easterly (2009). "Introduction: Thinking Big versus Thinking Small." In Cohen and Easterly (eds.) *What Works in Development. Thinking Big and Thinking Small*. Washington, DC: Brookings Institution, 1–23.

Costa-Gomes, M., V. P. Crawford and B. Broseta (2001). "Cognition and Behavior in Normal-Form Games: An Experimental Study." *Econometrica* 69(5): 1193–235.

Cox, J. C. (2004). "How to Identify Trust and Reciprocity." *Games and Economic Behavior* 46(2): 260–81.

Cox, J. C. (2008). "Preference Reversals." In C. R. Plott and V. L. Smith (eds.) *Handbook of Experimental Economics Results*. New York: Elsevier, 967–75.

Cramton, P. (1997). "The FCC Spectrum Auctions: An Early Assessment." *Journal of Economics and Management Strategy* 6(3): 431–95.

Crisp, R. (2006). *Reasons and the Good*. Oxford: Clarendon Press.

Crisp, R. (2008). "Well-Being." In E. N. Zalta (ed.) *The Stanford Encyclopedia of Philosophy*. Online. Available HTTP: <http://plato.stanford.edu/archives/win2008/entries/well-being/>, accessed November 21, 2012.

d'Aspremont, C., J. J. Gabszewicz and J.-F. Thisse (1979). "On Hotelling's 'Stability in Competition'." *Econometrica* 47(5): 1145–50.

Dasgupta, P. (2005). "What do Economists Analyze and Why: Values or Facts?" *Economics and Philosophy* 21(2): 221–78.

Dasgupta, P. (2007). "Reply to Putnam and Walsh." *Economics and Philosophy* 23(3): 365–72.

Davidson, D. (1970). "Mental Events." In L. Foster and J. W. Swanson (eds.) *Experience and Theory*. Amherst: University of Massachusetts Press, 79–101.

Davidson, D. (1974). "Psychology as Philosophy." In S. C. Brown (ed.) *Philosophy of Psychology*. New York: Harper & Row, 41–52.

Davidson, D. (1980). *Essays on Actions and Events*. Oxford: Clarendon Press.

Davidson, D., J. C. C. McKinsey and Patrick Suppes (1955). "Outlines of a Formal Theory of Value, I." *Philosophy of Science* 22(2): 140–60.

Davies, J. B., S. Sandstrom, A. Shorrocks and E. N. Wolff (2006). *The World Distribution of Household Wealth*. Helsinki: World Institute for Development Economics Research.

Davis, J. B. and D. W. Hands, eds. (2011). *The Elgar Companion to Recent Economic Methodology*. Cheltenham: Edward Elgar.

Davis, J. M. (1958). "The Transitivity of Preferences." *Behavioral Science* 3(1): 26–33.

de George, R. T. (2009). *Business Ethics*. Upper Saddle River, NJ: Prentice-Hall.

de Palma, A., V. Ginsburgh, Y. Y. Papageorgiou and J.-F. Thisse (1985). "The Principle of Minimum Differentiation Holds under Sufficient Heterogeneity." *Econometrica* 53(4): 767–81.

de Soto, H. (2000). *The Mystery of Capital: Why Capitalism Triumphs in the West and Fails Everywhere Else*. London: Black Swan.

Deaton, A. (2010a). "Instruments, Randomization, and Learning about Development." *Journal of Economic Literature* 48(2): 424–55.

Deaton, A. (2010b). "Understanding the Mechanisms of Economic Development." *Journal of Economic Perspectives* 24(3): 3–16.

Department of Education (US) (2005). "What Works Clearinghouse (WWC)." Online. Available HTTP: <http://www2.ed.gov/about/offices/list/ies/ncee/wwc.html>, accessed July 10, 2012.

Diewert, W. E. (1998). "Index Number Issues in the Consumer Price Index." *Journal of Economic Perspectives* 12(1): 47–58.

Dowe, P. (2004). "Causes Are Physically Connected to Their Effects: Why Preventers and Omissions Are Not Causes." In C. Hitchcock (ed.) *Contemporary Debates in Philosophy of Science*. Oxford: Blackwell, 187–96.

Driver, J. (2009). "The History of Utilitarianism." In E. N. Zalta (ed.) *The Stanford Encyclopedia of Philosophy*. Online. Available HTTP: <http://plato.stanford.edu/entries/utilitarianism-history/>, accessed November 21, 2012.

Duflo, E., R. Glennerster and M. Kremer (2004). "Randomized Evaluations of Interventions in Social Service Delivery." *Development Outreach* 6(1): 26–9.

Duhem, P. (1991 [1914]). *The Aim and Structure of Physical Theory*. Princeton, NJ: Princeton University Press.

Dworkin, G. (2010). "Paternalism." In E. N. Zalta (ed.) *The Stanford Encyclopedia of Philosophy*. Online. Available HTTP: <http://plato.stanford.edu/entries/paternalism/>, accessed November 21, 2012.

Dworkin, R. (1978). *Taking Rights Seriously*. Cambridge, MA: Harvard University Press.

Easterly, W. (2009). "Comment." In J. Cohen and W. Easterly (eds.) *What Works in Development. Thinking Big and Thinking Small*. Washington, DC: Brookings Institution, 227–32.

Economist, The (2009). "What Went Wrong with Economics." *The Economist*, July 16.

Edmond, C. and P.-O. Weill (2009). "Aggregate Implications of Micro Asset Market Segmentation." Cambridge, MA: National Bureau of Economic Research. 15254.

Ellsberg, D. (1961). "Risk, Ambiguity, and the Savage Axioms." *Quarterly Journal of Economics* 75(4): 643–69.

Elster, J. (1983). *Explaining Technical Change: A Case Study in the Philosophy of Science*. Cambridge: Cambridge University Press.

Elster, J. (1989). *Nuts and Bolts for the Social Sciences*. Cambridge: Cambridge University Press.

Elster, J. (1998). "A Plea for Mechanisms." In P. Hedström and R. Swedberg (eds.) *Social Mechanisms: An Analytical Approach to Social Theory*. Cambridge: Cambridge University Press, 45–73.

Elster, J. (2007). *Explaining Social Behavior: More Nuts and Bolts for the Social Sciences*. Cambridge: Cambridge University Press.

Fehr, E. and K. M. Schmidt (1999). "A Theory of Fairness, Competition, and Cooperation." *Quarterly Journal of Economics* 114(3): 817–68.

Ferguson, N. (2008). *The Ascent of Money. A Financial History of the World*. New York: Penguin Press.

Feyerabend, P. (1975). *Against Method*. London: Verso.

Fisher, I. (1911). *The Purchasing Power of Money: Its Determination and Relation to Credit and Crisis*. New York: Macmillan.

Fisher, R. A. (1935). *The Design of Experiments*. Oxford: Oliver & Boyd.

Flaherty, J. M. (2012). "Jobs, Growth, and Long-Term Prosperity: Economic Action Plan 2012." Ottawa, ON: Public Works and Government Services Canada.

Foster, J. B. and F. Magdoff (2009). *The Great Financial Crisis. Causes and Consequences*. New York: Monthly Review Press.

Franklin, A. (1986). *The Neglect of Experiment*. Cambridge: Cambridge University Press.

Frederick, S. and G. Loewenstein. (1999). "Hedonic Adaptation." In D. Kahneman, E. Diener and N. Schwarz (eds.) *Well-Being: The Foundations of Hedonic Psychology*. New York: Russel Sage Foundation Press, 302–29.

Frey, B. S. and S. Luechinger (2003). "How to Fight Terrorism: Alternatives to Deterrence." *Defence and Peace Economics* 14(4): 237–49.

Friedman, D. (1989 [1973]). *The Machinery of Freedom: Guide to a Radical Capitalism*. La Salle: Open Court.

Friedman, M. (1953). "The Methodology of Positive Economics." In *Essays in Positive Economics*. Chicago: University of Chicago Press, 3–44.

Friedman, M. (1962). *Capitalism and Freedom*. Chicago: University of Chicago Press.

Friedman, M. and A. J. Schwartz (1963). "Money and Business Cycles." *Review of Economics and Statistics* 45(1, part 2, Supplement): 32–64.

Friedman, Michael. (1974). "Explanation and Scientific Understanding." *Journal of Philosophy* 71(1): 5–19.

Frigg, R. and S. Hartmann. (2012). "Models in Science." In E. N. Zalta (ed.) *The Stanford Encyclopedia of Philosophy*. Online. Available HTTP: <http://plato.stanford.edu/entries/models-science/>, accessed November 21, 2012.

Frisch, R. (1933). "Editor's Note." *Econometrica* 1(1): 1–4.

Fudenberg, D. and J. Tirole (1991). *Game Theory*. Cambridge, MA: MIT Press.

Galison, P. (1987). *How Experiments End*. Chicago: University of Chicago Press.

Gasking, D. (1955). "Causation and Recipes." *Mind* 64: 479–87.

Gauthier, D. (1986). *Morals by Agreement*. Oxford: Oxford University Press.

Gibbard, A. and H. R. Varian (1978). "Economic Models." *Journal of Philosophy* 75(11): 664–77.

Gilboa, I. (2010). *Rational Choice*. Cambridge, MA: MIT Press.

Gilboa, I., A. Postlewaite, L. Samuelson and D. Schmeidler (2011). "Economic Models as Analogies." Online. Available HTTP: <http://www.ssc.upenn.edu/%7Eapostlew/paper/pdf/GPSS.pdf>, accessed December 5, 2012.

Glennan, S. (1996). "Mechanisms and the Nature of Causation." *Erkenntnis* 44(1): 49–71.

Glennan, S. (2002). "Rethinking Mechanistic Explanation." *Philosophy of Science* 69(S3): S342–S353.

Glennan, S. (2010). "Ephemeral Mechanisms and Historical Explanation." *Erkenntnis* 72(2): 251–66.

Goodin, R. (1986). "Laundering Preferences." In J. Elster and A. Hylland (eds.) *Foundations of Social Choice Theory*. Cambridge: Cambridge University Press, 75–102.

Gooding, D., T. Pinch and S. Schaffer, eds. (1989). *The Uses of Experiment: Studies in the Natural Sciences*. Cambridge: Cambridge University Press.

Graafland, J. (2007). *Economics, Ethics and the Market*. Abingdon and New York: Routledge.

Greene (2000). *Econometric Analysis*. Upper Saddle River, NJ: Prentice-Hall.

Grether, D. and C. Plott (1979). "Economic Theory of Choice and the Preference-Reversal Phenomenon." *American Economic Review* 69: 623–38.

Griffin, J. (1986). *Well-Being*. Oxford: Clarendon Press.

Grüne-Yanoff, T. (2008). "Game Theory." Internet Encyclopaedia of Philosophy. Online. Available HTTP: <http://www.iep.utm.edu/g/game-th.htm>, accessed December 6, 2012.

Grüne-Yanoff, T. (2009). "Learning from Minimal Economic Models." *Erkenntnis* 70(1): 81–99.

Grüne-Yanoff, T. (2012). "Old Wine in New Casks: Libertarian Paternalism Still Violates Liberal Principles." *Social Choice and Welfare* 38(4): 635–45.

Grüne-Yanoff, T. and A. Lehtinen. (2012). "Philosophy of Game Theory." In U. Mäki (ed.) *Philosophy of Economics*. Oxford: Elsevier, 531–76.

Guala, F. (2001). "Building Economic Machines: The FCC Auctions." *Studies in History and Philosophy of Science Part A* 32(3): 453–77.

Guala, F. (2005). *The Methodology of Experimental Economics*. Cambridge: Cambridge University Press.

Guala, F. (2006). "Has Game Theory Been Refuted?" *Journal of Philosophy* 103(5): 239–63.

Guala, F. (2008). "Paradigmatic Experiments: The Ultimatum Game from Testing to Measurement Device." *Philosophy of Science* 75(5): 658–69.

Guala, F. (2010). "Extrapolation, Analogy, and Comparative Process Tracing." *Philosophy of Science* 77(5): 1070–82.

Guala, F. and R. Burlando (2002). "Conditional Cooperation: New Evidence from a Public Goods Experiment." *CEEL Working Paper* 0210. Trento: Cognitive and Experimental Economics Laboratory, Department of Economics, University of Trento, Italy.

Gul, F. and W. Pesendorfer (2008). "The Case for Mindless Economics." In A. Caplin and A. Schotter (eds.) *The Foundations of Positive and Normative Economics: A Handbook*. New York: Oxford University Press, 3–39.

Guyatt, G., J. Cairns, D. Churchill *et al.* (1992). "Evidence-Based Medicine. A New Approach to Teaching the Practice of Medicine." *JAMA: The Journal of the American Medical Association* 268 (17): 2420–5.

Hacking, I. (1983). *Representing and Intervening*. Cambridge: Cambridge University Press.

Hacking, I. (1999). *The Social Construction of What?* Cambridge, MA: Harvard University Press.

Hahnel, R. and K. A. Sheeran (2009). "Misinterpreting the Coase Theorem." *Journal of Economic Issues* 43(1): 215–38.

Hall, N., J. Collins and L. A. Paul, eds. (2004). *Causation and Counterfactuals*. Cambridge, MA: MIT Press.

Hamilton, J. (1997). "Measuring the Liquidity Effect." *American Economic Review* 87(1): 80–97.

Hamminga, B. and N. De Marchi, eds. (1994). *Idealization in Economics*. Amsterdam: Rodopi.

Hands, D. W. (2001). *Reflection without Rules. Economic Methodology and Contemporary Science Theory*. Cambridge: Cambridge University Press.

Hanson, N. R. (1958). *Patterns of Discovery: An Inquiry into the Conceptual Foundations of Science*. Cambridge: Cambridge University Press.

Hardin, R. (1982). *Collective Action*. Baltimore, MD: Johns Hopkins University Press.

Hargreaves Heap, S., M. Hollis, G. Loomes *et al.* (1992). *The Theory of Choice: A Critical Guide*. Oxford: Blackwell.

Hargreaves Heap, S. and Y. Varoufakis (2004). *Game Theory: A Critical Text*. London: Routledge.

Harrison, G. W. and J. A. List (2004). "Field Experiments." *Journal of Economic Literature* 42(4): 1009–55.

Hausman, D. M. (1992a). *The Inexact and Separate Science of Economics*. Cambridge: Cambridge University Press.

Hausman, D. M. (1992b). "When Jack and Jill Make a Deal." *Social Philosophy and Policy* 9(1): 95–113.

Hausman, D. M. (2000). "Revealed Preference, Belief, and Game Theory." *Economics and Philosophy* 16(1): 99–115.

Hausman, D. M., ed. (2008). *The Philosophy of Economics. An Anthology*. Cambridge: Cambridge University Press.

Hausman, D. M. (2012). *Preference, Value, Choice, and Welfare*. Cambridge: Cambridge University Press.

Hausman, D. M. and M. S. McPherson (2006). *Economic Analysis, Moral Philosophy, and Public Policy*. New York: Cambridge University Press.

Hausman, D. M. and M. S. McPherson (2009). "Preference Satisfaction and Welfare Economics." *Economics and Philosophy* 25(01): 1–25.

Hausman, D. M. and B. Welch (2010). "Debate: To Nudge or Not to Nudge*." *Journal of Political Philosophy* 18(1): 123–36.

Hayek, F. (1944). *The Road to Serfdom*. Chicago: University of Chicago Press.

Hayek, F. (1960). *The Constitution of Liberty*. Chicago: University of Chicago Press.

Heckman, J. (1992). "Randomization and Social Policy Evaluation." In C. F. Manski and I. Garfinkel (eds.) *Evaluating Welfare and Training Programs*. Boston, MA: Harvard University Press, 201–30.

Heckman, J. (1996a). "Comment." *Journal of the American Statistical Association* 91(434): 459–62.

Heckman, J. (1996b). "Randomization as an Instrumental Variable." *Review of Economics and Statistics* 78(2): 336–41.

Hedström, P. (2005). *Dissecting the Social: On the Principles of Analytical Sociology*. Cambridge: Cambridge University Press.

Hedström, P. and R. Swedberg, eds. (1998). *Social Mechanisms: An Analytical Approach to Social Theory*. Cambridge: Cambridge University Press.

Hedström, P. and P. Ylikoski (2010). "Causal Mechanisms in the Social Sciences." *Annual Review of Sociology* 36(1): 49–67.

Heien, D. and J. Dunn (1985). "The True Cost-of-Living Index with Changing Preferences." *Journal of Business & Economic Statistics* 3(4): 332–5.

Heilmann, C. (forthcoming). "A Success Criterion for Nudge."

Hemingway, E. (1999). *True at First Light: A Fictional Memoir*. New York: Simon & Schuster.

Hempel, C. (1965). *Aspects of Scientific Explanation and Other Essays in the Philosophy of Science*. New York: Free Press.

Hempel, C. (1966). *The Philosophy of Natural Science*. Upper Saddle River, NJ: Prentice-Hall.

Hempel, C. and P. Oppenheim (1948). "Studies in the Logic of Explanation." *Philosophy of Science* 15: 135–75.

Hendry, D. and M. Morgan (1995). *The Foundations of Econometric Analysis*. Cambridge: Cambridge University Press.

Henrich, J., R. Boyd, S. Bowles *et al.* (2001). "In Search of Homo Economicus: Behavioral Experiments in 15 Small-Scale Societies." *American Economic Review* 91(2): 73–8.

Hesslow, G. (1976). "Two Notes on the Probabilistic Approach to Causality." *Philosophy of Science* 43: 290–2.

Hicks, J. R. (1956). *A Revision of Demand Theory*. Oxford: Clarendon Press.

Hill, A. B. (1965). "The Environment and Disease: Association or Causation?" *Proceedings of the Royal Society of Medicine* 58(5): 295–300.

Hindriks, F. (2008). "False Models as Explanatory Engines." *Philosophy of the Social Sciences* 38(3): 334–60.

Hitchcock, C. (2007). "How to Be a Causal Pluralist." In P. Machamer and G. Wolters (eds.) *Thinking about Causes: From Greek Philosophy to Modern Physics*. Pittsburgh: University of Pittsburgh Press, 200–21.

Hobbes, T. (1994 [1651]) *Leviathan*. In E. Curley (ed.) *Leviathan, with Selected Variants from the Latin Edition of 1668*. Indianapolis: Hackett.

Hoover, K. D. (2001). *Causality in Macroeconomics*. Cambridge: Cambridge University Press.

Hoover, K. D. (2003). "Nonstationary Time-Series, Cointegration, and the Principle of the Common Cause." *British Journal for the Philosophy of Science* 54: 527–51.

Hoover, K. D. (2004). "Lost Causes." *Journal of the History of Economic Thought* 26(2): 149–64.

Hoover, K. D. (2006). "Econometric Methodology." In K. Patterson and T. C. Mills (eds.) *The Palgrave Handbook of Econometrics*. Basingstoke: Palgrave Macmillan, 61–87.

Hoover, K. D. (2009). "Microfoundations and the Ontology of Macroeconomics." In H. Kincaid and D. Ross (eds.) *The Oxford Handbook of Philosophy of Economics*. New York: Oxford University Press, 386–409.

Hotelling, H. (1929). "Stability in Competition." *Economic Journal* 39(153): 41–57.

Hume, D. (1752). "Of Money." In *Political Discourses*, 2nd edn. Edinburgh: R. Fleming, 41–60.

Hume, D. (1960 [1739]). *A Treatise of Human Nature*. Oxford: Clarendon Press.

Hume, D. (1999 [1748]). *An Enquiry concerning Human Understanding*. Oxford: Oxford University Press.

Hyamson, M. (1937). *Mishneh Torah, Book I (The Book of Knowledge)*. New York: Jewish Theological Seminary.

Imbens, G. W. (2009). "Better LATE than Nothing: Some Comments on Deaton (2009) and Heckman and Urzua (2009)." Cambridge, MA: National Bureau of Economic Research. 14896.

Ireland, P. N. (2008). "Monetary Transmission Mechanism." In S. N. Durlauf and L. E. Blume (eds.) *The New Palgrave Dictionary of Economics*. Basingstoke: Palgrave Macmillan. Online. Available HTTP: <http://www.dictionaryofeconomics.com/article?id=pde2008_M000214>, accessed December 5, 2012.

James, A. (2009). "Academies of the Apocalypse?" *Guardian*, April 7.

Jeffrey, R. C. (1990). *The Logic of Decision*. Chicago: University of Chicago Press.

Kagel, J. and A. Roth, eds. (1997). *The Handbook of Experimental Economics*. Princeton: Princeton University Press.

Kahneman, D. (2011). *Thinking, Fast and Slow*. New York: Farrar, Straus and Giroux.

Kahneman, D., J. L. Knetsch and R. H. Thaler (1990). "Experimental Tests of the Endowment Effect and the Coase Theorem." *Journal of Political Economy* 98(6): 1325–48.

Kahneman, D. and A. B. Krueger (2006). "Developments in the Measurement of Subjective Well-Being." *Journal of Economic Perspectives* 20(1): 3–24.

Kahneman, D. and A. Tversky (1979). "Prospect Theory: An Analysis of Decision under Risk." *Econometrica* 47(2): 263–92.

Kalai, E. and E. Lehrer (1993). "Rational Learning Leads to Nash Equilibrium." *Econometrica* 61(5): 1019–45.

Kaldor, N. (1957). "A Model of Economic Growth." *Economic Journal* 67(268): 591–624.

Kaldor, N. (1961). *The Theory of Capital*. London: Macmillan.

Kandori, M., G. Mailath and R. Rob (1993). "Learning, Mutation, and Long Run Equilibria in Games." *Econometrica* 61(1): 29–56.

Kant, I. (1998 [1787]). *Critique of Pure Reason*. Cambridge: Cambridge University Press.

Kant, I. (2004 [1783]). *Prolegomena to Any Future Metaphysics that Will be Able to Come Forward as Science: With Selections from the Critique of Pure Reason*, ed. G. C. Hatfield. Cambridge: Cambridge University Press.

Karni, E. and Z. Safra (1987). "'Preference Reversal' and the Observability of Preferences by Experimental Methods." *Econometrica* 55(3): 675–85.

Keller, S. (2002). "Expensive Tastes and Distributive Justice." *Social Theory and Practice* 28(4): 529–52.

Kennedy, A. G. (2012). "A Non-Representationalist View of Model Explanation." *Studies in History and Philosophy of Science Part A* 43(2): 326–32.

Khan, B. Z. and K. L. Sokoloff (2001). "History Lessons: The Early Development of Intellectual Property Institutions in the United States." *Journal of Economic Perspectives* 15(3): 233–46.

Kincaid, H. (1996). *Philosophical Foundations of the Social Sciences*. New York: Cambridge University Press.

Kincaid, H. (1997). *Individualism and the Unity of Science: Essays on Reduction, Explanation, and the Special Sciences.* Lanham, MD: Rowman & Littlefield.

Kincaid, H. and D. Ross, eds. (2009). *The Oxford Handbook of Philosophy of Economics*. New York: Oxford University Press.

Kitcher, P. (1981). "Explanatory Unification." *Philosophy of Science* 48: 507–31.

Kitcher, P. and W. Salmon (1989). *Scientific Explanation*. Minneapolis, MN: University of Minnesota Press.

Klein, J. and M. Morgan (2001). *The Age of Economic Measurement.* Durham, NC: Duke University Press.

Knight, F. H. (1921). *Risk, Uncertainty and Profit*. Boston, MA: Hart, Schaffner & Marx; Houghton Mifflin Co.

Knuuttila, T. (2009). "Isolating Representations versus Credible Constructions? Economic Modelling in Theory and Practice." *Erkenntnis* 70(1): 59–80.

Koopmans, T. (1947). "Measurement without Theory." *Review of Economic Statistics* 29(3): 161–71.

Kreps, D. M. and R. Wilson (1982). "Sequential Equilibria." *Econometrica* 50(4): 863–94.

Krimsky, S. (2003). *Science in the Private Interest: Has the Lure of Profits Corrupted Biomedical Research?* Lanham, MD: Rowman & Littlefield.

Krueger, A. (2007). *What Makes a Terrorist: Economics and the Roots of Terrorism*. Princeton, NJ: Princeton University Press.

Krugman, P. (2009a). "How Did Economists Get It So Wrong?" *New York Times*, September 2.

Krugman, P. (2009b). *The Return of Depression Economics and the Crisis of 2008*. New York: Norton.

Kuhn, T. S. (1996 [1962]). *The Structure of Scientific Revolutions*. Chicago: University of Chicago Press.

Kuorikoski, J., A. Lehtinen and C. Marchionni (2010). "Economic Modelling as Robustness Analysis." *British Journal for the Philosophy of Science* 61(3): 541–67.

Laibson, D. I., A. Repetto and J. Tobacman (1998). "Self-Control and Saving for Retirement." *Brookings Papers on Economic Activity* 1998(1): 91–196.

Lawson, T. (1997). *Economics and Reality*. London: Routledge.

Layard, R. (2005). *Happiness: Lessons from a New Science*. New York: Penguin Press.

Levitt, S. and S. Dubner (2005). *Freakonomics: A Rogue Economist Explores the Hidden Side of Everything.* New York: William Morrow.

Lebow, R. N. (2010). *Forbidden Fruit: Counterfactuals and International Relations.* Princeton, NJ: Princeton University Press.

LeGrand, J. (1982). *The Strategy of Equality.* London: Allan and Unwin.

Lehtinen, A. and J. Kuorikoski (2007). "Computing the Perfect Model: Why Do Economists Shun Simulation?" *Philosophy of Science* 74: 304–29.

Lerner, A. P. and H. W. Singer (1937). "Some Notes on Duopoly and Spatial Competition." *Journal of Political Economy* 45(2): 145–86.

Levi, I. (1997). "Prediction, Deliberation, and Correlated Equilibrium." In *The Covenant of Reason.* Cambridge: Cambridge University Press, 102–16.

Levitt, S. D. and J. A. List (2007). "What do Laboratory Experiments Measuring Social Preferences Reveal about the Real World." *Journal of Economic Perspectives* 21(2): 153–74.

Lewis, D. (1973). *Counterfactuals.* Cambridge, MA: Harvard University Press.

Lichtenstein, S. and P. Slovic (1971). "Reversals of Preference between Bids and Choices in Gambling Decisions." *Journal of Experimental Psychology* 89(1): 46–55.

Lichtenstein, S. and P. Slovic (1973). "Response-Induced Reversals of Preference in Gambling: An Extended Replication in Las Vegas." *Journal of Experimental Psychology* 101(1): 16–20.

List, J. A. (2003). "Does Market Experience Eliminate Market Anomalies?" *Quarterly Journal of Economics* 118(1): 41–71.

List, J. A. (2004). "Neoclassical Theory versus Prospect Theory: Evidence from the Marketplace." *Econometrica* 72(2): 615–25.

List, J. A. (2006). "The Behavioralist Meets the Market: Measuring Social Preferences and Reputation Effects in Actual Transactions." *Journal of Political Economy* 114(1): 1–37.

List, J. A. (2007). "Field Experiments: A Bridge between Lab and Naturally Occurring Data." *B.E. Journal of Economic Analysis & Policy* 5(2). Online.

Little, D. (1991). *Varieties of Social Explanation.* Boulder, CO: Westview.

Little, D. (1998). *Microfoundations, Method, and Causation: On the Philosophy of the Social Sciences.* New Brunswick, NJ: Transaction Publishers.

Little, I. M. D. (1949). "A Reformulation of the Theory of Consumer's Behaviour." *Oxford Economic Papers* 1(1): 90–9.

Locke, J. (1988 [1689]). *Two Treatises of Government.* Cambridge: Cambridge University Press.

Logeay, C. and S. Tober (2004). "Explaining the Time-Varying Nairu in the Euro-Area." Luxembourg: Office for Official Publications of the European Communities.

Lomasky, L. (1987). *Persons, Rights, and the Moral Community.* New York: Oxford University Press.

Loomes, G. and R. Sugden (1982). "Regret Theory: An Alternative Theory of Rational Choice under Uncertainty." *Economic Journal* 92(368): 805–24.

Loomes, G., C. Starmer and R. Sugden (1991). "Observing Violations of Transitivity by Experimental Methods." *Econometrica* 59(2): 425–39.

Lucas, R. (1976). "Econometric Policy Evaluation: A Critique." *Carnegie-Rochester Series on Public Policy* 1: 19–46.

Luce, D. (2005 [1959]). *Individual Choice Behavior: A Theoretical Analysis.* Mineola, NY: Dover.

Machamer, P., L. Darden and C. F. Craven (2000). "Thinking about Mechanisms." *Philosophy of Science* 67: 1–25.

Mackie, J. (1974). *The Cement of the Universe: A Study of Causation.* Oxford: Oxford University Press.

Mäki, U. (1992). "On the Method of Isolation in Economics." In C. Dilworth (ed.) *Idealization IV: Structuralism, Intelligibility in Science.* Amsterdam and Atlanta, GA: Rodopi, 317–51.

Mäki, U. (1994). "Isolation, Idealization and Truth in Economics." In B. Hamminga and N. De Marchi (eds.) *Idealization in Economics*. Amsterdam: Rodopi, 147–68.

Mäki, U. (2001). "Explanatory Unification: Double and Doubtful." *Philosophy of the Social Sciences* 31: 488–506.

Mäki, U. (2005). "Models are Experiments, Experiments are Models." *Journal of Economic Methodology* 12(2): 30–315.

Mäki, U. (2009). "MISSing the World. Models as Isolations and Credible Surrogate Systems." *Erkenntnis* 70(1): 29–43.

Mäki, U. (2011). "Models and the Locus of Their Truth." *Synthese* 180: 47–63.

Maloney, B. and T. Lindenman (2008). "Behind the Big Paydays." *Washington Post*, November 15.

Marshall, A. (1961 [1920]). *Principles of Economics*. Amherst, NY: Prometheus.

Mas-Colell, A., M. Whinston and J. R. Green (1995). *Microeconomic Theory*. Oxford: Oxford University Press.

Maxwell, G. (1962). "The Ontological Status of Theoretical Entities." In H. Feigl and G. Maxwell (eds.) *Scientific Explanation, Space, and Time: Minnesota Studies in the Philosophy of Science*. Minneapolis, MN: University of Minnesota Press, 3–27.

McAllister, James W. (2004). "Thought Experiments and the Belief in Phenomena." *Philosophy of Science* 71(5): 1164–75.

McClennen, E. F. (1988). "Sure-Thing Doubts." In P. Gärdenfors and N.-E. Sahlin (eds.) *Decision, Probability, and Utility*. Cambridge: Cambridge University Press, 166–82.

McCloskey, D. N. (1983). "The Rhetoric of Economics." *Journal of Economic Literature* 21(2): 481–17.

McKelvey, R. D. and T. R. Palfrey (1992). "An Experimental Study of the Centipede Game." *Econometrica* 60(4): 803–36.

McMullin, E. (1985). "Galilean Idealization." *Studies in the History and Philosophy of Science* 16: 247–73.

Menger, C. (1963). *Problems of Economics and Sociology*. Urbana, IL: University of Illinois Press.

Merges, R. (2011). *Justifying Intellectual Property*. Cambridge, MA: Harvard University Press.

Miguel, E., S. Satyanath and E. Sergenti (2004). "Economic Shocks and Civil Conflict: An Instrumental Variables Approach." *Journal of Political Economy* 112(4): 725–53.

Mill, J. (1986) [1823]), *Essays on government, jurisprudence, liberty of the press, and law of nations*, Fairfield, NJ : A.M. Kelley.

Mill, J. S. (1844). "On the Definition of Political Economy; and on the Method of Investigation Proper to It." In *Essays on Some Unsettled Questions of Political Economy*. London: Parker, 120–64.

Mill, J. S. (1874 [1843]). *A System of Logic, Ratiocinative and Inductive*. New York: Harper & Brothers.

Mill, J. S. (1963a [1848]). *Principles of Political Economy*. In J. M. Robson (ed.) *Collected Works of John Stuart Mill*, vols. II and III. Toronto: University of Toronto Press.

Mill, J. S. (1963b [1861]). "Utilitarianism." In J. M. Robson (ed.) *Collected Works of John Stuart Mill*, vol. X. Toronto: University of Toronto Press, 203–60.

Mill, J. S. (2003 [1859]). *On Liberty*. New Haven, CT: Yale University Press.

Mirowski, P. and E. Nik-Khah (2007). "Markets Made Flesh: Performativity, and a Problem in Science Studies, augmented with Consideration of the FCC Auctions." In D. MacKenzie, F. Muniesa and L. Siu (eds.) *Performing Economics: How Markets are Constructed*. Princeton, NJ: Princeton University Press, 190–225.

Mishkin, F. S. (1996). "The Channels of Monetary Transmission: Lessons for Monetary Policy." Cambridge, MA: National Bureau of Economic Research.

Mitchell, S. D. (2009). *Unsimple Truths: Science, Complexity, and Policy*. Chicago: University of Chicago Press.

Moffitt, T. E., L. Arseneault, D. Belsky *et al.* (2011). "A Gradient of Childhood Self-Control Predicts Health, Wealth, and Public Safety." *Proceedings of the National Academy of Sciences* 108(7): 2693–8.

Morgan, M. S. (1990). *The History of Econometric Ideas*. Cambridge: Cambridge University Press.

Morgan, M. S. (2001). "Models, Stories and the Economic World." *Journal of Economic Methodology* 8(3): 361–84.

Morgan, M. S. (2012). *The World in the Model: How Economists Work and Think*. New York: Cambridge University Press.

Morgan, M. S. and M. Morrison, eds. (1999). *Models as Mediators. Perspectives on Natural and Social Science*. Cambridge: Cambridge University Press.

Morgan, S. L. and C. Winship (2007). *Counterfactuals and Causal Inference: Methods and Principles for Social Research*. Cambridge: Cambridge University Press.

Mullainathan, S. and R. H. Thaler. (2001). "Behavioral Economics." In N. J. Smelser and P. B. Baltes (eds.) *International Encyclopedia of the Social and Behavioral Sciences*. Oxford: Pergamon Press, 1094–100.

National Institute for Clinical Excellence (NICE) (2003). *NICE Guideline CG6 Antenatal Care: Routine Care for the Healthy Pregnant Woman*. London: NICE.

Neumark, D. and W. L. Wascher (2008). *Minimum Wages*. Cambridge, MA: MIT Press.

Nichols, S. (2002). "Folk Psychology." In L. Nadel (ed.) *Encyclopedia of Cognitive Science*. London: Nature Publishing Group, 134–40.

Niiniluoto, I. (2002). "Truthlikeness and Economic Theories." In U. Mäki (ed.) *Fact and Fiction in Economics: Models, Realism and Social Construction*. Cambridge: Cambridge University Press, 214–28.

Nik-Khah, E. (2005). "Designs on the Mechanism: Economics and the FCC Spectrum Auctions." Unpublished PhD dissertation, University of Notre Dame, Indiana.

Nik-Khah, E. (2006). "What the FCC Auctions Can't Tell Us about the Performativity Thesis." *Economic Sociology* 7: 15–21.

Nobelprize.org. (2012). "The Prize in Economic Sciences 2011," July 26. Online. Available HTTP: <http://www.nobelprize.org/nobel_prizes/economics/laureates/2011/>, accessed November 21, 2012.

Nordhaus, W. D. (2008). *A Question of Balance: Weighing the Options on Global Warming Policies*. New Haven, CT: Yale University Press.

Nozick, R. (1974). *Anarchy, State, and Utopia*. Oxford: Basil Blackwell.

Nussbaum, M. (2000). *Women and Human Development: The Capabilities Approach*. Cambridge: Cambridge University Press.

OECD (Organisation for Economic Co-operation and Development) 2011. *Divided We Stand: Why Inequality Keeps Rising*. Paris: OECD.

Osborne, M. (2004). *An Introduction to Game Theory*. Oxford: Oxford University Press.

Otsuka, M. (2003). *Libertarianism without Inequality*. New York: Oxford University Press.

Parfit, D. (1984). *Reasons and Persons*. Oxford: Oxford University Press.

Parkinson, C. N. (1957). *Parkinson's Law*. Cutchogue, NY: Buccaneer Books.

Paternotte, C. (2011). "Rational-Choice Theory." In I. C. Jarvie and J. Zamora-Bonilla (eds.) *The Sage Handbook of the Philosophy of Social Sciences*. London: Sage, 307–21.

Pearl, J. (2000). *Causation: Models, Reasoning and Inference*. Cambridge: Cambridge University Press.

Pender, J. L. (1996). "Discount Rates and Credit Markets: Theory and Evidence from Rural India." *Journal of Development Economics* 50(2): 257–96.

Peterson, M. (2009). *An Introduction to Decision Theory.* Cambridge: Cambridge University Press.

Pigou, A. C. (1932 [1920]). *The Economics of Welfare.* London: Macmillan and Co.

Plott, C. (1981). Experimental Methods in Political Economy: A Tool for Regulatory Research." In A. R. Ferguson (ed.) *Attacking Regulatory Problems.* Cambridge, MA: Ballinger, 117–43.

Plott, C. (1997). "Laboratory Experimental Testbeds: Application to the PCS Auction." *Journal of Economics and Management Strategy* 6(3): 605–38.

Popper, K. (1959). *Logic of Scientific Discovery.* New York: Basic Books.

Poundstone, W. (2008). *Gaming the Vote. Why Elections Aren't Fair (and What We Can Do About It).* New York: Hill and Wang.

Pratkanis, A. R. and A. G. Greenwald (1988). "Recent Perspectives on Unconscious Processing: Still No Marketing Applications." *Psychology and Marketing* 5(4): 337–53.

Putnam, H. and V. Walsh (2007). "A Response to Dasgupta." *Economics and Philosophy* 23(3): 359–64.

Ramsey, F. (1931 [1926]). "Truth and Probability." In *The Foundations of Mathematics and Other Logical Essays*, ed. R. B. Braithwaite. London: Routledge & Kegan Paul, 156–98.

Rapoport, A. and A. M. Chammah (1965). *Prisoner's Dilemma. A Study in Conflict and Cooperation.* Ann Arbor: University of Michigan Press.

Rasmusen, E. (2006). *Games and Information: An Introduction to Game Theory.* Oxford: Blackwell.

Ratcliffe, M. (2007). *Rethinking Commonsense Psychology: A Critique of Folk Psychology, Theory of Mind and Simulation.* Basingstoke: Palgrave Macmillan.

Rawls, J. (1971). *A Theory of Justice.* Cambridge, MA: Harvard University Press.

Rawls, J. (1993). *Political Liberalism.* New York: Columbia University Press.

Rawls, J. (2001). *Justice as Fairness: A Restatement.* Cambridge, MA: Harvard University Press.

Reiss, J. (2001). "Natural Economic Quantities and Their Measurement." *Journal of Economic Methodology* 8(2): 287–311.

Reiss, J. (2002). "Epistemic Virtues and Concept Formation in Economics." Unpublished PhD dissertation, London School of Economics.

Reiss, J. (2005). "Causal Instrumental Variables and Interventions." *Philosophy of Science* 72(5): 964–76.

Reiss, J. (2007a). "Do We Need Mechanisms in the Social Sciences?" *Philosophy of the Social Sciences* 37(2): 163–84.

Reiss, J. (2007b). "Time Series, Nonsense Correlations and the Principle of the Common Cause." In F. Russo and J. Williamson (eds.) *Causality and Probability in the Sciences.* London: College Publications, 179–96.

Reiss, J. (2008a). *Error in Economics: Towards a More Evidence-Based Methodology.* Abingdon: Routledge.

Reiss, J. (2008b). "Social Capacities." In S. Hartmann and L. Bovens (eds.) *Nancy Cartwright's Philosophy of Science.* Abingdon: Routledge, 265–88.

Reiss, J. (2010). "In Favour of a Millian Proposal to Reform Biomedical Research." *Synthese* 177(3): 427–47.

Reiss, J. (2011). "Third Time's a Charm: Causation, Science and Wittgensteinian Pluralism." In P. McKay Illari, F. Russo and J. Williamson (eds.) *Causality in the Sciences.* Oxford: Oxford University Press, 907–27

Reiss, J. (2012). "Counterfactuals." In H. Kincaid (ed.) *Oxford Handbook of the Philosophy of Social Science*. Oxford: Oxford University Press, 154–83.

Reiss, J. and P. Kitcher (2009). "Biomedical Research, Neglected Diseases, and Well-Ordered Science." *Theoria* 24(3): 263–82.

Resnik, M. D. (1987). *Choices: An Introduction to Decision Theory*. Minneapolis: University of Minnesota Press.

Ricardo, D. (1817). *On the Principles of Political Economy and Taxation*. London: John Murray.

Risse, M. (2000). "What Is Rational about Nash Equilibria?" *Synthese* 124(3): 361–84.

Roberts, J. T. (2004). "There Are No Laws of the Social Sciences." In C. Hitchcock (ed.) *Contemporary Debates in Philosophy of Science*. Oxford: Blackwell, 151–67.

Robeyns, I. (2011). "The Capability Approach." In E. N. Zalta (ed.) *The Stanford Encyclopedia of Philosophy*. Online. Available HTTP: <http://plato.stanford.edu/entries/capability-approach/>, accessed November 21, 2012.

Rodrik, D. (2007). *One Economics, Many Recipes: Globalization, Institutions, and Economic Growth*. Princeton: Princeton University Press.

Rosenberg, A. (1992). *Economics: Mathematical Politics or Science of Diminishing Returns?* Chicago: University of Chicago Press.

Ross, D. (2005). *Economic Theory and Cognitive Science: Microexplanation*. Cambridge, MA: MIT Press.

Ross, D. (2009). "Integrating the Dynamics of Multi-scale Economic Agency." In H. Kincaid and D. Ross (eds.) *The Oxford Handbook of Philosophy of Economics*. Oxford: Oxford University Press, 245–79.

Ross, D. (2010a). "Game Theory." In E. N. Zalta (ed.) *The Stanford Encyclopedia of Philosophy*. Online. Available HTTP: <http://plato.stanford.edu/entries/game-theory/>, accessed November 21, 2012.

Ross, D. (2010b). "Should the Financial Crisis Inspire Normative Revision?" *Journal of Economic Methodology* 17(4): 399–418.

Roth, A. E. (1986). "Laboratory Experimentation in Economics." *Economics and Philosophy* 2(2): 245–73.

Roth, A. E., V. Prasnikar, M. Okuno-Fujiwara and S. Zamir (1991). "Bargaining and Market Behavior in Jerusalem, Ljubljana, Pittsburgh, and Tokyo: An Experimental Study." *American Economic Review* 81(5): 1068–95.

Rousseau, J.-J. (2002 [1755]). "Discourse on the Origin and the Foundations of Inequality among Mankind." In S. Dunn (ed.) *The Social Contract and The First and Second Discourses*. New Haven, CT: Yale University Press, 69–148.

Royall, R. (1997). *Statistical Evidence: A Likelihood Paradigm*. London: Chapman & Hall.

Russell, B. (1967). *The Autobiography of Bertrand Russell*. London: George Allen and Unwin.

Sackett, D. L., W. M. C. Rosenberg, J. A. Muir Gray *et al.* (1996). "Evidence-Based Medicine: What It Is and What It Isn't." *British Medical Journal* 312(7023): 71–2.

Salmon, W. C. (1984). *Scientific Explanation and the Causal Structure of the World*. Princeton, NJ: Princeton University Press.

Salmon, W. C. (1989). *Four Decades of Scientific Explanation*. Pittsburgh: University of Pittsburgh Press.

Salmon, W. C. (1991). "Hans Reichenbach's Vindication of Induction." *Erkenntnis* 35(1): 99–122.

Salmon, W. C. (1992). "Scientific Explanation." In M. H. Salmon (ed.) *Introduction to the Philosophy of Science: A Text by the Members of the Department of the History and Philosophy of Science of the University of Pittsburgh*. Indianapolis: Hackett, 7–41.

Samuelson, P. A. (1938). "A Note on the Pure Theory of Consumer's Behaviour." *Economica* 5(17): 61–71.

Samuelson, P. A. and W. Nordhaus (1992). *Economics*, 14th edn. Boston, MA: McGraw-Hill.

Sandel, M. J. (1998). "What Money Can't Buy: The Moral Limits of Markets." The Tanner Lectures on Human Values, delivered at Brasenose College, Oxford May 11 and 12, 1998.

Sandel, M. J. (2012). *What Money Can't Buy: The Moral Limits of Markets*. London: Allen Lane.

Santos, A. C. D. (2010). *The Social Epistemology of Experimental Economics*. Abingdon: Routledge.

Satz, D. (2010). *Why Some Things Should Not Be for Sale: On the Limits of Markets*. Oxford: Oxford University Press.

Savage, L. J. (1972). *The Foundations of Statistics*. New York: Courier Dover Publications.

Scanlon, T. (1998). *What We Owe to Each Other*. Cambridge, MA: Harvard University Press.

Schelling, T. C. (1960). *The Strategy of Conflict*. Cambridge, MA: MIT Press.

Schelling, T. C. (1978). *Micromotives and Macrobehavior*. New York: Norton.

Schelling, T. C. (1999). "Social Mechanisms and Social Dynamics." In P. Hedström and R. Swedberg (eds.) *Social Mechanisms: An Analytical Approach to Social Theory*. Cambridge: Cambridge University Press, 32–44.

Schlimm, D. (2009). "Learning from the Existence of Models: On Psychic Machines, Tortoises, and Computer Simulations." *Synthese* 169(3): 521–38.

Schultze, C. and C. Mackie, eds. (2002). *At What Price? Conceptualizing and Measuring Cost-of-Living and Price Indexes*. Washington, DC: National Academy Press.

Sciolino, E. (2008). "Even France, Haven of Smokers, Is Clearing the Air." *New York Times*, January 3.

Selten, R. (1975). "Reexamination of the Perfectness Concept for Equilibrium Points in Extensive Games." *International Journal of Game Theory* 4(1): 25–55.

Selten, R. (1978). "The Chain Store Paradox." *Theory and Decision* 9(2): 127–59.

Sen, A. (1970). "The Impossibility of a Paretian Liberal." *Journal of Political Economy* 78(1): 152–7.

Sen, A. (1973). "Behaviour and the Concept of Preference." *Economica* 40(159): 241–59.

Sen, A. (1977). "Rational Fools: A Critique of the Behavioral Foundations of Economic Theory." *Philosophy and Public Affairs* 6(4): 317–44.

Sen, A. (1983a). "Accounts, Actions and Values: Objectivity of Social Science." In C. Lloyd (ed.) *Social Theory and Political Practice*. Oxford: Clarendon Press, 87–107.

Sen, A. (1983b). *Poverty and Famines: An Essay on Entitlement and Deprivation*. New York: Oxford University Press.

Sen, A. (1987). *On Ethics and Economics*. Malden, MA: Blackwell.

Sen, A. (1993). "Internal Consistency of Choice." *Econometrica* 61(3): 495–521.

Sen, A. (1999a). "Assessing Human Development: Special Contribution." In UNDP (ed.) *Human Development Report*. New York: Oxford University Press, 23.

Sen, A. (1999b). *Development as Freedom*. Oxford: Oxford University Press.

Sen, A. (2009). *The Idea of Justice*. Cambridge, MA: Harvard University Press.

Sen, A. and B. Williams (1982). *Utilitarianism and Beyond*. Cambridge: Cambridge University Press.

Shadish, W. R., T. D. Cook and D. T. Campbell (2002). *Experimental and Quasi-experimental Designs for Generalized Causal Inference*. Boston, MA: Houghton Mifflin.

Shanks, N. and C. R. Greek (2009). *Animal Models in Light of Evolution*. Boca Raton, FL: BrownWalker Press.

Shapere, D. (1982). "The Concept of Observation in Science and Philosophy." *Philosophy of Science* 49(3): 485–525.

Shapiro, M. and D. Wilcox (1996). "Mismeasurement in the Consumer Price Index: An Evaluation." *NBER Working Paper Series* 5590. Cambridge, MA: National Bureau of Economic Research.

Shoda, Y., W. Mischel and P. K. Peake (1990). "Predicting Adolescent Cognitive and Self-Regulatory Competencies from Preschool Delay of Gratification: Identifying Diagnostic Conditions." *Developmental Psychology* 26(6): 978–86.

Sidgwick, H. (1874). *The Methods of Ethics*. London: Macmillan.

Simon, H. A. (1953). "Causal Ordering and Identifiability." In W. Hood and T. Koopmans (eds.) *Studies in Econometric Method*. New York: John Wiley, 49–74.

Simon, H. A. (1959). "Theories of Decision-Making in Economics and Behavioral Science." *American Economic Review* 49(3): 253–83.

Simon, H. A. and N. Rescher (1966). "Cause and Counterfactual." *Philosophy of Science* 33(4): 323–40.

Singer, P. (1979). *Practical Ethics*. Cambridge: Cambridge University Press.

Skyrms, B. (2004). *The Stag Hunt and the Evolution of Social Structure*. Cambridge: Cambridge University Press.

Slovic, P. and S. Lichtenstein (1983). "Preference Reversals: A Broader Perspective." *American Economic Review* 73(4): 596–605.

Smith, A. (1904 [1776]). *An Inquiry into the Nature and Causes of the Wealth of Nations*. London: Methuen & Co.

Sober, E. (1987). "The Principle of the Common Cause." In J. Fetzer (ed.) *Probability and Causality: Essays in Honor of Wesley Salmon*. Dordrecht, Netherlands: Reidel, 211–28.

Spears, D. (2010). "Economic Decision-Making in Poverty Depletes Behavioral Control." *Center for Economic Policy Studies Working Paper 213*. Princeton, NJ: Center for Economic Policy Studies, Princeton University. Online. Available HTTP: <http://www.princeton.edu/ceps/ workingpapers/213spears.pdf>, accessed December 6, 2012.

Spirtes, P., C. Glymour and R. Scheines (2000). *Causation, Prediction, and Search*. Cambridge, MA: MIT Press.

Stahl, D. O. and P. W. Wilson (1995). "On Players' Models of Other Players: Theory and Experimental Evidence." *Games and Economic Behavior* 10(1): 218–54.

Stapleford, T. (2007). *The Cost of Living in America: A Political History of Economic Statistics, 1880–2000*. New York: Cambridge University Press.

Steel, D. (2004). "Social Mechanisms and Causal Inference." *Philosophy of the Social Sciences* 34(1): 55–78.

Steel, D. (2008). *Across the Boundaries. Extrapolation in Biology and Social Science*. Oxford: Oxford University Press.

Steel, D. (2011). "Causality, Causal Models, and Social Mechanisms." In I. C. Jarvie and J. Zamora-Bonilla (eds.) *The Sage Handbook of the Philosophy of Social Sciences*. London: Sage, 288–304.

Steiner, H. (1994). *An Essay on Rights*. Cambridge, MA: Blackwell.

Stern, N. H. (2009). *The Global Deal: Climate Change and the Creation of a New Era of Progress and Prosperity*. New York: Public Affairs.

Stiglitz, J. E. (2006). "Scrooge and Intellectual Property Rights: A Medical Prize Fund Could Improve the Financing of Drug Innovations." *British Medical Journal* 333: 1279–80.

Stiglitz, J. E. (2009). "The Anatomy of a Murder: Who Killed the American Economy?" *Critical Review* 21(2–3): 329–39.

Stiglitz, J. E. and L. J. Bilmes (2008). *The Three Trillion Dollar War: The True Cost of the Iraq Conflict*. New York: Norton.

Stiglitz, J. E., A. Sen and J.-P. Fitoussi (2010). *Mismeasuring Our Lives: Why GDP Doesn't Add Up*. New York: New Press.

Strevens, M. (2004). "The Causal and Unification Accounts of Explanation Unified—Causally." *Noûs* 38: 154–79.

Suárez, M., ed. (2009). *Fictions in Science. Philosophical Essays on Modeling and Idealization*. New York: Routledge.

Sugden, R. (2000). "Credible Worlds: The Status of Theoretical Models in Economics." *Journal of Economic Methodology* 7(1): 1–31.

Sugden, R. (2009). "Credible Worlds, Capacities and Mechanisms." *Erkenntnis* 70(1): 3–27.

Sugden, R. (2011). "Explanations in Search of Observations." *Biology and Philosophy* 26(5): 717–36.

Sumner, L. W. (1996). *Welfare, Happiness, and Ethics*. Oxford: Oxford University Press.

Suppes, P. (1970). *A Probabilistic Theory of Causality*. Amsterdam: North-Holland.

Thaler, R. H. and C. R. Sunstein (2003). "Libertarian Paternalism." *American Economic Review* 93(2): 175–9.

Thaler, R. H. and C. R. Sunstein (2008). *Nudge: Improving Decisions about Health, Wealth, and Happiness*. New Haven, CT: Yale University Press.

Titmuss, R. (1970). *The Gift Relationship. From Human Blood to Social Policy*. New York: New Press.

Tversky, A. and D. Kahneman (1974). "Judgment under Uncertainty: Heuristics and Biases." *Science* 185(4157): 1124–31.

Tversky, A. and D. Kahneman (1981). "The Framing of Decisions and the Psychology of Choice." *Science* 211(4481): 453–8.

Urbach, P. (1985). "Randomization and the Design of Experiments." *Philosophy of Science* 52(2): 256–73.

Urquiola, M. and E. Verhoogen (2009). "Class-Size Caps, Sorting, and the Regression-Discontinuity Design." *American Economic Review* 99(1): 179–215.

Vallentyne, P. (2012). "Libertarianism." In E. N. Zalta (ed.) *The Stanford Encyclopedia of Philosophy*. Online. Available HTTP: <http://plato.stanford.edu/entries/libertarianism/>, accessed November 21, 2012.

Vandenbroucke, J. P. (2008). "Observational Research, Randomised Trials, and Two Views of Medical Science." *PLoS Med* 5(3): e67.

Varian, H. R. (1992). *Microeconomic Analysis*. New York: Norton.

Varian, H. R. (2010). *Intermediate Microeconomics*. New York: Norton.

von Neumann, J. and O. Morgenstern (1944). *The Theory of Games and Economic Behavior*. Princeton, NJ: Princeton University Press.

Wallis, W. A. and M. Friedman. (1942). "The Empirical Derivation of Indifference Functions." In O. Lange, F. McIntyre and T. O. Yntema (eds.) *Studies in Mathematical Economics and Econometrics in Memory of Henry Schultz*. Chicago: University of Chicago Press, 175–89.

Walzer, M. (1983). *Spheres of Justice: A Defense of Pluralism and Equality*. New York: Basic Books.

Way, J. (forthcoming). "Explaining the Instrumental Principle." *Australasian Journal of Philosophy*.

Weber, M. (1949 [1904]). "Objectivity in Social Science and Social Policy." In M. Weber, E. Shils and H. Finch (eds.) *The Methodology of the Social Sciences*. Glencoe, IL: Free Press, 50–112.

Weber, M. (1968). *Economy and Society: An Outline of Interpretive Sociology*. New York: Bedminster Press.

Weibull, J. (2004). "Testing Game Theory." In S. Huck (ed.) *Advances in Understanding Strategic Behaviour*. New York: Palgrave, 85–104.

Weisberg, M. (2007). "Three Kinds of Idealization." *Journal of Philosophy* 104(12): 639–59.

Wilkinson, N. and M. Klaes (2012). *An Introduction to Behavioral Economics*. Basingstoke: Palgrave Macmillan.

Williams, B. (2011). *Ethics and the Limits of Philosophy*. Abingdon: Routledge.

Wimsatt, W. (2007). *Re-engineering Philosophy for Limited Beings: Piecewise Approximations to Reality*. Boston, MA: Harvard University Press.

Wolff, J. (2004). "Are There Moral Limits to the Market?" Unpublished manuscript, London School of Economics. Online. Available HTTP: <http://sas-space.sas.ac.uk/672/>, accessed December 5, 2012.

Wolff, J. (2006). *An Introduction to Political Philosophy*. Oxford: Oxford University Press.

Woodward, J. (1989). "Data and Phenomena." *Synthese* 79: 393–472.

Woodward, J. (2000). "Data, Phenomena, and Reliability." *Philosophy of Science* 67(Supplement): S163–S179.

Woodward, J. (2002). "What Is a Mechanism?" *Philosophy of Science* 69: S366–S377.

Woodward, J. (2003). *Making Things Happen*. Oxford: Oxford University Press.

Woodward, J. (2009). "Why Do People Cooperate as Much as They Do?" In C. Mantzavinos (ed.) *Philosophy of the Social Sciences. Philosophical Theory and Scientific Practice*. Cambridge: Cambridge University Press, 219–65.

Worrall, J. (2000). "The Scope, Limits, and Distinctiveness of the Method of 'Deduction from the Phenomena': Some Lessons from Newton's 'Demonstrations' in Optics." *British Journal for the Philosophy of Science* 51(1): 45–80.

Worrall, J. (2002). "*What* Evidence in Evidence-Based Medicine?" *Philosophy of Science* 69: S316–S330.

Worrall, J. (2007a). "Evidence in Medicine and Evidence-Based Medicine." *Philosophy Compass* 2: 981–1022.

Worrall, J. (2007b). "Why There's No Cause to Randomize." *British Journal for the Philosophy of Science* 58(3): 451–88.

Wright, C. (1969). "Estimating Permanent Income: A Note." *Journal of Political Economy* 77(5): 845–50.

Young, H. P. (1993). "The Evolution of Conventions." *Econometrica* 61(1): 57–84.

Index